Dragons
in
Distress

ASIA'S MIRACLE
ECONOMIES IN CRISIS

Dragons in Distress

ASIA'S MIRACLE ECONOMIES IN CRISIS

Walden Bello
and
Stephanie Rosenfeld

A FOOD FIRST BOOK
The Institute for Food and Development Policy
San Francisco

Library of Congress Cataloging-in-Publication Data

Bello, Walden F., 1945 –
Dragons in distress: Asia's miracle economies in crisis/Walden
Bello & Stephanie Rosenfeld
p. cm.
"A Food First book"
Includes bibliographical references.
Includes index.
ISBN 0-935028-54-4 (hard) : $19.95
ISBN 0-935028-55-2 (pbk.) : $12.95
1. Korea (South) — Economic policy — 1960 –. 2. Singapore —
Economic policy –. 3. Taiwan — Economic policy — 1960 –.
I. Rosenfeld, Stephanie, 1968 –. II. Institute for Food and
Development Policy (San Francisco, Calif.) III. Title. HC467.B45
1990
338.9—dc20   90-42475   CIP

Printed in the United States of America

10 9 8 7 6 5 4 3 2 1

To order additional copies of this book, please write or call:

The Institute for Food and Development Policy
145 Ninth Street
San Francisco, CA 94103
(415) 864-8555
Please add 15% for postage and handling ($1 minimum).
California residents add sales tax. Bulk discounts available.

Design and typesetting: Jabula Desktop Publishing
Cover design: Nancy Hom
Printed on recycled paper by Thomson–Shore

To Marilen ,
Jess and Luz Bello,
and May and Eddie Aaronson,
for everything

Contents

List of Tables

List of Illustrations

Preface

If one were to ask me when the idea for this book emerged, I would say in the early 1980s, while I was tied up in Washington, D.C., trying to lobby Congress, the White House, and the World Bank to cease aiding the Marcos regime in the Philippines. Again and again, I and my colleagues in the antidictatorship movement would come up against the rationale—especially at the World Bank—that aid to Ferdinand Marcos was part of an effort to turn the Philippines into another NIC, or "newly industrializing country."

Naturally, the question came up: What was going on in Taiwan and South Korea anyway, that made them models for the Philippines? The question led me to the growing literature on the NIC pattern of development, much of which extolled the undeniable fact of high growth rates while remaining silent on the political repression that seemed to be an indispensable feature of that growth. The NIC model, I found, was well on its way to becoming the new orthodoxy. Not only the Philippines but the rest of the third world was being measured against the performance of South Korea, Taiwan, Hong Kong, and Singapore.

Development Debacle: The World Bank in the Philippines, published by Food First in 1982, was, in part, a critical examination of the NIC strategy of export-oriented growth as applied in the Philippines. Something told me, however, that sooner or later, I would have to come to terms directly with the NIC experience. But in the mid-1980s, I had my hands full participating in the urgent effort to bring down the Marcos regime and cooperating with others on other priorities of peace research, like uncovering the different dimensions of the U.S.and Soviet military presence in East Asia and the Pacific and investigating the counterinsurgency strategy of low-intensity conflict that was unfolding in the Philippines.

The problem of economic development, however, had become my preeminent intellectual and moral concern. And, in the late 1980s, the increasingly obvious failure of both the Marxist collectivist model of development and the traditional nationalist strategy of import-substitution industrialization lent particular urgency to the need to investigate the question of whether the NIC model, in fact, offered a viable future for the third world.

The opportunity to pursue this research suddenly opened up in 1986, owing to the fortuitous conjunction of two developments: Marcos was ousted by the Filipino people and I was invited to join the Institute for Food and Development Policy (Food First) by its cofounders, Frances Moore Lappé and Joseph Collins. Seven intense years in Washington had taken its toll on my sanity and personality, and I was more than willing to jump at the excuse provided by the fall of the *ancien régime* to leave the city of power and other trips without feeling guilty. But perhaps even more decisive was Food First's offer to fully back a comprehensive investigation of the miracle economies of Asia. Living in San Francisco, I must confess, was a bonus.

Begun early in 1987, the NICs project initially covered South Korea, Taiwan, Singapore, and Hong Kong. After a few months, however, I decided to drop Hong Kong because political and economic trends there were increasingly being shaped overwhelmingly by the geographical proximity of China and the approaching devolution of the colony to that country in 1997. Over the next three and a half years, the project blossomed into a truly cooperative, international endeavor, drawing on the assistance, advice, and wisdom of scores of colleagues and friends on both sides of the Pacific. Coauthor Stephanie Rosenfeld joined the project in 1989 and quickly became an indispensable part of it, with her dedication, intelligence, and congenial company.

Stephanie and I are immensely indebted to all our present and past colleagues at Food First for their unswerving support of this project. We would like to mention, in particular, Frances Moore Lappé, Joe Collins, Tom Ambrogi, Viola Weinberg, Ann Kelly, Susan Galleymore, Marilyn Borchardt, Medea Benjamin, Kevin Danaher, Christopher Kashap, Victor di Suvero, Warren Mills, Denise Newman, Audee Kochiyama-Holman, Jon Christensen, Lorraine Coleman, and Ian McWilliam.

The assistance, advice, and insights provided by the following colleagues were vital to the completion of this study: John Cavanagh, Robin Broad, Hagen Koo, Bruce Cumings, Marc Cohen, Linda Gail Arrigo, Pharis Harvey, Tim Shorrock, David Satterwhite, Mike Fonte, Sheldon Severinghaus, Richard Doner, Lenny Siegel, Jomo Sundaram, Sharat Lin, Peter Hayes, Michael Borrus, Lyuba Zarsky, Henry Lo, Thomas Gold, Sergy Floro, Alice Amsden, and Marie Gottschalk.

In Korea, I was assisted immeasurably by discussions with Kelly Yim, Shim Sang-Wan, Soh Kyung-Sok, Lee So-Sun, Oh Jae-Shik, Choi Jang-Jip, Moon Chung-In, Kim Dae-Hwan, Tony Michell, Chul Kyu-Kang, Park Young-Ju, Imm Chai-Kyung, Lee Young-Ho, Park Y.C., Chung Chai-Sik, Roh Kim-Yung, Ahn Byong-Ok, Lim Sang-Taek, and Chang Shang-Hwan. Kim Jin-Soo, Lee Eun-Joo, and Lee Kyung-Hee provided invaluable contacts. Ed and Genell Poitras were the source not only of important insights but also warm hospitality. Chon Yu's translation of hundreds of pages of technical literature was superb. Interpreter Chang Shin-Hwan's daredevil skills in maneuvering through Seoul's *kyotongchiok* or gridlock on his motorcycle got me to most of my appointments at least ten minutes early, though with some risk to life and limb. Also valuable were the vigorous, wide-ranging dialogues with the officers of the Chonggye Garment Workers Union, the staff of the Christian Institute for the Study of Justice and Development, and the staff of the Korean Institute for the Study of Rural Societies. The members of the union at the Handok Heavy Metal Company in Inchon talked to me *en masse* at the factory, despite management attempts to break up the meeting. Finally, talks with Lee Ji-Hoon of the Korea Information and Resource Center, Chung Ki-Yul of the International Committee for Peace and Reunification in Korea, and Chung Minn of Young Koreans United did much to illuminate Korean realities.

In Taiwan, an equally long list of friends and colleagues guided me to an understanding of the island's economy and society: Chang Fu-Chung, Michael Hsiao, Su Ching-Li, Patrick Huang, Chin Pei-Hsiung, Ben Woo, Chen Win-Chen, Jackson Kuo, Stephen Lee, Ho Dwan-Fan, Chio Yi-Jen, Daniel Huang, Yao Chia-Wen, Lawrence Chung, Mao Yu-Kang, Jimmy Shang, Lou Mei-Wen, Hsu Ching-Fu, Lin Fou-Hsi, Chiou Hon-Yung, Lu Hsiu-Yi, Ailan Tsao, Ju Gau-Jeng, Hsieh Ming-Ja, Jim Tsai, Lin K. H., Lin Hsien-Kui, Wu Nai-Teh, Edgar Lin, Lin Chung-Chen, Wu Jieh-Min, Liang Ji-Jeng, Alfred Du, Wang Yi-Hsiung, and Shih Shin-Min. The leadership of the Democratic Progressive Party, the leading officers of the Labor Party, and the members of the union at Nanya Plastics in Kaohsiung all went out of their way to make sure I got not only a lot of information but also a good dose of Taiwanese hospitality. I must also register my personal gratitude to Talleyrand Lin of the Democratic Progressive Party staff for his excellent services as interpreter, and to Zhang Jie for assistance in translating documents.

I profited greatly from discussions with numerous colleagues and friends in Singapore, including oppositionists J. B. Jeyaretnam and Francis Seow. The others—without whose assistance this research would not have gotten off the ground—requested anonymity. This was a perfectly understandable request from people living in Lee Kwan-Yew's Brave New Isle. Also, I must thank Lily A. and her *barkada*, or gang, for giving me some insights into the dismal lives of Filipino domestics in Singapore.

Without support from well-motivated interns, this book would have taken much longer to complete. Particularly noteworthy were the contributions of Rodney Siegel, Paula Fomby, Amy Schwartz, Elpidio Morales, Blandina de Mesa, Jeanny Wang, and Jay Gonzalez. We would also like to thank Audrey Ordona, Maryam Maleki, Mary Claire Poslosky, Carol Lee, Jon Hangartner, Jin K. Won, John Goldsmith, and Peter Chang.

Generosity came in various forms, one of the most important being financial. Funding for the book came from the Maryknoll Fathers, Funding Exchange, the Women's Division of the United Methodist Church, Korea Joint Action Group of the National Council of Churches, the Levinson Foundation, the C.S. Fund, the Rubin Foundation, the Uniting Church of Canada, John Maher, Tim Maher, Kimo Campbell, and Ping and Carol Ferry. We are particularly indebted to Tom O'Brien and Gene Casper of Maryknoll, Victor Hsu of the National Council of Churches, Michael Hahm and Jiro Mizuno of the United Methodist General Board for Global Ministries, Beth Rosales and June Makela of the Funding Exchange, Rhea Whitehead of the Uniting Church of Canada, Jutta von Gontard of the Levinson Foundation, and Cora Weiss for securing funding for the book.

A number of individuals assisted the project in a variety of ways, from helping us obtain library and research privileges, to securing documents and periodicals that were difficult to acquire, to providing camaraderie and encouragement at critical points. These dear friends and colleagues include Rebecca Ratcliff, Barbara Gaerlan, Eric Crystal, Mike Cullinane, Totoy Castrence, Elsie Castrence, Johnny Fox, Amy Pascual, Edgardo Rodriguez, Joaquin Po, Willie Abesamis, David Spooner, Julia and Roger Estrella, Mary and Lewis Suzuki, Khoo Kay-Jin, Jane Cardosa, Jim Heddle, Dick and Girlie Ng, Marybeth Braun, Claire Schub, John Kelly, Tonette Garcia, Edna Pujeda, Laurie Schultz of Senator James Jeffords' office, and Congresswoman Nancy Pelosi of San

Francisco. Sunny Rosenfeld provided camaraderie and an absurd sense of humor that helped her sister get through this project.

Nancy Hom designed the colorful cover of this book, and for this both Stephanie and I are grateful, as we are to Gaen Murphree for her magnificent copyediting.

Parts of this book first came out as articles in popular publications, thanks to the interest and assistance of Sandy Close and Franz Schurmann of *Pacific News Service*, Amy Alina of the *Multinational Monitor*, Teddy Goldsmith and Patrick McCully of the *Ecologist*, Elizabeth Kirkendall of the *San Francisco Chronicle*, Doug Foster and Sara Miles of *Mother Jones*, Martin Khor of *Third World News and Features*, Tim Wise of *Dollars and Sense*, Paul Hoeffel of *Development Forum*, Sheila Coronel of the *Manila Times*, and Paulynn Sicam of the *Manila Chronicle*.

My wife Marilen put up with, though not without protest, my moods and anxieties and, together with the children, endured family affairs like Sundays at the office with the computer, photocopier, and super-burritos-to-go.

While acknowledging the invaluable help we received from all these fine colleagues, friends, loved ones, and acquaintances, Stephanie and I take sole responsibility for the facts and analysis contained in this book.

WALDEN BELLO
San Francisco
August 3, 1990

Introduction

The Rise and Crisis of the Dragon Economies

T here is nothing in it for us," responded Lee So-Sun, one of Korea's most respected labor leaders, when asked what benefits high-speed industrialization had brought to Korean workers.[1] Her words would have formed an apt caption to photos of workers lobbing Molotov cocktails at the thousands of riot policemen who seized the strategic Hyundai shipyard in late April 1990. The most dramatic of thousands of confrontations between labor and the power structure since 1987, the battle for the strategic shipyard underscored the fragility of the so-called Korean miracle.

But television footage of rebellious workers in Korea has not tarnished the widespread image of that country as a new Japan. Nor have photos of angry farmers demonstrating in Taiwan ruffled the picture of that island as an economic powerhouse. The common perception of these two countries, as well as of Singapore and Hong Kong, continues to be that offered by, among others, futurologist John Naisbitt, coauthor of the popular *Megatrends 2000*:

> Countries like South Korea, which were impoverished just decades ago, now challenge the U.S. and Japan with exports of automobiles, TV sets, ships, computers, and videocassette recorders and make Europe positively anemic.
>
> South Korea, Taiwan, Singapore, and Hong Kong have revolutionized the theory of economic development by showing the world how to skip over much of the industrialization phase and plunge into the information economy. They are expected to continue growing at annual rates ranging from 7 to 10 %, compared with about a 3 % growth for the U.S.[2]

To the ordinary American consumer with a Hyundai Excel or a Samsung VCR, Naisbitt's image of these countries as the emerging new giants from across the Pacific may well sound credible. But add some critical pieces of information—like the fact that both the engine and transmission of the Excel are designed in Japan, or that 85 percent of the value of a Korean color TV is made up of imported components from Japan, or that the Korean firm Samsung's VCR technology is licensed from a subsidiary of the Japanese conglomerate Matsushita—and the new dragons from the East begin to look less formidable. Indeed, one gets an image not of formidability but of fragility when one learns that even as South Korea, Singapore, and Taiwan rack up trade surpluses with the United States, they suffer chronic and huge trade deficits with Japan.

Popularizers like Naisbitt often pick up their ideas from academic specialists, and in this case, they are merely passing along what has become the orthodox view in the economics and development establishment. In this view, the newly industrializing countries or NICs have discovered the formula for economic development in the late twentieth century. The key ingredients of this formula, say the academics, are export-oriented production, cheap labor, an undervalued currency, free markets, and a minimum of state intervention. They are right on the first three elements of the formula, but they overemphasize the role of free markets and grossly underplay the activist role of the state. This misrepresentation of the NIC experience, however, has not prevented its being transformed into doctrine at the International Monetary Fund (IMF) and the World Bank, whence technocrats sally forth to all points of the vast third world bearing the same message: You too can be a Taiwan or a Korea, provided you can summon up the political will to make the painful but necessary structural reforms.

But such is the cunning of history that at the very moment that the economists and technocrats have enshrined the NIC model as the new orthodoxy, that very strategy is running out of steam in Taiwan, Singapore, and South Korea.[3] True, these economies continue to post 7 to 10 percent growth rates, but that is the glitter of half past high noon. The troublesome truth is that the external conditions that made the NICs' export successes possible are fast disappearing, while the long-suppressed costs of high-speed growth are catching up with these economies. It is the dangerous intersection of these trends that has led some Korean technocrats to fear that the halving of the growth rate from 12.2 percent in 1988 to 6.5 percent in 1989 may be but the prelude to a severe structural crisis.

To be sure, these countries are at a different stage of economic transformation relative to the third world. Their problem is not how to get out of the third world but, having just left it, how to avoid being hurled back into the third world.

The signals of distress are varied and often striking.

In Korea, workers launched over 7,000 strikes between the summer of 1987 and late 1989, or close to 10 per day—probably a world record for a labor force the size of that country's.

Farmers, formerly the mainstay of the ruling parties in both countries, fought pitched battles with police in Taipei and in Seoul as they protested policies opening the domestic market to a flood of U.S. agricultural imports. The technocrats have succumbed to American pressure, the farmers claim, and have boarded up the countryside. The farmers see resistance as the only alternative to extinction.

As aggressive protectionism limits the growth of exports to their main market, the United States, Korean exporters desperately scour the globe, from Siberia to Hungary, for new markets, but few hold real promise.

High-speed growth without environmental controls has converted Taiwan into a poisoned paradise of free-wheeling capitalism, leading increasing numbers of Taiwanese to a willingness to trade rapid growth for ecological equilibrium.

As wages rise in Taiwan and Korea, capital flees to sites in Southeast Asia, China, and the Caribbean that offer even lower wages.

Then there are the less visible symptoms of distress, like the quiet departure of increasing numbers of Singapore's educated work force, many of them to escape the pervasive authoritarian management of their lives that the ruling party says is necessary for their country's economic survival.

The Conditions of Growth

But before we examine the crisis of the East Asian NICs, it would be worthwhile to discuss briefly some of the conditions that enabled them to emerge as important players in the world economy, for these conditions also carried the seeds of their current distress. Three factors were especially critical: the NICs' "special relations" with the United States, their links with Japan, and the system of state-directed development that we shall call command capitalism.

The U.S. Connection

The East Asian NICs emerged as economies specializing in the export of labor-intensive manufactures during a particular period of the world economy that is now drawing to a close, a phase marked by the economic and political hegemony of the United States. In the early 1960s, following the example of Japan, the NICs tied their fortunes to the vigorously expanding U.S. market at a time when the United States was still the champion of a liberal international trading order.

The emergence of the United States as the guardian of the free market coincided with its assumption of the role of defender of the free world against communism. The place of South Korea and Taiwan at the frontlines of that global struggle had immense economic implications. For one, it entitled them to an Asian version of the Marshall Plan. Between 1951 and 1965, the United States pumped about $1.5 billion in economic aid into Taiwan—in addition, of course, to billions of dollars in military aid. U.S. aid financed 95 percent of Taiwan's trade deficit in the 1950s.[4] Economic aid to South Korea was even larger, coming to almost $6 billion between 1945 and 1978—almost as much as the total aid provided to all African countries during the same period.[5] More than 80 percent of Korean imports in the 1950s were financed by U.S. economic assistance.[6]

But an equally significant fallout from the status as frontline allies was that the U.S. benignly overlooked Taiwan and South Korea's protected markets and their tight regimes on foreign investment, even as the IMF, World Bank, and the General Agreement on Tariffs and Trade (GATT)—the institutions set up by the United States and its Western allies to safeguard free trade and the mobility of capital—were telling the rest of the third world to end their restrictions on imports and foreign capital. In fact, Korea's foreign investment code was one of the world's most restrictive. This was a critical advantage, since Korea's protected domestic market provided a secure base from which its subsidized conglomerates, or *chaebol*, launched their drive for foreign markets in the late 1960s and 1970s.

U.S.-led containment strategy had another positive fallout for the NICs: Vietnam. War in East Asia served as an engine of prosperity. Just as the Korean War pulled the Japanese economy from post–World War II stagnation, so did Vietnam provide a vital stimulus for economic takeoff in Korea and Taiwan. The war provided what Taiwan expert Thomas Gold describes as an "incalculable boost" to the Taiwanese economy in the form of U.S. purchases of agricultural and industrial commodities, spending for "rest and recreation," and contract work for local firms in Vietnam.[7]

Like Taiwan, South Korea benefited from U.S. purchases and recreational spending. But perhaps the most significant stimulus came in the form of the big Vietnam War–related construction contracts that firms like Hyundai were awarded as part of the offset arrangements under which the United States paid for the services of 50,000 Korean troops in Indochina. These arrangements are characterized as the "blood money" that "fueled the modernization and development of the country" by the main protagonist in *White Badge*, Ahn Jung-Hyo's acclaimed autobiographical novel about Korean troops in Vietnam. "And owing to our contribution," he continues, "the Republic of Korea, or at least a higher echelon of it, made a gigantic stride into the world market. Lives for sale. National mercenaries."[8] By the end of the war in 1975, overseas work contracts had reached a total of $850 million[9]—accounting for almost 20 percent of Korea's exports of goods and services. Given their start by the U.S. military in Vietnam, Hyundai, Daewoo, and other Korean construction giants went on to conquer the Middle East in the late 1970s and early 1980s.

The Japan Factor

"Those Asian nations where the economy has been a success story, such as Korea, Taiwan, and Singapore were all, at one time or another, under Japanese administration," asserts the right-wing nationalist Shintaro Ishihara in the controversial book *The Japan That Can Say "No."* "We are aware that some negative changes happened under Japanese administration, but it cannot be denied that many positive changes were left behind."[10] While Koreans would probably take strong exception to this claim, there is an element of hard truth in it.

The proximity of the two countries to an expansionist Japan led to their being colonized in the first half of the twentieth century. Colonization meant repression, but it was also a period of vigorous economic development. Not only did the military-tech-nocratic elite in Korea and the Kuomintang (KMT) elite in Taiwan inherit a relatively well-developed physical and educational in-frastructure from the Japanese after World War II, but the old colonial economic and cultural ties became vital assets in the context of a revived and dynamic Japanese economy during the 1960s and 1970s.[11]

As Japanese firms sought to escape the rising cost of domestic labor, their first choice of location became their former colonies, Taiwan and South Korea. As the NICs sought to emulate Japan's export success, Japanese trading companies handled international trade for Taiwanese and Korean firms, with an estimated 50 to 70 percent of Taiwan's exports passing through them.[12] And as Taiwanese and Korean industrialization took off in the 1970s, Japan provided a significant portion of the machinery and com-ponents utilized by NIC enterprises to turn out toys, bicycles, radios, television sets, and PC monitors for export. Japan was more tightfisted when it came to technology transfers, but, espe-cially as the United States lost its technological edge to Japan, the Koreans became dependent on licensing available Japanese tech-nologies in finished form to achieve their export successes, partic-ularly in consumer electronics, automobiles, and semiconductors. In the period 1962–80, Japan was the source of nearly 59 percent of approved technology licenses, while the United States ac-counted for only 23 percent.[13]

In the last three decades, a vigorous triangular trade in manu-factured goods has developed, with the United States providing the market for the NICs, and the NICs depending on Japan for the critical technology, machinery, and component inputs. The dy-namism of what political analyst Kent Calder calls the "emerging North Pacific political economy" stemmed from

> a highly unbalanced set of relationships through which South Korea and the other newly industrializ-ing countries imported heavily from Japan to support their industrial development, and exported heavily to the U.S. to cover these imports. Japan compounded the imbalances by itself exporting heavily to the United States, and importing from the United States less than half of what it exported. These imbalances

were supported financially through massive capital flows from Japan to the United States and, to a lesser degree, to South Korea and the other NICs as well. The system was kept in political as well as short-run economic equilibrium by huge U.S.-bound capital flows.[14]

By the mid-1980s, while the NICs were running multibillion dollar trade surpluses with the United States, they were running multibillion dollar trade deficits with Japan. The NICs export successes were undeniable, but they came at the price of extreme economic dependence on Japan. In 1988 Taiwan enjoyed a $10.4 billion surplus in its trade with the United States but suffered a $6 billion deficit in its commerce with Japan. In the case of Korea, the surplus with the United States in 1988 came to $8.6 billion, while the deficit with Japan amounted to nearly $4 billion. The Japanese connection, in short, was both an asset and a liability, and when Singapore, Taiwan, and Korea sought to move to a higher stage of development in the 1980s, the liabilities became all too prominent.

Command Capitalism

Among the myths surrounding the NICs is the idea that they are free market economies approximating the United States. And among those who casually passed on this "truth" was Ronald Reagan, who declared in his 1985 State of the Union address that "America's economic succcess...can be repeated a hundred times in a hundred nations. Many countries in East Asia and the Pacific have few resources other than the enterprise of their own people. But through free markets, they've soared ahead of centralized economies."[15]

Contrary to the views of Reagan and the neoclassical economists, however, the NICs, with the possible exception of Hong Kong, were hardly paragons of free trade. The laws of the market did operate in Singapore, Taiwan, and South Korea, but under the constraints or "guidance" imposed by state elites.

The technocratic state elite determined the direction of economic policy and did not hesitate to employ subsidies, preferential access to credit, investment incentives, and other market-violating administrative measures to achieve the targets that they set. If these measures subverted the "efficient allocation of resources" that would be brought about in the short term by unrestrained market forces, so much the worse for the market. In a very real sense, development in the NICs depended on "getting relative prices wrong," to use Alice Amsden's phrase.[16]

Export success, not efficient resource allocation, was the overriding goal of the technocrats. And to achieve export competitiveness, they were willing to distort the operation of market forces. Thus, the Korean state deployed credit resources and other subsidies to the chaebol to enable them to withstand short-term losses to achieve market share. In contrast, the Singaporean state's preferential treatment of foreign investors—its preferred export agents—via infrastructural subsidies and tax incentives ended up marginalizing the Singaporean business class. In all three countries, the state forcefully intervened in the labor market to press down workers' wages below market value in order to achieve competitiveness for NIC exports in the international market.[17]

Command capitalism, not free market capitalism, is the system that enabled the NICs to become major players in the world economy. True, the international market had the ultimate say. But the rigorous demands of international competition evoked in Singapore, South Korea, and Taiwan a system of forceful state intervention that distorted local markets and incurred short-term inefficiencies to win long-term effectiveness as exporters in a harsh world economy.

The Onset of Crisis

By the late 1980s, the NICs' external and internal environments had been radically transformed, and what had been key assets in the period of high-speed growth increasingly became liabilities.

Protectionism was preventing export expansion in the NICs' main markets, while the economic, environmental, and social costs of a strategy of industrialization imposed from above by an authoritarian elite spawned increasingly powerful opposition movements that directly challenged the NIC model. Moreover, in South Korea, Taiwan, and Singapore, the technocrats were forced to confront the same profound structural dilemma that was unraveling the NIC economy: rising wage costs were making the NICs unprofitable as sites for labor-intensive manufacturing at the same time that their continuing technological backwardness severely obstructed plans to create a more capital and skill-intensive, high-tech manufacturing base.

The Protectionist Threat

Once the guardian of the liberal trading order, the United States had been transformed by the late 1980s into an aggressively protectionist power. Given the same label of unfair trader pinned on Japan, the NICs became prime targets of the protectionist offensive launched in the latter years of the Reagan administration to contain the massive U.S. trade deficit. Indeed, with the dramatic decline of the Soviet threat and the deepening technological crisis wracking U.S. industry, the NICs, together with Japan, became the leading candidates to replace the Soviet Union as America's new enemy.

Economic hostilities against the United States' staunchest cold war allies were formalized in what was tantamount to a declaration of war issued by senior Treasury official David Mulford in October 1987: "Although the NICs may be regarded as tigers because they are strong, ferocious traders, the analogy has a darker side. Tigers live in the jungle, and by the law of the jungle. They are a shrinking population."[18]

The U.S. trade offensive has had several prongs.

In January 1989 the United States revoked the tariff-free entry of selected NIC imports under the General System of Preferences (GSP). While elimination from GSP nominally affected only about 10 percent of NIC imports, its main intent was to warn the NICs that even more drastic measures would be taken if they did not cooperate by taking steps to radically reduce their trade surpluses.

Voluntary Export Restraints (VERs) on NIC products have drastically reduced their penetration of the U.S. market. Restrictive quotas placed on Korean textile imports drastically reduced their rate of growth from 43 percent per year in the 1970s to less than 1 percent per year in the early 1980s. Tough restrictions have also limited Korean steel to less than 2 percent of total U.S. steel imports.

To make the NICs' imports even more expensive and less appealing to consumers, Washington forced the appreciation of the New Taiwan dollar and the Korean won by 40 percent and 30 percent, respectively, between 1986 and 1989. Acknowledging the efficacy of currency warfare, a high executive of a leading Korean textile firm reported, "We can absorb wage increases, but we can't take any more appreciation."[19]

Protectionist measures were coupled with an aggressive drive to abolish import restrictions and lower tariff barriers for U.S.

goods in the NIC markets. Threatened by the infamous Super 301—legislation that required the U.S. president to take retaliatory measures against those officially tagged as unfair traders—Korea and Taiwan have been forced to liberalize trade restrictions on thousands of services and commodities, from foreign banking operations to imports of cigarettes and beef.

Washington and U.S. corporations have teamed up to throttle unauthorized technology transfer to the NICs. While the government has sought to place restrictive covenants on intellectual property in the General Agreement on Tariffs and Trade, U.S. electronics companies have initiated technological warfare against Korean and Taiwanese clone makers, who have gained the reputation of turning out products even better and considerably cheaper than the originals. IBM, Texas Instruments, and Intel now stand to make hundreds of millions in royalty payments from Asian producers, who have no choice but to pay up, given their dependence on trouble-free entry to the U.S. market.

The techno-trade offensive has drastically curbed further expansion of exports from Taiwan and Korea to the U.S. market. Both countries' exports to the United States grew by only about 1 percent in 1988 over 1987, while imports from the United States rose sharply, by more than 75 percent in the case of Taiwan.[20] As the destination of NIC exports, the United States saw its share fall from 39 percent in 1987 to 32 percent in 1988 in the case of Korea and from 45 percent to 39 percent in the case of Taiwan. The American shock treatment has been quite effective.

Faced with a U.S. market that is becoming less hospitable, the NICs have been feverishly hunting for new markets. Efforts to export to Western Europe have intensified, but so have antidumping moves against NIC producers, especially the Koreans. In fact, many Taiwanese and Korean manufacturers assume that when the Economic Community becomes a unified market in 1992, their access to the continent will be severely limited.

NIC attempts to carve out a niche for their manufactured goods at the lower end of the Japanese market have had disappointing results. And the few NIC producers that have some success soon face a powerful protectionist alliance between bureaucracy and business. For instance, Korean knitwear manufacturers have been successfully intimidated by Japanese bureaucrats and garment makers to limit their exports to Japan—or else.

The prospect of markets in China, the Soviet Union, and Eastern Europe has received a lot of hype in the press, but recent developments have underlined the fact that these fragile postsocialist economies will generate no more than a fraction of the former U.S. demand. Moreover, the plans of the new market-oriented technocrats to shut down inefficient factories, lay off surplus labor, and radically reduce social subsidies will depress popular purchasing power and eliminate Eastern Europe and the Soviet Union as significant mass markets, at least in the short and medium term.

The immense difficulties of diversifying from the U.S. market in an increasingly protectionist world are suggested by the following set of statistics. In 1988 Hyundai sold over 300,000 Excel subcompacts in the United States. In contrast, in the same year it was able to sell only 20,097 in the European Community and a minuscule 150 in neighboring Japan.[21]

The Internal Costs of the NIC Model

As the NICs' external environment worsened, so did their internal environment. Among the internal costs of the NIC model was the crisis of agriculture. The subordination of agriculture to export-oriented industrialization in Taiwan and South Korea led to the serious erosion of the agrarian base of these economies. This might come as a surprise to many, since Taiwan and Korea are often cited as examples of successful agrarian reform. True, decisive land reform was enacted in both countries in the 1950s, and certainly, in Taiwan at least, higher agricultural incomes contributed to a rise in domestic demand that sparked early industrialization efforts.

Since then, however, it was downhill for the agrarian sector in both countries, as a massive net transfer of resources from agriculture to industry was effected to fuel export manufacturing beginning in the late 1960s. Low grain-price policies translated into low wages for urban workers, which in turn translated into competitive prices for Taiwanese and Korean exports. Low grain prices had another, perhaps not unintended impact: as rural incomes fell relative to urban incomes, young people left the countryside for the cities, where they provided the work force for the growing industrial sector.

Half-hearted rural development efforts failed to stem the agrarian crisis in the 1970s, and in the 1980s, the erosion of agriculture was speeded up by intensified U.S. efforts to completely dismantle tariff and nontariff barriers to U.S. agricultural commodities. Liberalization of agricultural imports was the quid pro quo for continued access to the U.S. market for NIC manufactured exports. The ultimate price, farmers realized, was the extinction of wide swaths of the agrarian economy.

Taiwanese and Korean technocrats were no help to the farmers, for the U.S. effort to open up protected agricultural markets, in fact, dovetailed with their view on how to make agriculture more efficient—eliminate surplus labor in the countryside and concentrate land in larger units to take advantage of the economies of mechanization. Bereft of sympathy from the very governments that once valued them as a secure base of electoral support, farmers in both countries took to the streets with the same message: the countryside is no longer going to serve as the sacrificial lamb for export industry.

Like agriculture, the environment has been a prime victim of the NICs' high-speed industrial growth. With state technocrats assuming that some degree of ecological destabilization was the price of economic growth, export-oriented industrialization telescoped into three decades processes of environmental destruction that took many more years to unfold in earlier industrializing societies.

The dimensions of the environmental crisis in Korea are only now coming to light, but what is known indicates that the situation is grave: world-record levels of sulphur dioxide concentration in Seoul's air, rain with high acid content, tap water with heavy metals at many times the official tolerance level, and nuclear reactors plagued by malfunctions and accidents.

Taiwan, it appears, is in a more advanced state of environmental decay. Not only are crops overdosed with pesticides, but agricultural land has been heavily contaminated with heavy metals from unregulated waste dumping by thousands of manufacturing establishments that located in the countryside as a result of the government's rural industrialization policy. Levels of air pollution considered hazardous in the United States are normal in many of Taiwan's urban areas.

Rapid environmental deterioration has not only produced the ubiquitous motorcyclist with a surgical mask weaving in and out of Taipei's hellish traffic; it has also provoked the rise of a multiclass, grass roots environmental movement. This movement fills the role that the labor movement does in Korea—that of presenting the status quo with its most powerful challenge. Resorting to direct action like plant occupations, local residents have been able to stop the establishment of key petrochemical facilities and nuclear plants. But growth-oriented KMT technocrats fear not only the movement's impact on local investments but also its long-term philosophical impact on the people. Indeed, a 1985 survey showed that 59 percent of respondents favored environmental protection over economic growth.[22]

The crises in agriculture and the environment aggravated what was already a profound crisis in the legitimacy of the authoritarian political systems that had imposed high-speed, export-oriented growth.

The People's Action Party of Singapore had pushed export-oriented growth as a means to strengthen its political legitimacy, while in Korea and Taiwan the state elites had sought to use economic development to neutralize what was widely perceived to be their illegitimate assumption of power. Prosperity, it was hoped, would buy legitimacy and excuse the repressive policies imposed to achieve high-speed growth.

By the mid-1980s, however, it was clear that this strategy of purchasing legitimacy was not working. Instead, both the economic model and the power structure that imposed it were losing legitimacy. In Singapore, there was growing disaffection with the longstanding alliance between the authoritarian Lee Kwan-Yew regime and transnational capital, which had marginalized local business, emasculated labor, and subjected the population to pervasive political control. In Taiwan and Korea, decades of labor repression created working classes that were alienated from the paradigm of export-oriented growth. Indeed, in Korea, labor's attitude bordered on the insurrectionary, making nearly impossible the institutionalization of Western-style collective bargaining processes.

Rising opposition pressure from the social groups that had been marginalized by the NIC strategy of growth forced a gradual democratization of the political process. But precisely because labor and other groups had been so strongly repressed in the pursuit of high-speed development, political decompression did not lead to the creation of a new consensus around the traditional strategy of growth but to a politics of polarized struggle over the distribution of income, sectoral priorities, the trade-off between environmental and economic priorities, and the direction of development itself. Late industrialization, followed by late democratization, promoted not consensus but divergent views on economic priorities. As one report on Korea aptly put it, "the country's new-found democratic politics are putting wage push, labor unrest and demands for welfare expenditure in the way of continued super-growth."[23]

But clearly there was no alternative to democratization, whatever its limitations and however late it might be. For example, in Singapore, the one East Asian NIC that resisted democratization, opposition nevertheless expressed itself in a way that threatened the viability of the old economic model, as the very middle class that the Lee Kwan-Yew regime had envisioned as the base of a future high-tech economy expressed its discontent by emigrating in large numbers.

One of the key lessons of the NIC experience is that there is no alternative to democratic participation in the making of economic policy, and the longer democracy is postponed, the more difficult will it be to create the necessary social consensus to underpin a strategy of economic development.

The Structural Squeeze

Coinciding with the rise of protectionism and the eroding legitimacy of the model of export-oriented growth was the worsening structural squeeze on the economy. Throughout the 1960s and early 1970s, cheap labor was the chief asset that provided NIC exports with their competitive edge. But by the late 1970s and 1980s, the drying up of labor reserves from the countryside and militant labor organizing created strong upward pressures on wages that raised labor costs in the NICs significantly above those in other third world countries that were moving fast to adopt export-oriented growth policies. In 1988, for instance, the average monthly wage stood at $643 in Taiwan, $558 in Hong Kong, $401 in Singapore, and $610 in Korea. In contrast, the figure was $132 in Thailand, $129 in Malaysia, and $209 in Indonesia.[24]

In the view of NIC technocrats, the solution was to move their economies away from dependence on labor-intensive manufacturing processes to more skilled, higher-value-added production. Singapore's technocrats took the boldest step along this path in 1979, when they decreed a wage correction policy that raised unit labor costs by 40 percent over the following six years. Contrary to expectations, however, most transnational corporations refused to automate their production processes or shift to producing high-tech commodities, preferring to move their investments to other low-wage sites. The onset of a deep recession in 1985–86 forced the Singaporean technocrats to retreat and return to the old strategy of attracting multinationals with the promise of a cheap labor force, a policy that was increasingly dependent on bringing in more low-wage foreign workers from Thailand, Malaysia, and other neighboring countries.

In rhetoric, Taiwan's technocrats also committed themselves to a high-tech future. In practice, however, their strategy was to back only a few high-tech projects, especially in electronics, while the island's manufacturers continued to concentrate on low-tech, labor-intensive investments. To slow the inevitable loss of competitiveness, Taiwan's capitalists either transferred their manufacturing operations to China and other low-wage countries or, following Singapore's example, began importing foreign workers who were paid from a third to half the average wage of the Taiwanese worker. In Taiwan, this rear-guard strategy has led to the emergence of a two-tier labor force, composed of poorly paid foreign workers and better paid local workers—a sure-fire formula for social and political conflicts in the near future.

South Korea was, for a time, buffered from the consequences of rising wages by its ability to organize its labor force into an efficient manufacturing system that could take advantage of economies of scale. But a 60 percent rise in wage costs between 1986 and 1989 pushed the technocrats toward the two-pronged policy of transferring low-tech, labor-intensive manufacturing to Southeast Asia, China, and other low-wage countries, while moving domestic production toward high-tech manufacturing.

The government laid out ambitious plans to develop the ultra-advanced 64 megabit DRAM (dynamic random access memory) chip, artificial intelligence computers, videodisc players, and even a Korean rocket to launch satellites. But the Koreans were soon up against the moment of truth: their complex of basic and intermediate industries was still inadequate to sustain significant high-tech manufacturing, and they did not have adequate numbers of trained technical personnel to support self-sustaining technological innovation. Skilled personnel were not as easy to clone as VCRs and IBM personal computers. And it was the pool of scientists and engineers that would make the difference in the vicious competition with Japan and the United States in the frontiers of high technology.

The coming together of protectionism in Western markets, the internal political crisis of the NIC model, and the structural squeeze in the economy posed a formidable threat to the strategy of high-speed export-oriented industrialization. To surmount the

developing crisis meant more than just macroeconomic adjustments in the basic paradigm. Continued economic transformation
demanded fundamental changes in the strategy, direction, and
quality of growth, but this could only come about with a profound
change in the very structure of political and economic power.
Some of the key elements of an alternative paradigm will be
suggested later.

In 1984, at a time that the East Asian NICs were the star per-
formers in the world economy, a confidential study by the Central
Intelligence Agency's Office of Global Issues predicted that "the
change in the composition of the NICs will more likely be the
result of a country falling from its [sic] ranks rather than advancing
to the status of an industrial country."[25] Accurate forecasting is
not the CIA's forte, but recent developments have rendered this
particular prediction credible.

This is, in broad strokes, the argument of this book. The succeed-
ing chapters will attempt to provide a detailed portrait and analysis of the development, dynamics, and dimensions of the crisis of
the NIC model in Korea, Taiwan, and Singapore. But crisis, as the
Chinese say, is also opportunity, and at various points in this study
new directions of economic transformation for the NICs will be
explored.

PART I

Korea: A Model Unravels

Introduction to Part I

Shortly before the tumultuous events in Tiananmen Square in June 1989, a new doctrine of development was gaining currency among Chinese Communist party intellectuals. Aptly named neoauthoritarianism, it was explicitly derived from the experience of Singapore, Taiwan, and, in particular, South Korea. Proponents of the doctrine asserted that the lesson that South Korea held for China was that development depended on economic liberalization and that the latter could only be achieved through "a combination of free enterprise and an ostensibly temporary period of benign autocracy."[1] Or as one Chinese academic expressed it, in more mundane terms:

> It is impossible to believe that any real democratic reforms can take place in the near future...I like democracy, just as I like the free market. But in both cases, I think it will take a strongman to get us there.[2]

Chinese intellectuals were becoming enamored with a model with which many Western economists had been infatuated for about two decades. And, to South Korean technocrats, nothing was perhaps more gratifying than to become regarded as a role model by former enemies as the latter tried to solve the dilemma of maintaining the Communist party's monopoly of power while dismantling China's socialist economy. Indeed, in the mid-eighties, the Korean technocrats had reason to be satisfied and the Chinese had reason to be dazzled: South Korea's powerhouse economy grew by an astounding 12 percent a year in 1987 and 1988, probably the highest rate of growth in the world. The International Monetary Fund, usually slow to praise other third world economies, called it an "impressive expansion, unequaled elsewhere in the world."[3] And in September 1988, South Korea's entry into the ranks of developed nations was marked by the impressive Seoul Olympics.

But had South Korea really arrived? Were the Chinese justified in joining the ranks of Seoul's admirers? The massacre of student demonstrators clamoring for more political and economic freedom at Tiananmen Square in June 1989 underlined what it would cost to apply the South Korean model to China. And a year after the Seoul Olympics, it was increasingly evident to South Korea's military-technocratic leadership that the concatenation of factors that had created the so-called miracle was coming apart. The GNP growth rate was cut in half. Labor was in open rebellion, and there was no end in sight. The massive U.S. market that had served as the locomotive of Korea's economy for nearly thirty years was closing up, with the United States forcing the appreciation of the won (the Korean currency) and explicitly threatening trade sanctions on South Korea. An uneven process of democratization was eroding the monopoly over setting economic priorities that had been exercised by the technocratic elite and big business, forcing them to consider the demands of social groups that did not share the "consensus" on high-speed, export-oriented growth. And it was becoming clear that the vision of moving from dependence on labor-intensive industries to a skill-intensive or high-tech economy was encountering significant technological and structural obstacles.

Moreover, two of the greatest costs of high-speed, export-oriented growth were coming to the fore of public consciousness. The revelation in August 1989 that a significant portion of the country's tap water was seriously contaminated with heavy metals and other pollutants brought home the seriousness of environmental destruction. And increasingly militant demonstrations by farmers exposed the depth of the crisis that had been visited on the countryside by a strongly urban-biased pattern of industrialization.

Korea faced a triple crisis by the late 1980s: the erosion of the legitimacy of the model of authoritarian, export-oriented industrialization and of the institutions that sustained it; an agro-environmental disaster set off by high-speed growth; and a profound crisis of the economic structure. The depth of the crisis was pointed out by President Roh Tae-Woo himself: "The old political, economic, and social systems and orders started to crumble, and we have thus had to grapple with the formidable task of building new systems and orders to replace them."[4] Economic Planning Minister Cho Soon, the nation's top technocrat before being fired in March 1990, was more somber, warning that the unraveling of the old growth formula could lead to a situation in which "our economy will collapse like some of the Latin American countries," such as Argentina.[5] Yet alarmist rhetoric was not matched by innovative solutions to the worsening crisis. Roh, Cho, and virtually the whole corps of senior technocrats, as well as the chieftains of the country's *chaebol* or conglomerates, remained imprisoned by the paradigm of export-oriented growth. The solution, Roh said, was for Koreans to put their "heart and soul" into another export campaign, as they did in the 1960s and 1970s.

This treatment of the South Korean economy is not intended to be another contribution to the admiring literature on the subject of how and why the miracle occurred. It seeks, instead, to understand the origins and dynamics of the current crisis of the Korean route to development. It explores the unfolding of the contradictions that threaten the viability of high-speed, export-oriented growth as an engine for sustained development in the 1990s.

1

The Making of an Insurrectionary Working Class

The past three years, 1987–1990, have seen the shattering of a number of myths about the process of industrialization in Korea, popular with Western commentators. Among them is the image of a docile working class laboring twelve hours a day out of Confucian respect for their employers. Yes, Korean workers were worked to the bone. Yes, they were highly motivated. But the eruption of labor since 1987 has underlined the point that Confucian piety was not the mainspring of the energies of Korea's workers.[1] Indeed, the working class that barged into the center of Korea's political stage and grabbed the world's attention with 3,500 strikes in the hot summer of 1987 evoked images of the European working classes in the nineteenth century: rebellious, uncompromising, and passionately class conscious.

A Class Matures, in Anger

One cannot understand the uncompromising streak of the Korean working class without referring to the circumstances of its growth. The transformation of the work force in any society is accompanied by great social and cultural dislocation and alienation. In Korea these stresses were exacerbated by the speed of the process. While the urban working class was born in the period of Japanese colonialism in the first half of this century, its growth was concentrated in a brief twenty-year period from the mid-1960s to the mid-1980s. As a percentage of the total labor force, farm labor declined from 65 percent in the early 1960s to 38 percent in the early 1980s. The working class's industrial core shot up from 10 percent in 1965 to 23 percent in 1983, while workers in the services rose from 31 percent to 47 percent.[2] Indeed, the speed with which this class expanded and reached a critical mass was paralleled in few other societies.

The swiftness of its growth, however, was but one of several factors that conditioned the formation of working class consciousness in Korea. Central to the emergence of a militant stance was an economic strategy that depended fundamentally on the harsh and systematic exploitation of labor. Labor emerged as the key factor of production in the program of export-oriented growth pushed by the Korean military-technocratic elite beginning in the mid-1960s.

In the savage competition that emerged for the markets of the advanced industrial countries, the advantage devolved to the country that was most successful at keeping down the cost of labor. And Korea's elite was supremely successful at keeping labor cheap. From the early 1960s until 1987, the wages of Korean workers were consistently lower than those of workers in Singapore, Hong Kong, and Taiwan. At the beginning of 1987, before aggressive unionism brought about the big wage gains of the past three years, the hourly pay of Korean manufacturing workers was 11 percent of United States' workers, 14 percent of Japan's, 75 percent of Taiwan's, and 80 percent of Hong Kong's.[3] But low wages were only one element in the Korean formula for success. Another was the long working day. A 1986 international survey by the International Labor Office found that Korean workers worked the longest hours—an average of 54 hours per week. Instead of declining over time, hours worked per week actually rose from 50.5 to 54.3 between 1975 and 1983.[4] In fact, the twelve-hour working day is still common. As the foreman of a medium-size wood-processing firm in Inchon told me, "We operate around the clock, with two shifts of twelve hours each. But we're not unusual. Koreans like to work hard. Don't judge us by American standards."[5] American standards were, in 1986, 40.5 hours per week.[6]

The secret of Korea's success lay in the combination of long working hours, cheap labor, and the organization of this cheap labor force into a highly efficient system of production. This formula produced "labor costs per unit of output [that]...undercut almost every competitor in sight."[7]

While these were the main ingredients of the Korean formula for profitability, not to be underestimated was the contribution of another cost-saving measure: minimal investment in safe working conditions. While there are laws requiring industrial safety, notes one authority, they "are almost useless in practice...because employers do not follow the rules and regulations set out in the laws, workers lack proper knowledge of work-induced health hazards, and [because of] the lack of trained professionals and proper equipment to prevent and to treat work-related illnesses."[8] Needless to say, the results of cutting costs on safety have been simply horrendous: Korea has the world's highest rate of industrial accidents, with an average of 5 workers killed daily and another 390 injured.[9] The country also leads the world in the rate of occupation-related illnesses, with 2.66 per 11 persons suffering from work-related illnesses and injuries, compared to 0.61 for Japan, 0.70 for Taiwan, and 0.93 for Singapore.[10]

Women Workers on the Cutting Edge

The centrality of cheap labor in global competition led both domestic and foreign export manufacturers to a preference for women workers in the early years of the industrialization process. The target group were unmarried women aged sixteen to twenty-five with at least a middle-school education.[11] Notes one study for the International Labor Office:

> Girls are preferred not only because their discipline is better, but also because female production wages are, on average, almost 50 percent of male wages. There is little evidence that women are less productive than men, and it is therefore much more profitable to employ women.[12]

Women thus became the fastest growing section of the labor force, both in industry and the services, and "Kong Soonie" (a Korean name equivalent to Rosie the Riveter) became "in great part, responsible for the Korean miracle."[13]

Indeed, so prominent are gender-based differences in pay and treatment that economist Alice Amsden describes the structure of labor thus: "At the top in Korea is the new, male labor aristocracy of the firms that dominate the more capital- and skill-intensive sectors. At the bottom are the 'factory girls,' young women whose low wages and long working hours support the international competitiveness of labor-intensive industries."[14]

There is undoubtedly an element of exaggeration at work here, for under the government–big business slogan of "growth first, distribution later" both men and women workers have had to endure low wages. In 1985, for instance, 87 percent of South Korean workers earned less than the 507,254 won per month ($638) that the government estimated to be the minimum cost of living for a family of four.[15] Still, when the data is broken down according to sex, female workers are, in fact, significantly more exploited than male workers. While 13.2 percent of male workers received wages below the single worker's minimum cost of living in 1985, the figure for women workers was a far larger 63.9 percent.[16]

Moreover, in the social organization of work, patriarchal authority was used as a means of discipline, with few female workers promoted to supervisory positions.[17] More generally, male workers, claims labor specialist Jeong Taik-Lee, had more job stability, engaged in less labor-intensive operations, enjoyed more freedom from overseers' interference, and were more easily coopted by employers.[18]

The control of women workers, in fact, extended beyond the factory. With most of them being rural migrants packed into company-provided housing,

> their dormitory lives were totally controlled. The dormitory functioned as a mechanism by which workers' lives at work and off work were integrated and thus, employers could maximize their control over workers. Roommate shifts were frequently undertaken so that formation of social ties was minimized.[19]

It is probably true that despite growing inequality in income rapid growth has made less widespread in Korea the sort of severe penury that is the normal condition of marginalized workers elsewhere in the third world. But if there is any sector of the working class that approaches this condition of extreme poverty, it is single women factory workers. One account of the daily life of the mostly women workers in the Bucheon electronics complex in Seoul captures this quality of living at the edge of existence:

> Even with the wage increases [of 1988]...factory workers in Bucheon live mostly on *ramyon*—instant noodle soup. Out of a minimum wage of 122,000 won per month [$168], [a worker] has to pay rent (60,000 to 70,000 won a month on average for a small flat), and water and heat (30,000 won on average). The rest is spent for food. A movie or even a beer is a rare, if not unthinkable, luxury. The only "liquor" these workers can afford is *soju*, an indigenous "whiskey" costing only 300 won a bottle. The workers argue that the

minimum cost of living for a single man is at least 222,000 won per month; for a woman, a little higher. Saving is impossible. The most painful moment for these factory workers is when members [of the family] or friends come to visit. They cannot afford a visitor even a decent meal, much less a little travel or pocket money for their sisters or brothers.[20]

The combination of low wages and long working hours for women has undoubtedly contributed to two phenomena. One is that Korea's percentage of women under twenty-five who are unmarried is the highest in the world (see table 1.1).[21] The other is a low population growth rate of 1.4 percent per year. In other words, it is very likely that the severe exploitation of women workers was a key factor in inducing this demographic transition to lower population growth rates, generally attributed to higher levels of living in already developed countries. As one reconstructed technocrat expressed it, in classic Orwellian fashion, a factor in the decline of fertility rates

> was the increase in employment opportunities for women in developing industries, encouraging [women workers] to postpone getting marriage [sic] and to have fewer children. Because these employ- ment opportunities initially were mainly in labor-in- tensive industries, women with no more than a primary school education were the first to benefit from the expanded opportunities.[22]

And, with no trace of irony, he concluded that "the impact of industrialization on fertility was highly egalitarian in the early period of growth."[23]

The stereotype of female docility made women central to the plans of both domestic and foreign firms. But the harsh exploita- tion produced an unforeseen and unwanted side effect: the sub- missiveness into which women have been traditionally socialized gradually gave way to combativeness. The reluctance to partici- pate in struggles for workers' rights observed among women workers in many other areas of the third world was not as marked in Korea. Choi Jang-Jip, the country's foremost student of labor, claims that the "Korean case, at least of the 1970s, sharply diverges from such a general pattern. In the past ten years in Korea, the women workers have really been the driving force not only to bestow on the nascent labor movement a dynamic character but

Table 1.1

Percentage of Single Women Ages Twenty to Twenty-four in Selected Third World Countries

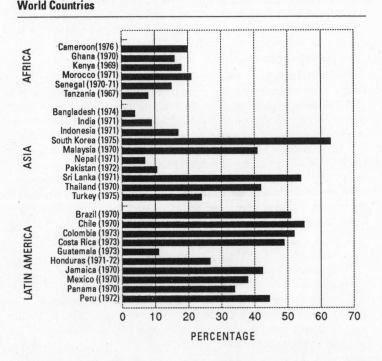

PERCENTAGE

Source: U.S. Commerce Department data, cited in Tony Michell, "From LDC to NIC: The Republic of Korea: Employment, Industrialization and Trade, 1961–82" (Unpublished manuscript, Seoul, February 1988), p. 136.

also to actually lead it at the grassroots level."[24]

Militarism and Management

Making the strategy of export-oriented development work meant systematically preventing working class organization and defusing incipient class consciousness. Defenses were created at both the enterprise and state levels.

At the enterprise level, Korea's business class evolved a particularly repressive management culture—an extremely hierarchical and centralized system of decision making and discipline that bordered on the militaristic. Koreans, in fact, refer to the chaebol as military companies, and, indeed, "workers in many Korean construction companies are expected to obey orders and work with the same discipline as soldiers in the army construction and engineering commands."[25] The influence of military culture and discipline is often direct since retired officers have extensive involvement in the management of private enterprises.[26]

Management sought not only unquestioning discipline but total control of the production process. Firing was not to be disputed, workers were rarely allowed to share information on company matters, and the role of worker-manager was nonexistent.[27] Moreover, as You Jong-Il points out, while management urged workers to apply their knowledge to the production process, the line was firmly drawn at decision making: "Employers would not let their prerogatives [be] compromised by involving workers in the decision making process even if that could enhance workers' cooperation in the production process."[28]

Among the chaebol it is perhaps Hyundai, Korea's second-largest conglomerate, that exemplifies Korea's militaristic and hegemonistic management culture. Hyundai's founder, Chung Ju-Yung, is said to live "with a religious belief in military-like command and unconditional obedience from employees."[29] Chung warned workers that "I will never allow a union in my corporation. There can be a union only over my dead body."[30] This militaristic frame of mind, which pervaded Hyundai's management, reflected an attitude towards labor as a force to be "tamed" by means fair and foul, including hiring large gangs of *kusadae*, or toughs, to kidnap, beat up, and intimidate workers.[31]

Not surprisingly, not only did Hyundai's iron fist not work, it provoked a similarly militaristic response from Hyundai workers. Insurrectionary is the only apt description of the great strikes at the Hyundai shipyard in 1974, 1988–89, and 1990. One observer of the 1988–89 strike—an epic 109-day insurrection—asserted that the militaristic management style was perhaps an even more fundamental reason for the uprising than wages: "Although they wanted higher wages, money wasn't their top grievance. Above all, they hate the way bosses order them around: They want their human dignity reaffirmed."[32]

The State and Labor Control

But unlike in Europe or in the United States, control of the labor force in Korea has evolved primarily as the responsibility of the state, with the firm playing a subsidiary role. As one prominent technocrat put it, "Korean entrepreneurs have developed a habit of delegating intra-firm labor-relations to the government and of devoting minimal efforts to reduce the potential sources of labor disputes by themselves."[33]

The state's leading role in repressing labor has been a constant in post–World War II Korea. Following the collapse of the Japanese colonial government in 1945, the U.S. military government crushed the left-wing Chun Pyong, or General Council of Korean Trade Unions, which was active in organizing left-wing People's Committees throughout the country. From 1,980 unions with a membership of 553,408, the Chun Pyong was radically reduced in a few years to a mere 13 unions with 2,465 members.

Under the conservative government of Rhee Syng-Man in the 1950s, labor was kept under control via the Federation of Korean Trade Unions (FKTU), which was officially an organ of the ruling party. When Maj. General Park Chung-Hee came to power in May 1961, one of his junta's first decrees was the dissolution of unions, using as a pretext the ferment of labor during the short-lived government of Premier Chang Myon. Under Park's long reign from 1961 to 1979, the Korean state evolved into the central mechanism for "socializing" labor to carry out its role in the strategy of export-oriented growth.

There are three key reasons for the prominence of the Korean state as an instrument of labor control during the Park period. One, the state became the leading agency in economic development. Two, the state functioned as the manager of a program of forced-march industrialization that would telescope in Korea processes and their concomitant tensions and contradictions that took decades to unfold elsewhere. Third, Korea's mode of insertion into the global economy—export-oriented growth—required the global, suprafactory coordination and repression of the labor force to be effective.

In the effort to systematically demobilize labor, the government constructed three lines of containment: legal, ideological, and repressive. All three were drawn together to form a nearly impenetrable mesh during the Park regime.

While the Park regime eventually removed the formal ban on unions that it had imposed upon taking power, the terms under which unions could function were so restrictive as to eliminate the possibility of any genuine independent organizing. The predominant legal instruments of state control have been the Labor Union Law and the Labor Disputes Adjustments Law, and their subsequent amendments.

The Labor Union Law basically subjected unionizing to government control by giving the latter "the right to order the union to change its decision or make the decision null and void."[34] Later revisions that further emasculated unionism included one that prevented unions from cooperating, forming, or contributing to a political party; and another that banned collective bargaining beyond the union local, thus preempting the solidarity, technical cooperation, and strength in numbers that could emerge with industrywide associations.

The Labor Disputes Adjustments Law essentially outlawed strikes by stipulating a complicated and lengthy process for resolving disputes. By law a strike could not take place until three months after a dispute occurred and the appropriate investigations, appeals, and counterappeals had taken place. Moreover, the government could intervene and impose compulsory arbitration in disputes occurring in export industries and all other industries that the president of the country chose to designate as being in the "public interest." The Labor Disputes Adjustments Law also banned "third parties" from involvement in union affairs—an ill-disguised measure against church activist groups like the Urban Industrial Mission and the Young Catholic Workers, which played a key role in assisting workers to form unions.[35]

In addition to these two basic laws, there were other measures designed to create an airtight legal system against independent union organizing. The formidably titled Law Concerning Special Measures for Safeguarding National Security expanded compulsory government arbitration to all industries in 1971, meaning that most labor disputes came under the jurisdiction of administrative agencies whose ruling became final and binding.[36] The Labor-Management Council Law sought to supplant union power by creating councils made up of an equal number of representatives of management and labor, the function of which was ostensibly "to seek peace in industry and make a contribution to the development of the national economy."[37]

With labor bound by a thousand and one legal chains, it is not surprising that some labor experts claim that no strike that has taken place in Korea in the last three decades has really been "legal."

Korea's rulers have always been sensitive to the fact that an economic strategy based only on force or legal dicta would be highly unstable. Thus efforts were expended to formulate and institutionalize mechanisms of ideological containment of the working class. Perhaps the most important of these corporatist efforts was the Factory *Saemaul* (New Community) Movement, which aimed to put labor on an ideological "war footing" against the Communist enemy to achieve production objectives set by the technocrats and the conglomerates. On the one hand, Factory Saemaul attempted to exploit the traditional high value placed on collectivism and patriotism to achieve the high-speed industrialization that Park regarded as the basis of his government's legitimacy. On the other hand, Factory Saemaul work teams, which operated on such principles as "work hard without being conscious of the closing hour of work" and "workers should behave toward employers as sons to their fathers," were actually a means to subvert unions. And in many cases, they served as a means to militarize the factory atmosphere.

The state-promoted Factory Saemaul Movement plugged into conglomerate management's efforts to artificially incorporate workers through different variants of the family-enterprise ideology. The chaebol sought to create the image of the Confucian employer, with incentives like cheap meals, bonuses, night classes for workers, and sports tournaments. Among the more advanced efforts at cooptation was that at Samsung, which cultivated a "'family'-oriented managerial philosophy that offered workers what management believed to be a Garden-of-Eden working environment by Korean standards. In return, Samsung workers were expected to refrain from the tempting fruit of the union tree."[38]

While the objectives of Factory Saemaul and the chaebol's family-enterprise ideology were transparent to most workers, the impact of periodic ideological campaigns in the 1970s must not be underestimated, especially in the context of the prevailing red-hot ideological rivalry with North Korea. As labor expert Choi Jang-Jip asserts:

> The crudely defined "enterprise family" ideology in Korea is likely to have a real effect in fostering workers' ideological conformity and compliant mentality when it is plugged into the "national security" ideology with emphasis on a state of quasi-war from the Northern threat, repeatedly evoked by the state. Now workers' contributions to export production by hard work becomes equivalent to their patriotic efforts for

nation-building and national defense. Certainly this ideology is instrumental in creating a corporative and authoritarian workshop atmosphere which prevails in Korea's factories, where incipient delinquency and rebellion is either brain-washed away or shamed because an individual worker can hardly stand the moral pressure.[39]

But in the last analysis, the family-enterprise ideology was ineffective; indeed, the image was turned around, with labor arguing that if the company was indeed a family, "workers were treated more like family servants rather than sons and daughters."[40]

Thus, nothing could replace force and repression as the prime instruments for keeping the working class in its place in the program of cheap labor–dependent export-oriented growth. Indeed, one of the distinctive features of the Korean state is that the evolution of the internal security apparatus was greatly determined by the need to surveil and repress labor as part of a broader economic strategy. In Park's development program, Choi observes, the Korean Central Intelligence Agency (KCIA) played a central role in separating "the planning and implementation processes from any external political influences and controls, thereby minimizing 'distortion' and 'irrationality.' It explains why the EPB [Economic Planning Board] and the intelligence agency possess a close relationship."[41]

The KCIA labor-control program involved not only infiltrating factories with hundreds of agents to monitor dissenters but also making the government-recognized union leadership an adjutant of the state. This meant, above all, having a pliable set of officers for the nationwide Federation of Korean Trade Unions and key national unions like the Chemical Workers Union. KCIA agents attended meetings of the central committees of the national unions and regularly intervened in elections to get candidates of their choice elected. Even though close government surveillance did not necessarily ensure that every election had the appropriate outcome, it did mean that no uncooperative leader could win election at the national level.[42]

At the local level, behind-the-scenes cooperation regularly took place between management and the local police, who made a daily report on labor activities to higher authorities. Indeed, the state security agents' intrusion into even labor-management negotiations on wages led one labor specialist to remark that they deserved to be classified as a third party and thus legally banned from the process according to the Labor Disputes Adjustments Law.[43]

The KCIA was reorganized as the National Security Commission in the aftermath of Park's assassination in 1979, but it continued to maintain a Committee to Counteract Labor Insurgency, with agents planted throughout the country.[44] Indeed, what little space was won for free labor organizing in the last years of Park was eliminated under the seven-year reign of President Chun Doo-Hwan, who seized power in a May 1980 coup that cut short the brief period of democratic ferment after Park's death. The state divested industrywide unions of the right to serve as workers' representatives in centralized collective bargaining and disbanded other broad formations like the militant Chonggye Garment Workers' Union, thus depriving workers of the ability to exercise their collective voice beyond the factory level. In the space of less than four years, all existing independent unions were destroyed. Blacklisting was systematically employed and about 1,000 labor activists were interrogated and intimidated on the basis of such lists.[45] With state repression heightened at every level, the smallest labor protest took on an insurrectionary character.

The Struggle for Labor Rights

"Historically," notes labor scholar Kim Seung-Kuk, "there has been a close relationship between weak, unorganized labor movements and the outbreak of radical, violent activities."[46] Indeed, the history of the 1970s and 1980s, when the Korean working class matured amidst the state's and business's supreme efforts to keep the working class weak and atomized, is peppered with strikes and labor actions that can only be described as bordering on the insurrectionary.

Perhaps the most dramatic and significant labor struggle of the 1970s was that of the Chonggye Garment Workers' Union (CGWU). The CGWU struggle was marked by a creative combination of tenacity, self-sacrifice, and confrontational tactics that made it the symbolic center of the nascent Korean labor movement in the 1970s.

A brief background on the conditions of work in the textile and garment industries is essential to understanding the confrontational character of the CGWU struggle. The labor force in both industries was predominantly made up of terribly underpaid female workers. In the textile industries in the 1970s and early 1980s, wages were 80 percent of the national average. In the garment industries, wages averaged 70 percent or less of the national average for manufacturing as a whole, and the number of hours worked per month exceeded the manufacturing average by ten or more hours in most years. Equally as oppressive were health conditions: in the textile factories, hearing loss was reported for many workers who had toiled for five to ten years.[47]

Within these industries, probably the worst conditions were found in the Peace Market section of Seoul, where over 20,000 workers labored for over a thousand sweatshops. After numerous attempts to publicize the plight of the garment workers were rewarded only with police repression, Jeon Tae-Il, a key CGWU organizer, set himself on fire in November 1970 with the cry, "Do not mistreat the young girls."[48]

Jeon's sacrifice set the standard for his coworkers. As one observer notes, "Jeon's sacrifice gave his fellow Peace Market garment workers not only the birth of a labor union but also a sense of solidarity, self-awareness, and efficacy of collective action."[49] His mother (simply called Mochin or Mother), Lee So-Sun, filled his role as symbolic leader and was arrested several times leading militant mass actions. Following Jeon's example, leaders of the union tried to commit suicide by setting themselves on fire or jumping from buildings. Demonstrations, sit-ins, and hunger strikes became the instruments of a legendary struggle that finally brought the reluctant employers to the negotiating table.

Indeed, Jeon's sacrifice set the standard not only for the whole labor movement but for other egalitarian struggles as well. Suicide became a not unusual method of upping the ante in strikes and wage negotiations,[50] as well as an instrument of the nationwide antidictatorship struggle.[51] As Jeon's brother, himself a tested leader of the CGWU, told us in an interview, "Though my mother does not wish to see more suicides by students, unfortunately many more students and workers will sacrifice themselves.... Suicide is the expression of passion for the people, of the purest love. I cannot tell you when it will cease to be an instrument of protest."[52]

The Chonggye struggle was one of several insurrectionary labor actions that served as milestones on the long march to the great working-class explosion in the summer of 1987. The bitter struggle at the Dong-Il Textile Company in the mid-1970s was marked by

Table 1.2

Unionization Rate, by Sex, 1963–1985

	Union Membership as Percentage of Regular Employees in Nonfarm Sector				
	1970	1973	1977	1980	1985
Male	20.1	20.4	22.7	18.5	15.9
Female	19.7	20.5	28.5	23.6	15.2
Total	20.0	20.4	24.3	20.1	15.7
Union Membership (in thousands)	473	548	955	948	1004

Source: You Jong-Il, "Capital-Labor Relations of the Newly Industrializing Regime in South Korea: Past, Present, and Future" (Unpublished paper, Harvard University, Cambridge, Mass., April 1989), p. 19.

"sit-in demonstrations, the workers' fast at Myundong Cathedral, a demonstration by about 70 women workers who stood nude, forming a human wall in front of riot police, an attack by male workers on women workers by throwing human excrement over them, mass dismissal, and detentions."[53] In February 1974, one thousand women staged a massive sit-in at the Bando Trading Company; in September of that same year 2,500 workers occupied the Hyundai shipyard; and early in 1980, miners took control of the town and mines of Sabuk in what came to be known as the Sabuk Uprising.

These actions had several features worth stressing at this juncture. First, while most were waged for limited goals like reinstatement of fired workers, higher pay, and genuine unions, the absence of fair collective bargaining institutions forced workers into radical, insurrectionary actions. Second, women in light-manufacturing industries spearheaded the most militant actions of the 1970s.[54] Prior to the great labor insurrection of 1987, the rate of unionization was highest in the late 1970s and "it was female workers (secondary sector) who were leading this union expansion" (see table 1.2).[55] Third, while the strikes were led and initiated by workers, many labor leaders received training and assistance from the Urban Industrial Mission (a worker support group associated with the Protestant churches), the Young Catholic Workers, and scores of students who became factory workers to assist union-organizing efforts. In the late 1960s, church support was instrumental in organizing some 40,000 workers at one hundred enterprises.[56] As previously noted, so crucial was church support in such milestone actions as the Dong-Il Textile Company strike that the state banned "third parties" from involvement in union affairs under the Labor Disputes Adjustments Law.

A period of heavy repression under Chun Doo-Hwan separated the militant labor actions of the mid to late 1970s from the labor insurrection of the past three years, following President Roh Tae-Woo's promise of democratization. But the intensity of labor's rebellion in the late 1980s can only be fully appreciated by placing labor's situation in the larger socioeconomic canvas of the early and mid-1980s.

A Background of Growing Inequality

Undoubtedly contributing to the radicalization of working class consciousness was the growth in inequality in both income and status. On the one hand, it is often pointed out that compared to other third world countries Korea has had a less uneven distribution of income at the time of industrial takeoff. For instance, while the top 10 percent of the population in Korea receives 28 percent of household income, in Brazil this same group receives over 50 percent.[57] Korean workers, however, do not compare themselves to their Brazilian or other third world counterparts; instead they situate their experience of deprivation historically. In the popular memory Korea emerged from the Korean War of 1950–53 with "incomes among poverty-stricken Koreans...at bare-subsistence level and very equal."[58] Inequality began to become an issue in the 1970s, as a result of the decision to undertake export-oriented industrialization in the 1960s. From being roughly equal, rural income fell precipitously to 67 percent of urban income in 1970.[59]

The 1970s and early 1980s saw an intensification of inequality. In the crucial twenty-year period from 1965 to 1985, the share of income going to the bottom 40 percent of the population declined from 19.3 percent to 17.7 percent, while the share going to the top 20 percent rose from 41.8 percent to 43.7 percent (see table 1.3).[60]

Indeed, within the top 20 percent of the population, it was "the top 10 percent, the senior managers and owners of major enter-

Table 1.3

Income Distribution, 1965–1985

Income Group	Share of Income (%)					
	1965	1970	1976	1980	1982	1985
Lower 40%	19.3	19.6	16.9	16.1	18.8	17.7
Middle 40%	38.9	38.8	37.8	38.5	38.2	38.6
Upper 20%	41.8	41.6	45.3	45.4	43.0	43.7

Source: Economic Planning Board data, cited in *Korea Report* 1, no. 4 (September–October 1987), p. 7.

prises, who have increased their share of the income."[61] But worsening income distribution was far from the whole story; it was both the perception and the reality of the growth of a more uneven ownership of visible wealth—land, property, and financial assets—that caused the greatest ill will. The figures, in fact, reflected this trend: the share of property (rents, profits, and dividends), as opposed to wages and salaries, rose from 12.7 percent of the national income in 1975 to 18.6 percent in 1981.[62]

Conspicuous consumption by the rich, something that was much less evident in the 1970s, began to rankle public consciousness by the late 1980s; particularly disconcerting was the importation of luxury cars like Mercedes-Benzes and BMWs. Among other things, this indicated "an increasing willingness to display...wealth publicly."[63] How explosive this phenomenon of "defiantly conspicuous" consumption (as the *Financial Times* put it) had become was stressed by the Presidential Commission on Economic Restructuring:

> ...The question of fairness has been raised as a result of the visible wealth accumulated by the rich. The unbridled pursuit of wealth by the upper class through various privileges and their conspicuous consumption have fanned the feeling of relative poverty among the ordinary people.[64]

Workers' increasing anger at conspicuous consumption was further inflamed by the crisis in home ownership and housing that worsened in the mid-1980s. Owning a house has steadily become a distant dream for a good many Koreans, as ownership of private landholdings has been concentrated in fewer and fewer hands.

According to the Korea Research Institute on Human Settlements, 65.2 percent of all private landholdings nationwide are now concentrated in the hands of 5 percent of the population.[65]

The crisis is most evident in Seoul, the capital city. Already in 1970 more than half of Seoul's population was renting, squatting, or literally homeless. By 1985 this figure had shot up to 60 percent, or over 6 million people.[66]

Owing to strong state controls over the use of real estate, the creation of shantytowns by squatters appears to have been less marked in Seoul than in other third world cities. What has transpired instead is a tremendous overload on existing housing. As one study succinctly describes the problem:

> The result of so few housing options open to poorer groups is a high proportion of renters and a high degree of overcrowding in the existing housing stock. If there is little or no increase in the housing options open to poorer groups, the tendency is for increasing numbers of people to crowd into existing dwellings. In 1986, 60 percent of Seoul's population lived in rented accommodation and the proportion in rented accommodation has grown in recent decades. In 1985, the poorest 30 percent of the population had an average of two square meters per person and three families per house. It is common for one family to live in one or two small rooms and often, three generations live together—in some cases in one room.[67]

Indeed, the government was forced to admit in a 1988 report that the total supply of housing units nationwide fell 40 percent short of the number of households.[68]

While doubling up—or even tripling up, as some 24 percent of Seoul's population did[69]—in rented housing appeared to be the dominant solution, squatting was nonetheless widespread. While Seoul does not have the gaping shantytowns found in other third world cities, squatter communities do exist and their residents "live in daily fear of having [their shacks] torn down by the authorities."[70] The authoritative Christian Institute for the Study of Justice and Development estimates that Seoul has 2 million squatters—out of a total population of 9.6 million.[71]

Many of these shantytowns were settled in the early sixties, during the first phase of export-oriented industrialization, by people evicted from the old urban center and by rural migrants streaming into Seoul. Once peripheral, the land on which these communities were built became valuable as Seoul expanded and is now slated for redevelopment. Evictions began in the name of beautification for the 1988 Olympics, but eventually redevelopment will end up evicting 3.5 million people from 230 slums.[72]

As the process of eviction created more homeless in the late 1980s, land speculation by the chaebol led to skyrocketing housing costs throughout the country, with prices rising at a rate of 50 percent in some parts of Seoul.[73] The price of an average small Seoul apartment reached $225,000 in 1989, the same level as in the San Francisco Bay Area in California—in a country where per capita GNP was less than $5,000![74] This meant that not only were the working class and the poor being priced out of home ownership, but the middle class as well. As one account pointed out, "a fairly well-paid white-collar worker with a monthly salary of US$1,000 would have to save an entire salary for three years just to buy 3.3 square meters of land in downtown Seoul, based on the present price of land."[75]

Rising income inequality, conspicuous consumption, and the housing crisis jarred the sensibility of a people who had been socialized by the government to the myth of a relatively egalitarian Korea, and the engendered dissatisfactions fueled the flame of labor's rebellion in the late 1980s to an even greater intensity. By then, suspicion of wealth had become so deeply ingrained that one ruling party legislator remarked, "The mood of the country is like a people's court in a communist country."[76]

The Great Labor Offensive, 1987–90

When labor launched its massive organizing offensive in the summer of 1987 following Chun Doo-Hwan's ouster and his successor Roh Tae-Woo's democratization decree, the movement's center of gravity had shifted from the textile and garment industries to the heavy industries dominated by such conglomerates as Hyundai and Daewoo. The centrality of these industries in the new organizing drive underlined that much of the working class had been formed by the priority government had placed on heavy and chemical industries in the 1970s. In contrast to the young female rural migrants in textiles and garments that formed the base of the union organizing drive in the 1970s, the most militant workers' unions in the late 1980s tended to be dominated by males, workers with an urban background, and workers with higher education. The educational dimension, You Jong-Il points out, was significant:

> Increasingly higher educational attainments of the second generation workers have resulted in an increased level of assertiveness. The percentage of those with high school or more education among the skilled and semi-skilled workers in the machinery sector, for instance, rose from 17.6 percent in 1967 to 59.3 percent in 1984. It is not hard to guess that it will be much higher among the young workers. For instance, in the Korea Export Industrial Complex located in south Seoul, over 90 percent of new entrants have [a] high school diploma. These young workers have been the driving force behind the current confrontations.[77]

Between the summer of 1987 and late 1989 more than 7,100 labor disputes erupted throughout Korea (see table 1.4).[78] And the number of unions more than doubled, from 2,725 in June 1987 to 7,358 by the end of 1989.[79] All industries were rocked by strife. Strikes hit not only domestic firms but also key foreign-invested enterprises like Motorola and IBM. But it was the conglomerates like Daewoo and Hyundai that bore the brunt of working class fury.

The epic struggle at Hyundai Heavy Industries is perhaps the one key struggle that will continue to shape relations between labor and the state-chaebol alliance for a long time to come.

Hyundai is a classic militarized company, run as the *Financial Times* described it, "like a boot camp," with a regulation Hyundai haircut and uniform.[80] Over the years workers accumulated tremendous resentments against Hyundai management, not only because of low wages but, perhaps even more so, because of the repressive management style, personified by authoritarian founder Chung Ju-Yung, who took it "as a personal insult that any worker should strike for better conditions and wages."[81]

The concentrated geography of the big factories and huge industrial complexes that served as the base of the heavy and chemical industries (HCI) drive in the 1970s unwittingly provided the infrastructure for the Hyundai insurrection. Eleven Hyundai affiliates were located in the industrial city of Ulsan, where Hyundai workers and their families accounted for one out of every three persons in a total population of 650,000. Thus unionization proceeded with lightning speed following Roh's democracy decree.

Taken by surprise, Hyundai management sought to create yellow (company) unions to counter the militant groups. It was not able, however, to prevent the formation of the Council of Labor Unions of the Hyundai Group (CLUHG), made up of genuine unions from twelve factories. Management reluctantly acknowledged that the CLUHG was legal and said that its constituent unions would serve as partners in collective bargaining. Immediately, however, it set out on a two-year campaign to convert the CLUHG into company unions through such measures as bribes, intimidation, and even kidnapping by company-hired kusadae. But just when management appeared to have emasculated the CLUHG leadership, the shipyard workers at Hyundai Heavy Industries broke away from the company-backed union in December 1988, set up an alternative union, and demanded wage raises and the reinstatement of fired union leaders.

Thus began an epic 109-day battle for the strategic Hyundai shipyard, which involved violent attacks on blue-collar workers by company thugs, aided by white-collar workers. But private security forces could not contain the strike, forcing Hyundai management to once again seek the assistance of the state's repressive agencies. At the end of March 1989, 14,000 policemen stormed the shipyard from land, sea, and air, using tear-gas firing helicopters against workers. The police occupied the workers' dormitories and hunted down union leaders, many of whom were forced underground. After a few months of trying to project the image of being a neutral arbiter between capital and labor, the Korean state reverted to its traditional role of being the ultimate defender of the chaebol.

"We wanted to tame them," said a Hyundai official after the strike, expressing the essentially repressive relationship of Korean capital to Korean labor.[82] But management's victory was likely to be Pyrrhic: the Hyundai struggle and other bitter labor confrontations throughout the country underlined the immense difficulty of getting labor to be a willing partner in the development strategy promoted by the state-chaebol alliance.

The Impossibility of Consensus

An insurgent working class is the inevitable product of two key features of the Korean economic experience: "late industrialization," followed by "late democratization." To catch up with the

Table 1.4

Labor Disputes, 1975–1989

Disputes							
1975	1976	1977	1978	1979	1980	1981	1982
133	110	96	102	105	407	186	88

Disputes						
1983	1984	1985	1986	1987	1988	1989
98	113	265	276	3,749	1,833	1,532[a]

Source: You Jong-Il, "Capital-Labor Relations of the Newly Industrializing Regime in South Korea: Past, Present, and Future" (Unpublished paper, Harvard University, Cambridge, Mass., April 1989), p. 36; Yonhap, "Yonhap Wraps Up Year's Labor Developments," Foreign Broadcast Information Service, *East Asia: Daily Report*, December 13, 1989, p. 29.

[a] First ten months only.

Western industrial powers, Korea launched a state-led, conglomerate-based, and repression-imposed strategy of industrialization. The costs were so high in terms of worker alienation that when the long-postponed democratic *apertura* came in the late 1980s, conflicts were exacerbated instead of mitigated. The opening revealed that precisely because the Korean strategy for industrial growth had been based so greatly on severe exploitation and repression, workers not only did not share the "consensus" around export-oriented growth but were positively alienated from it. It also revealed that an authoritarian and militarist management method can create effective and efficient production systems so long as an aura of invincibility surrounds its main promoters. Once that aura dissipates, labor discipline and production efficiency can unravel pretty fast, as they did between 1987 and 1990.

Park Chung-Hee sought economic development to build legitimacy for the chaebol-military-technocrat power structure, but ironically his draconian methods eventually subverted his goal. Instead of reaping the respect of the Confucian worker, he and his successors harvested the bitter resentment of the class-conscious proletarian who could not care less if the formidable export machine broke down.

This dissenting perspective was expressed angrily by Lee So-

Sun, mother of Jeon Tae-Il and a labor leader in her own right: "The government says the economy is successful. But only a few benefit from the economy....There is nothing in it for us."[83] A young metalworker in Inchon told us confidently: "We, the workers, will set our own agenda."[84] As the late 1980s have shown, that agenda includes more than the right to organize unions and strike for higher wages; it challenges some basic prerogatives of capitalist management. As one observer noted, "Last year [1988], the focus was better wages and the right to organize unions, but now workers want a say in how their companies are run. They're calling for equal control over personnel management and profit distribution. No longer do they think of business as a personal asset subject to an owner's whim."[85]

If consensus is impossible, is it nevertheless still possible to develop a modus vivendi between labor and capital that would not depend principally on force? This would be difficult, given the fact that the state has so closely identified itself with the interests of the chaebol that it has been unable to credibly develop a neutral image in workers' eyes. In the United States and Europe the state was able to project an image of being distanced from the immediate interests of capital, opening up the space for collective bargaining between labor and business. In contrast, by aligning itself with business to create a solid phalanx of opposition to labor in the thirty years of high-speed industrialization, the Korean state provided no significant safety valves for working class resentments, no space for a moderate workers' movement to emerge. The temper of the times was captured by one reporter's observation that the "sharp increase and the emergence of union leaders in their 20's has led many unions to take hard-line struggles rather than trying to negotiate, and moderates have sometimes been called 'pro-management' and ousted from the union leadership."[86]

At this late date, no common rules for collective bargaining have emerged to channel unionism along Western lines nor is evolution along the Japanese company union model now possible. As one commentator put it:

> Company and government officials still talk optimistically of molding Korean unions after their Japanese counterparts. But the parallels between Korea and Japan don't seem to hold for labor. Japan solved its labor problems early on its road to industrial development, in the 1950's, under a democratic system that

permitted union activity. Workers were organized in
company unions, and made to feel they shared in
corporate decisions. Worker loyalty hardened because wages increased as companies grew.

The comparable point in Korea's industrial
development came 15 years ago, but union activity
wasn't allowed until three years ago, and worker
bitterness remains, even after pay increases that have
brought their median salary to two-thirds the income
of white-collar employees.[87]

Integrating or coopting labor into the dominant socioeconomic
order has been a difficult task for elites everywhere. But in Korea,
it promises to be especially difficult, for what is demanded is no
less than a swift transformation of capital-labor relations from the
boot-camp management methods of command capitalism into
those characteristic of advanced social democracies.

In fact, after nearly three years of labor ferment, in the beginning
of 1990 the chaebol-backed government appeared to have given
up even on cosmetic attempts to accommodate labor and shifted
decisively back to repression. On January 20, 1990 the Roh government declared the new, militant Korean Trade Union Congress
(better known as *Chonnohyop*) illegal because "it is leading a
vicious conflict with an ideology of class struggle for the liberation
of labor."[88] Over 300 intelligence agents, it announced, would be
deployed to seventy-one industrial complexes "in order to follow
and investigate impure elements infilitrated into the workplace."[89]

2

The Rise of Command Capitalism

The state's repression of labor was done in the service of its strategic objective: high-speed industrialization. Park Chung-Hee saw economic development as the key to his regime's legitimacy. To achieve this goal, labor was to be the instrument and business was to be the partner, albeit a subordinate one. The Park regime was, in fact, successful in bootstrapping Korea through the earlier phases of industrial growth, and while labor was massively repressed and the intelligentsia was alienated, the ability to deliver a growth rate of nearly 10 percent per year between 1965 and 1980 did evoke tolerance, if not legitimacy, for the government from the urban middle class and other social strata.

It was not simply the economic growth that blunted discontent, but the perception that the state was indeed an agent of development that stood above social classes, though its policies might favor selected groups. During the Park period the conglomerates were certainly allowed to grow rich, but they were also perceived to be instruments of development. These perceptions were not limited to Koreans. The image of the strong state standing above business interests and promoting development attracted the attention of many third world intellectuals, who were otherwise dismayed by the Korean government's repressive, anti-Communist policies.

But this perception began to change during the Chun Doo-Hwan era. The chaebol began to be seen as having become too big to control and were perceived in fact to have corrupted the state. No longer could the state be seen as standing above social classes like the old Confucian bureaucracy. In the popular mind, the state had become captive to the chaebol, and this struck a massive blow at the ideological validity of the state's exhortations to "sacrifice for the national good" and "promote growth first, redistribute later." The new mood of cynicism was expressed by a legislator who asked, rhetorically, "Is the Sixth Republic the Chaebol Republic or the Speculation Republic?"

In this chapter and the next, we shall analyze the emergence of command capitalism, discuss the complementarities and contradictions between the state and the chaebol in the process of Korean development, and explore the conditions that have emerged to render this historic alliance an anachronism in the public mind.

Development from Above

In his 1985 State of the Union address, President Ronald Reagan claimed that

> America's economic success...can be repeated a hundred times in a hundred nations. Many countries in east Asia and the Pacific have few resources other than the enterprise of their own people. But through...free markets, they've soared ahead of centralized economies.[1]

Unfortunately, reality differed from what Reagan and his orthodox economic advisers sought to pass off as truth. Korea did not represent the triumph of free enterprise and the free market. If anything, Korea is one of the few successful cases of state-led economic growth in the postwar period, where presidential command supplanted the market as the main motor of economic development.

The salient role of the Korean state in economic development cannot be divorced from its domination by the military under cold war conditions for nearly thirty years. Essentially, the current Korean political regime descends from the May 1961 illegitimate assumption of power by Maj. Gen. Park Chung-Hee and his cabal of young colonels. This fact is important because whether under Park, Chun Doo-Hwan, or Roh Tae-Woo, the military-dominated state has attempted to erase its essential illegitimacy by fostering rapid economic development. In this tacit social compact, citizens were expected to tolerate the banishing of their political rights in exchange for prosperity.

This social compact was conditioned by the cold war context in three ways. First, ideological competition with Communist-led North Korea for the allegiance of the people of South Korea was based partly on the issue of economic performance. Second, since socialist ownership of the means of production was precluded by the vehemently anti-Communist ideology of the regime and its American sponsor, the regime settled for ideologically tolerated methods that could still achieve the centralization and concentration of resources it saw as necessary for rapid economic growth, namely, strong state intervention and forceful guidance of the economy. In a way, Korea was in a better position to ignore the neoclassical, free market biases of its sponsor in the realm of the economy precisely because it played such a critical political and military role in the larger containment strategy of the United States. Third, the Korean War bequeathed a massive, oversized army to South Korea at a time when other social and political forces had been weakened. With the landlord class diminished by land reform, politicians and businessmen tainted with corruption, and intellectuals and students on the defensive ideologically in an atmosphere of McCarthyism, the military was the only force with enough clout to impose its vision of the country's future.

That vision of a brave new Korea was articulated principally by Park. An admirer of the Meiji Restoration in Japan and a former officer in the Japanese colonial army, Park dismissed democracy and proposed instead "a great leap forward toward economic growth."[2] His reasoning was that "for such poor people like the Koreans, on the verge of near starvation, economics takes precedence over politics in their daily lives and enforcing democracy is meaningless."[3]

The subordination of business interests to state-directed economic objectives was brought about early in 1961, when Park made a deal with the business elites that had fallen into disrepute because of their corrupt dealings during the previous government of Rhee Syng-Man. The essence of the arrangement, asserts a former technocrat under Park, "was that the government would exempt them [the business elites] from legal punishment and they in return would pay off their obligations to 'nation building through industrialization.'"[4] Thus was born the enduring chaebol-government relationship, with business in a decidedly subordinate position.

Park's vision, patterned after what he perceived to be the Meiji experience in Japan, was to use "millionaires" to create a "national capitalism."[5] For Park, the primordial reality of modern economic life was the dominance of giant corporations; the challenge was to tame them for what he perceived as the public interest:

> One of the essential characteristics of a modern economy is its strong tendency towards centraliza-

tion. Mammoth enterprise—considered indispensable, at the moment, to our country— plays not only a decisive role in the economic development and elevation of living standards, but further, brings about changes in the structure of society and the economy....Where the appalling power of mammoth enterprise is concerned... there is no competition...Therefore, the key problem facing a free economic policy are coordination and supervisory guidance, by the state, of mammoth economic strength.[6]

But there was another reason for Park's preference for "mammoth enterprises": in contrast to hundreds or thousands of small and medium enterprises, they could be subject to a "narrower span of administrative control."[7]

A Capitalism Sui Generis

For most of the Park period (1961–1979), the laws of the market did operate but under the severe constraints of a command economy. The dynamics of what could be called command capitalism was captured by one of Park Chung-Hee's economists:

Economic decisionmaking has been overwhelmingly a top-down process. In the 1960s many government offices, including economic ministries, were staffed by retired army generals and colonels. Because the President himself was a retired army general, Korea's economic decision-making process was very close to the "General Headquarters"—"GHQ"—style, in which the President himself made all major decisions and settled policy disputes among his senior officials. Many Koreans complained that Korean economic policy in the 1960's was managed by command. Nevertheless, the GHQ style turned out to be very effective in initiating development and achieving the Park government's top priority of rapid growth.[8]

Whether its initiatives were called market conforming, market managing, or market leading, the Park government ran a tight economic ship. This meant, first and foremost, laying down from above the strategic thrust of economic growth. In the 1960s, Park identified the thrust as *Suchul ipquk*, or nation building through exports. In the 1970s, it was the so-called HCI drive, a coordinated effort to develop heavy and chemical industries as Korea's industrial base.

To achieve its economic goals, the state manipulated the chaebol with a variety of attractive incentives and strong sanctions. Park rewarded his "millionaires" with markets and medals, but he also made it clear to them that he would wield the stick if necessary. There was a strong coercive dimension to the state-chaebol relationship, according to Song Byung-Nak, a technocrat under Park: "The export targets agreed upon between the government and individual firms were taken by businessmen as equivalent to compulsory orders. Firms that failed to achieve their export targets without a plausible excuse ran the risk of heavy administrative sanctions from the government."[9]

The overwhelming dominance exercised by the state and, particularly, by the executive over business actors in the first phases of Korean industrialization has led some commentators to the conclusion that the epithet Korea Incorporated is probably more appropriate than Japan Incorporated:

> The chairman of "Korea, Inc." has been the President himself, while business groups such as Samsung, Hyundai, Lucky-Gold Star, and Daewoo have been its production units. The relationship between the government and business groups in Japan has been nearly bilateral or horizontal, whereas, in the case of Korea, it has been vertical or hierarchical.[10]

The key incentives and sanctions employed to manipulate the "president's production units" were access to credit, export promotion and protectionism, tax policy, and foreign investment policy. A brief examination of these policies reveals the hegemonic role played by the state in the early period of Korean industrialization.

Credit Policy

One of the first acts of the military regime upon coming to power in 1961 was to nationalize the commercial banking system. By 1970 the government had come to control an astounding 96.4 percent of the country's financial assets.[11] While the government sold its shares in the commercial banks in 1983, it continued to maintain strong administrative controls. Throughout the past thirty years, then, the government had in its hands an exceedingly powerful instrument to encourage the chaebol to pursue certain policies and to punish them when they went astray.

The expansion of the chaebol has been fueled, for the most part, by debt rather than retained earnings. In the 1980s, for instance, only 9.9 percent of manufacturing sector activity was financed from retained earnings or capital increases. The rest was supported with credit derived from government-owned or controlled financial institutions.[12] The government, it must be pointed out, encouraged this dependence by setting real interest rates that were either negative or close to zero.

Secure access to government-controlled credit made it possible for the chaebol to pursue expansion plans that were expensive, risky, or unprofitable in the short term. For the Korean state technocrats, the key consideration was gaining and expanding market share in export markets, even at the risk of short-term losses. The price of this secure cash-flow guarantee was a severe loss of independence. Government technocrats, using the power of the purse, have not hesitated to declare a chaebol bankrupt or to force corporate restructuring or mergers. One of the most recent examples of this power was the decisive dismantling in 1985 of the Kukje-ICC conglomerate, the seventh largest chaebol, as its four creditor banks declared it bankrupt at the urging of the government. As one banker put it, "Anytime the government chooses to close a company or break it up, it can do so. All it has to do is call the so-called Korean commercial banks, which it controls, and tell them not to refinance a company's debt."[13]

Export Promotion and Market Protection

Secure access to credit for compliant firms was coupled with other incentives. To make up for the losses or paper-thin profit margins of Korean exporters as they battled for market share through savage price competition, exporters were provided with a variety of export subsidies, including low tax rates on income earned from exports, accelerated depreciation allowances, and duty-free import of selected components under specified conditions.[14]

Also, exporters were compensated for participating in the government's export-at-all-costs program by being allowed to sell their goods in the domestic market at inflated prices. More generally, protectionism via tariff and nontariff barriers was an important element in Korea's industrialization strategy, contrary to the orthodox, freemarket interpretations of the Korean experience that reigned among Western economists in the 1970s. According to Richard Leudde-Neurath's valuable study, the share of freely importable commodities in total import volume fell from 55.6 percent in 1968 to 46.9 percent in 1974 to 38.8 percent in 1978, before recovering to 61.6 percent in 1980.[15] Korea's protectionist structure is, of course, no longer a matter of academic dispute but an accepted reality in the light of the U.S. government's aggressive attempts to open up the Korean economy in recent years.

Protectionism did not, however, translate into coddling vested interests, as in many other third world countries—at least not in the 1960s and 1970s. As economist Hong Won-Tack has pointed out, "the government did not allow…entrepreneurs to enjoy a lackadaisical life with monopolistic rents."[16] It threatened to allow imports whenever domestic prices of the protected industrial commodities went too far out of line from international prices both to defuse consumer discontent as well as prevent superprofits from domestic transactions from spoiling the firms' export-oriented investment plans.

Tax Policy and Infrastructure

Tax policy was also used to influence the chaebol. Exporters were exempted from the indirect tax on income earned from their export sales; and from 1961 to 1972 exporters enjoyed a 50 percent cut from the normal corporate and income tax levied on export earnings. On the other hand, tax audits constituted an extremely powerful threat that could be deployed against recalcitrant chaebol. As one analyst pointed out,

> Because of the many informal transactions concerning the allocation of bank and foreign credit, as well as land speculation, dual accounting and bookkeeping was common among firms that borrowed heavily from the banks, putting the firms in an even more vulnerable position if threatened with a tax investigation. Not a few firms folded as a result of tax investigations, and the punishment for tax fraud included penalty taxes as well as criminal prosecution.[17]

Provision of infrastructural services functioned in much the same double-edged fashion. In the 1970s the government set up industrial estates where export firms could purchase industrial sites at greatly discounted prices. It also provided exporters with low fees for services like electricity, water, transportation, and communications. But failure to meet export targets could provoke the disconnection of electricity on the orders of the Ministry of Trade and Industry (MTI).[18]

Foreign Investment Policy

In terms of its impact on development, probably the most underestimated incentive has been the state's foreign investment policy. Perhaps more than any other single factor, this policy has been responsible for the emergence of the chaebol as the dominant force in the domestic economy.

Local enterprises were protected from foreign investors in those areas in which the state wanted to develop local production capability—in practice, nearly all areas of manufacturing. While Korea has relied greatly on foreign loans—raising its foreign debt to some $46.7 billion by 1988—it is described by one progovernment publication as "one of the few countries with highly restrictive foreign investment regulations."[19] Foreign investment was practically nonexistent prior to 1962, and afterwards government policy ensured that foreign investment, unlike in Singapore, for example, did not crowd out local entrepreneurs. Indeed, the policy was to see how much foreign investors could be controlled and at the same time used to promote local business via technology transfers. The favored arrangement was joint ventures, in which the local partner owned at least 50 percent of equity. Three-fourths of all foreign-invested firms, in fact, had less than half of equity in foreign hands.[20] Majority foreign-owned firms were permitted only "in such exceptional cases as entirely export-oriented investments, highly technologically intensive projects, projects for Korean residents abroad, or investment in the Free Trade Zones."[21]

Controls on foreign investment were, in fact, tighter than what was set out in the foreign investment code. Not only were foreign investors banned from many sectors of the economy, but the screening process weeded out applications from many sectors that were supposed to be open.[22] Applications were viewed not only from the vantage point of the letter of the law but were judged according to unpublished guidelines. Moreover, bureaucrats enjoyed a wide degree of administrative freedom, which could result in the veto of an otherwise perfectly legal application if officials felt it did not serve the national interest. Government officials also frequently intervened to renegotiate contracts with foreign-invested firms on matters like increasing domestic content of the firms' output or raising export targets. Moreover, firms were requested to provide sensitive information about their operations—information that on "several occasions...ended up in the hands of domestic competitors or was otherwise used against the foreign firm."[23]

In the past few years, the contribution of foreign investment to gross capital formation was only 1.2 percent. The value of foreign investments in Korea is currently estimated at $3.78 billion, compared to $16.8 billion in Singapore.[24] The difference is not accounted for by the degree of state intervention; both states are highly interventionist. It stems from the attitude toward foreign capital. Singapore has used multinationals as the main agents of development, whereas South Korea has used local capitalists, with foreign firms regarded mainly as organizations to be milked for technology.

Korea is, in fact, one of the few countries in the third world that has applied stringent nationalist controls on foreign investment and not only gotten away with it but made the policy a success. It is not surprising, then, that many third world countries regard Korea's foreign investment policy as a model, while eschewing other aspects of the development strategy like the extreme reliance on the U.S. market and the repression of labor.

The Technocratic Overlords

The Park period saw not only the consolidation of the military as the nation's political elite but also the emergence of a technocratic elite that assumed command of economic policy. Three agencies staffed by technocrats, many of them U.S. educated, assumed responsibility for planning and macroeconomic surveillance. Policy-making was not a smooth process but emerged as a result of debates and compromises among these three agencies and Park's personal economic advisers.

On one side was the Ministry of Trade and Industry, which generally favored expansionary policies involving huge amounts of government expenditure. On the other side was the Ministry of Finance, which, like finance ministries all over the world, was biased toward noninflationary growth, less spending, and less state regulation of business. The Ministry of Finance was also more permeable than the Ministry of Trade and Industry to pressures and advice by influential external agencies like the International Monetary Fund.

Above these two ministries—and often the swing factor in policy debates—was the Economic Planning Board (EPB), a super-agency that became the main instrument of Park's export-first strategy. Organized in 1961 and staffed by U.S.-trained economists, the EPB acquired a directive capability that rivaled, if not outstripped, Japan's vaunted Ministry of Trade and Industry (MITI). The EPB was endowed with the power not only to engage in macroeconomic planning but also to implement plans by allocating the budget, evaluating all major private and public projects for which public funds would be spent, and coordinating foreign aid and foreign investment.[25] Heading up the EPB was the deputy prime minister, who doubled as chairman of the Council of Economic Ministers. While interministerial rivalries were undoubtedly strong, the EPB's commanding position was assured by the annual scrutiny it conducted of each ministry's budget.[26]

Strong support from Park helped insulate the EPB from pressures from interest groups like the chaebol. As a consequence, claims analyst Choi Byung-Sun, "unlike other government agencies, the EPB is relatively autonomous from any particular group in society. This institutional autonomy permits the EPB to maintain a broader economic policy perspective, provide relatively objective analysis...and, therefore, render a unique service to the president and the nation."[27] The EPB thus acquired "an unrivalled capacity for swaying between contractionary and expansionary policies," adds Kim Byung-Kook, in contrast to the trade and finance ministries, which "had a narrower sectoral interest and [were] less competitive in sweepingly changing gears and aggressively following new political and economic signals."[28]

But influential though the EPB was, the most powerful economic agent was the presidential dictator himself. Park took a hands-on approach that involved, among other things, a monthly export-promotion conference, close surveillance of the progress of exports, and rewards for successful exporters. That the president's was the ultimate word on the economy was revealed in the adoption of the heavy and chemical industries (HCI) drive in the early 1970s. Not only were many chaebol dragged reluctantly into this ambitious effort to transform Korea's economic structure, but the plan evoked "guarded skepticism" from EPB technocrats. As a result, the formulation of the plan was highly centralized in the

Blue House (Korea's White House) and removed from the scrutiny of the EPB.[29]

Undoubtedly, some venality marked the relationship between the economic bureaucracies and the chaebol during the Park period. Nonetheless, the combination of a relatively weak business class and strong support from a president who derived his power not from the business elite but from his undisputed control of the military, contributed to making the EPB and other agencies relatively immune from private interests. During the Park period there was little of the "colonization" of state agencies by well-organized and traditionally powerful upper-class interests that one finds, say, in the Philippines and Latin America. That colonization—and its destructive impact on the legitimacy of development strategy—was to occur later, in the Chun Doo-Hwan period. And one of the factors that provided the material basis for that later colonization was a breathtaking transformation that took place in the second decade of Park's rule, the so-called HCI, or heavy and chemical industries, drive.

The HCI Drive

Industrial deepening was the strategic aim of the HCI drive. By creating, literally from scratch, basic or strategic industries like iron and steel, petrochemicals, electronics, machinery, shipbuilding, and transport equipment, Park and his technocrats sought to give more depth and integration to the economic structure, as well as make Korea less dependent on imports of key intermediate and basic goods. Though it was essentially an import-substitution process, HCI did not signify an inward turning. HCI was, in fact, conceived as a new phase of Park's export- first strategy, the idea being to move from low-valued-added, labor-intensive exports to higher-valued-added, capital or technology-intensive exports. As one analyst noted, HCI "embodied the planners' belief that Korea could achieve import-substitution and export upgrading simultaneously by moving into an emerging niche in the world market for standardized capital and intermediate goods."[30]

Not only did market forces play a relatively peripheral role in the adoption of the HCI program, but political factors had a significant influence. President Richard Nixon's withdrawal of a whole division of U.S. troops from Korea in the early 1970s and President Jimmy Carter's declared intention to withdraw the rest in the late 1970s greatly alarmed the Park regime and led it to see

HCI partly as a "policy of defense industrialization."[31] The heavy and chemical industries that were the program's priority targets would provide the industrial infrastructure for defense production and enable Korea to absorb defense technologies transferred from the United States, such as making tanks, howitzers, and aircraft.[32]

Not surprisingly, orthodox economists, especially foreign advisers like World Bank technocrats, recoiled from what they saw as Park's Great Leap Forward. As even the EPB was skeptical, the HCI drive was mainly a presidential initiative, deliberately withdrawn from the scrutiny of the EPB. "The Plan," claims Chu Yun-Han, "was prepared by a close-knit group of economic advisers around Park and working with the MTI [Ministry of Trade and Industry] and the largest firms."[33] When the EPB, in the mid-1970s, advised going slow, Blue House economists instead accelerated the pace of economic expansion.

The centralization of decision making was dictated not only by opposition or caution on the part of key technocratic groups. Tight centralization was also demanded by the need to monitor and control proliferating activities of the chaebol, Park's preferred agent of economic transformation, and by the need to supervise the expanding role of state enterprises. Amidst opposition from World Bank and IMF economists, public enterprises were founded for such strategic areas as petroleum, chemicals, and iron and steel. As a portion of total investment, public enterprise investment rose from almost 19 percent in 1970 to over 33 percent in 1975.[34]

The drive to develop heavy industry was all-out: in the key two-year period, 1977–79, 80 percent of investment in manufacturing was devoted to heavy industry. To finance this feverish activity, Korea resorted to massive foreign borrowing, with the foreign debt rising from $2.2 billion in 1970 to $27.1 billion in 1980. Between 1977 and 1981, 45 percent of the financing of heavy and chemical industries came from foreign loans.[35] The rest was siphoned from domestic savings, through such mechanisms as the National Investment Fund, which absorbed employee pensions as well as a fixed portion of all bank deposits.[36]

Breakneck expansion threw the economy into sharp disequilibrium as light industry was starved of capital, production capacity outstripped demand in the HCI sectors, and inflation accelerated. These trends were exacerbated by the OPEC-decreed hike in oil prices in 1979 and the downturn in world trade. These adverse trends strengthened the hand of the more conservative economists at the EPB and the IMF, leading to the imposition of stabilization measures meant to cool an overheated economy. Stabilization via tight monetary and fiscal policies led to a rise in the rate of business failures and a drop in real wages, creating the economic context for the political unrest that resulted in the assassination of Park in 1979 and Chun Doo-Hwan's power-grab in 1980.

But as the economy moved from recession to growth in the early 1980s, it became clear that the HCI program had transformed Korea's economic structure. In 1970 heavy and chemical industrial exports came to only 12.8 percent of total exports; by 1985 their share was up to nearly 60 percent. In the same period, the export share of light industry fell from 69.6 percent to 37.5 percent.[37]

Ambiguous Legacy

The HCI drive yielded an ambiguous legacy. On the one hand, it validated the strategy of making integrated national industrialization as the core element of sustained economic development. By the mid-1980s the performance of many of the new capital-intensive industries had refuted the doctrinal bias of the World Bank and the IMF against heavy industry and state enterprises in third world development programs. Perhaps the most glittering success was the Pohang Iron and Steel Corporation (POSCO), the creation of which had been opposed by the World Bank. By the mid-1980s POSCO had become one of the most efficient steel makers in the world, producing a ton of iron and steel with half the manpower of British Steel.[38]

More important, HCI became the springboard of the renewed Korean export offensive in the mid-1980s. POSCO, for instance, was central to Korea's transition from an exporter of labor-intensive commodities to an exporter of higher-value-added, technology-intensive products, since it "was able to provide related industries with a steady supply of steel products at low prices, thus sharpening Korea's competitive edge in such industries as shipbuilding, automobiles, construction, and electronics."[39]

The HCI program provided the platform from which Hyundai catapulted itself to control a substantial share of the U.S. market for subcompact cars in the late 1980s. HCI also enabled Korea to become by the late 1980s the world's second largest shipbuilding power and a major exporter of construction and engineering

services. As economist Tony Michell points out, HCI "was conceived as a long-term strategy, which would ultimately yield a
higher growth rate than further investment in textiles. This became steadily more true as trade barriers rose in the later 1970s
and early 1980s. Indeed, the resumption of high growth rates in
the 1980s would have been impossible without investment in
accordance with the Plan."[40]

Yet the transformation must not be overstated. While exports
did indeed shift decisively to more sophisticated, technology-intensive products, Korea's dependence on imported intermediate
and capital-goods imports remained high. For instance, most
machines for the country's growing industrial plants are still
imported[41] and many of the critical components that make up
Korea's finished goods exports need to be imported, mostly from
Japan. Although trade with the United States began to swing into
surplus in the early 1980s—reaching over $4 billion by 1985—
Korea's great dependence on Japan was unchanged, as indicated
by the $3 billion Korea-Japan trade deficit in 1985. Indeed, as of
1985 it was estimated that the amount of imported input requirements per $100 worth of Korean output came to $30.6—up from
$26.2 in 1970.[42]

The positive spin-offs of the HCI drive must, moreover, be
balanced against the severe costs HCI imposed on Korean society.
For one, the HCI drive rapidly expanded the working class while
imposing militaristic management to keep the lid on wages—the
perfect formula for generating a rebellious labor force that
despised the ruling elite's developmentalist ideology. HCI also
wrought havoc on Korea's environment, as pollution controls
were forgotten, neglected, or opposed by business and government authorities as a drag on the pace of economic expansion.

Under the HCI program, small and medium businesses were
systematically starved of capital, leaving this sector in permanent
instability and lacking in dynamism, and stoking the resentment
among the petty and medium bourgeoisie against both the technocrats and the chaebol that would flame into political opposition
during the late 1980s.

Finally, the HCI drive propelled the chaebol from being subordinate "production units" of the state, to use Song Byung-Nak's
image, to becoming massive conglomerates with a stranglehold
on the nation's economic life and a corrupting influence on state
elites. Like Dr. Frankenstein, Park had created a creature whose

behavior increasingly eluded the control of his successors at the Blue House.

3

From Command Capitalism to the Chaebol Republic

The chaebol have, in recent years, achieved a reputation as controversial as that of the *keiretsu* in contemporary Japan and the oligopolies of the United States. The comparison is not unmerited. In 1988 the combined revenues of the top four chaebol—Samsung, Hyundai, Lucky-Goldstar, and Daewoo—topped $80 billion, or an astonishing 60 percent of Korea's total gross national product of $135 billion.[1]

In 1982 out of a total of 35,971 firms registered in the manufacturing sector, firms belonging to the top 30 conglomerates numbered only 271, or less than one percent. Yet these 271 firms accounted for 40.7 percent of sales; 33.2 percent of the value added in production; 37.2 percent of fixed assets; and nearly 20 percent of employment.[2]

Other indicators reveal an even higher degree of monopolization of economic activity. Measured in terms of market share, the average share of the top three producers in all manufacturing industries was 62.0 percent in Korea, compared to 56.3 percent in Japan.[3] In terms of sales, the ten largest chaebol accounted for a staggering 72 percent of total sales in 1987. Such high degrees of concentration have prompted one analyst to claim that "Korea has an extremely high level of aggregate concentration by the standards of industrialized non-Communist nations, particularly when adjusted for the size of the economy."[4]

The chaebol are striking not only in their size but also in their global range. Hyundai, for instance, has become a household name on account of the subcompact Excel's smashing success in the U.S. market in 1987 and 1988. In the late 1980s, Hyundai, Samsung, Lucky-Goldstar, and Daewoo—the top four chaebol—were regulars in *Fortune*'s list of the 500 leading industrial groups outside the United States.[5] (See table 3.1 for additional data on chaebol performance.)

Table 3.1

Performance of Top Ten Chaebol, 1988 (in Millions of US$)

Group	Turnover	Net Profits	Net Worth
Samsung	31,760	439	2,466
Hyundai	28,445	353	3,893
Lucky-Goldstar	23,322	306	3,269
Daewoo	15,547	-173	3,178
Sunkyong	9,550	152	1,260
Ssangyong	6,452	202	1,864
Hyosung	4,336	5	667
Hanjin	4,203	82	585
Kia	3,748	56	635
Korea Explosives	3,531	91	1,337

Source: *Business Korea* 7, no. 5 (November 1989), p. 22.
Note: The original figures are in won. The conversion rate used here is $1=669 won.

A brief survey of three of the top conglomerates reveals the impressive diversity of their productive activities.

Samsung, Korea's top chaebol, was listed by *Fortune* as the twentieth largest non-U.S. international company in 1987. Made up of thirty-eight companies, Samsung produces more than three thousand different products.[6] It owns Korea's largest semiconductor company, its largest electronics firm, its largest trading company, as well as hotels, newspapers, insurance companies, and shares of leading banks. In 1988 Samsung racked up $32 billion in sales, though its profits came to only $439 million—a not untypical spread for Korea's highly leveraged chaebol. A truly international conglomerate, Samsung derives the bulk of its income from exports and boasts one hundred forty outposts overseas, twenty-seven of them subsidiaries, including two research institutes in the United States.

Hyundai, the second-largest conglomerate, had a turnover of $28 billion in 1988 and made $352 million in profits. Hyundai has forty-five subsidiaries, three of which are in the United States, one in Canada, one in the Netherlands, and one in Indonesia.[7] Hyundai is Korea's biggest automaker, its biggest shipbuilder, and its leading civil engineering firm. It is less diversified than Samsung, being concentrated in heavy industries, though it recently made a bold foray into semiconductors, computers, and computer accessories.

Perhaps the chaebol that has displayed the most meteoric rise in recent years is Daewoo, the fourth largest conglomerate, which sold $16 billion worth of goods but registered a loss in 1988. Perhaps more than the older chaebol, Daewoo grew mainly through the aggressive acquisition of firms in unrelated fields. Daewoo, made up of thirty companies employing 70,000 workers, is in mineral extraction, civil engineering, textiles, chemicals, trading, consumer electronics, hotels, securities trading, machinery, automobiles, semiconductors, computers, and defense industries. Like Samsung and Hyundai, Daewoo is global in its reach, having offices or subsidiaries in the United States, Canada, Britain, France, West Germany, Malaysia, Panama, Nigeria, the Sudan, Japan, and Hong Kong. Its auto-assembly subsidiary, Daewoo Motor Company, is a joint venture with General Motors.

Scandal and Success at Samsung

A close look at Samsung reveals the key features of chaebol economics, among them continuing family control despite great size and diversity, the volatile combination of corruption and bold strategy, orientation toward gaining market share as opposed to short-term profit maximization, and expansion through escalating debt rather than through retained earnings or public offerings of stocks.

Despite its enormous size and diversity, Samsung continues to be controlled by the family of the late patriarch Lee Byung-Chull. With family domination maintained through an elaborate series of cross shareholdings, nepotism and paternalism are vital parts of Samsung's corporate culture, as is a volatile combination of corruption and bold—some would say reckless—expansionism.

What eventually became Samsung was founded as a small trading company in Taegu by Lee Byung-Chull in 1938. It was, however, in the aftermath of the Korean War that Lee pulled off the economic coups that established his business as more than just another enterprise. He established a sugar-refining plant and a textile company, and the strong control he was able to achieve over these commodities, plus his purchasing of nearly half the shares in commercial banks in the 1950s, led many to regard him as "the richest man in Korea."[8]

Shortly after the May 1961 coup, the new military regime accused Lee of illegally accumulating funds and taxed or confiscated a substantial amount of his wealth.[9] But as part of a "compensatory entrepreneurship" scheme worked out with the military regime, Lee was allowed to continue in business provided he agreed to participate in Park's export-first strategy. This was not the last time, however, that scandal would touch Samsung. It occurred once again when Samsung moved into fertilizer production in the mid-1960s by building the country's first privately owned fertilizer plant. When the plant was about 80 percent complete, scandal again broke out over Lee's trading and financial operations, and he was forced to donate the plant to the state.[10]

Lee, nevertheless, obtained a second absolution by wholeheartedly throwing himself into Park's export drive. From 2 percent of total sales in 1960, exports rose to over 18 percent in 1965 and to over 50 percent in 1980.[11] In the 1970s, Samsung became a key player in the government-promoted HCI program. It established a petrochemical plant and a shipbuilding subsidiary and moved into consumer electronics, acquiring the necessary technology through foreign licensing and joint ventures with foreign corporations such as Japan's Sanyo.

Samsung's modus operandi in the 1970s and 1980s paralleled that of the other chaebol. Its diversified structure allowed it to offset losses in some subsidiaries with profits in others and to channel earnings to its most strategic units. But Samsung's massive sales were not matched by its relatively minuscule net profits; in 1988, for instance, out of sales of $32 billion, its net profit came to only $439 million.[12] With retained earnings providing a fragile base for expansion, Samsung came to rely on subsidies from the government, particularly loans that often carried a negative real rate of interest. By the early 1980s, almost 70 percent of all bank loans went to the conglomerates.[13] And among them, the top five conglomerates, including Samsung, received 20.3 percent of total bank loans in 1980.

The result was a highly leveraged conglomerate. In Korea, notes one account, "debt-equity ratios run at five or six to one, which would scare even the debt-defying Hongkong Chinese (see table 3.2)."[14] Samsung's debt-equity ratio in 1988 was 502, above the average of 484 for the leading thirty chaebol. For specific subsidiaries, the debt ratio was even worse. In 1987 the ratio for Samsung Construction was 992 and that for Samsung Semiconductor and Telecommunications stood at 764.[15] Moreover, borrowed funds got shunted from one Samsung subsidiary to another, thus giving the whole operation a fragile financial structure that could, at any moment, collapse like a house of cards.[16]

Table 3.2

Debt-Equity Ratio of Ten Leading Chaebol, August 1988

Group	Debt-Equity Ratio (%)
Samsung	502
Hyundai	429
Daewoo	488
Lucky-Goldstar	408
Hanjin	492
Ssangyong	226
Sunkyong	355
Korea Explosives	189
Dong Ah	2,930
Lotte	121
Average for top thirty chaebol	484

Source: *Business Korea* 7, no. 5 (November 1989), p. 23.

Access to preferential credit was especially critical for chaebol trying to crack export markets. Like the Japanese conglomerates, Samsung and other Korean exporters have sought not short-term profitability but the gradual acquisition and consolidation of market share, which often means foregoing substantial profits and even taking losses in the first few years of carving out an export market.

Samsung's venture into microwave ovens provides a good illustration of the chaebol's strategy of carving out a market amid short-term—and often medium-term—losses. One out of three microwave ovens now sold in the United States is made by Samsung, which manufactures about 80,000 a week. Yet this feat was achieved by initially absorbing significant losses. Samsung got its break when J.C. Penney, one of the biggest U.S. retailers, asked if it could produce a $299 oven, at a time when its production costs per unit were far above that price. The conglomerate's response is recounted by business consultant Ira Magaziner:

> Samsung was being asked for a few thousand ovens only. On top of that, Penney's order would mean designing a whole new oven and taking heavy losses, all in the name of gaining a fraction of the U.S. market. But in Suwon, Samsung's managers were ecstatic. They promised Penney anything it wanted. To

deliver, they promised [Samsung's microwave specialist] any investment he needed. They still put no pressure on him for profits. All they wanted was production and a doorway into a major foreign market.[17]

But after a few more years of absorbing losses, Samsung was, by the early 1980s, ready to turn a profit in global competition with giants like the U.S. firm General Electric. As Magaziner notes,

In 1983, it cost GE $218 to make a typical microwave oven. It cost Korea's Samsung only $155. Then we broke the costs down: assembly labor cost GE $8 per oven, Samsung, only 63 cents. The difference in overhead labor—supervision, maintenance, setup—were even more astounding: for GE it was $30 per oven; for Samsung, 73 cents. GE was spending $4 on materials handling for each oven; Samsung, 12 cents. The biggest area of difference was in GE's line and central management—that came to $10 per oven. At Samsung, it was 2 cents. What the companies got for their money was the most disturbing figure of all. GE got four units per person each day. Samsung got nine. And once their volume increased, Korean costs could go even lower.[18]

GE eventually decided to source its microwave production to Samsung, making the Korean firm the biggest maker of microwave ovens in the world by the late 1980s.

But cost competitiveness in many lines of consumer electronics is fleeting; and in certain products, like microwave ovens and videocassette recorders, it may be very fleeting. This is especially the case when labor costs and the value of the Korean currency are escalating. By the late 1980s, Samsung's competitive edge in consumer electronics products appeared to be eroding and market shares became millstones around the conglomerate's neck. At the same time, Samsung's traditional products, like food, textiles, and paper, were marked by stagnant earnings in the fiercely competitive domestic market. To surmount a developing profitability crisis, Samsung's management decided once again to expand—this time into higher-value-added, technology-intensive products like semiconductors, which promised higher profit margins.

But going into semiconductors involved even more massive investments than consumer electronics—an estimated $625 million between 1984 and 1987. And on the two occasions that Samsung launched dramatic bids in semiconductors, the international market did not cooperate. When it unveiled its 64 kilobit dynamic random access memory (DRAM) chip in 1983, an oversupply of memory chips forced prices down rapidly. And when it started producing the even more sophisticated 256K DRAM chip in April 1986, memory chip prices fell to their lowest point ever. Already by 1984 Samsung accounted for over 6 percent of all bank borrowings by the 30 major chaebol.[19] If Samsung was to survive, it needed even greater access to credit. Samsung's profitability crisis was reflected in its low 1.5 percent return on sales in 1988. This figure was only marginally better than the average return on sales of the top thirty chaebol—a minuscule 1.3 percent.[20]

Credit, Cannibalism, and Speculation

Greater access to resources was opened up to the chaebol in the early and mid-1980s by three developments: liberalization of the banking system, conglomerate cannibalism, and hothouse speculation in property.

The chaebol acquired greater control of the nation's financial system as a result of a structural adjustment program imposed on the Korean economy by the IMF in the early 1980s, following dislocations created by the HCI program. Under pressure from the United States, the Korean government began to open up the domestic market to more intensive foreign penetration. The chaebol were dismayed, and to pacify them—as well as satisfy the antistate bias of the IMF—the government offered the chaebol freer access to and greater control of financial markets.[21]

In 1982 as the government divested its controlling shares of the five national commercial banks, the chaebol made moves to try to gain equity control of these institutions. Though the government revised the banking law to prevent a single person from owning more than 8 percent of a bank's stock, the chaebol apparently found various means to circumvent the law through the use of multiple agents or dummies. As a study by the Christian Institute for the Study of Justice and Development noted, "In not a few cases, the real stockholding share of each chaebol in a given bank goes beyond the limit of eight percent."[22] True, the state did retain administrative control of the banks; but the chaebol's ability to acquire significant influence—if not minority control—in the big commercial banks was a giant step towards tilting the government-chaebol balance of power in their favor.

In addition to the commercial banks, the chaebol also moved to control other financial institutions. A large proportion of the stocks of local and regional banks, for instance, passed into the control of the chaebol.[23] Of the twenty-six Korean insurance companies, eleven were under the ownership of one chaebol and most of the rest were jointly owned by several conglomerates.[24]

IMF pressure on the state to end its ownership of the commercial banks was motivated by a desire to end the latter's monopoly on the financial sector. The result, however, was not what the neoclassical, free-market economists expected: an immense concentration of credit in the hands of the chaebol. The top thirty conglomerates had secured $55 billion in bank credit. Including loans from nonbanking financial institutions, the total credit acquired by the top thirty chaebol came to $65 billion—an amount equivalent to almost 39 percent of Korea's 1988 GNP and 41 percent of the chaebol's combined 1988 turnover.[25]

Moreover, concentration of bank credit was, in fact, even tighter if one considers the proportion of total bank credit held by the top five chaebol, which came to 22.7 percent in 1988. As in recent years, Samsung was the top corporate debtor, accounting for $3.5 billion or close to 6 percent of bank loans and guarantees.[26]

For all intents and purposes, the government had lost its tight grip on the chaebol's dealings in the financial market. Despite the Central Bank's nominally tight credit policy and its urging that the conglomerates reduce their exposure by selling shares in the stock market, seventeen of the thirty leading conglomerates increased their bank loans in 1988. Bank loans were preferred to capitalization in the stock market, according to some observers, because the chaebol family owners feared losing control of their conglomerates.[27] "Already," said one member of the Financial Committee of the National Assembly, "the Sixth Republic has lost its power to control strictly the conglomerates' bank credit."[28]

Aside from expanding via loans acquired through increasing control of the banking system, the chaebol extended their activities through cut-throat mergers and acquisitions. Indeed, it is claimed that in the 1980s the chaebol have grown mainly through mergers and acquisitions.[29] Some of the targets were state enterprises, which were acquired under the privatization program propelled by the IMF and the chaebol. Other targets were private enterprises, acquired in a distinctly unfriendly fashion. Indeed, chaebol often ate up chaebol. The most celebrated case of chaebol cannibalism occurred in 1985 when the Kukje-ICC conglomerate, the seventh largest in the country, was dismantled by the Chun government at the apparent instigation of other chaebol. Hanil Synthetics was said to have acquired controlling shares of the troubled conglomerate at below market rates, while another chaebol, Dongkuk Steel, bit off Kukje-ICC's construction and machinery subsidiaries.[30]

But perhaps the most controversial cash-generating tactic that the chaebol resorted to in the 1980s was speculation in real estate. In 1988 the leading thirty chaebol had expanded their real estate holdings to 429 million square meters of land valued at some $15 billion, plus some 45,000 square meters of buildings.[31] Of the total holdings, land set aside for plant construction was just below 10 percent, the rest apparently being reserved for speculation. In the first half of 1989, the chaebol stepped up their acquisition of land, purchasing an additional 46.2 million square meters valued at $1.5 billion, despite government attempts to restrict their ability to borrow money.[32]

With land prices skyrocketing several hundred percent just in the first half of 1989,[33] the chaebol were making windfall profits through speculative investment and apparently plowing profits back into speculation rather than production. As one trade journal angrily claimed, "While complaining about the nonavailability of money for their productive investment, chaebol spend huge sums on land and securities which are not urgently needed."[34]

Perhaps more than any other factor, rampant speculation in real estate pushed public opinion against the chaebol in the late 1980s. Not only were middle-class and working-class people angered at the way they were being deprived of home ownership by rising land prices, but the public at large began to perceive that the link between profits and production on which rested the fragile legitimacy of the chaebol had snapped. The chaebol were increasingly scorned as rentiers instead of being respected as producers.

Corruption of a Partnership

Public perception of the chaebol as rentier capitalists grown too powerful for the good of the nation was reinforced by the conviction that the state-chaebol relationship had become extremely corrupt under Chun Doo-Hwan, the successor of the comparatively austere Park Chung-Hee.

When Chun first came to power in May 1980, he tried to defuse popular anger at the blood spilled by his troops during the Kwangju Massacre with a number of antichaebol initiatives designed to get the conglomerates to sell off subsidiaries not related to their main lines of business.[35] Specifically, the government ordered 26 conglomerates to dispose of 166 unaffiliated companies by 1984. The program ended up as a failure. Some companies were indeed sold off, but as Tony Michell points out, "many of the companies which were to be disposed of were small and had voluntarily associated themselves with the *chaebol* in order to get access to credit, marketing, and information."[36]

Chun also promised a new deal for small and medium businesses (those employing less than 300 people), which made up over 98 percent of manufacturing establishments in 1982. This sector had been systematically starved of credit under the Park regime, yet studies showed that despite favoritism to the chaebol the productivity of small and medium firms had grown faster than that of large firms in the period 1970–79.[37] In the early reformist flush of the Chun government, guidelines were set up to channel the bulk of credit to small and medium enterprises. But like the effort to get the conglomerates to rid themselves of some subsidiaries, this reform soon stalled: after rising to 39.3 percent in 1983, the share of bank credit going to small and medium businesses dropped to 33.6 percent in 1985.[38]

Indeed, the Chun regime not only failed to stem the power of the chaebol but negotiated a new modus vivendi as well. It was, however, one that was bound to destroy the precarious legitimacy of the government-chaebol alliance that Park had painstakingly constructed. While Park promised the chaebol rewards if they supported the policy of export-led growth, Chun apparently promised favors if the conglomerates contributed to his personal and political slush fund. While bureaucratic venality had undoubtedly existed under Park, under Chun it went beyond the range of the acceptable.

Chun's means of securing personal financing from the chaebol was to establish the Ilhae Foundation, to which the chaebol patriarchs were pressured to contribute. They did—in large sums. Hyundai, POSCO, and Samsung all kicked in about 4.5 billion won (about $6 million) each. Hyundai's head, Chung Ju-Yung, was delegated bag man, with the task of collecting 30 billion won (about $40 million) from various businesses in three years' time.

Those who did not cooperate found their fortunes at grave risk. Those who did sometimes made their fortune from others' misfortunes. For instance, the Kukje-ICC conglomerate, according to its former chairman, was dismantled because its management had not completely buckled under Chun's extortionist pressure. His group refused to give money to the Ilhae Foundation and gave only a paltry sum to another of Chun's fundraising fronts, the Saemaul Undong, or New Community Movement. When Kukje was disbanded, its steel subsidiary was, as noted earlier, given to Dongkuk Steel and a substantial portion of its stocks was sold below market value to Hanil Synthetics. Both Dongkuk and Hanil were, interestingly enough, major contributors to the Ilhae Foundation.[39]

The Chaebol Republic

The increasingly controversial chaebol-government alliance led some technocrats and economists to break with the pro-chaebol consensus, at least in rhetoric. No longer unusual was the following sentiment expressed by technocrat Hong Won-Tack:

> Perhaps due to the snowballing effect of wealth accumulation, there has been an extreme concentration of economic activities in the hands of a small number of big business groups that goes well beyond the limit justifiable by scale economies. Extreme over-extension of a given entrepreneurial talent implies poor management of the extended group's business activities and frequent gigantic-scale cases of failure. In Korea, the entrepreneurial ability of the chosen few businessmen has been unreasonably exaggerated, and there has occurred a tremendous waste of resources in the hands of these chosen few.[40]

Indeed, some early figures in the new, democratically elected government of President Roh Tae-Woo positioned themselves on the populist end of the spectrum. Thus Deputy Prime Minister Cho Soon was said to favor a policy that sought "to check the expansion of conglomerates, promoting instead a greater role for small and medium-sized businesses."[41] Another key figure, presidential economic adviser Moon Hi-Gab, adopted populist rhetoric in justifying the need for legal restrictions on landownership to control chaebol speculation in real estate: "Land is both a public utility and a commodity. Due to its scarcity, private ownership should be limited and the government has a duty to regulate private ownership to help as many people as possible share their right to use the available land."[42] Cho and Moon also backed a controversial reform to force the use of real names in financial transactions, which would facilitate the progressive taxation of financial gains and the imposition of a capital gains tax system.

These technocrats were responding to what they perceived as an alarming phenomenon. No longer was it just the working class that was alienated from the traditional formula for development, but the legitimacy of the state-chaebol alliance and the whole strategy of chaebol-led growth was eroding among Korea's swing factor, the middle class. Thus, the resentful voices of the professionals and owners of small businesses ware added as one more centrifugal element in Korea's volatile brew of "late industrialization and late democratization." Seventy-two percent of Koreans, the Korea Gallup Poll revealed, perceived a severe gap between haves and have-nots, with nearly half attributing this condition to land speculation and other nonproductive activities.[43]

But despite the current defensiveness, the government's reliance on the chaebol as the locomotive of Korean growth is so profound that the government-chaebol relationship is likely to remain essentially intact. The thrust of the current reforms is not to bust the conglomerates but to curb the most abusive features of chaebol power. Some discipline and rationalization have always followed in the wake of overheated expansion. In the first years of both the Park government and the Chun regime, there was an initial period of soak-the-rich rhetoric, but the state elite and the corporate elite eventually settled into their fundamentally complementary roles as soon as business showed proper deference to the new regime and the latter began to get uneasy about the mass expectations aroused by its populist language.

Indeed, in the face of continuing social turmoil, the timid technocratic apertura toward the workers and small and medium capital in the first two years of Roh Tae-Woo steadily narrowed. In 1989 and 1990 several moves marked a gradual return to the old, comfortable arrangement. The government decided to contribute a substantial sum to bailing out the financially mismanaged Daewoo shipyard. This was followed by the government's sending 14,000 troops to evict workers from the strike-ridden Hyundai shipyard at the end of March 1989—an action that was repeated scarcely over a year later. The reversion to the old way of doing things speeded up with the banning of the new militant

Chonnohyop labor federation that sought to supplant the traditional government influenced Federation of Korean Trade Unions (FKTU). Finally, in March 1990, Planning Minister Cho Soon and his team of reformist technocrats were replaced by figures more favorable to chaebol interests. As one observer explained it,

> Faced with trouble, the economic boffins reacted the way most people do: they reached back to the past. In South Korea, that means resurrecting the idea of Korea, Inc. Big business groups, the much-maligned *chaebol*, are now expected to kick the export machine into high gear. Gone is the idea of domestic demand as the motor for the economy, gone is the idea of building up small and medium industries.[44]

There is, however, one difference from previous periods that is likely to make it difficult for the old formula to work under the Roh Tae-Woo government: the strong, democratic opposition of Korea's newly mobilized masses.

4

Sacrificing Agriculture

L abor was not the only social group that paid a high price for the policy of high-speed industrialization. Though not in as brutal a fashion, Korea's farmers have had to bear a significant share of the costs of the development strategy. Korea's agricultural economy is today in a state of profound crisis, and this dismal condition is directly related to the success of urban-biased export-led growth.

Farming today is an extremely risky activity, accompanied by high levels of debt and an equally high rate of suicide. A few statistics would underline the erosion of what once was considered the society's most valued occupation, that of being the producer of the food that sustained the whole population.

Consider, for example, that in the first six months of 1989 alone, some twenty-one farmers took their own lives, apparently out of frustration at their inability to secure a mate from the rapidly thinning ranks of agrarian women of marriageable age.[1]

Consider also that the portion of the population living in rural areas dropped from 56 percent in 1965 to 17 percent in 1988. This was not only a relative decline but a precipitous drop in absolute terms: from 15.8 million to 7.8 million people. The rate of migration from the countryside to the cities has been one of the highest in the world, approaching an average of almost 400,000 yearly during the mid-1980s. The vast majority of these migrants have been young men and women, and their departure has resulted in a rapidly aging agricultural work force: the portion of the agricultural work force age fifty or over leapt from 19 percent in the early 1980s to almost 33 percent by the end of 1988.[2]

In the past few years, discontent has been translated into militant political action, with a clearcut political message: We will no longer be sacrificial lambs. More than anything else, government acquiescence to U.S. pressure to open up Korea's agricultural markets has convinced farmers of their essentially marginal status in the reigning development model. Farmers have finally realized that their elimination is the quid pro quo for a grand compromise that would allow the chaebol continued access to the U.S. market and thus maintain the momentum of export-oriented industrialization.

The great trade-off is consistent with the Korean technocratic elite's traditional approach to the agrarian question since export-first became doctrine in the 1960s. This perspective is echoed in policy statements that view as positive a drastic reduction of the rural population, following the example of the United States. Rather than a force to be tapped for national development, the peasantry has been seen through technocratic lenses as an obstacle to growth, a force to be approached mainly as a problem in political management.

The Ambivalent Legacy of Land Reform

That farmers are second-class economic citizens might come as a surprise to those who have been told that South Korea's is one of the few recent cases of successful agrarian reform in the third world. But a closer look reveals the profound ambivalence with which Korea's successive governing elites have approached the countryside.

Land reform was decreed in South Korea in the late 1940s by the conservative Rhee Syng-Man regime, which really had little choice in the matter given the period's great social and political flux and ideological competition. Rhee Syng-Man's government, installed by the United States Army occupying Korea south of the 38th Parallel, had been preceded by the short-lived Korean People's Republic, which had decreed the dispossession of the landlords and the redistribution of land in the aftermath of the Japanese surrender.[3] This was a very popular move, since the landlords had become discredited as Japanese collaborators during Japan's thirty-five-year colonial occupation of the peninsula. But though American military authorities dissolved the KPR in the south, its land reform program was implemented and expanded above the 38th Parallel by a Communist-led transition government that had assumed power with the approval of the Soviet Army that had occupied the area. In this atmosphere of heightened political and ideological competition, land reform became the key to popular legitimacy in a country where 60 percent of the population lived in the countryside. Thus, with a great deal of reluctance, the landlord-backed Rhee regime enacted a land-reform law with two core provisions: limitation of farm ownership to no more than three hectares or 7.5 acres, and the banning of tenant farming.

Not one hectare was, however, redistributed until the outbreak of the Korean War in the summer of 1950, "whence came a revolutionary dispossession in all but the 'Pusan perimeter' holding area," by peoples' committees cooperating with the occupying North Korean Army.[4] This was the moment of truth for the Americans, who realized that unless land reform passed from law to reality, any noncommunist regime in the south would be plagued by fundamental instability. Thus, in Bruce Cumings's classic description,

> After Rhee clamoured back to Seoul, the Americans refused to resituate his herd of lords on the land. Thus redistribution created a vast mass of small-holding peasants and quieted the countryside, while landlords received state bonds convertible to industrial wealth. Basically the Americans were trying to fashion industrialist silk purses out of agrarian sow's ears—part of the capitalist class-making in which they have engaged throughout the Third World. But rarely have they been helped by the revolution they sought to deny, as in Korea.[5]

There is no denying that Korea's land reform was sweeping and that it did install a mass of smallholders as the dominant force in the countryside. The number of tenant-farmer households dropped from 86.2 percent in 1945 to 26.4 percent in 1960.[6] But the reform was by no means complete. Over 40 percent of the land scheduled for redistribution was actually not transferred because owners were able to disguise themselves as tillers or register land titles to their sons or other relatives.[7] Moreover, the ban on tenant-farming was subsequently weakened, as this exploitative land-tenure arrangement made a comeback in the 1970s and 1980s.[8]

The Subordination of the Countryside

But the return of tenancy was not the problem in the years following the land reform. The problem lay in the fact that land reform was seen only as a political-management program, not as a central element in an integrated policy of economic development. This narrow perspective was evident in the Rhee regime's policies that discriminated against agriculture and the well-being of the rural population, even as the reform was in motion.

While the regime did not have a coherent industrialization program, some of its policies had the effect of favoring urban industry over agriculture. One policy that had more than a passing impact was that of keeping grain prices low in order to blunt economic and political discontent in the cities. This was achieved partly through the indiscriminate importation of U.S. agricultural surpluses under Public Law 480, which depressed grain prices below the cost of production. The low pricing policy for grain, combined with the failure to follow the land reform of the early 1950s with essential support services like effective agricultural credit systems, extension services, and technological assistance, resulted in a significant degradation of rural living standards and increased rural emigration. This conjunction of cheap labor streaming in from the poor countryside and cheap grain subsidizing the costs of this work force constituted an indispensable condition for the emergence of import-substitution industrialization, a largely unplanned process of replacing formerly imported consumer goods with local products.

Thus, while manufacturing grew at an average rate of 10 percent per year between 1957 and 1960, agriculture grew by only 1.6 percent.[9] A measure of the widespread rural distress created by these haphazard pro-urban policies was the loss of 1.3 million rural residents to the cities in just five years, between 1955 and 1960.[10]

The countryside thus subsidized the first phase of South Korean industrialization in the postwar period. So did it subsidize the second, export-oriented phase. This did not, however, seem inevitable in the first years after the historic military coup of May 1961. Park Chung-Hee, who took pride in being a "farm boy," appeared to promise a new deal for the countryside. Under his direction, agricultural credit cooperatives were merged with the Agricultural Bank, resulting in an enlarged flow of credit to the rural areas and contributing to the rise in the agricultural growth rate from 1.6 percent per year in 1957–60 to 8.8 percent in 1962–65.[11] The infusion of credit into the countryside, claims one account, generated greater rural demand that "set in motion supplementary growth in industries catering to the home market and hence produced derived growth throughout the economy."[12] Indeed, for a time it seemed that agriculture would be the designated locomotive for growth.

Betrayed Again

Nonetheless, the modest increase in rural credit flows did not signify a basic change in the urban-industrial bias of economic policy. Indeed, by the mid-1960s, the Park regime had adopted a full-scale program of export-oriented industrialization that reversed the countryside's gains earlier in the decade. Central to this policy was the same mechanism of real resource transfer and urban pacification that had operated under the Rhee government: low prices for rice and other grains. The difference was that the low-grain-price policy was systematically utilized to subsidize industry. As one analyst put it, under Park "low grain price policies were adopted as a means of surplus extraction....The state was, in effect, engaged in forming an export-oriented entrepreneurial class that was competitive in world markets. Keeping wage costs low facilitated this economic development strategy."[13]

The impact of the late-1960s drive to promote industrial exports at the expense of agriculture is evident in the statistics. While the farm population rose slightly from 14.6 million in 1960 to 15.8 million in 1965, reflecting the pro-agriculture thrust of the early Park period, it dropped to 14.4 million in 1970. Even more striking was the plunge in farm household income from rough parity with urban household income in 1965 to 67 percent of the latter by 1970.[14]

Organized opposition to the urban-industry–biased strategy was weak because land reform had eliminated a politically articulate and potentially obstructionist landlord class and replaced it with a fragmented smallholding mass that was incapable of mounting strong opposition to a strong military-backed state.[15] Nonetheless, rural discontent festered, becoming painfully evident in the burgeoning slums in and around Seoul. It flared into a spontaneous uprising in August 1971 at Songnam, a large slum outside Seoul, most of whose residents were former farmers.[16] By the early 1970s, the countryside was impinging on the Park regime's consciousness as a serious problem that could threaten the government's stability. In the context of the always-paranoidal competition with North Korea, the authorities feared that rural discontent could become the Achilles' heel of the south: a dissatisfied peasantry could serve as the point of entry for North Korean guerrillas.[17]

The Great Cooptation of the 1970s

The regime's response to the rural crisis, again falling within the realm of mere political management, was a four-pronged rural development program consisting of a revitalization of the rural credit system; a grain policy of buying dear and selling cheap; a campaign to plant so-called miracle rice instead of traditional rice varieties; and the *Saemaul Undong*, or New Community Movement.

The flow of government credit to the rural areas escalated in the early 1970s—a trend shown by the rise of borrowings for agricultural credit from the Bank of Korea from 1,377 million won in 1969 to 78,565 million won in 1974.[18] But typically credit delivery was also used to extend and consolidate centralized control of the countryside. Governing the allocation of government credit was the National Agricultural Cooperatives Federation (NACF), a giant bureaucracy that funneled funds to some 17,600 "cooperatives" to which over 2.2 million farmers belonged at the height of the rural development thrust in the late 1970s. The NACF's power over the mass of unorganized smallholders was enhanced by its monopoly over two other critical government functions: the management of the pricing and delivery of fertilizer and pesticide, and the buying of grain from the farmers at harvesttime. This concentration of power in one agency enabled the regime to take away or reduce with one hand what it gave as credit with the other.

A new double-pricing policy was the second component of Park's rural-development strategy. The government bought grain from the farmers at artificially high prices at harvesttime, then sold it on a subsidized basis to urban consumers in the off-season. The tilt towards the farmer was genuine: rice became Korea's most protected commodity, selling at twice the world-market price. Equally genuine was the concomitant subsidy: by 1982 the deficit of the double-pricing program came to $686 million, or 34 percent of the total government budget deficit.[19]

The third prong of the Park program was the drive to get farmers to plant miracle rice, which was then touted worldwide as the panacea for every problem, from low rural incomes to food deficits to political instability. A variety of incentives, including higher government prices for the *Tong-il* or Indica variety than for the traditional *Ilban* or Japonica rice, resulted in more than 70 percent of paddy land being planted to Tong-il by 1977. But in a fashion typical of Park's command capitalism, incentives were mixed with sanctions. When massive propaganda campaigns failed, local agricultural officials resorted to force to meet quotas. Rooting out rice fields planted to traditional rice was a common practice.[20] In one county, for instance, the popular press reported that "the head of that *myun* [county] and 10 officials went with sickles and hooks to 750 *pyung* [1 pyung equals 4 square yards] of rice field owned by three farmers and pulled out, cut down or trampled on all of the young rice plants because the farmers had planted Ilban instead of the new strains."[21]

Planting Tong-il (Unity) did result in higher yields, but it also incurred much higher costs than Ilban in the form of greater applications of fertilizers and pesticides, the prices of which were controlled by the government. Application of fertilizer per hectare rose from 162 kilograms in 1970 to 299 kilograms in 1980.[22] Pesticide use rose even more dramatically, by over 330 percent between 1974 and 1976.[23] Aside from the negative impact on the environment and farmers' health, the high chemical input involved in growing Tong-il left producers with escalating expenses and uncertain profit margins. For instance, in just one year, 1978, the 100 percent rise in outlays for fertilizers and other chemicals was the highest increase registered in all categories of expenditure of the Korean farming household.[24] This in turn contributed to increasing indebtedness: between 1972 and 1978, a period that marked the height of the Tong-il campaign, average liabilities per farm household skyrocketed nearly eight times, from 14,000 won to 111,061 won.[25]

The government-sponsored miracle-rice program not only began the process of burying the Korean farmer in debt, but it eventually turned out to be a costly dead end as well. The Tong-il program was eventually unraveled by the strain's susceptibility to disease and by continued consumer loyalty to the traditional varieties. With higher urban incomes in the 1980s, urban consumers were willing to pay a premium for the more familiar taste of the traditional Japonica varieties. Defying the officials, farmers rapidly turned their backs on the bureaucrats' choice. In 1979 land devoted to traditional rice accounted for less than one third of total paddy land; by 1985 it had gone up to nearly three quarters.[26]

The fourth prong of the government's attempt to secure the loyalty of the peasantry was the Saemaul Undong, or New Community Movement. Ostensibly a campaign to mobilize the rural masses for self-reliance, Saemaul organized farmers into cooperative production teams and into work brigades to repair roads, bridges, and other rural infrastructure. Under Saemaul's "beautification" program, a number of villages were completely rebuilt and relocated, "although this may have been confined mainly to 'show villages' visible from national highways."[27]

Farmers were also pressured to replace their thatched roofs with sturdier and more "beautiful" metal or Mediterranean-style tile roofs. Some 2.4 million homes or about a third of all Korean houses, saw their roofs replaced—something that would have been impossible without rigid quotas imposed on local leaders by the Saemaul bureaucracy.[28] Pressed to meet their targets, local officials often used coercive techniques to overcome peasant resistance to costly "home improvement." According to one eyewitness account,

> If several farmers in a village were reluctant to replace the traditional brush fences around their houses with cement walls, jeep loads of men from the county seat might arrive and simply tear down all the brush fences. Similarly, there were occasions when house owners who were unwilling to make the substantial investment necessary to replace their thatched roofs with composition or tile might return home from a market trip to find the thatch gone and their homes open to the sky.[29]

Beautification was expensive. Thus, like the Tong-il program with which it was coordinated, Saemaul bequeathed a legacy of debt to the rural population. And it was not only debt that made the rural population wary about tile or corrugated roofing but also common sense: as one study noted, "tile and corrugated roofing provide less insulation for houses, thus possibly reducing warmth in winter and insulation against heat in summer."[30]

But Saemaul was, above all, an intense campaign of moral and ideological indoctrination meant to defuse peasant dissatisfaction after years of neglect and to mobilize the peasantry behind a central government constantly worried about its legitimacy. It was an ambitious effort to invigorate centralized state control of the dispersed smallholders that used the traditional rural government and police bureaucracies while bypassing them at the same time.

Korea specialist Robert Wade characterizes the movement circa 1983 in this fashion:

> While emphasizing higher productivity and community participation in local projects, it has placed special stress on education in the politics of the government and its leader. Though identified with President Park it remains today, under President Chun, a centrally important organization for economic and political mobilization, with its own hierarchy stretching from village...leaders right up to the Secretariat in the Blue House, the office of the President himself. Indeed, it can be understood as South Korea's equivalent of a mass vanguard party, such as the KMT in Taiwan.[31]

In retrospect, what judgment are we to make of the impact of Park's rural development program in the 1970s? Regime apologists claim that it was essentially successful, since in the space of just five years (1970–75) the average annual income of rural households went from 67 percent of that of urban households to parity.[32] However, this claim is misleading, as one rural specialist points out, because the average rural household was larger than the average urban household—with five members compared to four—so that, on a per-worker basis, the income of the urban industrial worker was still higher than that of the rural worker.[33] Moreover, it is difficult to say that rural income rose significantly when claims to part of that income in the form of debt increased at an even greater rate. Thus, while farm income and assets grew three times between 1975 and 1980, debt increased ten times.[34]

What little real gains the farmers made were not likely to be lasting, for the main thrust of the whole rural-development effort was to be palliative rather than to integrate agriculture into a coherent national economic-development program. Like Rhee's land reform in the 1950s and Park's own agricultural initiatives in the early 1960, Park's rural-development enterprise in the 1970s was geared to delivering short-term economic prosperity. This limited vision was due to the failure of Park's technocrats to articulate a role for agriculture in a long-term development strategy, and the priority that Park assigned to establishing centralized control over the peasantry and securing political legitimacy among them.

What was perhaps the strongest outcome of the rural-development program endured only a few years. Constantly wooed with pork barrel benefits—channelled to them at strategic moments, like elections—the rural areas did become strongholds of support for the ruling party.[35] This support, however, was not able to weather the volatile combination of deepening structural crisis and flagrant government corruption that hit the countryide in the mid-1980s.

The Crisis Deepens

The government's Band-Aid approach to the rural crisis fell apart in the mid-1980s in the face of a deepening crisis and spreading rural discontent. When a 1988 farmers' demonstration in front of the National Assembly in Seoul turned into a riot, the Korean ruling elite realized that it was faced not just with a protest over irrigation taxes and price policies but also with a class that was shaking off government control and organizing as an independent political force.

That conditions in the countryside were worsening was underlined by the figures on farmers' income and indebtedness. From parity in 1975, the height of the rural-development program, average rural household income dropped to 84 percent of average urban household income in 1980 and rose weakly to 89 percent in 1986.[36] But perhaps more alarming were the figures on farmers' debt. The number of rural households in debt rose from 76 percent in 1971 to 90 percent in 1983 and to an astounding 98 percent in 1985.[37] Between 1975 and 1985, average farm household income increased 6.6 times and farm assets 6.3 times, while farm debt rose by almost 63 times, or at almost 10 times the rate at which income and assets increased (see table 4.1).[38] By 1988, 17 percent of total farm debt was incurred to make payment on past debt, leading one observer to note that "the farmers are trapped in a vicious cycle in which they 'repeatedly pull out the bottom rock and stack it atop the top rock.'"[39]

The escalating farmers' debt and unrelieved out-migration of the young and the able were symptoms of a massive debacle: the long-standing failure of government planners to integrate agriculture into a national economic-development strategy.

Rural initiatives, which were dictated mainly by political expediency, could easily be overturned by opposition from strong pressure groups. Thus, in the early 1980s, discontent among urban

Table 4.1

Comparative Growth Rates of Farm Household Income and Debt, 1975–1985

	1975	1980	1981	1982	1983	1984	1985
Income (in thousand won[a])	873	2,693	3,688	4,465	5,128	5,549	5,743
Growth Rate (%)	—	—	36.9	21.1	14.8	8.2	3.5
Debt (in thousand won[a])	33	338	437	830	1,285	1,784	2,024
Growth Rate (%)	—	—	29.2	89.8	54.9	38.8	16.1

Source: Park Chan-Hee, "The Reality of the Four Trillion Won Farm Household Debt," *Chosun,* March 1987.

[a] $1 = 669 won as of 1989. The won has greatly appreciated in value relative to the dollar in the past ten years.

consumers and pressure from the International Monetary Fund to reduce the deficit from grain subsidies led the government to subvert its policy of buying grain at a high price. But to defuse the rural discontent sure to be triggered by a direct move, the mechanisms involved were subtle. One method was to release government rice stocks onto the market at harvesttime, thereby "artificially depressing rice prices at a time the farmers would have to sell."[40] Another method of depressing prices was to not announce the buying price before a commodity's planting season. For instance, in 1985–86, in an effort to reduce its purchases of barley, the government did not announce its buying price before the November planting. This ensured that both the purchase price of barley and its volume would drop; and volume did drop to an all-time low that harvest season.[41]

But an even more damaging legacy of the technocratic inability to integrate agriculture into a national development model was that Korean agriculture was turned into what one writer described as the "sacrificial lamb" to ensure the continued viability of the dominant export-oriented industrialization strategy.[42] As the 1980s progressed, Korean farmers began to realize that in the face of U.S. trade pressure, the government had all but boarded up the Korean countryside in exchange for keeping the American market open to Korean manufactured exports. For Korea's technocrats, farmers had become, at best, marginal to their vision of Korea's future, at worst, an element to be weeded out.

While the U.S. press has successfully portrayed South Korean agriculture as a highly protected sector, in fact, since the 1950s the viability of Korean agriculture has been consistently eroded by U.S. trade policies, including the PL-480 program, which dumps U.S. agricultural surpluses in the third world. Between 1973 and 1983, for instance, grain imports—particularly wheat, corn, and beans—skyrocketed by almost 300 percent.[43] The lower prices induced by these imports discouraged domestic production and dropped the self-sufficiency ratio from 27 percent in 1965 to 6 percent in 1983 for wheat, from 36 percent to 2.7 percent for corn, and from 100 percent to 25.7 percent for beans. Indeed, as one analyst claims, "imports of wheat and cotton from the U.S. have already resulted in the disappearance of Korean farms growing those crops."[44]

Korea is now the third largest importer of U.S. agricultural products, at a current cost of $3.2 billion.[45] Indeed, on a per-capita basis, Korea now consumes more U.S. farm products than any other foreign nation.[46] Half of Korea's total food imports come from the United States.[47] When it comes to certain strategic imports, U.S. trade dominance is even more marked: 95–100 percent of soybean imports, 74 percent of wheat, and 70 percent of cotton.[48]

Relentless U.S. trade pressure was cutting off the Korean farmers' last avenues of retreat. This was illustrated forcefully by the impact of the opening of the tobacco market in 1988. Upon reducing trade barriers to U.S. cigarettes, the government encouraged tobacco farmers to shift production to other crops, like red peppers. But an almost 10 percent increase in fields planted to pepper drastically lowered the market price, resulting in vast unsold stocks and bankrupting many farmers.

The current mood of desperation was captured by writer Hwang Ui-Pong:

> As the planting season loomed in the spring of 1989, farmers were confused: "Hey," they asked each other, "what are we going to plant?" We have to plant rice no matter what, but wheat has been a lost cause for a long time—imported soybeans have grabbed more than 80 percent of that market; a few years ago, the garlic market was hot, but seed garlic is in short

supply now and western cigarette imports have already forced reductions in tobacco acreage. We just don't have a crop to plant. In the end, the farmers reached the inescapable conclusion that they were caught in a vicious cycle that runs like this: "First, a crop is opened to imports, which causes collapse of that crop. That triggers, in turn, mass flight to another crop, which causes over-production, which causes the bottom to drop out of prices. Which causes penniless farmers."[49]

As they reviewed their options for planting in 1989, "the farmers concluded that barring extraordinary good luck, about all they could plant in 1989 was red peppers, setting the stage for an inevitable replay of the massive 1988 disruptions triggered by the over-planting of red peppers."[50]

A similar dislocation is likely to accompany the opening up of the beef market. Under U.S. pressure, the government allowed the importation of 14,500 tons of beef in 1988 to meet 10 percent of domestic demand. The quota was raised by over 325 percent to 50,000 tons in 1989, and further raised to 58,000 tons in 1990.[51] By 1997 the beef market will be fully open, according to U.S. negotiators.[52] Since foreign beef can be sold for as low as a quarter of the domestic price, these moves are likely to have a more massive impact on Korean agriculture than other instances of market opening and are likely to bankrupt a substantial number of the almost 50 percent of Korea's farmers who depend in varying degrees on raising cattle.[53]

The consequences of market liberalization did not escape government technocrats. As one Korean official warned, "A further acceleration of farm import liberalization at this stage is certain to pauperize...farmers and hollow out the rural economy, with serious social and political consequences."[54] Committed as they were to the priority of keeping the U.S. market open to the chaebol's manufactured exports, government technocrats were unlikely to develop the political will to stem the disappearance of Korea's class of small peasant farmers. Indeed, it was questionable if the technocrats' concern for the future of the countryside stemmed from anything more than fear of the potential political clout of rebellious farmers.

The devastating impact of market liberalization, farmer bankruptcies due to high levels of debt, and rural emigration was in fact moving the land-tenure system back to a pre-1950s structure

Table 4.2

Trends in Land Tenancy in Korea, 1945–1981

	1945	1960	1972	1980	1981
Total farmland (in hectares[a])	2,207	2,025	2,298	2,196	2,188
Tenanted area (in hectares[a])	1,407	273	404	435	488
Percentage of total farmland cultivated by tenants	66.7	13.5	17.7	19.8	22.3
Total farm households (in thousands)	1,999	2,329	2,415	2,156	2,030
Tenant farm households (in thousands)	1,723	615	809	800	942
Tenant farm households as percentage of all farm households	86.2	26.4	33.5	37.1	46.4

Source: Pak Ki-Hyuk, "Farmland Tenure in the Republic of Korea," in *Land Tenure and the Small Farmer in Asia*, FFTC Book Series, no. 24 (Taiwan: FFTC, 1983), p. 116.

[a] 1 hectare = 2.5 acres.

of land tenure. Though the number of full or part-time tenant households had dropped from 86.2 percent of rural households in 1945 to 26.4 percent in 1960, it rose to 46.4 percent in 1981 and to an astounding 64.7 percent in 1985 (see table 4.2 for 1945–81 figures).[55] In the mid-1980s, tenancy arrangements were typically made by verbal contract for about one year, with rent usually set at 40 to 50 percent of the annual yield, and with both parties knowing that the relationship violated the land-reform laws.[56]

The return of tenancy was apparently propelled principally by rural emigration, as many of those leaving rented out their own land to their neighbors. With the worsening of rural economic conditions in the mid-1980s, emigration escalated, with 34,000 farmers leaving for the cities in 1986, 41,000 in 1987, and 50,000 in 1988. From 20 percent of the total population in 1985, the rural population dropped to 17 percent in 1988. It was mainly young people who left the countryside raising the average age of the rural work force. Close to 33 percent of all farmers, as noted earlier, are now over fifty years of age.[57]

These demographic trends also presented the technocrats with an opportunity to argue for a "rationalization" of agricultural production by raising the upper limit on landownership from 3 to 10 hectares. In the technocrats' view, the crisis of agriculture lay in the "growing inefficiency" of small-scale agriculture: the structure of small landholdings—the average size of which was slightly over 1 hectare—hindered mechanization and the achievement of economies of scale necessary for efficient production.

The technocrats' agenda was the introduction of large-scale commercial farming, and this agenda found favor among certain sectors of a countryside that was rapidly being differentiated by the rural crisis. As the poorer families sold out and left for the cities, the number of rural families owning more than 1.5 hectares jumped from 15.5 percent to nearly 17 percent between 1988 and 1989. Families with more than 2 hectares increased by over 8 percent.

Having been socialized to the priority of export-oriented industrialization, the technocrats were markedly unsympathetic to the rural economic and cultural system that had sustained Korea for centuries. Indeed, for these economists, a large rural population was an obstacle to the realization of their limited vision of agrarian modernization: more efficient food production. Thus they favored eventually bringing the rural population down to less than 10 percent of the total population, a perspective brazenly expressed by a legislator-technocrat of the ruling party who proposed special lending facilities to "support the consolidation of land so as to accelerate structural adjustment and reduce the farming population."[58]

Indeed, if it had been more cost-effective to import food than to produce it in Korea, these technocrats would probably not have opposed the death of Korean agriculture. This basic lack of sympathy for the rural masses made the technocrats not only good spokespersons for the commercial farming agenda of the richer farmers but also weak negotiators vis-à-vis U.S. agricultural interests seeking to dump U.S. surpluses on Korea.

The Farmers' Rebellion

The mid-1980s saw the collapse of the institutions of cooptation that the Park regime had constructed in the 1970s. This stemmed not only from farmers' perception of bureaucratic indifference and the technocrats' weak-kneed stance in the face of the U.S. trade assault, but also from corruption. Just as Chun Doo-Hwan perverted the government-chaebol relationship, so did his lieutenants subvert the fragile alliance between the ruling regime and the farmers.

Already, at the end of the Park era, the Saemaul was running out of steam. As one study of Saemaul village forestry activities observed, "People are more and more reluctant to provide their time and efforts on a cooperative basis and without pay."[59] Later, under the command of Chun's brother, Chun Kyung-Hwan (also known as Little Chun), the Saemaul movement was more swiftly transformed from a pseudo–grass roots movement into a centralized bureaucracy that became, in one description, "a fourth branch of government which now appears to have forced its influence on many of the country's legislative, executive, and judicial bodies."[60] The Saemaul bureaucracy in fact degenerated further into a mechanism for strong-arming donations from big business and diverting them into various projects from which the Chun family siphoned off personal profits—in much the same fashion as the Ilhae Foundation served as a front for funneling funds to President Chun. One controversial project engineered by Little Chun was the illegal import of 24,000 head of cattle in 1983, which apparently triggered a rapid fall in the price of beef, leading to a massive slaughter of cattle, bankruptcy for many farmers, and a debt crunch for the estimated 1 million farm households engaged in cattle raising. Chun, in contrast, apparently profited from the tragedy to the tune of 10 billion won or $7.3 million dollars, from the sale of the imported cattle.

Corruption on a massive scale merely accelerated the demise of the system of government patronage in the countryside and the emergence of the farmers' movement as an autonomous political force. In 1987 and 1988 a wave of farmer protests swept the country, organized around the key threats to the survival of the farm family: imports of foreign products, unfair domestic prices for farm products, unreimbursed appropriation of land, the onerous water tax, and the lack of a fair system of health insurance for farmers.[61] This surging movement was often born out of violent confrontation with combat policemen, with farmers' groups arming themselves with "automated tillers, tractors, and other farm machinery...not to mention farm implements, tools, and now even fire bottles."[62]

The pace of organization was unexpected and unprecedented. In 1986 and 1987 free farmers' societies began to sprout in counties throughout the countryside, and by 1989 there were about fifty of them. On March 1, 1989, twenty of these groups joined about eighty former district chapters of the activist Catholic Farmers' Association and fifteen groups formerly affiliated with the Protestant Farmers' Association to form the *Chonnongnyon,* or National Alliance of Farmers' Movements. The founding of the Chonnongnyon was the first time Korean farmers had organized themselves at the national level to press autonomously for farmers' interests.

While much more effort will be necessary to translate the surging farmers' movement into a voice powerful enough to shape national policy, it is clear that the Korean peasantry will no longer remain pliable, molded by political regimes to serve their schemes to stay in power or discarded by technocrats as an obstacle to development. As one farmer put it, "Farmers today will never again be the simple farmers of yesterday. Farmers today know that we are the masters of history. We know that we are ahead of any other group in the struggle for individual rights."[63]

5

The Toxic Trade-off

I f the countryside was plunged into ruin by a contradictory
policy of defusing farmer unrest in the short-term while sacrificing agriculture on the altar of export-oriented industrialization in the long-term, the environment has been devastated by the
tacit technocratic assumption that some degree of environmental
destruction is the price of economic growth.

"Some," however, is a fairly elastic term. And when we are
talking about a program of high-speed industrialization that tele-
scopes into three decades transformations that took many more
decades to transpire in the United States and other advanced
industrial countries, "some" can be quite enormous.

Indeed, the enormity of the ecological damage in Korea is only
now becoming discernible, its extent being underlined to ordinary
citizens by the government's admission in August 1989 that a
substantial amount of Korea's tap water is dangerously contaminated with heavy metal. But what is known even now about the
different dimensions of the environmental crisis drives one to the
conclusion that the price of saving the environment may well be
a radical reversal of past economic policies.

Deforestation and Chemical Poisoning in the Countryside

Korean government propaganda paints the country as having
an exemplary reforestation program. This claim, however, must
be placed against the extensive deforestation that predated the
better publicized crises of Southeast Asian forests. As a 1981
government report admitted, Korea's "once extensive forests have
been greatly reduced by years of harvesting for fuel and timber."[1]
Presently, as in Thailand, only one third of Korea is covered by
trees of substantial size, and most of these are found in the inac-
cessible mountains of northeastern Kangwon Province.[2]

Farming in the lowlands has depended on a steady flow of water from the once-forested highlands. Forest destruction triggered an ecological chain reaction. River flows became more erratic, leading to serious problems of drought and flooding. Erosion and soil loss caused by flooding reduced the productivity of agricultural land. Erosion and soil depletion also increased siltation in rivers and other bodies of water, which diminished the rivers' capacity to carry water, leading to more frequent flooding. And as the number of dams increased under the government's hydroelectric and irrigation programs, so did the severity of the siltation problem. According to a United Nations report, "Reservoirs filled rapidly and their capacities declined steadily, thus reducing the capacity to provide water during droughts and to prevent flooding during monsoon periods."[3]

Equally as devastating as deforestation in terms of its impact on the rural environment has been the more intensified application of fertilizers and pesticides as a result of the government-sponsored program to promote high-yielding varieties of rice.

Koreans are increasingly aware of the carcinogenic properties of the pesticides that have become an integral part of rice production. The dangers from pesticides have proliferated in recent years. Pesticide runoff is a major cause of groundwater pollution, exposure to pesticides substantially increases the risk of cancer, and pesticide residues in food heightens the threat not only of cancer but of other physical maladies. In Korea, pesticide use jumped over twenty-six times between 1967 and 1985, from 1,577 metric tons to over 42,300 metric tons, making Korea one of the highest

Table 5.1

Trends in Pesticide Use in Korea, 1967–1985

	1967	1977	1980	1983	1985
Metric tons	1,577	9,574	15,178	24,692	42,300
Percentage increase	0	507	59	62	71

Source: Vute Wangwacharakul, "Trade, Investment, and Sustained Development" (Paper presented at the ESCAP/ADB Meeting on Trade, Economics, and Environmental Sustainability, October 23–27, 1989), p. 51; Christian Conference of Asia/Urban Industrial Mission, "National Report: South Korea" (Paper presented at CCA URM Consultation, September 8–13, 1987), p. 29.

consumers of pesticides in the world on a per hectare basis (see table 5.1). In 1978 pesticides were applied on average eight and a half times a year; by 1984 the figure was twenty times a year.[4]

Like pesticides, petroleum-based fertilizers have been found to have environmentally destructive effects. In South Korea, heavy fertilizer use has been promoted not only by the government's miracle rice campaign but also by the spread of illegal tenancy relations. The insecurity of the new tenants, says writer Phyllis Kim, pushes them to "use huge amounts of fertilizer *now*, to get as much as they can out of the land while they still have it...[leading to] eventual exhaustion and desolation of the soil."[5] By the early 1980s, fertilizer applied per hectare in the Korean countryside had reached 380 kilograms. A comparison made in the mid-1970s showed that per hectare fertilizer consumption in Korea was over six times that of the United States and thirteen times the world level.[6]

Excessive use of petroleum-based fertilizers like urea has led, in many countries, to loss of soil fertility due to deficiencies in sulfur, which was present in traditional sources of fertilizer. Massive application of urea is also associated with zinc losses, which have put more and more farmland out of production in many Asian countries. Chemical fertilizer runoffs have also been associated with the contamination of groundwater, rice fields, and the rice crops with heavy metals like cadmium and mercury. In Korea, according to one impassioned account,

> Fertilizer pollution has reached a serious level.... Already some farmland has been found to be polluted by mercury and the rice grown on it has been found unfit for human consumption. In Japan, if they found this kind of polluted rice, the government would buy it up, but our government never has surveyed the situation or exposed the facts nor would it buy the rice if it was found to be bad.[7]

Many cases of mercury poisoning have been registered, perhaps the most notorious being the contamination of all six members of the Koh Un-Sok family in Tamyang, Cholla-Namdo, in March 1978. Their rice field was found to contain mercury at levels far above the national average. Lack of effective monitoring of and controls on fertilizer use was also evident in a survey of rice and vegetables in the Kimhae area, which found an astonishingly high rate of cadmium—7.6 ppm (parts per million), as opposed to a legal upper limit of 1.0 ppm in Japan and 0.5 ppm in the United States.[8]

Many farmers have, in fact, become so distrustful of their methods of growing food that, as in Taiwan, they have taken up the practice of growing vegetables and rice organically for their own consumption while marketing the chemically grown produce.[9]

Degrading the Urban Environment

The urban environment has, if anything, deteriorated even more rapidly than the countryside under the impact of unregulated high-speed industrialization.

The Greenhouse Effect and Air Pollution

It is claimed that the greenhouse effect, for instance, is already noticeable in key urban-industrial concentrations—a product of the combustive mixture of accelerated deforestation, the concentration of carbon dioxide and other industrial gases, and more intense heat from smokestack industries. One recent report notes that between 1973 and 1987, the period in which the cities of Pohang and Ulsan became huge industrial complexes, the mean air temperature rose by 0.5 and 0.4 degrees centigrade, respectively.[10]

Air pollution has reached intolerable levels. A 1978 World Health Organization study tagged Seoul's air as having "the highest sulphur-dioxide content of the world's major cities."[11] A decade later that dubious honor has gone to Shenyang and Milan, but Seoul is still in fourth place.[12] High levels of sulfur dioxide (SO_2) have also been recorded in Inchon, Pusan, Ulsan, Masan, Anyang, and Changweon.[13]

So polluted is Seoul's air that, according to a Seoul National University study, 67 percent of the rain falling on that city contains enough acid to pose a hazard to human beings.[14] Acid rain and other industrial fallout have been especially damaging to farmland close to factories. As one government report admitted,

> In some areas, farmers have reported that their crops were damaged by neighboring industrial facilities, and the yield from rice and barley crops substantially reduced. Recently, several industries in the Yeocheon Industrial Complex were ordered to compensate

nearby farming households...for crop damage that
had been inflicted over the years.[15]

Undoubtedly, motor vehicles are a source of air pollution, especially in Seoul, and by 1989 an estimated 1 million cars clogged
Seoul's streets. [16] Still, statistics from just a year earlier showed
that cars were responsible for only 34.5 percent of air pollution. A
study earlier in the decade revealed that the transportation sector
accounted for only 8 percent of sulfur dioxide emissions. Eighty-
seven percent of sulfur dioxide emissions came from the industrial
and commercial sectors.[17] This was not surprising since the annual
growth of pollution-intensive industries between 1976 and 1985
was 11.4 percent (see table 5.2).[18]

The government ordered desulfurization facilities in the late
1970s, but it caved in to the demands of high-speed industrialization based on cheap, high-sulfur oil. It agreed to postpone implementation until 1985 in the face of a threat from the oil refineries
that they would raise prices by 20 percent if the decree were
applied immediately.[19] Thus, it has only been recently that industries and motor vehicles have been obliged to use the more
expensive Bunker-C oil, which has a lower sulfur content. Currently, the import and sale of high-sulfur oil is illegal, but Seoul
city officials "admit that there are frequent violations of this
rule."[20]

The same tolerant government attitude toward polluters is
evident in two other instances. None of Korea's coal-burning
power plants—which generate 23 percent of electricity—contain
pollution-treatment facilities for noxious gases like sulfur dioxide
and nitrous dioxide (NO_2).[21] Chlorofluorocarbons (CFCs) have
been universally condemned for their contribution to depleting
the ozone layer, yet South Korea continues to build a new CFC
plant, contravening the 1987 Montreal Protocol that restricted the
production of CFCs.[22] Not only did environmental regulations
appear rather late, in 1978, but, as one government report admitted, "the fines are too low to make it profitable to comply and
convert [sic] noncompliance is frequent."[23]

The problem, one might add, lies not in the state's capacity for
enforcement; the Korean government's record in strong-arming
industries to move along certain preferred policy paths is impressive. Rather, it lies in the lack of desire for enforcement on the part
of government technocrats who are committed to high-speed
growth as an article of faith.

Table 5.2

Average Annual Growth of Selected Pollution-Intensive Industries in Korea, 1976–1985

Industry	Percentage Growth
Industrial chemicals[a]	8.9
Other chemicals[b]	13.3
Electrical machinery	18.3
Iron and steel	16.3
Paper and paper products	11.1
Food products	13.0
Total[c]	11.4

Source: Vute Wangwacharakul, "Trade, Investment, and Sustained Development" (Paper presented at the ESCAP/ADB Expert Meeting on Trade, Economics, and Environmental Sustainability, October 23–27, 1989), p. 48.

[a] Includes basic chemicals and synthetic resins but excludes fertilizers.
[b] Includes drugs and medicine.
[c] Includes other manufacturing industries and production sectors, such as mining and quarrying, electricity, gas and water.

Water Pollution

Like air pollution, water pollution has reached critical levels. The Han River, which runs through Seoul, and the Nakdong River, which serves as the main artery for Pusan and Taegu, have been especially damaged by effluents. By stimulating the growth of organic materials like algae, sewage and industrial wastes result in high biological oxygen demand (B.O.D.), thus depriving fish and other aquatic animals of their normal supply of oxygen. While largely untreated domestic sewage is partly responsible for the high B.O.D. in the Han and Nakdong rivers, industrial wastes contribute some 55 to 77 percent of the B.O.D. load.[24] In the late 1970s, there were reports of deformed fish in the Han River, and water pollution became so bad that, for public health reasons, two major intakes for the Seoul municipal water system had to be relocated upstream, some thirty kilometers from the city.[25] According to one expert, the Han River was "incomparably worse than, for instance, the Hudson River in New York."[26]

Water pollution has apparently become an even greater threat to public health since then. In August 1989 government investigators discovered that water at ten purification plants contained heavy metals such as iron, manganese, and cadmium at up to two times the official tolerance level. Also, neutral detergents were detected at seven to twenty times the official tolerance level in tap water in the Pusan and Puyo areas. Ammoniacal nitrogen generated by human and animal wastes was discovered at nearly ten times the tolerance level in the Seoul area, and bacteria at five times the tolerance level was found in nine out of the forty-six water-purification facilities in the country.[27] Much of Korea's water had, for all intents and purposes, become unsafe to drink.

Industry, the government investigation found, was a major culprit: 19 percent of more than 25,600 factories equipped with waste-water treatment facilities were either not using them or using them improperly.[28]

The enormity of the problem was indicated by the Ministry of Construction's estimate of what it would take to make the nation's water supply suitable for drinking: $3.3 billion to build eighty-four sewage treatment plants by 1996, and another $2 billion to replace aging water pipes and upgrade 19 percent of the nation's water purification plants by 1995.[29]

Even this huge outlay to contain water pollution may not be enough if the chaebol and foreign multinationals go on with their plans to substantially upgrade the petrochemical sector in the 1990s. Petrochemical plants rank very high in terms of their impact on water pollution and public health.[30] The chaebol are planning to set up six big integrated petrochemical complexes between 1991 and 1993, complete with naphtha crackers (plants that produce ethylene and raw materials needed to make plastic) and associated downstream facilities.[31] Meanwhile, the U.S. firm Dupont, which was thwarted in its bid to build a titanium dioxide plant in Taiwan by that country's environmental movement, has been given the go-ahead to build a similar factory in Korea, thanks to a U.S. government threat to impose trade sanctions on Korea if it refused Dupont's application for investment.[32]

It is not only rural and urban areas that are threatened by severe water pollution but also the coastal lands and waters. Large industrial complexes like the Masan Export Processing Zone and the massive Ulsan industrial complex discharge their effluents directly into the ocean, victimizing, a government reports admits, Korea's aquaculture:

> Since 1966 there have been reports of industrial waste-water related damage to fishing and aquaculture near the Ulsan industrial complex. Other coastal areas have periodically reported estimates of significant damage to fishing. Masan Bay, which was formerly an excellent fishing area, has by decree been closed to fishing and shell fishing. Aquaculture in the Ulsan area is also poor, but fishing has not been banned. Oyster and shellfish aquaculture in these areas have declined and compensation for these losses is being considered. Inchon Harbor is closed to commercial fishing.[33]

The Toxic-Waste Issue

Water pollution is part of a bigger problem confronting the nation: toxic-waste disposal. The problem is not merely at the level of implementing environmental regulations but at the even more basic level of knowing the magnitude of the problem. In 1983 government data revealed that 269,000 tons of hazardous waste were being generated annually.[34] Yet an earlier report by the Ministry of Energy and Resources estimated that in 1978 some 4,900 industrial plants produced 27,000 tons of waste daily, some 6 percent of which were considered toxic and requiring special treatment and disposal by law.[35] This added up to 591,000 tons of toxic waste produced annually or more than twice the 1983 estimate.

Korea's incipient environmental legislation provides for strict controls on mercury, cadmium, lead, chromium, arsenic, organophosphorus, polychlorinated biphynels (PCBs), and alkalies. But a Ministry of Energy report conceded that the machinery to effectively implement the law is simply absent: "The efficacy of these [environmental] laws, especially in rural areas, is unknown...since there is no information regarding actual practices, the level of adherence to these standards, or whether the appropriate expertise is available for determining if the pollutant concentrations require the rigorous procedures described by the law."[36] In this context, it concluded, "it is possible that industrial waste disposal could be the most serious future environmental problem facing Korea."[37]

The Factory Environment

For a long time, the factory environment was effectively closed to monitoring by the media and organizations interested in workers' health and safety in the interests of national security. With limited democratization has come a wider peek into working conditions, and this has revealed a veritable chamber of horrors. The country leads the world not only in the rate of industrial accidents but also in the rate of fatal occupation-related illnesses.[38] For every eleven persons, 2.66 are suffering from work-related illnesses, compared to 0.61 in Japan, 0.70 in Taiwan, and 0.93 in Singapore.[39]

Many worker deaths occur from exposure to such chemicals as toluene, mercury, cadmium, and lead. Reliable figures are hard to get, but the magnitude of the problem is indicated by the fact that in just a two-month period, June–July 1988, nine workers died from chemical poisoning.[40] Ministry of Labor statistics reveal that chemical poisoning still lags behind pneumoconiosis and hearing problems as a work-related illness. Nonetheless, with more and more chemical-intensive high-tech industries being established in Korea, deaths and illnesses are likely to mount in the absence of more stringently applied health and safety rules. The electronics industry, for instance, uses 250 different kinds of chemicals.[41] In the face of a likely explosion of chemical poisoning, says one expert, Korea is unprepared: "We just do not have enough time or manpower or proper equipment to treat and test patients. Testing and treating patients intoxicated by a chemical needs special training, and we have very few professionals with sufficient knowledge of chemistry."[42]

The Nuclear Threat

Perhaps the most threatening shadow cast over the Korean environment is that of nuclear power.

In the past few years, Korea's high-speed industrialization has become severely dependent on nuclear power. With nine reactors operational and two under construction, nuclear power now accounts for 53 percent of total electricity generation. Indeed, the percentage of total power that comes from nuclear plants is greater for Korea than for any other country in the world.[43] Owing to nuclear power, Korean technocrats assert, "Korea is virtually insulated from the dangers of oil price fluctuations."[44]

Today's nuclear energy infrastructure (see table 5.3) owes itself to Park's grandiose vision of building forty-four plants by the year 2000 in a country smaller than the state of Ohio. While the escalating costs of construction in the early 1980s forced the Chun regime to shelve thirty of the planned plants, Korea's nuclear lobby continues to confidently project an even greater role for nuclear power despite Three Mile Island and Chernobyl.

Nuclear Interest Groups

The ambitious Korean nuclear power program may not serve the interests of the Korean people but it does serve several powerful foreign and domestic interests.

A key interest group that has poured much effort into securing a nuclear Korea is the international nuclear power industry. U.S. firms, in particular, strengthened their lobbying efforts as they were confronted with the collapse of the U.S. market for reactors in the 1970s, owing to strong opposition from the antinuclear movement. As energy specialist Peter Hayes notes, it is hardly coincidental that "it was not until the international nuclear industry's domestic markets started to dry up in the mid-70's that South Korea announced its grandiose plans for 44 nuclear plants by the year 2000."[45]

Korea became a prime market for the U.S. nuclear industry, with Westinghouse securing six out of twelve orders for reactors. Other U.S. firms carving out a share of the market were Combustion Engineering, which supplied the reactors for two plants; General Electric, which supplied the generators used in six plants; Bechtel, which supplied architectural and engineering services for four plants; Gilbert Associates, which provided the same services for two plants; and Sargent and Lundy, which supplied services for two plants.[46] While data on the profitability of Korea's nuclear program are difficult to obtain, the program's magnitude is suggested by the government's admission that the costs of nuclear units seven and eight came to 2,004 billion won, or $3 billion.[47] Apparently, even more lucrative were nuclear plants eleven and twelve, scheduled for completion by the mid-1990s: total costs were estimated at $4.4 billion, a significant portion of which went to the U.S. suppliers, GE, Combustion Engineering, and Sargent and Lundy.[48]

Given the high financial stakes involved, it is not surprising that corrupt means have been employed to secure orders. It is reliably

Table 5.3

Commercial Nuclear Plants in Korea, 1989

Plant	Site	Type	Reactor Supplier
Korea Nuclear 1	Near Pusan	PWR[a]	Westinghouse[b]
Korea Nuclear 2	Near Pusan	PWR	Westinghouse
Korea Nuclear 3	Wolsung-Kun	PHWR[c]	AECL[d]
Korea Nuclear 5	Near Pusan	PWR	Westinghouse
Korea Nuclear 6	Near Pusan	PWR	Westinghouse
Korea Nuclear 7	Yonggwang	PWR	Westinghouse
Korea Nuclear 8	Yonggwang	PWR	Westinghouse
Korea Nuclear 9	Near Yeongju	PWR	Framatome[e]
Korea Nuclear 10	Near Yeongju	PWR	Framatome
Korea Nuclear 11[f]	Yonggwang	PWR	Combustion Engineering[g]
Korea Nuclear 12[f]	Yonggwang	PWR	Combustion Engineering

Source: Frank Nipkau, "South Korea: Dream Land for Nuclear Energy" (Unpublished paper, 1988), p. 1; *Business Korea* 7, no. 6 (December 1989), pp. 51–54.

[a] Pressurized light-water-type reactor.
[b] Based in the United States.
[c] Pressurized heavy-water-type reactor.
[d] Based in Canada.
[e] Based in France.
[f] Contract for construction concluded.
[g] Based in the United States.

reported, for instance, that the selection of Combustion Engineering to construct nuclear units eleven and twelve involved kickbacks to former President Chun Doo-Hwan and his brother Chun Kyung-Hwan.[49] What is beyond doubt is that, whether oiled by bribes or other means, Korean orders have played a key role in propping up the U.S. nuclear industry in its lean times.

Another set of actors with a keen interest in the nuclear energy program is the conglomerates. They have been drawn to the field by the government's aggressive localization program, which seeks to supply construction, architecture and engineering services, turbines and generators, and finally, the nuclear reactors themselves from domestic sources. The prospect of substantial profit margins from government contracts has made the industry a prime area of investment for firms like Hyundai Engineering and Construction and Korea Heavy Industries Corporation (KHIC). So strategic is the nuclear industry in the plans of some chaebol that Hyundai, for instance, has reportedly sent over 1,000 employees to specialized training centers in Korea and abroad to speed up the transfer of nuclear energy technology to the firm.[50]

Indeed, nuclear energy has become the field for some of the fiercest battles among the chaebol. Hyundai, for instance, managed to secure the lucrative construction contract for nuclear units four through eight, but it was elbowed aside by the team of Dong Ah Construction and KHIC for the construction contracts for units nine and ten. Hyundai initially got a fat $395 million contract to build units eleven and twelve, but the contracts were rescinded shortly after they were granted, reportedly owing to pressure from KHIC.[51] Hyundai regained the contract for construction, but KHIC became the prime beneficiary in terms of nuclear technology when it was designated as a partner of the reactor supplier Combustion Engineering.[52]

A third interest group with a huge stake in nuclear energy is the state technocratic elite, particularly if one considers the "fit" between nuclear power and the state-directed, highly centralized character of Korean high-speed industrialization: of all energy technologies, nuclear power is perhaps the most amenable to central control. As pointed out by one energy expert, "Centralized energy sources reinforce centralized economic activity of all kinds and thereby further the tendency of industrialization generally to concentrate population, culture, employment, production, and so forth increasingly."[53] But it is not only economic activity that is centralized by centralized energy sources, as energy specialist Zalmay Khalilzad makes clear:

> Emphasis on electricity centralization has been accompanied by centralization of the electricity bureaucracy and general political centralization, involving increased political penetration and control of the rural areas and rural dependency on urban areas, especially on the capital cities.[54]

Thus, the fact that in Korea 53 percent of electric-power generation is now provided by nine nuclear units represents not only a centralization of energy but also increased economic and political power for central authorities, specifically the energy ministry, the state technocratic elite, and the ruling elite.

Nuclear power, in short, is not congenial to democracy, and at their most candid, the technocrats regarded this as a virtue. In the words of one Ministry of Energy report,

> Development of nuclear energy will...not be restrained by public opinion. Though little in the way of scientific polling has been done, all seem to agree that there is no opposition to atomic energy in any form outside the universities. Much of this probably goes back to the Confucian respect for scholarship. There is general inclination to accept the opinions of experts and little inclination to get involved with issues that do not seem to have very immediate concern to the individual.[55]

The aspirations of the civilian technocratic elite have jibed with the ambitions of the military elite that wields the ultimate power in the state. For the latter, nuclear energy is the route to the development of nuclear weapons. The military has been especially interested in gaining access to nuclear fuel reprocessing technology, which enables one to separate plutonium—the key ingredient in nuclear weapons—from spent reactor fuel. Though the United States blocked a French-Belgian deal to transfer nuclear-reprocessing technology to South Korea in 1976, South Korean officials apparently continue to harbor ambitions to acquire the fast breeder reactor (FBR), which separates out plutonium in the process of enriching spent fuel. Fast breeder reactor core design, safety analysis, and sodium handling, states the Ministry of Science and Technology, are being studied "to prepare for the commercial operations of FBRs in [the] near future."[56]

Why the interest in developing nuclear weapons via commercial reactor technology? According to energy specialist Peter Hayes, the reason lies in the South Korean elite's desire to lessen its dependence on the U.S. military in deterring the perceived threat of invasion from North Korea. "A South Korean near-nuclear option," he writes, "might suffice in South Korean eyes to substitute for the U.S. nuclear threat against North Korea."[57] Indeed, "South Korea is likely to acquire reprocessing capability in the early 1990's whatever the U.S. thinks or does if they perceive North Korea to be obtaining that capability."[58]

Two recent developments are likely to accelerate this trend toward "nuclear self-reliance." One is increasing evidence that North Korea may have a nuclear-reprocessing facility capable of removing plutonium from spent nuclear fuel.[59] The other development is U.S. Army plans to substantially reduce its forces in Korea from one division to one brigade and associated support units.[60] Faced with a similar prospect of losing Big Brother in the early 1970s, the South Korean regime, it might be recalled, launched its policy of defense industrialization to further the goal of self-reliance.

Towards a Korean Chernobyl?

The threat to the environment and the community posed by the commercial and military nuclear program has been highlighted by several recent incidents and revelations.

In an effort to downgrade public fears about nuclear waste disposal, the Minister of Energy and Resources claimed in May 1988 that "ten years of waste can be stored in a space smaller than the size of a swimming pool."[61] However, in December of that same year radioactive wastes were discovered in a village near the Kori nuclear power plants in Gyongnam, including a contaminated rubber glove and vinyl shoe covers.[62] A $3 million fine was assessed against the Korean Electric Power Company (KEPCO), but this did not deter the dumping of more radioactive waste—in the very same village.[63] These two incidents brought home to Koreans the ineffectiveness of low-level nuclear waste disposal, contrary to the assurances of the Ministry of Energy and Resources. Public fears have also risen with reports of the high incidence of leukemia near two unnamed power plants.[64] These fears are not unfounded since the risk of getting cancer from low levels of radiation appears to be four times as high as previously estimated, according to the U.S. National Research Council.[65]

Added to the difficulty of disposing low-level radioactive waste is the problem of storing or disposing of spent nuclear fuel. So far spent fuel has been stored in pools at each reactor site. These sites, however, are likely to reach their limits by 1990.[66] There are apparently no firm plans to deal with the problem, though there has been talk in official circles of constructing a centralized "retrievable storage site."[67]

The accident record at Korea's nuclear plants is alarming. Operations were long shrouded until recently, when investigations conducted by the new Korean National Assembly early in 1988 shed light on them. The evidence was chilling. Since the first nuclear plant went into operation in 1978, there have been 193 accidents that have halted operations in seven plants.[68]

Perhaps the most serious accident occurred on November 25, 1984, at the country's only heavy-water reactor plant at Woolsung, when heavy water leaked. According to one account, the accident was "brought under control with much difficulty," and had repair efforts failed the resulting accident would have been one on the scale of the Three-Mile Island disaster.[69] Recently, late in 1988 the brand-new nuclear unit nine broke down after only fifty days of operation, after "two bolts slipped out of the generator," though Korean officials denied that any leakage of radioactivity took place.[70] Horror stories about the impact on health of working in the nuclear power plants are now surfacing, including one case in which the wife of a nuclear plant worker aborted two deformed fetuses.[71] Again, such reports acquire sinister significance in the light of a new finding by the U.S. National Research Council that there exists "a much greater danger of mental retardation among babies exposed in the womb to low-level radiation from 8 to 15 weeks after conception."[72]

The accident record (see table 5.4) underlines the validity of the controversial 1982 secret assessment of the Korean nuclear energy program done for the World Bank by nuclear expert Salomon Levy. "The organization and the relevant documentation to control safety," asserted Levy, "are still far from being in place in Korea."[73] He charged that construction schedules were given priority over the implementation of the safety standards set by the U.S. Nuclear Regulatory Commission. Among Levy's other findings were too few trained technicians, causing severe strain on existing manpower; trainees who were allowed to keep taking exams until they passed; and the inability of many Korean operators to understand operating manuals written in English.[74]

Part of the problem lay with the failure of Westinghouse and other nuclear vendors to impose quality controls on subcontractors like Hyundai, which Hayes describes as having achieved a reputation for "reckless success in industrial construction."[75] But a major obstacle to nuclear safety lies in reactor design, that is, with the vendors. For instance, Combustion Engineering's design for nuclear units eleven and twelve "has never been tested and could be dangerous," according to Westinghouse.[76] Westinghouse reactors themselves, however, have been afflicted by a variety of mechanical and design defects, causing many of the twenty-four plants operating in the United States to be shut down early in 1979,

Table 5.4

Official Accident Record of Korean Nuclear Plants, 1978–1988

	1978	1979	1980	1981	1982	1983
Units in operation	1	1	1	1	1	3
Suspensions caused by						
machinery problems	15	5	8	5	3	13
human error	1	2	0	1	1	3
other	1	2	0	1	1	2
Total suspensions	17	13[a]	8	7	4[a]	18

	1984	1985	1986	1987	1988	1978–1988
Units in operation	3	4	6	7	8	
Suspensions caused by						
machinery problems	13	14	21	11	6	114
human error	1	3	4	5	3	24
other	2	13	8	10	4	44
Total suspensions	16	30	33	26	13	185[a]

Source: *Business Korea* 7, no. 6 (December 1989), p. 54.

[a] Totals as found in original.

owing to cracked welds, cracked bolts, and defects in coolant pumps and piping. Similar problems discovered in Westinghouse reactors in Korea were compounded by "poor quality control, shoddy construction, and inadequate standards for equipment."[77]

Then there are the generic problems associated with light-water reactors, the most common model in Korea, including the inability to refine calculations of reactor-core meltdown probability and the lack of knowledge about how and to what extent equipment ages under nuclear conditions.[78]

Two hundred and fifty-five items in Korean nuclear reactors were recommended for improvement by the U.S. Nuclear Regulatory Commission after the Three Mile Island accident. Eight years later the Korean parliamentary investigation discovered that thirty-four of these items had not yet been dealt with satisfactorily.[79]

Despite heightened public concern, however, Korea's technocrats continue to behave as if Three Mile Island and Chernobyl did not happen. The dream of a nuclear Korea persists: at a conference in the spring of 1989, a team of government, industry, and university experts proposed the construction of "55 new nuclear power plants with production capacity of 1 million kilowatts each by the year 2031 to meet the ever-increasing energy demand."[80]

The Environmental Movement

Environmental groups have existed in Korea since the 1970s. For the most part, however, these groups were small and connected with churches or based in universities. Since the start of the democratization process in the summer of 1987, however, environmental consciousness has been transformed from being the possession of marginalized small groups into the driving force of an incipient grass roots mass movement.

While the Korean environmental movement is not yet on the scale and militance of the environmental movement in Taiwan, it shares the same exciting beginnings in localized protests focusing on concrete issues. These protests have not been strictly environmental in motivation, being triggered as well by anger at the forced entry of U.S. products and populist resentment at conspicuous consumption by the upper class. Since the summer of 1987, grass roots protests have been directed at U.S. cigarette imports, harmful imported ingredients of locally manufactured noodles, U.S. fruit imports treated with the chemical alar, and excessive consumption of foreign commodities.

Of all the incipient environmental movements, the antinuclear movement is, perhaps, the most advanced. In April 1989, sixteen environmental organizations formed the National Headquarters for the Nuclear Power Eradication Movement. The movement's potential was underlined by the joint declaration against the construction of reactors eleven and twelve in Yeongkwang made by the presidents of ten universities in the region.[81] While the movement has some distance to travel before it can reverse the drive to nuclear power, the technocrats have acknowledged its potential. "Korea's nuclear power plant construction program faces stiff public resistance, most notably from environmentalists, affected by the continuing trend towards democratization," the director-general of the Ministry of Energy's Electric Power Bureau recently admitted. He added that "securing plant sites has become an increasingly difficult task."[82] Not the least of citizens' motivations is the fact that the price of land has declined in areas surrounding nuclear plant sites.[83]

Conclusion

The destruction of the environment in Korea has been tacitly accepted by government technocrats as one of the costs of high-speed development. When combined with the fascination with nuclear power's capacity to centralize energy generation, economic production, and political control, this perspective or philosophy has had extremely damaging consequences. Korea's technocrats have managed to compress into 30 years the processes of environmental destruction that took several generations to achieve in earlier industrializing societies.

Can the environment be saved in Korea? The trends evoke pessimism, in spite of the appearance of a militant environmentalist movement. One thing is certain though: saving the environment will demand the abandonment of the paradigm of export-oriented, capital-intensive, high-speed development.

6

High Tech:
Solution or Illusion?

K orean development is at a critical juncture. Not only are the costs of export-oriented growth in the form of the rural debacle and the environmental disaster becoming more and more apparent, but what has long been the foundation of the economic strategy, low-cost labor, is being eroded by rising wages as the working class awakens to its exploitation and its potential power. To counter the loss of competitiveness in labor costs, the chaebol-government alliance is pushing a new strategy for continued high-speed growth: moving Korean industry decisively into high-technology, higher-value-added production. To government technocrats this means upgrading technology in traditional industries like textiles and garments and launching Korea into the frontiers of microelectronics, mechatronics, automobiles, aerospace, biotechnology, and superconductors.[1] In other words, the strategy envisions no less than taking on the big boys themselves—the United States and Japan.

How capable is Korea of acquiring or developing the core technologies of the cutting-edge industries?

The Dimensions of Dependence

In the past few years, technology-acquisition by Korean conglomerates has been pursued through three channels: aggressive licensing of advanced technologies from foreign suppliers; a feverish localization program promoting the domestic production of key components of strategic products like automobiles; and substantially upgraded research and development programs.

Despite Korea's record of translating borrowed technology into export success, several trends evoke skepticism about its ability to make the technological breakthroughs that would enable it to successfully compete with the United States and Japan in the frontiers of high technology.

One is the continuing heavy dependence on licensing almost all key advanced technologies from Japan and the United States. The list includes wafer fabrication in semiconductors, engines and transmissions in cars, computer-aided design and manufacturing in textiles and garments, hardware and software design in computers, and videocassette recorder and facsimile technologies in consumer electronics. Korea's genius has been to marry licensed (and often unlicensed) technology to efficient manufacturing processes and cheap labor. This has not, however, led to the development of substantial design and product innovation. Production via licensed technology, no matter how seemingly efficient and low cost, may not be accompanied by the technological deepening essential for self-sustaining innovation.

That this is, in fact, the case is further suggested by the continuing heavy dependence of Korea's exports on Japanese inputs, which manifests itself in the massive trade deficits with Japan even as surpluses are registered in trade with the United States. Japanese imports alone now make up a third of the value of Korean exports. For instance, every time Korea exports a computerized lathe or other machine tool, 35 to 45 percent of the gross profit is pocketed by Japanese manufacturers of computer-guidance equipment.[2] Japanese inputs account for between 20 percent and 30 percent of the value of a Korean car. In many key electronics exports, the proportion is even higher: 85 percent of the value of a Korean-produced color TV set is accounted for by Japanese parts. Seventy to 90 percent of the components of a Korean laptop computer come from Japan and account for more than 60 percent of its price.[3]

Perhaps the frankest assessment of the state of Korean high tech comes from Kim Woo-Choong, chairman of Daewoo, who admits that "Korean development is largely...promoted by foreign supplies of parts and equipment, and sustained by the technical know-how of foreign partners."[4] The same conclusion is offered by a senior official of the Economic Planning Board, Korea's planning superagency: "We have grown so fast we could not accumulate technology."[5]

Not only is licensed foreign technology of limited value in terms of technological diffusion but its costs are increasing dramatically. The price of obtaining foreign technology in the form of licensing and royalty payments doubled from $58 million to $115 million between 1977 and 1982.[6] By 1987, the figure was up to $574 million; and in 1989, Korean firms paid out $1.2 billion in royalty payments.[7] Today, the terms at which leading-edge firms like IBM, Texas Instruments, and Intel are willing to license their technologies can wipe out much of the already precarious margin of profits the Koreans derive from their exports, particularly for products at the low end of the market.

Limitations of the Technical Infrastructure

Research and development expenditures are one indicator of how serious an effort is being mounted to develop high-tech capability. While some estimates place Korean R&D spending at 2 percent of gross national product, this figure is probably inflated. Government R&D in 1988, in fact, came to only 0.4 of GNP, a level lower that even that of Taiwan.[8] As for private R&D, recent data show that the 1980s were a lost decade for Korean industry from the point of view of modernizing plants and equipment and upgrading R&D. According to some analysts,

> The worst part of the Chun [Doo-Hwan] era was the neglect of new investment in plants and equipment, introduction of new technologies, and development of new products—all attributes of a healthy export-oriented economy. The trend was intensified by the presence of ample opportunities to make quicker returns by investing in property and service-related industries. Those industries, often condemned as economically unproductive and even socially unethical, flourished during the 1980's. Analysts argue that businesses, big or small, were busy sizing up such windfall opportunities, shifting the money they earned from manufacturing to the service sector.[9]

Instead of being channeled into R&D, an estimated $16.5 billion in chaebol funds, as mentioned earlier, are currently tied up in land, luxury hotels, and golf courses.

But the failure to develop self-sustaining technological innovation is not traceable solely to the lack of government R&D support and the chaebol's failure to invest in new equipment and R&D. Even if they were willing to throw more capital into R&D, the chaebol would run into the limitations of Korea's infrastructure of technical personnel. While Korea's pool of engineers and scientists is proportionally larger than that of most developing countries, it is rather small in comparison with that of Japan and the United States, who are Korea's main competitors in high tech. For every 10,000 people in the Japanese labor force, there are 240 engineers. In the United States, the proportion is 160 per 10,000. But in Korea, there are only 32 per 10,000 workers.[10]

A brief look at the situation in selected industries reinforces the sense that Korea is still quite a distance from developing the capability for internal innovation. There are only an estimated 200 personal-computer architecture engineers in the whole of Korea[11]—a very serious constraint on Korea's ambitions to move beyond cloning U.S. or Japanese computers. There is not one scientist employed in the whole auto-parts industry, and less than 9 percent of the work force in this sector is skilled.[12] Less than 50 percent of the total number of employees in the critical software industry have college degrees.[13] And only 450 out of the 11,450 doctorate holders in science and engineering are reported to be working in private companies.[14] These figures support the profile of Korea's technical personnel offered by Sheridan Tatsuno of Dataquest: "At one end, you have a few highly trained research scientists. At the other, a host of recent graduates from Seoul National University. What is scarce is that middle level of trained and experienced engineers that provide the infrastructure for technological innovation."[15]

Training significantly more scientists and engineers in the next few years will run up against the backward research and engineering facilities of most Korean colleges and universities and against the continuing brain drain. According to Sheridan Tatsuno and John Wilson, the flow of engineering and science graduates to the United States makes "the recruiting prospects for fast-growing companies...grim."[16] True, the chaebol have launched an aggressive attempt to recruit expatriate Korean technical personnel, but of the 7,200 scientists and engineers estimated to have studied and remained in the United States since 1968, 6,000 continue to reside there.[17] And in the next few years, Korean R&D will feel the impact of the departure of highly trained Korean specialists who temporarily took leave from their jobs in the United States to help set up some cutting-edge industries, like semiconductors.

Innovation in the Conglomerate Cocoon

Another factor that may seriously constrain the development of self-sustaining technological capability is the precarious status of small and medium firms in Korea, owing to the dominance of the chaebol.

The chaebol have been most effective in amassing capital and marrying borrowed technology to large-scale manufacturing processes based on cheap labor. Conglomerate power may well be effective in laying the first stages of industrialization with foreign technology. It is questionable, however, if the conglomerates can provide an institutional context that encourages innovation. The history of the microelectronics industry in the United States underlines the lesson that creating a climate that encourages creativity is probably more critical than throwing huge amounts of capital at a problem. It was Intel, Fairchild, Texas Instruments, and other relatively small start-ups that won the battle in semiconductors, driving out the big but ossified corporations of the vacuum-tube era ion electronics RCA, Sylvania, GE, Westinghouse, Philco-Ford, and Raytheon.[18]

True, to survive in the long term, smaller firms eventually hooked up with the surviving giants—for example, both Microsoft, which specializes in software, and Intel, a microprocessor pioneer, have teamed up with IBM. Yet, especially in the early phases of product innovation and marketing, the smaller firms have a pioneering boldness, creative spirit, and agility that the big conglomerates do not possess. In the United States, in fact, in many key industries there has developed a rough division of labor wherein small firms produce the innovations and the bigger corporations translate those innovations into efficient mass production.

In Korea this division of labor does not exist because smaller firms are so severely short of resources due to the government's past policy of encouraging the rise and monopolistic dominance of the chaebol. For instance, only thirty out of 11,450 Ph.D.s in science and engineering are employed in small enterprises.[19] For the most part smaller firms serve not as independent innovators but as satellites to which the chaebol farm out contracts.

Recently, the probable negative impact on R&D of the chaebol's monopolization of resources has been underlined by the fact that while the chaebol's expenditures on R&D remain low, their investment in real estate and securities for speculative purposes has skyrocketed.[20] The estimated $16.5 billion in chaebol funds that are currently tied up in land, luxury hotels, and golf courses could have gone instead into R&D—if the chaebol were really serious about developing self-sustaining technological capabilities.

Without the development of a viable R&D infrastructure and an industrial structure that encourages technological innovation, Korea's high-tech aspirations are likely to be stillborn. The demands of challenging Japan and the United States for hegemony in the frontiers of high technology are only now becoming clear to Korea's technocrats. Capital, efficient assembly, cheap labor, and hard work—the old ingredients of success—are no longer enough. As the Korea Institute of Economics and Technology sees it, in many high-tech areas "our technology in assembly work is not too far behind that of the advanced countries. We are, however, more than ten years behind in the area of research and development. It is said that our high-tech industry, which is far behind the advanced countries, needs urgent attention just to survive beyond the nineties when the industry will open its doors completely."[21]

7

Textile's Troubles

The difficulties of switching from labor-intensive to high-technology production processes are perhaps best illustrated in Korea's textile and garments industry, which has gone from being a "sunrise" to a "sunset" industry in just three decades.

Initially responsible for catapulting Korea to the ranks of the world's top exporting nations, the textile and garment industry began prospering in the protected domestic market of the 1950s and went into high gear in the 1960s and 1970s. Between 1962 and 1975, the industry grew at a phenomenal 16 percent a year, largely from the momentum of exports. The industry reached its zenith around 1971, accounting for 53 percent of total exports of $1 billion.[1] At 20 percent per year, growth was even more phenomenal in the 1970s, although textile and garment exports began to decline as a percentage of total exports. By the early 1980s, however, crisis began to overtake the industry, with growth precipitously dropping to 5 percent between 1979 and 1984.[2]

Although electronics overtook textiles and apparel as the country's top export earner in 1988, the textile and garments industry continues to be a vital, albeit ailing, sector of the economy. It currently accounts for a quarter of the value of Korea's exports, and in mid-1980s it employed some 783,000 people out of a manufacturing work force of 3.3 million, making it the largest single sector for nonagricultural employment.[3] Despite rising protectionism in its key markets, Korea is the world's third largest textile exporter, after Italy and West Germany, and supplies approximately 9 percent of the world's textiles.[4] The industry's biggest markets are the United States and Japan, with the first accounting for some 37 percent of exports and Japan for 14 percent.[5]

Like other sectors of the economy, the textile and garments industry has witnessed a steady concentration of ownership over the last decade.[6] Indeed, the rise of the chaebol and the textile industry are intimately intertwined since a good number of the current chaebol began as textile producers, and used profits from textiles to expand into more capital-intensive and more risky ventures. As one observer notes, "It is popularly believed that garment factories were set up by large conglomerates in order to generate cash quickly for investment elsewhere and that promising managers are transferred to other parts of the conglomerates."[7]

Samsung, Sunkyong, Hyosung, Kolon Daenong, Taekwong, and Daewoo are among the conglomerates built up from textiles.[8] Daewoo, in particular, illustrates the strategic use of textiles as a springboard to conglomerate status. Starting as a solitary textile firm, Daewoo's fortune was made through the clever manipulation of textile quotas the United States imposed on Korean exports in the early 1970s. Anticipating that quotas would be imposed and knowing that the allocation of quotas within Korea would be based on the export performance of each firm in the recent past, Daewoo decided to accelerate its textile exports to the United States at any cost, including low profit margins.[9] When quotas were in fact imposed, Daewoo's decision paid off as it was awarded nearly 40 percent of Korea's total export quota to the United States.[10] The dynamics of subsequent expansion are described by Kim Byong-Kuk, biographer of Daewoo founder Kim Woo-Choong:

> The abundant cash flow from its flourishing textile exports to the United States stocked Daewoo's coffers with sufficient funds to empower Daewoo to make a round of new acquisitions for expansion into other strategic business areas and consumer products. At this juncture, Daewoo's successes in securing substantial shares of the textile market in the United States and in establishing its reputation as a supplier of quality products enabled it to expand further into the European markets. Kim Woo-Choong [Daewoo's founder] cleverly perceived opportunities to export other light industry and consumer products to these markets....The worldwide stage was well prepared and the curtain was rising for Daewoo's big leap forward.[11]

Nevertheless, despite its domination by big business, there appears to be more maneuvering space for small and medium manufacturers in textiles and garments than in many other industries. The garments sector, for instance, is marked by a dual structure, wherein the very large firms produce for overseas markets while the smaller establishments cater to the domestic market and occasionally subcontract to the large companies. The smaller firms undoubtedly survive because of cheap and overworked labor. Just how cheap and overworked this labor was during the expansive years of the industry is indicated by the fact that between 1970 and 1982, wages in the garments industry averaged 70 percent or less of the average wage in manufacturing, while the number of hours put in by garment workers exceeded the manufacturing average by ten hours or more per month in most years.[12]

In the past few years, however, the textile and garments industry has been hit by a profound crisis brought about by the harsh conjunction of three forces: rampant protectionism; savage competition from other low-wage third world countries; and cost-effective automation of the textile and garments industries in the advanced industrial countries.

The Impact of Protectionism

Since the mid-1950s, pressure from domestic manufacturers has spurred governments in the advanced industrial countries to subject textile and garment exports from Japan and the third world to a growing web of voluntary export restraints. The Multifiber Agreement (MFA), negotiated in 1974, was a milestone in world trading history that served to formalize and legitimize a regime of bilateral restrictive agreements on synthetic fibers. By the early 1980s, agreements with thirty-four countries ensured that 80 percent of all textile and apparel imports from developing countries into the all-important U.S. market would be subjected to restrictions.[13] Internationally, 14 percent of the textile trade and 40 percent of the apparel trade were covered by the MFA. And throughout most of the world, trade not covered by MFA quotas was subject to heavy tariffs.

Korea's textile exports were particularly hard hit. While exports shot up at the phenomenal rate of over 43 percent per year in the 1970s, they grew at less than 10 percent in the years 1979–84. In 1977 a renegotiation of the MFA allowed only an 8.6 percent annual growth in Korean textile imports into the United States. Permissible annual growth was even more drastically scaled down to less than 1 percent under MFA-III in 1981.[14] These moves to restrict Korean textile and garment imports on the part of the United States were paralleled in Europe. And in the late 1980s, Japan, Korea's second-biggest export market, signaled that it would move in the same direction when Japanese knitwear producers brought charges of dumping against Korean garment makers. The Koreans quickly agreed to impose restraints on knitwear exports to Japan.

The Threat from Below

Even as protectionist barriers were rising against Korean textile exports, the industry's competitive position was being assaulted by third world producers with even lower labor costs.

Between 1972 and 1982, real wages in the Korean textile industry rose by 103 percent, while labor productivity went up by only 40 percent.[15] What labor organizing could not achieve under conditions of repression, the economics of the labor market did: wages rose inexorably, noted the World Bank, because of the emergence of "a general shortage of unskilled labor, a shortage brought about by falling birth rates and rising education levels."[16] Whatever the cause, Korea's wage cost advantage over fellow NIC Hong Kong was reversed in the early 1980s, and what was initially a slight wage-cost disadvantage over South and Southeast Asian producers has widened significantly. Today the average cost per hour of a textile operator in South Korea comes to $2.87, compared to $2.44 in Hong Kong, $0.65 in India, $0.68 in Thailand, $0.40 in China, and $0.26 in Sri Lanka (see table 7.1).[17]

For Korea the main threat comes not from other NICs, whose wages are also rising, nor from South and Southeast Asia, but from China, whose average wage costs were about seven times lower than Korea's in 1989. In the last decade, China has enjoyed a meteoric rise as a textile power; it is now the world's largest textile producer and the sixth largest exporter.[18] Possessed with three advantages over Korea—lower wages, less restrictions on the growth of exports given its status as a late entrant in the world textile trade, and a greater capacity for retaliating against restrictions[19]—China has been displacing Korea in the U.S. market. The dynamics of this bitter competition are described by the World Bank:

Table 7.1

Comparative Labor Costs in the Textile Industry, Spring 1989

Country	Average cost per operator hour (in US$)	Ratio to U.S. cost (%)
NICs		
Hong Kong	2.44	25
South Korea	2.87	30
Taiwan	3.56	37
Selected developing countries		
China	0.40	4
India	0.65	7
Indonesia	0.23	2
Philippines	0.64	7
Thailand	0.68	7
Selected industrial countries		
Japan	13.98	144
United States	9.71	
West Germany	13.17	136

Source: Werner International, "Spinning and Weaving Labor Cost Comparisons" (New York, Spring 1989).

In 1973, Korea's share of the U.S. market for textiles was about 1.3 per cent while China's was nonexistent. By 1978 both Korea and China possessed about 2.8 per cent of the market. By 1982 China had taken a clear lead as its share rose to 8.6 per cent while Korea's rose to 6.5 per cent. This experience was repeated in an even more striking fashion in the U.S. import market for clothing. While Korea's share stagnated at 17.3 per cent over 1978-82, China's grew sharply from 1.1 per cent to 7.8 per cent.[20]

"Just as East Asia ousted Japan from the U.S. market for clothing," concludes the report, "so does China now threaten the East Asia group."[21]

The Threat from Above

Assaulted from below by low-wage competitors in other developing countries, the Korean textile and garments industry also faced a threat from advanced countries exploiting advances in cost-effective automated or semi-automated technology. The development of open-ended spinning and shuttleless weaving systems has reduced the labor intensity of textile production, boosting the capacity of U.S., European, and Japanese textile manufacturers to counter the low-wage advantage of manufacturers in Korea, Taiwan, and Hong Kong. The elements of this minirevolution introduced by advanced microelectronics are described by the World Bank:

> New open ended rotor spindles offer a 40 per cent saving in manpower over traditional ring spindles. Weaving has been automated by the advent of shuttleless and multiphase looms that operate at higher speeds and can cope effectively with fashion changes when married with electronic monitoring systems. Knitting has been transformed by the combining of fabric and garment stages into one, increasing enormously the flexibility, through computer control of handling the design of high fashion items.[22]

In garment manufacturing, computer-aided design, combined with laser-beam cutting and high-speed sewing machines, have successfully automated the preassembly phase. And in their search for ways to get the jump on Asian competitors, U.S. garment manufacturers found a novel way of marrying high tech with low wages to achieve low costs. This was to "perform the capital-intensive tasks in the United States, while taking advantage of low wages in the Caribbean for the assembly and post-assembly stages. This allows low production costs and a quick turn around time."[23]

This avenue was made possible by the Reagan administration's Caribbean Basin Initiative, which granted members of the Caribbean Economic Community a special access program that allowed their textile and garment exports broader access to the U.S. market provided that the pre- and post-assembly stages took place in the United States. Assembled items were then imported into the United States under Item 807 of the tariff code, which levied import duties only on that portion of value added to the commodity outside the United States.[24]

The Squeeze on Textiles and Its Consequences

This three-front assault on Korean textiles and garments created a severe profit squeeze. Profitability, measured by the ratio of profit to total assets, decreased from 3.2 in textiles and 3.8 in apparel in 1973–77 to 0.6 and 1.8 in 1978–84.[25]

In response to the crisis, Korea's textile and garments firms are adopting a two-pronged strategy. One prong consists of relocating the mass production of low-quality textiles to third world countries, especially in Southeast Asia and the Caribbean. Already, thirty-seven textile firms have set up shop in the Caribbean, a move that allows them to exploit low-cost labor, circumvent quota restrictions on Korean exports, and benefit from the tariff reductions of the Caribbean Basin Initiative.[26] The other prong is focusing domestic production on upscale, higher-value-added fabrics and garments, a move that "should soften the consequences of increasing competition in the lower-quality end of the market from lower-cost Asian textile producers as well as maximize the value of quotas placed on Korean exports in the U.S. and EEC."[27]

There are two major obstacles to an easy process of structural adjustment. One is the opposition it is likely to provoke. Retrenchment and restructuring already brought down the level of employment from 760,000 to 720,000 in 1981–84. This was just the start, for according to the World Bank, "It would appear that the bulk of the adjustment in costs and productivity is yet to come, and that it will very likely mean reduced employment."[28] Readjustment has provoked and undoubtedly will continue to provoke strong opposition from the 20 percent of the manufacturing work force that is in textile and garments, already one of the most militant sectors.

The other barrier to successful restructuring is the staggering capital requirements of moving upmarket. Over the years the volatile mix of complacently relying on cheap labor and channeling profits from textiles to the so-called sunrise industries has left textile machinery obsolete. While only 31 percent of spinning machines were more than ten years old in 1980, by 1983 nearly 45 percent were at least a decade old. In the same period, the percentage of decade-old looms increased from 31 percent to 51 percent.[29] Korea's textile industries are 29–45 percent automated, compared to 50.9–70.5 percent for Japan's.[30] And private investment in textile technology in Korea is only one-eighth that in Japan and the United States.[31]

Moreover, investment in new machinery will not necessarily result in improved trade performance if design capabilities and marketing networks are not simultaneously upgraded; and in these two areas, the Koreans are rather weak, having for so long produced low-quality clothing according to the specifications of U.S. retailers. Again, the World Bank has some illuminating words on the problems confronting Korean producers in this area:

> The upmarket move is not without its risks. Three may be most readily identified. First, there is limited room in the upmarket segment and manufacturers cannot move en masse into this area. Mergers, bankruptcies, retrenchment will necessarily be involved in the process. Second, there is much competition up there and it is of a nature that LDC's are not particularly strong in. Retailing networks are important. Advertising is important. Price is not the sole consideration. Hence production efficiency may be necessary but not sufficient. Third, the demand for upmarket products is highly income-elastic and, therefore, more prone to large swings over business cycles. Recessions hit upmarket firms hard (unless they are very, very upmarket).[32]

The competition in the upscale market is represented by such firms as the West German manufacturer and exporter Hugo Boss, which has managed to successfully offset the lower labor costs of the Korean and other Asian producers by differentiating its products through design and quality, and efficiently automating whatever can be automated in the production process. Hugo Boss and other West German textile and apparel makers have been so successful at raising labor productivity through automation that Korea's labor productivity has dropped to one-sixth of West Germany's.[33] What the Koreans are up against as they try to move upmarket is indicated in the following account:

> The West Germans in general have overcome the "differentiation" problem by concentrating on the upper-to-middle market for contemporary classic clothing. The Boss solution is to introduce sharply styled suits, in Italian fabrics, which are less extreme in design and less expensive than those of other designers such as Giorgio Armani.

But the West Germans have also developed highly efficient systems of production. Given that so large a part of clothing production is in the labour-intensive area of stitching—and there is little scope for automation in this area—the most efficient companies concentrate investment in all the other areas to ensure that their machinists' time is used effectively.

Boss has been automating the production process at its main factory in Metzingen, near Stuttgart, since the 1970's. This year it completed a programme of fully automating its systems for storing raw materials and shipping the garments.

It has also introduced computer-aided design and pattern planning to speed up the process of designing garments and preparing for production. Boss is now installing a computerized cloth-cutting system to ensure that the cloth is cut as accurately as possible, thereby minimizing waste.[34]

Competing in the upscale market against such companies as Hugo Boss will necessitate installing computer-aided design and computer-aided manufacturing processes, plus massive investment in design differentiation, marketing, and advertising. This can only be accomplished by a sharp, immediate reversal of the traditional flow of funds from the textile and garments sector to those industries designated strategic or sunrise by the government and the chaebol.

A Sunset Industry?

The road to successful readjustment has been made even more difficult by two recent developments. The first is the rapid appreciation of the formerly undervalued won by 25 percent in the period 1987–90. "We can absorb wage increases but we can't take any more appreciation," one textile manager complained in May 1988, predicting that by the year's end, some 30 percent of small and medium textile and garment manufacturers would be driven to bankruptcy.[35] The second ominous development is the likelihood that the Korean domestic market will gradually open up, on account of trade pressure from the United States. This would mean that both cheap clothing from Bangladesh and China and high fashion from the United States and Japan will be poised to give

Korean manufacturers a run for their money in the home market as well.

The formidable structural and trade obstacles to successful restructuring are apparently leading some technocrats to write off textiles and garments as a sunset industry. While the government promised in January 1990 a $4 billion plan to restructure the industry, it remains to be seen if the intent is not merely rhetorical. Many analysts had little doubt that the textile and garments industry was what the Presidential Commission on Economic Restructuring had in mind when it recommended in October 1988 that "to restructure industries, the labor and capital employed in declining industries must be shifted to growing industries."[36] If carried out, such a policy would have a highly negative social impact, displacing workers, creating massive unemployment among the largest segment of the manufacturing labor force, and bankrupting many thousands of small and medium entrepreneurs. Further, it would concentrate even more economic power in the chaebol, who already dominate the preferred high-tech industries.

But setting aside for one moment issues of justice and equity, it is fair to ask if, in terms of economic effectiveness alone, channeling investment from textile and other labor-intensive industries to key high-tech, science-intensive industries is likely to pay off. Is concentrating on high tech the key to Korea's sustained growth? The next two chapters, which investigate the automobile and electronics industries, will attempt to shed some light on the consequences of the critical choices currently being made by the technocratic and economic elite.

8

Ambition and Frustration
in the Auto Industry

The automobile industry is the largest branch of global manufacturing. Some 2,000 to 3,000 components go into the
manufacture of a car, giving the industry a fairly strategic
role in an advanced economy in light of the forward and backward
linkages it has with other sectors.[1] It is not surprising then that the
health of the economy of advanced countries is often measured by
the condition of their auto industries. And it is also not surprising
that many developing countries seeking to make the transition to
full-fledged industrial status assign strategic priority to the
development of a motor vehicle sector.

In the early 1960s, the Korean government approached auto
manufacturing as a priority sector to be developed through determined protectionism and subsidies. Today's statistics suggest that
the technocrats picked a winner. By 1988 over a million cars and
trucks a year were churned out by Korea's three auto manufacturers, and slightly over half of them were exported.[2] (See table
8.1 for additional data on Korea's position in car production
worldwide.) Nearly 40 percent of the $6.5 billion trade surplus
with the United States in 1988 was said to be accounted for by the
export of automobiles and auto parts.[3] Pride of place among the
exporters belonged to Hyundai, which introduced the best-selling
import subcompact Excel to the U.S. market in 1987 and 1988.

The numbers do reveal an impressive achievement. But they do
not tell the whole story. Indeed, they cloak the many serious trade,
technological, and structural obstacles that are now catching up
with the industry and threaten to slow its so-far dynamic pace. To
understand the emergence of these limits, it would be useful to
briefly trace the historical development of the industry.

Table 8.1

Car Production Worldwide, 1989

Country	Cars Produced (in thousands)
Korea	941
Western Europe	13,535
Japan	8,442
United States	6,959
Mexico	672
Brazil	746
Eastern bloc	2,459
World total	35,244
Korean production as percentage of world total	2.7

Source: *DRI World Automotive Forecast Report,* reproduced in *Financial Times,* January 8, 1990, p. iv.

Stages of Development

Under strong government guidance, auto manufacturing in Korea went through roughly five stages. Phase one, early experimentation, took place in the 1950s. Out of largely trial-and-error techniques came the first complete Korean car, the Cheval, a handmade and rather primitive Jeep-type vehicle whose body was made out of steel drums cut and bent by hand.[4]

Strong government guidance developed during the second stage, the strictly assembly phase, which lasted from around 1962 to the late 1960s. Government policy provided tariff exemptions for imported parts and components, tax breaks for assemblers, and infant-industry protection via a ban on the import of "completely built-up," or assembled, cars. Foreign cars like the Toyota Corona and the Ford 20M were imported on a "completely knocked down" or "semi–knocked down" basis and then assembled by domestic manufacturers who relied almost completely on foreign firms for engine, transmission, parts, and body technologies.[5]

In the third phase, beginning in the late 1960s, the government aggressively stepped up its drive to localize production, with the Ministry of Commerce and Industry announcing its intention to increase the local content portion of cars to 100 percent by 1972.

This did not mean that everything that went into a car was produced in Korea. In fact, a "locally produced" item was loosely defined. An engine was considered local if the combined price of all its parts produced locally was 30 percent or more of its total price. A part used for the assembly of the engine was, in turn, considered local if the combined price of all its subparts produced locally was 30 percent or more of its total price, and so forth until the car was completely knocked down to the last nut and bolt.[6] Thus, the official definition of localization overemphasized actual local content.

This initial ambitious goal of achieving 100 percent localization was modified in 1976, when the government redefined a "Korean car" to be one "whose production could be localized above 90 percent, whose chassis could be produced without any imports, and whose body style was never introduced by a foreign firm."[7] With access to foreign exchange and retention of tariff exemptions based on performance in meeting localization requirements, the government provided for strong incentives for the development of more independent manufacturing and technological capabilities. Hyundai was the most successful of the assemblers, achieving a "96 percent domestic content" with its bestselling Pony—the predecessor of the Excel—by 1984.[8]

The fourth phase of the industry, from the late 1970s to around 1988, was marked by several features, most notably, a more aggressive emphasis on exports, rationalization of production, and a more determined quest for core technologies.

The strong export push stemmed from the technocrats' belief that the profitability of the industry depended on achieving economies of scale, which meant that the domestic market alone, limited as it was, would not be sufficient. Indeed, the technocrats saw export markets not as complementary to but as a substitute for the domestic market. This thinking stemmed from the logic of export-oriented industrialization: if cheap labor was to be Korea's main weapon in the battle for export markets, then a significant domestic market based on prosperous car-buying consumers was out of the question. This perspective had one additional consequence that slowed the creation of a domestic market: since cars were expected to be purchased only by the rich, they were regarded by bureaucrats as sources of revenue for the state. In the early 1980s, the buyer had to pay twelve major taxes on an automobile before it was delivered, plus five other taxes while operating the car.

Rationalizing production was a euphemism for moderating competition among the conglomerates and dividing up the market, on the theory that this would bring about a more efficient use of capital. In 1981 the government moved to reserve the production of passenger cars for Hyundai and Saehan (a joint venture between Daewoo and General Motors) and allocate the manufacture of light trucks to a joint venture between Kia and Dong-Ah.

In addition to the export push and the rationalization of production, more aggressive technology-acquisition strategies marked the fourth phase. Daewoo, for instance, managed to acquire managerial control of Saehan (later renamed Daewoo Motors), freeing it to push a technology-acquisition strategy that was not fully dependent on GM. In contrast, traditionally independent Hyundai, motivated by the same technological imperative, entered an equity tie-up with the Japanese Mitsubishi Motors, giving the latter a 10 percent stake in Hyundai Motors in exchange for technical assistance.

The fifth and current phase of the industry is marked mainly by a discovery of the importance of the domestic market, triggered by a coincidence of weakening exports due to protectionism and an appreciating won and rising domestic demand due to the higher wages and salaries won by workers over the past three years. Roughly half of Hyundai's production in 1989, for instance, was destined for the domestic market.[9]

Two Routes to Technological Autonomy

The development of self-sustaining technological capability has been an overriding objective of the technocrats and entrepreneurs who dominate the auto industry. The key conglomerates, however, have followed different routes to this goal. While Daewoo has attempted to develop technological know-how through joint ventures, Hyundai has taken a more independent path. When Daewoo entered into a fifty-fifty joint venture with GM in the early 1970s, it hoped to travel the fast track in assimilating automobile technology as well as gain an international marketing network. The results have been, on balance, dismal.

For one thing, GM's international corporate objectives constrained the development of Daewoo's automaking capabilities. Daewoo's production of the subcompact Lemans, for instance, was determined primarily not by Daewoo's priorities but by GM's international strategy of sourcing lower-end vehicles for the U.S. market to its third world affiliates to take advantage of their cheaper labor force.[10]

In terms of technology acquisition and assimilation, Daewoo, during the period that it was under the thumb of GM's management, was constrained to follow what auto analyst Hyun Young-Suk describes as "a strategy based on dependency. It depended on GM for major auto parts and components as well as for technologies required for automobile assembly and overall management. In these circumstances, the Korean local partner has done relatively little to develop its own technologies for products or production management."[11]

The transfer of management control to Daewoo in 1982 did not appreciably change things. While some R&D work was sited in Korea, the firm's capacity for self-sustained technological innovation has remained low. As Kim Woo-Choong, chairman of the Daewoo group, admitted, "The upstream [automobile] industry in Korea is still in a very primitive stage. And the Korean industry must operate in partnership with overseas industries to secure necessary parts, equipment, and know-how. The Korean-made subcompact Lemans, for example, contains over 40 percent non-Korean parts."[12]

GM not only made a minimal contribution to developing Daewoo's technological capabilities but it also constrained the Korean partner's marketing potential. While Hyundai developed several models to meet changing market conditions, Daewoo was stuck with two models for five years, the Lemans and the midsized Royale. The Lemans was actually an alias for the output of GM's world car project, which aimed to make a few standardized vehicles for all markets; developing one model for one country was against GM's policy.[13] Daewoo's bad luck was compounded by the fact that the model, supplied by GM's West German subsidiary, had failed completely in the European market. This was, in the words of one analyst, "an extreme example of inappropriate technology transfer embodied in the product itself."[14]

An even more egregious example of the constraints imposed on Daewoo by the joint venture with GM was the latter's blocking an effort by Daewoo to sell the Lemans in Eastern Europe, on grounds that that market belonged to GM's 100 percent–invested European affiliates.[15]

Seeking a fast track to technology and international marketing contacts, Daewoo has so far gotten very little of either from GM. Instead, its priorities have been dominated by the sclerotic international sourcing and marketing strategy of a corporation that is acquiring the reputation of being the dinosaur of the auto industry. The results are evident in the statistics: while Hyundai racked up an astonishing 73 percent of exports in 1988, Daewoo accounted for only 13 percent.[16]

Hyundai Motors has followed a strategy quite different from Daewoo, one that stresses managerial independence, aggressive methods of technological acquisition, and in-house innovation. The effort seems to have met with some success. Hyundai now accounts for close to 65 percent of all Korean motor vehicle production. And its Excel subcompact is a household word in the United States.

Strategic talks on joint ventures with Ford in 1972 and GM in 1981 foundered on Hyundai's refusal to yield managerial independence and to limit its access to the U.S. market.[17] To avoid falling into heavy dependence on one source, the firm diversified its sources of technology. From 1962 to 1986, its technology licenses totalled fifty-seven, and these were drawn from thirty-one firms in nine countries; Daewoo, in contrast, had twenty-six licenses, drawn from eight firms in five countries.[18] Moreover, Hyundai licensed relatively advanced technologies from multiple sources in a less packaged form than Daewoo, giving its engineers a greater challenge—and a more intense learning experience—in the process of integration.[19]

But Hyundai also illustrates the limits on the ambitions of a latecomer from a newly industrializing country to become a major player in the extremely technologically competitive auto industry. For despite these efforts at developing in-house capacity for innovation, Hyundai has not yet achieved a genuine capability to develop core technologies (see table 8.2). The transmission of the best-selling Excel is designed and produced in Japan by Mitsubishi, which also designs the engine. Body styling, which is especially critical in attracting buyers, is also beyond Hyundai's capability: the Excel's style is drawn from an Italian design.[20]

Hyundai performs a largely integrative role, says Kim Byung-Kook in his excellent description of the making of the Pony:

Table 8.2

Sources of Technology at Hyundai Motors

Stage	Year	Product	Source of Product Technology	Source of Production-Management Technology
Assembly	1967–1974	Cortina	United States	Ford, Hyundai
Early internalized production	1975–1981	Pony	Japan, England, Italy	Mitsubishi, Hyundai
Late internalized production	1982–present	Excel, Sonata, Stellar	Japan, Italy	Hyundai, Japan

Source: Hyun Young-Suk, "A Technology Strategy for the Korean Industry" (Paper prepared for International Motor Vehicles Project Forum, Acapulco, Mexico, 1989), p. 12.

The role of Hyundai's technicians and engineers was reduced to that of drawing specifications of the body, changing the Mitsubishi specifications to meet the local requirements [for the car to pass the government definition of a "Korean car"]; and integrating the parts and components from various foreign sources.[21]

Less charitable was the judgment of a Mitsubishi Motors representative that Mitsubishi does all the critical design work while Hyundai constructs the pieces and puts them together.[22]

The integrative role is not to be scoffed at. Hyundai's learning how to integrate different components and technologies was a major advance—a vital step that Daewoo missed by taking the easier route of accepting finished or packaged auto technology from GM without being given the secrets of this technology. Indeed, no other third world–owned manufacturer has been able to attain the sophisticated level of manufacturing engineering that Hyundai has achieved through technological diversification, integration, and learning by doing. But this skill remains at the level of manufacturing engineering, not product engineering, or the capability to design the core components of the automobile. Hyundai itself admits that while it is on par with established automakers in manufacturing technology, it is below them when it comes to product technology and far below them in design and system technologies.[23]

In a world of swift technological change, Hyundai has realized that the price of continuing competitiveness is a connection with a Japanese giant, Mitsubishi. Mitsubishi has provided not only technology but also foreign outlets for Hyundai. It has, however, exacted a price: a rise in its equity in Hyundai Motors from 10 to 15 percent. As in the GM-Daewoo relationship, the more powerful partner has not hesitated at times to pull the rug out from under its Korean associate. For instance, when the Excel made spectacular inroads into the U.S. market, Mitsubishi employed the design it had offered Hyundai and made its own low-priced subcompact—an almost exact replica of the Excel—and sold it under the Mitsubishi brand name as the Precis. Mitsubishi did nothing to differentiate the Precis from the Excel, except for a slightly different body design and the implication that in purchasing the Precis, buyers were getting the real thing. Hyundai, in other words, might be said to have tested the market for its supposed corporate ally Mitsubishi.

Ambition and Reality in the 1990s

Despite its initial successes, Hyundai and the other Korean vehicle manufacturers face immense challenges in the fierce battle for the international automobile market that is expected to unfold in the 1990s.

First, rising protectionism will severely limit the Koreans' access to the most strategic global markets, the United States and Europe. Stringent local-content requirements—similar to those imposed by Korea—will limit import penetration of Europe, while a significant rise beyond the current export level of 300,000 vehicles to the United States is likely to increase pressure for the imposition of restraints on Korean car imports.

Second, in order to retain their current market share, Koreans have to be quicker to update their models and increase their variety. Korean exports are now concentrated on the lower end of the market, and that segment is now reaching saturation.[24] The profit margin for the Excel, the price of which begins at a low $5,395, is said to be tiny.[25] Indeed, Hyundai may well be losing money in its effort to gain market share. Low prices, however, are not the only key to increasing or maintaining market share. Updating a model is essential, but it was only in late 1989 that Hyundai updated the Excel model it had been selling for three years in the United States—definitely a long time to keep selling the same model in a highly competitive market.[26] "They sold 700,000-plus of the Excel model over several years without changing it, and they just ran out of buyers," observed one auto consulting firm. "They didn't get the next generation of styling on stream fast enough, and the market changed rapidly on them."[27]

To increase their profits, the Korean automakers will also have to go upmarket. This is especially urgent because, contrary to a fashionable theory, the Japanese are not abandoning the lower end of the market to the Koreans. Mitsubishi's marketing of the Excel clone, the Precis, and the development of even more sophisticated models of the Toyota Tercel, the GM Geo Prizm, and the Honda Civic belie this supposed trend.[28] But manufacturing more-profitable luxury models requires a technological sophistication, investment capability, and marketing expertise that the Koreans still do not possess. Hyundai did launch the upscale Sonata in 1989 to compete with such formidable models as the Honda Accord and the Toyota Corolla. So far, however, this move has not met with success: the Sonata, which is intended to compete in the crowded $10,000–$15,000 range, has not been able to carve out a clear niche, forcing Hyundai to radically lower its export projections in 1989.[29]

The third major obstacle faced by the Koreans is the need for greater technological innovation and more-cost-effective production. The Korean formula for success so far has been to marry foreign technology to efficient manufacturing and cheap, hard-working labor. These elements will no longer suffice. Without independent technological innovation there is a danger that the Korean firms will be converted into subsidiaries or minor partners of the big Japanese and American firms. Yet the Koreans have not yet been able to deploy the massive resources required for being on the cutting edge of technological innovation. No reliable figures exist for the R&D expenditures of Hyundai Motors or Daewoo Motors, but a generous estimate of the R&D budget for all Korean firms in 1988 was 3 percent of turnover.[30] This may, in fact, be diminishing given the chaebol's increasing preference for investing their funds in land, apartments, golf courses, and stocks rather than in production capacity and R&D. The Japanese firm Honda, on the other hand, spends in the region of 5 percent of sales on R&D, an effort that employs 20 percent of its work force.[31]

Advanced product technology, however, is only one dimension of effective production. An increasingly critical role is played by the revolutionary changes in the organization of production, or manufacturing engineering, which have been pioneered by the world's most efficient producers, the Japanese. The Koreans have not assimilated these changes yet, nor, for that matter, have the Americans and the Europeans. Indeed, the reason why, despite its tie-up with GM, Daewoo has had a poor track record is that "the key technology in today's auto industry—Toyota-style production—is not in GM's power to transfer."[32]

Japan's organizational edge stems principally from two innovations. One is the so-called just-in-time (JIT) production, or Toyota system, which consists of eliminating waste, providing "zero defects," and keeping inventory to a minimum through close cooperative ties with component suppliers located nearby who can assure almost 100 percent top-quality deliveries. The other innovation is a work force that is well-motivated because it is empowered to make decisions on the shop floor. The link between production efficiency and worker decision making is underlined by analysts Kurt Hoffman and Ralph Kaplinsky:

> Once a JIT structure is adopted, zero-defect policies must be utilized. This requires the line-worker to be responsible for quality control (QC) rather than the • specialized QC department, for if there are any defects the whole line will rapidly grind to a halt. By its nature quality control—and more important, the rectification of errors—necessitates decision-taking. In addition, giving responsibility to the base of the production hierarchy also flows from flexibility in production since the worker is no longer subservient to the same extent to the moving and unchanging production line.[33]

The Korean manufacturers are gravely disadvantaged on both counts. Both Hyundai and Daewoo have had problems instituting a JIT system. For although the assemblers, especially Hyundai, have achieved relatively high manufacturing standards, their domestic component suppliers continue to provide parts marked by high cost and low quality. As one student of the industry describes them, the suppliers are "small scale, hardly investing in R&D and copying marketed items. In the whole auto-parts industry, there is no [sic] one scientist employed and the proportion of skilled workers is 8.6 percent."[34] This state of affairs is not solely the suppliers' fault but stems in great part from years of official neglect of small and medium-size firms in favor of the chaebol.

What this means is that to maintain and achieve higher levels of production quality, Hyundai and the other assemblers must rely even more on distant Japanese and U.S. component suppliers, making a JIT system all but impossible. Although, by the loose definition of local content, it is claimed that 98 percent of the components of Korean automobiles are produced in Korea, in fact, asserts one expert, "considerable amounts of Japanese parts and materials are used in those components."[35] One reliable estimate is that between 20 and 30 percent of the value of a Korean-made car is imported from Japan.[36] Another account pegs the actual localization rate at just 50 percent.[37]

Aside from supplier difficulties, another obstacle in the diffusion of JIT technology in Korea has been Japan's reluctance to transfer many elements of JIT technology. Certainly in the case of Hyundai, "Japanese producers definitely felt at risk in transferring their production organizational know-how" to an upstart firm that was viewed as a future threat to Japanese domination of the industry.[38]

But even more problematic than the assimilation of JIT technology is the absence of a participatory work force. Both Daewoo and Hyundai have been known for their authoritarian systems of production, which treat workers like inanimate cogs in a machine. A system based on unthinking workers may not have posed a hindrance in the first stages of the industry, especially if the workers were disciplined and hardworking, but it has become dysfunctional in a mature industry striving for higher degrees of efficiency and quality.

Indeed, precisely on account of the authoritarian production system, the trend in Korea is away from a well-motivated work force. In 1988 assemblers and their suppliers had to halt production an average of twenty-seven days because of strikes. Probably worst hit was Daewoo, which experienced ninety days of work stoppage and lost an estimated $2.2 billion in sales.[39] Whereas the average wage of Korean workers went up by 60 percent between 1987 and 1990, that of autoworkers has gone up by nearly 100 percent.[40]

Contrary to the belief of the chaebol, it is not wage raises that are in the way of profitable production. These raises can easily be absorbed by a more efficient system of production based on greater worker motivation and decision making. The problem is the archaic, authoritarian relationship between management and labor at Hyundai and Daewoo. Comparing labor-management relations at Korean and Japanese firms, Hyun Young-Suk writes that

> workers' attitudes are very important in auto plants; Japanese history has shown that efficient production systems, including the Toyota system, are most fruitful when managers and workers trust each other and workers are considered not as a source of problems but as a source for continuous innovation.[41]

One must, of course, be wary of idealizing the Japanese system. As some observers have pointed out, a greater latitude for decision making and initiative is often accompanied by higher levels of stress and overworking. Nonetheless, morale, motivation, and decision making seem to be positively correlated.

Finally, among the key barriers to the Korean auto industry are constraints preventing the development of a viable domestic market. A great deal of the strength of the established American, European, and Japanese automakers stems from their domestic market base. Maintaining and expanding their domestic market share, in fact, continues to be the primary goal of their production and marketing strategies, with maintaining and expanding export markets a secondary, albeit critical, goal. The Korean auto industry, on the other hand, has been guided by an export-first strategy, and its early successes, as noted above, were built in part on cheap labor—an approach that worked against the creation of a domestic auto market.

That domestic demand is now the engine of the industry is a development that neither the technocrats nor the chaebol expected, though they are taking full advantage of it. In the first half of 1989, protectionism abroad and the rising won brought Korea's auto exports down to 177,430, a nearly 29 percent decrease from the same period in 1988. But domestic sales, spurred by workers' higher wages, rose by 45 percent, to 311,737.[42] Ironically, had they not been saved by higher incomes brought about by worker militance, Hyundai Motors and Daewoo Motors—two of the country's most aggressively antiunion firms—would have faced a severe overproduction crisis.

But despite the windfall from rising domestic demand, the technocrats and the chaebol continue to be ambivalent about domestic demand–led growth, which they uniformly label inflationary in the fashion of IMF bureaucrats. They still look to the export market as the real engine of growth and fear the higher wages demanded by a domestic demand–centered strategy will merely further erode the country's exporting capability. They are also apprehensive that a local market–oriented strategy will provide organized labor with tremendous clout and institutionalize regular wage increases at the expense of profits.

This perspective lies behind policies that continue to prevent the speedy development of the domestic market. Though Korea's cities are now experiencing massive traffic jams owing to the underdevelopment of the transportation infrastructure, automobile ownership is still very low relative to population. In 1987 there were only 20 cars per one thousand people in Korea, compared to 49 in Taiwan in the mid-1980s, 74 in Mexico, 116 in Argentina, 233 in Japan, 417 in West Germany, and 555 in the United States.[43] Perhaps the most onerous of these policies is the government's deliberate effort to make car ownership prohibitively expensive. In 1981, for instance, the ratio of total taxes to the factory price of the Pony in the local market was 44.4 percent, compared to 20.2 percent for a similar subcompact in Japan, 24.5 percent in the United Kingdom, 21.8 percent in Italy, and 4.6 percent in the United States.[44] The average operating cost of an automobile in Taiwan comes to only 71 percent of the cost in Korea. In Malaysia it came to 39 percent of the Korean cost, in Singapore 49 percent, and in Hong Kong 46 percent.[45] While it is true that some special consumption taxes were eliminated or reduced in 1989, policies informed by the technocrats' view that automobile ownership is a luxury continue to make it expensive to own and operate a car and act as a strong brake to the development of a domestic market.

But an even more strategic threat to the development of a domestic market is the trend towards greater and greater inequality in income distribution. This development not only prevents most Koreans from buying Korean cars but also promotes conspicuous consumption of foreign products—especially cars—by the rich and nouveau riche, who would rather splurge on imported BMWs and Mercedes-Benzes than on Sonatas or Excels.

In sum, threatened with protectionism in Korea's key export markets yet extremely hesitant to develop the domestic market, the government and auto industry might be unwittingly setting the stage for a strategic debacle.

Figure 8.1:

Tie-ins between Korean Manufacturers and Foreign Automobile Corporations

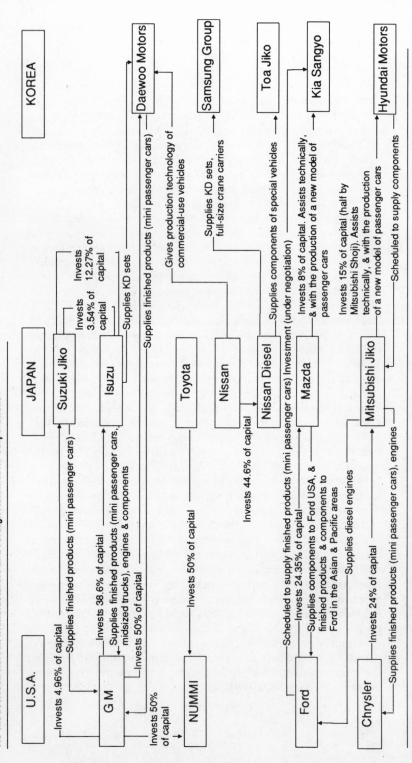

Source: Koichi Shimokawa, "Development of the Asian NIEs' Automobile Industry and Future Prospects of the Global Division of Labor — Japan, ROK, China-Taiwan, and Thailand." Paper prepared for the International Motor Vehicle Policy Forum, Acapulco, Mexico, May 9, 1988, p. 2.

Towards Subsidiarization?

Confronted with more intense competition in the 1990s, the Korean auto industry is at a decisive juncture. It may either continue on the road to technological independence, or it may give up the aspiration to become a powerful independent player and, like Taiwan's auto industry, seek a subordinate niche in an international division of labor dominated by the Japanese and American giants.

Daewoo, it seems, has, with its continuing tie-up with GM, opted for the latter path. The question is, confronted with even bigger challenges in the 1990s, which road will Hyundai take? There are indications that given its difficulties in sustaining export market shares and developing a self-sustaining technological capability, stubborn Hyundai is also being nudged towards the Daewoo solution. The Korean conglomerate has given Mitsubishi a 15 percent equity stake in its motor vehicle subsidiary in exchange for more technological inputs. Moreover, it has integrated itself into Mitsubishi's worldwide production plans in selected models like the Debonair. As automobile specialist Konomi Tomisawa observes,

> At the time of a model change for Mitsubishi Motors' top-of-the-line model "Debonair," Hyundai Motor decided to produce the same model under the name "Grandeur." They have been able to reduce costs by putting Hyundai Motor in charge of producing metal mold and processing, while Mitsubishi Motors produces the floor panels and cross member panels; reciprocal export ensues.[46]

It is too early to tell which trend will prevail. But it is clear that Korea's manufacturers figure prominently in the international strategies of the big guns of the industry for the life-and-death struggles of the 1990s, when an excess production capacity of 20 percent in the international auto industry will bring about a brutally competitive environment.[47] (See figure 8.1 for more on the links between Korean and international automobile firms.) As one observer asserts, "The Japanese automobile manufacturers are starting to incorporate [Korea, Taiwan, and other] countries into their international strategy. An attitude to seek coexistence with the enterprises in those countries in order to survive through the age of international competition is beginning to manifest itself."[48] To survive the big shakeout of the 1990s, the Koreans may well have to become what they have expended so much effort to avoid: de facto subsidiaries of the big powers of the automobile industry.

9

Chaebol Dreams
and Silicon Realities

E lectronics, South Korean industry's "wunderkind," is also seen by the technocratic elite and the chaebol as the decisive arena of their strategy to transform Korea from a cheap-labor export platform into a high-tech powerhouse. Today, chaebol like Samsung boast of leaping from one R&D triumph to another, such as the development of the capability to mass produce the advanced 4-megabit DRAM (dynamic random access memory) chip.[1] As in the auto industry, however, a dangerous gap is emerging between chaebol dreams and silicon realities.

Started only thirty years ago, electronics has grown into one of the country's largest industrial sectors, accounting for $21.5 billion, or 14.8 percent, of Korea's GNP of $145 billion in 1988 (see table 9.1).[2] Electronic products also passed textiles and garments as Korea's prime exports in 1988, accounting for $13 billion, or 25 percent, of the country's total exports of $52 billion.[3] The past few years, in particular, have witnessed white-hot expansion, with annual growth at close to 30 percent and exports rising at an incredible 43 percent per year between 1986 and 1989.[4] Korea now ranks sixth in the world in terms of total electronics production, and in the area of consumer electronics, it is topped only by Japan and the United States.[5]

Electronics production began in Korea in 1958, when Goldstar brought out its first radio. In the 1960s and early 1970s, Korea became a favored location for foreign electronic companies. Attracted by Korea's low-wage, hardworking, and repressed labor force, leading-edge electronic firms like Fairchild Semiconductors, Toshiba, Motorola, and Signetics relocated the labor-intensive assembly operations of their global production processes to Korea. In the late 1960s and 1970s, fully foreign-owned firms and joint ventures dominated exports, accounting for some 80 percent of exports in 1968.[6]

Table 9.1

Korean Electronics Industry, 1983–1988

	1983	1984	1985	1986	1987	1988[a]
	Production (in billions of US$)					
Electronics/electrical	6.7	8.4	8.5	12.1	17.4	21.5
GNP	75.0	81.0	83.0	95.0	119.0	145.0
	Electronics/Electrical as % of GNP					
	8.9	10.3	10.2	12.7	14.7	14.8
	Exports (in billions of US$)					
Electronics/electrical	3.3	4.6	4.6	7.4	11.2	13.0
All merchandise	24.0	29.0	30.0	35.0	47.0	52.0
	Electronics/Electrical as % of All Merchandise Exported					
	7.3	15.9	15.2	21.3	23.6	25.0

Source: John Wilson and Sheridan Tatsuno, "South Korea: Following the Leader?" *Strategic Issues* (Dataquest, San Jose, Calif.), February 1989, p. 4.

[a] Estimate.

Many foreign firms came in as joint ventures with Korean companies, and this arrangement facilitated some transfer of technology in the manufacture and packaging of consumer electronics products, electronic parts, and simple semiconductor devices. The bulk of such electronic components were not difficult to master since they embodied relatively simple technology.[7]

By the mid-1970s, mastery of assembly techniques, low-level technological diffusion, and reverse engineering methods enabled domestic producers, who monopolized the domestic market, to move into exporting simple electronic commodities. As the quality of these exports rose, many foreign companies began to find an OEM (original equipment manufacturer) or supplier relationship with Korean firms a better bargain than setting up production facilities in Korea itself. An OEM arrangement was convenient for a variety of reasons. According to analyst Morris Crawford,

> One compelling factor is that it gives the buyer components at low cost without surrendering control over technology. Another is that the OEM contract is most easily handled by engineering and managerial staffs of supplier companies. The main tasks are procurement and assembly; technological demands are not of a high order, as the most advanced components and parts are usually imported or provided by the buyer.[8]

Perhaps the most successful cases of OEM agreements are Samsung's supplying General Electric with microwave ovens and Daewoo's supplying IBM PC clones to the U.S. manufacturer Leading Edge.

A major boost to the development of Korea's exporting capabilities came in the early 1980s, courtesy of Apple and IBM. Both the Apple II and IBM PC had open architecture, which meant that they lent themselves to easy cloning by any electronics shop in Seoul that could obtain commercially available, nonproprietary components to duplicate the circuit board at the heart of the computer. Although Apple came down hard on cloners, IBM tacitly allowed cloning of its PC to make it the industry standard. When simple cloning technology was married to the capital reserves of the chaebol, the stage was set for the manufacture and export of thousands of IBM PC clones in the mid-1980s.

Korea's semiconductor industry began with the establishment of foreign subsidiaries or joint ventures that specialized in the labor-intensive process of wiring together packaged chips in wafers shipped in from Japan and the United States. Recently, however, Korean electronics has astonished the world by moving in a big way to the high-tech front end of the semiconductor industry: the fabrication of silicon wafers on which are imprinted dies or chips like diodes or integrated circuits.[9] Korea now mass produces 256-kilobit and 1-megabit DRAM (dynamic random access memory) chips and is attempting to acquire the capacity to produce 4-megabit DRAMs. It is currently the third largest producer of semiconductors in the world, after Japan and the United States, accounting for almost 4 percent of world production.[10]

As in other areas of industry, the evolution of the electronics industry has been marked by the hegemony of the chaebol. The current structure of Korea's electronics industry is characterized by what electronics analyst Geoff Crane calls a pernicious imbalance between big business and small and medium-size enterprises.[11] Some 80 to 85 percent of Korea's roughly 1,300 electronics companies are small or medium-size enterprises, yet production is dominated by a few chaebol. Indeed, electronics is dominated by the so-called Big Four—Samsung, Lucky-Goldstar, Daewoo, and Hyundai—which between them account for more than 55 percent of total output.[12]

Despite its high-speed development, however, Korea's electronics industry is plagued by many of the same structural problems that have affected the automobile manufacturers—problems that continue to render the technological foundations of the industry extremely shaky. These obstacles become painfully evident in an examination of the industry's three main sectors: consumer electronics, computers, and semiconductors.

The Vicissitudes of Consumer Electronics

Of all three electronics sectors, consumer electronics is Korea's biggest earner of U.S. dollars. In terms of production capacity, Korea is the third-largest producer of color television sets in the world, the second-largest producer of videocasette recorders and microwave ovens, and the third-largest producer of black-and-white TV sets. These facts are impressive, but they conceal the major problems now overtaking the consumer electronics sector: Korean manufacturers are severely dependent on foreign technology; they continue to depend on Japanese suppliers for crucial parts and components; and they are stuck at the low, unprofitable end of the market for popular consumer commodities.

As the battle for export markets heated up in the past few years, acquisition of foreign technology via licensing became a substitute for indigenous development, which is regarded as time-consuming, unreliable, and expensive. This is especially the case with highly popular, sophisticated products like videocassette recorders (VCRs). Thus, all three of the top Korean VCR manufacturers—Samsung, Goldstar, and Daewoo—acquired their technology from one source: the Japanese corporation JVC, a subsidiary of Matsushita, which owned the patent. The terms of the licensing included tight restriction on exports up to the year 1985 and high royalty payments to JVC. For every VCR manufactured, as much as 1,300 Japanese yen (or $10) are said to be remitted to JVC.[13] In 1987 royalty payments to JVC came to about $50 million, which was more than 6 percent of the three companies' exports of $800 million.[14]

In 1988 the Korean companies upgraded their VCR exports—not through indigenous R&D but through joint ventures with the Japanese giants, such as that between Samsung and Toshiba. Under a fifty-fifty joint venture, Samsung would manufacture 30,000 VCRs a month for export under the Toshiba brand name. Given the heated competition among the conglomerates, Goldstar's response was predictable; it decided to enter into negotiations with Hitachi rather than independently upgrade local VCR know-how.[15] The price of these new licensing deals has been steep: according to one report, the Japanese are now collecting as high as 10 percent of Korean VCR sales revenues.[16]

Parts and components dependence on Japan is, as in the automobile industry, quite heavy. Thus, even after years of assembling color TVs, 85 percent of the value of a Korean-produced TV set is accounted for by Japanese parts.[17] A conservative estimate of the Japanese content in Korean-manufactured VCRs is 20 to 40 percent.[18] Overall, the electronics industry currently relies on Japan for over 70 percent of its component imports.[19]

Even an intense drive to localize parts cannot compensate for years of neglect towards the small and medium firms that make up the suppliers and components sector. As one authority sees it, the parts and components bottleneck will not be resolved anytime soon. Dependence on Japan will continue, and it "could take one or two decades to build up a sufficient supply" of electronic components.[20]

In the meantime, because core electronic parts such as microwave oven doors and VCR decks are not available locally, production of such a strategic export as the VCR, as one trade journal puts it, "depends on the whims of Japanese headrum makers."[21] More than just whim may be operating here, according to microelectronics specialist Michael Borrus: "There is a lot of evidence that in order to slow down the speed with which a Goldstar moves upmarket in the VCR market, the Japanese have been withholding key critical components to prevent the Koreans from emerging as even tougher competitors than they are across the product line."[22]

The same dynamics have apparently stymied the manufacture of radiocassette players. These are mainly imported from Japan, partly for lack of indigenous technological capability, but also because "Japanese makers are reluctant to supply key parts and components to their Korean counterparts."[23]

An emerging problem is that the Korean producers are being bottled up at the low end of the market in a variety of key exports, including televisions, VCRs, and microwave ovens. The pattern seems to be, at least in the case of VCRs and camcorders, that Japanese firms come in and dominate all segments of a market for the first four or five years, then move to the higher end of the market, to more value-added and price inelastic—and hence more expensive—versions, leaving the low end of the market for the Koreans, who were constrained from entering the export market by technology-licensing restrictions during the hot years. The problem is that, especially after the novelty of a product wears off, profits at the low end of the market are marginal. "While Japanese firms are selling large-sized, high-resolution and multi-function TV's with several hundred dollars of profit for one set," says one account, "Korean firms must live with small profits generated from selling less sophisticated models."[24]

The problem has become rather acute in recent years on account of a concatenation of circumstances. With price levels at the low end quite rigid, the appreciating Korean won and rising wages for Korean workers have created an unprecedented situation of booming demand and great losses.[25] "Samsung...faces a conundrum," notes one account.

> The more products it sells in the U.S., the more money it loses. Korea's other two VCR manufacturers, Goldstar Co. and Daewoo Electronics Ltd., are also victims of their own success.
>
> Because of rocketing labor costs and the strength of the Korean currency, production costs in Korea are rising much faster than U.S.-based prices for VCRs. The result is collapsing profit margins. Indeed...Samsung lost money on every unit it exported to the U.S. last year.[26]

The same situation holds for microwave ovens, once the cash cow of the Korean consumer electronics industry: the big three Korean electronics firms found themselves exporting at a loss in 1989.[27]

As some observers have asserted, the Koreans are caught in a trap of their own making. To gain market share and drive the Japanese from the lower end of the market, they cut prices—even at the cost of profits. But having gained the low end of the market, the Koreans cannot now drive up their prices for that would send consumers back to Japanese VCRs, color TVs, and microwave ovens, which are higher-priced but have cutting-edge, high-tech features and enjoy a reputation for high quality. Indeed, the depreciation of the yen early in 1990 wiped out the price edge of many Korean exports and moved consumers back to Japanese products at the lower end of the market.

The Koreans have tried to acquire technology for more profitable state-of-the-art VCRs, but the stringent terms of agreement with the Japanese have prevented them from fully exploiting export markets. For instance, in 1988 Heung Yang Corporation came out with a sophisticated eight-mm VCR system with a built-in six-inch color TV, the HY-8050; but Heung Yang's agreement with Sony prevented it from exporting the HY-8050 to the European market.[28] And, of course, the surest money-makers—the top-of-the-line technology that brings in monopoly rents for a few years—won't be transferred by the Japanese until after the market peaks. At that point, the Japanese may find it more profitable to have the Koreans produce their mature product lines under OEM arrangements or in return for hefty royalties while they concentrate production on the more profitable, pioneering models.

Stymied with the VCR, the Koreans hope to break into profitable production with the camcorder. Agreements with the Japanese, however, have so far prevented Koreans from exporting camcorders; but even when they do begin to export camcorders, Koreans will have to be wary of the Japanese, who are not likely to vacate the low end of the market as quickly as they did in the case of the VCR. As a Samsung executive asserted, "Since most parts for camcorders still are made only in Japan...we can't afford to upset the Japanese too much by undercutting their prices, or they may cut off our supply."[29]

Plans for making profits on facsimile (fax) machines, one of the hottest-selling electronic innovations, have run up against the same constraints. Korean firms have been virtually shut out of export markets during the critical growth years because of anticompetition restrictions in technology agreements with the Japanese giants who control over 90 percent of the international fax market. Thus, according to industry projections, while the international market for faxes will reach 4,710,000 units by 1990, Korean production will reach only 200,000 units for both the local and export markets.[30] When the Korean export machine finally gets going, it will hit an already mature market and face the same paradox of gaining market share while either losing money or making very little.

The Computer Industry: Doomed to Cloning?

Korea's computer industry began in the early 1980s with very small Korean firms, usually "one-room outfits, stashed away in the back streets of Seoul, geared merely to the rapid and often surreptitious assembly of a look-alike Apple."[31] The 8-bit Apple Computer was built with open architecture, that is, with commercially available, nonproprietary components, making reverse engineering and assembly relatively easy.[32] Cloning became more popular when IBM came out with its 16-bit PC (personal computer). Like the first Apple models, the IBM 16-bit PC was designed with open architecture, perhaps deliberately so. As computer industry expert Lenny Siegel puts it, "IBM's hardware was easy to make or buy. Microsoft, the designer of the IBM PC's operating system, willingly licensed it to other manufacturers. And IBM's design was open, allowing—in fact, encouraging—other manufacturers to build add-on equipment to enhance the power of the PC. But it was IBM's size—its dominance of the entire data-processing market—that allowed Big Blue to define the standard."[33] When Chips and Technologies and companies like it placed IBM-compatible PC circuitry, or chip sets, on the open market, "virtually any efficient Asian assembler or U.S. marketer could clone even the most recent IBM product."[34]

Korean companies, especially the chaebol, married the low technology demands of PC assembly with low wages and efficient production lines to stake their claim on the domestic market and move into export. Daewoo Telecom scored a major success when it landed an OEM contract to provide the U.S. dealer Leading Edge with 270,000 PCs to be sold in the United States under the Leading Edge brand name. Since 1985, 500,000 Daewoo-manufactured PCs have been sold in the United States. Daewoo's success was followed in 1988 by Hyundai, which in that year sold 150,000 PCs—marketed under the Hyundai brand name—to capture some 3 to 4 percent of the highly competitive PC market.[35] From $19 million in 1983, Korean computer sales leaped to $260 million in 1987.[36] That year Korea produced 1.1 million IBM-compatible PCs, 60 percent of which were shipped to North America.[37]

But as the market tires of low-end "knock-off" IBM clones and the Japanese and the Americans introduce more sophisticated models like the IBM PS/2 with its new microchannel technology, the weaknesses of Korea's computer industry are becoming clear. As in consumer electronics, the key obstacles lie in components and technology. The parts bottleneck is underlined by Michael Borrus:

> If you take apart any of the leading [Korean] clones, the guts of the system is often foreign components not produced in Korea. Some of the monitors may be produced at this point in Korea but more often than not that technology may come from Japan. The components may come from Chips and Technology in the U.S., at least the hard part, the disk drives, recording and memory storage stuff may come from Japan or Singapore. But if it's from Singapore, it's part of the operations of one of the major U.S. or Japanese companies.[38]

To obtain advanced technologies to upgrade their 16-bit PC offerings, the conglomerates have again resorted to the quick but expensive route: importing technology via foreign licenses. Indeed, with only an estimated two hundred PC architecture engineers in the whole of Korea,[39] this route was practically unavoidable.

Samsung's 16-bit PC was manufactured under license from the NEC Corporation of Japan; Daewoo enlisted technology from the United States' Microsoft Corporation for its advanced 16-bit model; and Goldstar's 16-bit PCM-24 model derived technological assistance from Italy's Olivetti, in which the U.S. electronics giant AT&T has a 25 percent share.[40]

With the trend toward 32-bit PCs, firms that had only begun to produce upgraded 16-bit PCs with foreign assistance have moved into even greater dependency. For its 32-bit PC, Hyundai, for instance, has used architecture and software developed by Tolerant Systems of San Jose, California, licensed disk-drive technology from the Japanese firm Fujitsu, and bought printer know-how from Canon.[41] Like the engineers in Hyundai's automobile subsidiary, those at Hyundai Electronics were performing mainly an integrative role, that is, integrating foreign technologies into one computer system. Certainly, this was not an achievement to be downgraded, but it did not indicate a significant capability for technological innovation. Indeed, despite chaebol propaganda about their R&D expenditures, Siegel doubts that the Koreans are doing a lot of R&D, claiming that "they are content with cheaply assembling the hardware and using somebody else's software."[42]

As in consumer electronics, the Koreans are trapped in an ambivalent relationship with the Japanese, given their heavy dependence on the latter for key imported components like disk drives and keyboards. And they are extremely frustrated with the strong Japanese reluctance to share state-of-the-art technology, which consigns them to the low end of the market in computers and computer peripherals. The Koreans, for example, are desperate to get into the dot matrix printer market, but, as one account describes it,

> This technology is controlled by the Japanese. The chaebol are having to either license Japanese designs or develop proprietary machines that skirt Japanese patents. The Japanese licensing options yield older technology and often come with significant restrictions on the amounts Korean licensees can export. On the other hand, in-house development is expensive and time-consuming.[43]

If the Japanese are reluctant to license dot-matrix-printer technology, they are extremely possessive when it comes to top-of-the-line laser-printer technology. "Canon let us have their impact printer technology only after they had moved to laser technology," recounted one senior Hyundai manager. "I tried several times to get Canon's laser printer technology, but in all cases, they denied it."[44]

While the Koreans are desperately running after the Japanese technological leaders, they are, in turn, being chased by U.S. computer companies armed with threats of lawsuits for patent infringement. After years of allowing Asian computer makers to clone its products almost at will—in order to make IBM systems the world standard—IBM is cracking down. With the introduction of its new PS/2 line of PCs—on its way to becoming the new world standard—IBM is demanding as much as 5 percent royalties on future sales of PS/2 and older PC clones, and retroactive royalties on previous sales of the older PC (AT and XT) clones. Samsung,

Hyundai, Goldstar, and the rest might have no choice but to pay up, a move that is likely to have severe consequences since "as little as 5 per cent royalties could be devastating to South Korean PC makers because they work on such narrow profit margins."[45] Korea's computer makers may not yet be threatened by trade barriers, but their bottom lines are now at the mercy of the aggressive techno-protectionism of U.S. firms.

But the Americans and the Japanese are not the only problems. Confident that the chaebol could face down foreign competition in the domestic market, the government liberalized the import of PCs in 1987, a move that resulted in a flood of Taiwanese IBM-compatible PCs selling at half the price of Korean models but offering better quality. Korean-made computers were apparently selling at four times their export price in the domestic market, to make up for the low prices at which the computers were sold in export markets in order to increase and maintain market share. Ironically, therefore, while the big-volume Korean producers were challenging the Taiwanese in export markets, they were in danger of losing significant segments of their profitable home market to the Taiwanese.

The difference, according to one account, boiled down to the fact that small and medium components and parts suppliers in Taiwan are less disadvantaged than their Korean counterparts. While some accounts exaggerated the Taiwanese edge in components production and overlooked Taiwan's own financial and technological constraints, this edge does appear to exist. Without policies that systematically favored huge conglomerates while starving smaller manufacturers of capital, Taiwan had been able to develop a parts and components sector that was more dynamic and mature than Korea's, enabling Taiwanese computer makers to do more of their sourcing locally, thus making them more price competitive.[46]

In addition to heavy dependence on foreign technology and components in the area of computer hardware, another weakness of the Korean computer industry—indeed, some would say, its Achilles' heel—is the embryonic state of its software technology. Korea's deficit in the software trade came to $14 million in 1987; of its software imports of over $22 million, some 83 percent came from the United States and Japan.[47]

Korea lags behind in both application software and system software, and is fifteen to twenty years behind the United States in the latter area.[48] Korea has only 392 software producers, and of this number only 81 specialize 100 percent in software. The rest are underfunded hardware and software houses that are vulnerable to slight external market changes.[49] Added to the scarcity of firms specializing in software is another problem: less than 50 percent of the total number of employees in the software industry have college degrees.[50]

Again, this dismal state of affairs owed itself to the computer industry's being overwhelmingly dominated by the chaebol, which discouraged the development of software in several ways. First, they concentrated resources on the development of hardware and installed whichever U.S. system or application software was popular or profitable. Second, the chaebol were singularly unsuited for pioneering in software development. As author George Gilder observes in the case of the United States, bigness might be dysfunctional when it comes to creating software:

> Software is chiefly a product of individuals working alone or in small teams with minimal capital. Between 1975 and 1985, some 14,000 new software firms rose up in the United States, lifting the U.S share of the world software market from under two-thirds to more than three quarters. Since 1985, U.S. software output has grown faster even than Japan's. Software comprises a four times greater share of computer industry revenues in the United States than in Japan, and the United States produces more than four times more marketed software.[51]

Finally, the chaebol's focus on export markets has discouraged domestic software development by encouraging the domestic proliferation of the hardware and software operating systems of the foreign firms for which the chaebol built computers on an OEM basis.[52] Proliferation has discouraged the emergence of a standardized operating system, a condition that creates a costly handicap for the development of domestic software. As computer consultant Morris Crawford notes in his study of the Korean computer industry, software proliferation means,

> that any program written for a particular system is specific to that system and may not be used on others. There can be few economies of scale, for the cost of writing application software can be shared by only a limited number of buyers. Software costs per unit are high, as there is no mass marketing. The prospects of

profits from writing software is slight, and the business doesn't appear attractive.

Another important cost of not having a standard operating system is the added difficulty of networking, which is essential for large-scale corporate computer systems that tie microcomputers into larger mainframe and minicomputers. But networking is unlikely to work when its components are using different systems. Information stored in one system can rarely be retrieved from another based on a different operating system. In these circumstances, potential users shy away from computers.[53]

The proliferation problem—and the poor health of the domestic software sector generally—is likely to be exacerbated by recent government policy decisions, especially the 1987 Software Program Production Act. This measure was meant to bring in foreign investors who would spin off technology to their local counterparts in the software industry. It has apparently had the opposite effect: aggressive U.S. and Japanese firms, which offer their software at 20 to 30 percent less than domestic producers, have rushed in, making standardization even more difficult and threatening the very existence of the high-cost domestic small- and medium-size producers.[54]

The software bottleneck is a strategic one. Without standardization and a healthy software sector, there is unlikely to be strong demand for computers in the domestic market, which will be essential for the survival of the computer industry if export markets become unprofitable or unreliable. As Gilder has pointed out, it was the thousands of U.S. software firms created since 1981 that "transformed the computer from an esoteric technology into a desktop appliance found in 20 percent or more of American homes and ubiquitous in corporate workplaces."[55]

Semiconductors: An Industry Built on Sand

The hottest segment of the Korean electronics industry is semiconductors. Production of integrated circuits and other types of semiconductors in 1988 came to $6 billion, more than 90 percent of which was exported.[56] Korea is now one of the world's top producers of semiconductors.

As noted earlier, Samsung and other chaebol are no longer content with just remaining in the labor-intensive phase of wiring together wafers, but are moving into the front-end process of fabricating the wafers themselves—that is, imprinting integrated circuits into a silicon substrate.[57] In contrast to the assembly phase, the wafer-fabrication process is highly capital and technology intensive. Seventy percent of total cost is accounted for by facilities and equipment depreciation, while labor represents just 12 percent.[58] In slightly over six years, the Korean chaebol—in particular, Samsung, Hyundai, Lucky-Goldstar, and Daewoo—have telescoped decades of technological development in Japan and the United States, producing 64-kilobit, 256-kilobit, and 1-megabit DRAM chips in rapid succession, by furiously borrowing, buying, and licensing foreign technology. Now a consortium composed of Samsung, Goldstar, and Hyundai is attempting to develop the advanced 4-megabit DRAM chip.

Needless to say, the opposition is formidable. The Japanese are said to have a technological lead of at least one or two generations over the South Koreans in the DRAM chip, on which the Koreans are focusing their mass-production efforts.[59] In the late 1980s, the Japanese were sending customers samples of 4-megabit chips while the Koreans were still struggling to come up with a prototype.[60] Indeed, asserts expert Kenneth Flamm,

> The Japanese right now can place 4 megabit and 16 megabit chip technology basically on line whenever they want. It's available. It's there. It's just a question of timing for them and what's most profitable. So I think the Japanese remain firmly in control of the DRAM segment of the industry.[61]

In terms of investment, Japan's chip makers poured around US$4.5 billion into semiconductor-related plant and equipment in 1988 alone, more than the total South Korean investment to that date.[62]

Nonetheless, the Koreans' breathtaking pace has elicited praise from industry analysts. "Against all odds," says one recent report, "Korea is creating a viable semiconductor industry. The price has been high and there have been a lot of embarrassing failures along the way. But the Koreans finally look like they will make it, a testament to the impeccable determination and deep pockets of the chaebol."[63]

But has Korea really arrived? Other observers are not so optimistic. *Business Korea Electronics*, usually a cheerleader for Korea's chaebol, writes that "Korea's semiconductor industry may...resemble a house built on sand in more ways than one."[64] And indeed, there are several formidable obstacles. Perhaps foremost is the quality of the DRAMs being produced in Korea, which are said not to be competitive with Japanese and U.S. memory chips. The Korean DRAM, claims one specialist, has "a very high set of failure rates associated with it...and the yields on their manufacturing processes aren't very high. So, if one's getting a high failure rate and low yields, then you're not a state-of-the-art producer, even though you may be able to produce one."[65] Another obstacle is that the materials and equipment for semiconductor manufacturing are virtually all imported. These technologically ultra-sophisticated items come from the United States and Japan, and with the crisis of the U.S. semiconductor equipment industry, increasingly only from Japan.[66] For instance, like U.S. firms, Korean firms must depend on Japanese firms like Nikon and Canon for the critical "steppers" that engrave the circuitry image on silicon wafers.[67]

This dependence on Japanese firms, which are increasingly reluctant to share technology with their Korean rivals, can only grow as the line widths of the circuits etched on wafers continue to decrease, from the current 0.8 microns (a micron is the width of a human hair) to 0.5 microns by the early 1990s, necessitating more sophisticated and almost totally automated production technology.[68] Despite their deep pockets, the chaebol cannot devote cash and brains to developing semiconductors and semiconductor manufacturing technology at the same time. The dependence on Japan is likely to increase.

Chip development is also likely to rely more heavily on the acquisition of foreign technology than on chaebol R&D. There are some claims that the chaebol plan to invest as much as 18 percent of revenue from semiconductor sales in R&D.[69] This must be viewed with skepticism, however, given the chaebol's already-mentioned propensity to devote resources to high-yielding real estate and stock market investments. A more frenzied attempt to buy or license foreign technology is the most likely route. To fabricate its semiconductors, for instance, Hyundai "bought electrically erasable programmable logic device (EEPLD) from...International CMOS Technological Inc. (ICT) of San Jose. SRAM [static random access memory chip] designs are from MOS Electronics Corporation (Mosel), also of San Jose; ASIC [application specific integrated circuits] design software from LSI Logic Corp. of Milpitas, California; and Hyundai's DRAMs [dynamic random access memory chips] are thanks to, not one, but three companies: Inmos Corp., Texas Instruments Inc., and Vitelic Corp."[70]

Recently, reversing a trend of Japanese reluctance to share technology with the Koreans, Hitachi agreed to license its 1-megabit DRAM technology to Goldstar. Lucrative royalties from the Koreans are likely to be one of Hitachi's motivations.[71] Another could be a desire to develop strategic corporate ties that would allow the Japanese giant to penetrate the increasingly attractive Korean market with its own semiconductors and other products. According to one account,

> Japanese companies are changing their sales strategy vis-à-vis South Korea, which has had rapid and high growth and which now is viewed as a consumer market and not just as a production base. Thus one of the motives for deciding to provide technology was to establish a cooperative structure that could be developed into joint ventures that would include sales.[72]

But the most likely explanation for the Hitachi move fits the pattern evident in the area of consumer electronics: the Japanese sell obsolete technology to the Koreans for the low end of the market while they develop the high-end and highly profitable frontier products. Says one analyst: "While one megabit DRAMs are currently the industry standard, Japanese producers are gearing up to produce chips that can hold four times as much information. Hitachi apparently can guarantee itself a stable source of one megabit DRAMs through Goldstar, while concentrating on the more complicated and expensive four megabit market."[73]

Hitachi's move appears even shrewder in light of the fact that the price of 1-megabit DRAMs fell by two-thirds in 1989, owing to a slump in the U.S. personal computer industry.[74] What Goldstar has been trumpeting as a coup is actually the acquisition of rights to a money-losing commodity. Hitachi, on the other hand, has traded the insecurity of marketing 1-megabit DRAMs for the security of guaranteed royalty payments.

It is important to note, however, that the Japanese do not have a monopoly when it comes to passing obsolete or less-than-state-of-the-art technology to the Koreans. One of the senior executives of Intel, a U.S. firm with which Samsung has a technology exchange agreement, suggested that Intel was supplying the Koreans with technology "at least two generations old."[75] Gilder affirms that "many of the [semiconductor] technologies sold abroad were already obsolescent....US entrepreneurs may well have exploited the Koreans more than the Koreans exploited them."[76]

But whether to the United States or Japan, royalties paid for foreign licenses are a big drain on semiconductor sales, especially when Korean manufacturers like Samsung and Hyundai are producing mainly the low-end DRAMs, where prices are volatile and profit margins paper thin. In fact, following the pattern in VCRs, the Koreans are said to be absorbing large losses in the memory chip trade.[77] Expanding their markets to achieve greater volume and thus generate more profit is often not an option, since many agreements, except for some in memory chips, "restrict Korea's market to clearly defined regions or countries (usually to Asia or Korea)."[78]

This heavy dependence on foreign technology has now added a new complication: infringements on patents and copyrights held by the U.S. and Japanese giants. The Koreans are particularly vulnerable to this threat because, as one report points out, "much of the technology is provided by small Silicon Valley companies who may not legally control everything that they provide."[79] The result is likely to be costly lawsuits, as semiconductor giants like Intel and Texas Instruments (TI) have followed IBM's example and gone after the cloners. TI has successfully sued Samsung for patent violations, and the latter has agreed to make royalty payments reported at $25 to $95 million.[80] Intel has successfully sued Hyundai for marketing an EPROM (erasable programmable read-only memory chip) using a proprietary design; Hyundai has yet to settle.[81] In its suit against Samsung, TI reportedly demanded an amount equivalent to 15 percent of the Korean company's semiconductor sales; if this constituted the terms of the settlement, the results would be devastating for Samsung and the other Korean memory chip makers. As in the VCR and PC business, royalty payments could reach a level that would simply make continued production just to gain market share unviable.

Even if the chaebol were to now focus on R&D, it would not provide a sure route to profitability in the medium and long term because of problems in finances and technical personnel. Despite their reputation as engines of capital accumulation, the chaebol's pockets aren't deep enough when it comes to the formidable capital requirements of moving to the frontier of semiconductor production:

Table 9.2

Supply and Demand Forecast for Technical Personnel in Electronics and Electrical Sector, 1990–2000

	Ph.D.	M.A.	B.A.
		1990–1993	
Supply	410	2,423	22,091
Demand	638	9,367	14,578
Difference between demand and supply	-228	-6,944	7,513
	Ph.D.	M.A.	B.A.
		1994–1996	
Supply	342	1,869	19,470
Demand	474	7,613	10,270
Difference between demand and supply	-132	-5,744	9,200
	Ph.D.	M.A.	B.A.
		1997–2000	
Supply	456	2,492	25,960
Demand	815	16,092	17,475
Difference between demand and supply	-359	-13,600	8,485

Source: Korea Advanced Institute of Science and Technology data, reproduced in *Electronics Korea* 2, no. 6 (April 1989), p. 17.

For one thing, catching up in semiconductors and other capital-intensive fields will require huge investment outlays for research and capital equipment....Korea's industrial giants already are highly leveraged, with liabilities outweighing assets by 5 to 1 or more. Bank loans to the 30 biggest chaebol typically account for a third of all lending by Korean banks, and political pressures are building to reduce that dominance of the credit market. Clearly, Korean companies will have to find new sources of capital if they are to meet their new commitments.[82]

Given the enormous absorption of resources by the semiconductor industry, the issue, according to another analyst, becomes not so much whether Korea can mobilize the necessary capital to catch up with the United States and Japan but, even more fundamentally, whether "the industrialization strategies that have been undertaken with regard to chips in particular make sense" from the point of view of Korea's level of economic development.[83]

The technical personnel shortage is perhaps an even greater challenge than the capital barrier, since scientists and engineers cannot just be cloned overnight. Stopgap measures like the hiring of the so-called high-tech guerrillas from Japan—technicians who moonlight in Korea on weekends—are likely to have limited impact.[84] And in the next few years, R&D is likely to feel the impact of the departure of highly trained Korean semiconductor specialists who temporarily took leave from their jobs in the United States to return to Korea to help set up the semiconductor industry. "Having fulfilled their mission," notes one writer, "many are now returning to their overseas situations, where they prefer the management style. This new drain makes the underlying insufficiencies all the clearer."[85] (See table 9.2 for figures on the growing personnel deficit in the electronics sector.)

Sometimes chaebol representatives candidly admit the limits of their corporation's ambitions. For instance, one senior executive of Daewoo claimed, perhaps too harshly but essentially accurately: "You just don't have the foundation in South Korea. The people aren't skilled. You're just renting space in Korea. China could do the same thing."[86]

Conclusion

Despite impressive advances in the past thirty years, Korea's electronics industry faces formidable barriers in its effort to move into the frontier of the technology. As in other industries, the secret of Korean success lay in being able to marry licensed foreign technology to an efficient manufacturing process and cheap labor. Where the Koreans have excelled, in particular, is in perfecting an efficient manufacturing process. It is to this process that they have plugged different products, from VCRs to TVs to computers, with impressive results. As analyst Ashoka Mody describes it,

> Daewoo has this truly impressive facility where they
> assemble their TVs, VCRs. The nature of the opera-
> tions is very similar except you have different com-

ponents. As long as you have systems for doing that, you have great efficiency in selling your products. What these fellows seem to be exploiting is the huge scale economies that they seem to be getting in an organizational sense.[87]

But in the late 1980s, Korea's edge in manufacturing technology was being blunted by the rise in workers' wages, the continuing low level of development of the parts and components sector, and the continuing dependence on the United States and Japan for product technology and design innovation. The Koreans were essentially efficient mass cloners, but without the ability to innovate they were consigned to turning out products for the low end of already mature markets with obsolete technology. In the late 1980s, the trend in consumer electronics, computers, and semiconductors was everywhere the same: like overextended armies, the chaebol were either making marginal profits or incurring losses in the process of defending their market shares.

Cheap labor was the cutting edge of the Korean export machine in the 1960s. In the early 1970s and early 1980s, the edge was provided by manufacturing efficiency. By the late 1980s, efficient manufacturing systems could no longer suffice, even as the essential key to profitability in the highly competitive world of microelectronics—technological innovation—still lay beyond the grasp of the chaebol. Electronics had been designated as the decisive arena in Korea's drive to achieve advanced-country status. The chaebol and the government trumpeted R&D advances, but on closer examination, these claims were flimsy. Indeed, the Koreans' decision to take on the United States and Japan in high-tech electronics as the key to industrial advance was beginning to shape up as a strategic mistake.

10

Korea's Economy at the Crossroads

Today, Korea has reached a perilous point in its development, as all the accumulated tensions, resentments, and failures of past political and economic choices come to a head. The Korean economy is in the grips of three crises: the rapid erosion of the legitimacy of the model of high-speed export-oriented industrialization, an agro-environmental debacle, and a profound structural crisis of the economy. It is the conjunction and intersection of these crises that make the current situation particularly volatile.

The Crisis of Legitimacy

Park Chung-Hee promoted high-speed industrialization in order to gain legitimacy, working on the theory that if you deliver growth and higher living standards, people will willingly forego democratic choice. He was wrong. His particularly repressive brand of catch-up or late industrialization—imposed by the military, guided by the technocrats, and spearheaded by the chaebol—instead exploded in a democratic revolution.

Moreover, contrary to the hopes of many Korean technocrats, especially some of the reformists now surrounding President Roh Tae-Woo, the late democratization that has followed is not likely to leave the model of high-speed export-oriented growth unchallenged. The very repression used to ram through the strategy of gaining export competitiveness via cheap labor so alienated vast sectors of the population, particularly the working class, that it sacrificed any sort of long-term consensus on the model. Thus, instead of forging agreement on the priority of economic growth, late democratization in Korea has focused debate on wealth-and-income distribution issues. As the working class sees it, because they were never consulted on the matter, they are exonerated from responsibility for the continuing health of the development model. And they regard the 60 percent rise in average wages between 1987 and 1990 as the restoration of their rightful and long-postponed share of the fruits of Korea's economic growth. To the ordinary worker, the priority issue is not maintaining Korea's competitiveness in world markets but rectifying the worsening distribution of income.

It is not only the model that is in danger of losing its legitimacy, but the institutions that imposed it. The longtime justification of the chaebol—their alleged superiority in accumulating the capital resources necessary to invest in vast productive ventures—has been shattered by revelations that they have been pouring their money instead into high-profit speculative investments in land, buildings, and golf courses. The tie between wealth and production—always tenuous in the minds of Koreans—has snapped. And the conspicuous consumption displayed by the chaebol elites and their families, with their Mercedes-Benzes, Gucci bags, and imported designer clothes, can only exacerbate the rising anti-conglomerate sentiment.

This feeling is not confined to the working class. The middle class has been angered by the sharp rise in land prices triggered by chaebol speculation, which has increasingly made home ownership an unrealizable dream. And farmers on the edge of bankruptcy seethe with rage as they realize that the entry of competing U.S. agricultural imports has been the price exacted to ensure that the chaebol's manufactured products have continued access to the U.S. market.

The state's image as a neutral promoter of economic growth has been another victim of the process of late industrialization followed by late democratization. While the austere Park Chung-Hee could credibly project the image of a state whipping economic interests into line in the pursuit of economic development, his successor Chun Doo-Hwan came to represent a state whose mission and direction had been perverted by chaebol wealth. And today the continuing failure of President Roh Tae-Woo's government to rectify the chaebol's scandalous concentration of wealth has reinforced the perception that technocratic command can no longer constrain the overwhelming power of the conglomerates. Whereas Park was regarded as the CEO of Korea, Inc., Roh Tae-Woo is seen as the front man of the Chaebol Republic.

The Agro-Environmental Debacle

The second crisis wrenching the Korean mode of late capitalist development stems from the massive negative impact on agriculture and on the environment of the overwhelming priority assigned to high-speed industrialization.

One bitter fruit of this policy is an agricultural economy whose vitality has been eroded by years of subordination to the dynamics of export-oriented industrialization. Long a secure constituency of the government party, the farmers finally awakened in the mid-1980s and were in a state of virtual rebellion by the end of the decade. They are now trying to avert, desperately, the tragic denouement of the rural crisis: the extinction of much of Korean agriculture by the flood of cheap foreign grain, meat, and fruits.

As peasants become aware of their looming extinction should the current technocratic policies continue to reign, popular consciousness is catching up with an environmental crisis that has been brewing for some time. Koreans have been jarred to the crisis by food that has been steadily poisoned by a chemical-intensive agriculture and tap water that, even the government admits, is unfit for human consumption. The realization is quickly spreading that food and water contamination is just the tip of the iceberg—that in three decades the technocrat-chaebol alliance has managed to telescope processes of environmental destruction that took many generations to bring about in earlier industrial societies. As ecological awareness grows stronger, Korea's ambitious nuclear energy program, once regarded as the gem of technocratic development, has been transformed into the dark symbol of the environmental irrationality of the "hard" economic and energy path that Korea has been forced to travel.

The Structural Crisis

The third crisis is tearing at the heart of the economy itself. The Korean edge in export markets traditionally consisted of a simple formula: the efficient organization of cheap labor by the big conglomerates. By the 1980s this formula was obsolete. Greater working-class organization added impetus to normal upward pressures on wages to make Korean hourly wages the highest among the East Asian NICs in 1988.[1] When combined with the appreciation of the won forced by United States pressure, higher wages were making Korean exports uncompetitive, and increasingly, in many products and product lines, hard won market shares could only be maintained by taking losses.

Clearly, the export-oriented, cheap-labor economy was no longer viable. But instead of fashioning a new model of growth in which higher worker incomes and a more equitable distribution of wealth would serve as the motor of growth and development, the technocrat-chaebol alliance formulated a response that lay within the parameters of the discredited paradigm. This response was two-pronged: relocate labor-intensive firms or production processes to low wage areas, especially in Southeast Asia and the Caribbean, and focus domestic industry on more capital- and skill-intensive production. The technocratic vision was to make Korea a high-tech producer competitive with Japan and the United States.

The outward flow of Korean investment escalated in the late 1980s. In the first four months of 1988 alone, $392 million in investments surged outward, or close to 40 percent of all Korean investments in the twenty years between 1968 and April 1988.[2] Leading the exodus are the chaebol: Samsung, for instance, is transferring some of its labor-intensive electronic operations to the Philippines, Mexico, Turkey, and Thailand; while Goldstar is opening up electronics subsidiaries in Indonesia, Mexico, Turkey, the Philippines, and China.[3]

But not only the giants were on the move. As of early 1988, seventy-four textile and apparel firms—most of them small or medium-size companies—had set up operations abroad, with the number expected to go up to one hundred by 1989. The departure of textile and garment firms was paralleled by many of the smaller auto-parts manufacturers and by the country's footwear power-houses, which dominate key segments of the United States market with their OEM-commissioned Reebok and Nike sneakers. Like their counterparts in the textile and garments sector, the footwear manufacturers set in motion a strategy of having their Southeast Asian plants produce lower-quality footwear "while factories at home...concentrate on the high quality end of the market."[4]

Moving labor-intensive processes abroad is the easy part. Focusing domestic industries on high-tech, technology-intensive items is likely to be much more difficult. As we have seen in our survey of key industries, the chaebol remain highly dependent on foreign technology that they borrow, license, or simply steal. Their capacity for self-sustaining technological innovation in industries like electronics and automobiles—the cutting edge of Korea's export drive—is still quite low. Additionally, the national educational and research infrastructure to support technological upgrading across the board remains underdeveloped. Moreover, the approach of "picking winners" or concentrating resources on the efficient assembly of selected high-tech or medium-tech products like Excels and VCRs has left behind a very unevenly developed industrial structure, leaving strategic enterprises highly dependent on the Japanese for a wide range of inputs from car transmissions to computer disk drives to VCR tape decks.

Nevertheless, the technocrat-chaebol alliance is intent on moving into high tech in the massive and dramatic fashion characteristic of the conglomerates. Massive expansion of the petrochemical industry is on the agenda for the 1990s. And in a recent report, the Korea Institute of Economics and Technology (KIET), the influential government think tank, has called for the investment of some $33 billion in microelectronics, mechatronics, aeronautics, new materials, fine chemistry, and biochemistry in the period 1990–94.[5] Semiconductors are the centerpiece of the high-tech drive, with the government and chaebol laying out ambitious plans to develop the ultra-advanced 64-megabit DRAM.[6] Aside from the high-speed upgrading of microelectronics, the technocrats' plans include making artificial intelligence computers, developing a Korean rocket to launch satellites, creating a robot for seabed work and a deep-sea exploring vessel for manganese mining, and developing a superspeed linear electric train with a speed of 300-500 kilometers per hour.[7]

Putting aside the Alice-in-Wonderland quality of some of these proposed projects, the enormous allocation of resources to high tech is likely, in the period of slower economic growth that Korea is entering, to clash with the workers' and middle class's demands for more investment in social welfare, an improved quality of life, and a cleaner environment. Instead of promoting social peace, the high-tech focus is likely to exacerbate conflict, and the government's budgetary and tax policies are likely to become the object of bitter battles between pressure groups with contradictory priorities. Just cleaning up the country's contaminated water supply will cost $5.3 billion between 1990 and 1996.[8] In other words, having clean water to drink and clean air to breathe may well translate into scrapping plans for more nuclear reactors and shelving ambitions to mass produce the 4-megabit memory chip.

Focusing on high tech in the midst of a retrenchment of labor-intensive activities is likely to have a massive impact on employment. With high-tech's much lower need for unskilled and semi-skilled labor,   structural unemployment is likely to rise rapidly.

Already there are disturbing signs of this trend. According to one estimate, if one were to add the underemployed, the "precariously employed," and the seasonally unemployed to the figure of the officially unemployed, the current real unemployment rate would reach 17 to 20 percent of the work force.[9] Indeed, a recent survey of graduates of four-year Korean universities showed that fully 40.1 percent were unemployed in 1989, compared to 25 percent in 1985.[10] "Korea," observes one account, "is in a transition phase, moving from labor-intensive industries to those requiring greater concentrations of financial and technological resources. Factory and office automation is leaving a lot of people out in the cold."[11] And some of those college graduates left out in the cold are taking to suicide as an alternative to unemployment.[12]

The technocrat-chaebol elite's continuing obsession with exports might, in fact, bring about an even more radical and premature hollowing out of Korea's economy. For maintaining Korea's share of export markets might demand the departure not only of labor-intensive industries but even of many capital-intensive, high-tech operations. Locating these operations in developed countries would provide a way for the chaebol to get around the threat of high tariffs and meet stringent localization requirements for investors, such as European Economic Community rules that could require that as much as 80 percent of an automobile produced there must be sourced locally for it not to be subject to tariffs.

Thus, in just the past few years, a huge chunk of Korean investment has migrated, not to cheap-labor areas but to high-wage markets. Hyundai was compelled to open up an auto-manufacturing subsidiary in Canada. Daewoo has opened up a VCR plant in Britain and a microwave oven plant in France; Lucky Goldstar has set up electronics subsidiaries in the United States, Britain, and West Germany. And Samsung has spawned electronics units in Britain, Portugal, Spain, the United States, Hungary, and France.[13] Indeed, North America and Europe accounted for over 41 percent of total overseas investments of Korean firms as of April 1988.[14] This movement is likely to accelerate; for instance, between 1990 and 1993, Samsung plans to raise its electronics production abroad from 5 percent of its total production to 25 to 30 percent.[15]

This hemorrhage of productive capital is likely to render even more tenuous the link between conglomerate prosperity and domestic welfare, further eroding the legitimacy of the chaebol-dominated model of growth. Originally formulated as an escape route from an increasingly uncompetitive cheap-labor economy, the decision to challenge the Japanese and the Americans in the frontiers of high tech is leading Korea instead to an economic Waterloo. Awareness of this probability is dawning on some technocrats. As one former high official of the influential government think tank, the Korean Development Institute, warns, "old formulas for keeping the economy on track—usually technocratic solutions developed in a political vacuum—are no longer appropriate given the new socio-political environment."[16]

But is there an alternative to export-oriented high-tech industrialization?

Towards an Alternative Model of Growth

Though no coherent alternative approach to development had emerged in the late 1980s, the different elements of such a strategy have been coming together in the discussions and debates swirling around the economic crisis in progressive, liberal, and even some government circles. Perhaps the first element of a viable alternative model would be dismantling the chaebol and focusing state support on and channeling capital resources to small and medium manufacturers. This would reduce inequalities in the distribution of wealth, destroy the monopolistic stranglehold on investment resources, and spur innovation. This idea is not really radical. Periodically, the state has moved forcefully to dismantle inefficient chaebol. Moreover, at the beginning of both the Chun and the Roh governments, there was much discussion among technocrats about cracking down on the chaebol and channeling government support and credit to small and medium enterprises. In both cases, however, plans were subverted by chaebol power and by the technocrats' realization that they ultimately needed the chaebol as much as the chaebol needed them. Thus, dismantling the chaebol would greatly depend on a new coalition of political and social forces coming to political power.

The second element of an alternative paradigm would be substituting the domestic market for export markets as the locomotive of development. In fact, with exports plummeting and domestic incomes rising due to union activity in 1988 and 1989, the domestic market has become the de facto engine of economic growth. Paradoxically, the labor organizing efforts so bitterly opposed by the antiunion chaebol was what saved them from a crisis of overproduction, as protectionism abroad drastically scaled down projected sales.

But fortifying the domestic market would necessitate not just wage increases but legislated measures of social reform designed to radically rectify the worsening distribution of income, implement urban land reform, and thus prevent the further concentration of real estate in the hands of the chaebol and the rich. Domestic demand would be further stimulated by a massive financial aid program to save agriculture and by substantial government and private spending for the antipollution equipment needed to slow environmental deterioration. In other words, greater equality and a better quality of life could serve as the stimulus of economic growth, though the latter might be more moderate in its pace compared to the double-digit rates of past years.

While some of the technocrats might be open to certain reforms, as a rule they are suspicious of any development strategy based principally on domestic demand. In the manner of their technocratic kin, the IMF bureaucrats, they regard such a strategy as inflationary, and they share the chaebol's fear that domestic-demand-led growth would provide labor with tremendous power by institutionalizing ever-rising wages at the expense of profits. But perhaps the most profound obstacle is the fact that despite periodic downturns in international demand they remain fundamentally wedded to the view that export markets are the strategic engine of growth. And in this view, a policy of raising domestic incomes translates into less competitiveness in export markets.

The third element of an alternative development model would be a movement towards the economic integration of North Korea and South Korea. Again, this would hardly be radical, since under pressure from popular sentiments from both sides of the 38th Parallel, both governments have, at least rhetorically, expressed their desire for political and economic unification. Among other things, cooperation with the north, with its hydroelectric resources, would drastically lessen the need for nuclear power. Also, the integration into a unified mixed economy of 20 million more Koreans would significantly enlarge the domestic market and consolidate its position as the engine of the economy.

The fourth element would be a less-indiscriminate export policy. Reducing the emphasis on exports would, in fact, enable Korea to pursue a more-sophisticated export strategy. This approach could have a number of innovative features. One thrust might be to focus on selected products and deepen the technological capacity and support infrastructure to manufacture them effectively, instead of spreading resources too thin by trying to compete with the Japanese and Americans across the whole range of commodities. Another feature would be an effort to drastically lessen the dependence on the current fashions and fluctuations of a few Western markets by developing cooperative trade and technology agreements with Eastern bloc countries and the third world. Trade and technology ties with the third world could be based on the provision of low-tech or medium-tech products geared to an appropriate technological mix for those countries— like versatile power-tillers and energy-efficient, low-polluting means of public transportation.

Korea could, in fact, pioneer in the creation of trade and technology relationships that would not replicate the one-way, exploitative ties between the United States or Japan and the third world. To take one example, the Association of Southeast Asian Nations (ASEAN) and Korea might negotiate strategic alliances that would give one another free access to each other's markets while fostering the joint development and sharing of selected advanced technologies like semiconductors and computers. Such an arrangement would help redress the currently dangerous dependence on Japan and the United States for trade and technology.

Lastly, an alternative development model must incorporate the people into active, democratic determination of the direction of the economy. As we have seen, a major reason for the unraveling of the old model was that the majority were deliberately excluded from economic decision making, from the level of the firm to the level of national policy. To feel part of a national enterprise—and thus to be willing to sacrifice consumption for the sake of investment—people must participate in formulating the enterprise. Technocratic management may be superficially efficient, but in the end it is not effective. Democratic decision making, on the other hand, may be messy on the surface and seem inefficient in the short term, but in the end it is probably the most effective form of management.

These are, in broad strokes, the features of a new paradigm. What is yet to be mustered is the courage to break with the unworkable past and find the will and imagination to forge an alternative economic future.

Taiwan In Trouble

Introduction to Part II

More than South Korea, Taiwan symbolizes the new prosperity of the NICs. "An Embarrassment of Riches," "Awash With Money,"and "Filthy Rich" are some typical newspaper headlines that proclaim the island's supposed affluence. On the surface the admiration appears to be merited. Today per capita income in Taiwan stands at $6,053, substantially above South Korea's $4,040. And owing to large, successive trade surpluses, the island's foreign exchange reserves reached $69 billion by early 1990 — the same level as Japan's.

Judged by some of the common indicators used to measure social welfare, Taiwan's performance is equally impressive: infant mortality is down to eight per thousand; 25 percent of college-age youth are enrolled in college; and there are twenty-seven television sets and eight motor vehicles per one hundred people.[1] Walking down Taipei's streets, where the young flaunt the latest designer clothes, one encounters a middle-class society, at least in health and in dress.

The image transformation wrought by prosperity is striking. Taiwan in the 1950s and 1960s was the pariah of the third world, the island refuge to which the Kuomintang (KMT) fled after being defeated by the Communists on the Chinese mainland in 1947–49. Today, though it is not a member of the United Nations and has diplomatic relations with only twenty-six nations, Taiwan's cash is being courted by scores of third world countries, sometimes overtly, most often covertly.

But it is not so much the cash that has attracted other third world technocrats and political elites to the island; it is Taiwan's example as a "free market success." In recent years Taiwan has been transformed from a political pariah to a model, and its attractiveness has been enhanced by the contrast it presents to the failed experiments in socialist development and protectionist, import-substitution industrialization in China and other third world countries.

Technocrats and would-be technocrats have been taught that while the economies that failed focused on producing for stagnant domestic markets, Taiwan and the other NICs were smart to hitch their wagons instead to the expansion of foreign markets, particularly the U.S. market. They have been told that while the failures protected high wage rates, Taiwan used cheap labor to win trade wars abroad, which then rebounded domestically in the form of prosperity. They learn that while the failures overvalued their currencies, the undervalued New Taiwan dollar was one of the key reasons for export success.

Export-oriented industrialization, dirt-cheap labor, and an undervalued currency indeed made up the basic formula for Taiwan's high-speed growth. The problem with the orthodox explanation is what it leaves out. Among the elements not mentioned is the historical context that allowed the Taiwanese formula to work: the Taiwanese success is a product of a specific historical period marked by intense cold war competition and U.S. supremacy in the international economy.[2] Although mentioned earlier, three considerations, in particular, are worth stressing. First, Taiwan had relatively easy and privileged access to the most prosperous market on earth at a time of international economic expansion when the United States was still committed to a liberal international trading order. Second, Taiwan was hardly an exemplar of free market economics. It protected its domestic market, like other third world countries. But since it was a frontline ally in the struggle against Communism, the United States benignly overlooked the heavily protected Taiwanese domestic market, even as the International Monetary Fund, the World Bank, and GATT (General Agreement on Tariffs and Trade) were telling the rest of the world to end their restrictions on imports and foreign investments. This was important since the protected domestic market served as a springboard from which local firms could launch their assault on the international economy.

Third, war, as the old adage goes, produces misery for some and prosperity for others. The Vietnam War was an "El Dorado," to borrow Bruce Cumings' phrase, not only for Korea but also for Taiwan, boosting the island's economy with U.S. military purchases of agricultural and industrial goods, spending for rest and recreation, and contract work for Taiwanese firms in Indochina.[3]

These were a few of the favorable conditions surrounding the Taiwanese takeoff to industrial status, and they were part of an evanescent international context that can never be recaptured.

In the mid-1980s, however, such doubts about the replicability of the model of export-oriented industrialization were brushed aside by KMT technocrats as sour-grapes carping by third world intellectuals, and dismissed as leftist quibbling by orthodox economists. For nothing succeeds like success. And did not export-oriented growth deliver an average annual growth rate of nearly 10 percent between 1960 and 1980?

By 1990, however, both the doubts and the doubters had become more credible. Some uncritical third world technocrats and first world economists continue to extoll the Taiwanese Miracle. However, the debate has moved away from the question of the replicability of that growth elsewhere to the more fundamental issue of the desirability of pursuing a strategy of export-oriented industrialization Taiwan-style. And the participants in the debate are no longer just academics or policymakers, but the people of Taiwan themselves.

It is not that the growth rate has plunged significantly, or that the glitter of prosperity is in danger of disappearing soon. Most of the superficial indicators remain positive, although as in Korea, the floor dropped from under the stock market in the first half of 1990, wiping out the personal wealth of an estimated four million investors.[4] What really alarms many Taiwanese are the high costs of growth, which burst into the open in the last few years.

A farmer's protest on May 20, 1988, which ignited Taipei's worst riot since the late 1940s, drove home the reality that one of the costs of the primacy of export-oriented industrialization was the erosion and, increasingly, the extinction of Taiwan's agriculture. A burgeoning environmental movement underlined the reality that unregulated industrialization had created an environmental nightmare, with most of the island's rivers suffering from serious pollution, agricultural produce manifesting high levels of contamination by heavy metals, and air that was considered unfit to breathe for nearly 62 days out of one year. Scores of strikes broke out in the aftermath of the KMT government's lifting of martial law in July 1987, emphasizing the workers' point that the "miracle" had been built on their exploitation and that it was time to claim the benefits that were rightfully theirs.

The high costs of high-speed growth were overtaking Taiwan just as it became clear that the export-dominated economy was entering a profound structural crisis. It had lost its edge in cheap labor to other third world competitors, yet was finding it extremely difficult to make the transition to a high technology–based export economy.

That the island's entrepreneurs continued to rely on low-cost labor to provide their competitive edge in export markets was underlined by the migration of Taiwanese businesses to low-wage havens in Southeast Asia, the Caribbean, and China in order to escape rising wages and labor unrest in Taiwan. Firms ignored the KMT government's half-hearted efforts to get them to upgrade their production processes or shift to producing high-tech commodities. Taiwan was shaken when word leaked out early in 1990 that Y. C. Wang, head of the formidable Formosa Plastics, was scouting China as a possible site for a key petrochemical facility—a naphtha cracker—to avoid rising wages and the increasingly effective environmental movement. It was reported that a quarter of Taiwan's enterprises were ready to follow him to the capitalist Mecca across the Taiwan Straits, where profit-making would not be hampered by a free labor movement and pollution controls.[5] Earlier, in 1988, a poll taken of owners of 1,000 manufacturing companies and 300 service enterprises revealed that only a third were willing to continue investing in Taiwan and a tenth were planning to emigrate.[6]

To be sure, Taiwan in 1990 was not yet in a critical state, as Korea was. But the two countries were saddled with the same dependence on a labor-intensive manufacturing base. And both were plagued by the same debilitating problems of agricultural decline, environmental degradation, and worsening labor-management relations. Indeed, it seemed only a matter of time before Taiwan was overtaken by the crisis that had already gripped Korea.

Rising economic disaffection was paralleled by growing political alienation. In fact, they fed off one another, since export-oriented growth has been imposed from above by the ruling Kuomintang (KMT) regime, which had ensconced itself forcibly on the island after its defeat at the hands of the Communists on the Chinese mainland in the late 1940s. Thus, a widespread desire to be free of authoritarian rule combined with farmers' anger at agricultural policy, workers yearning for a better deal for labor, and environmental consciousness at the grass roots to reduce the KMT's percentage of popular vote from 70 percent to 59 percent during the legislative elections in December 1989.

The crisis of political legitimacy and the emerging crisis of economic strategy were intertwined.

The following chapters examine, in some detail, different aspects of the crisis of the reigning economic model, focusing in particular on the agro-environmental disaster created by the subordination of agriculture and environment to the needs of high-speed industrialization; the erosion of the legitimacy of the institutions and agencies that imposed export-oriented industrialization, particularly the KMT and its corps of technocrats and KMT-linked business groups; and the profound structural crisis of the export-dominated economy, stemming from the failure to make the transition from labor-intensive production to high-tech processes and exports as local labor costs have risen and competition has intensified in export markets.

11

Agriculture: The Road to Extinction

On the afternoon of May 20, 1988, a small but loud group of farmers from Yunlin County gathered in front of the Legislative *Yuan*, Taiwan's highest law-making body, in the middle of Taipei. The farmers were demanding, among other things, cuts in taxes on fertilizers and an increase in the amount of rice purchased at subsidized prices.[1] According to one account, the farmers "accused the government of ignoring their welfare for the past four decades under an economic program stressing industrial development."[2] By nightfall, this angry demonstration had triggered Taiwan's worst riot in decades, and it took 2,000 policemen to contain eighteen hours of rioting.

Most taken aback by the riot was the KMT government, which had boasted for years of having a solid alliance with Taiwan's small farmers, a relationship that had been forged by a sweeping land reform program carried out in the early 1950s.

Taiwan's land reform has been universally acknowledged to be one of the world's most successful. Carried out between 1949 and 1953, the enterprise went through three phases: rent reduction, sale of public land confiscated from the Japanese, and finally a land-to-the-tiller program. With a quarter of Taiwan's private farmland changing hands in the process, the reform altered the island's social landscape: families owning all or part of the land they tilled rose from 61 percent to 88 percent of all families; and tenant families plummeted from 39 percent to 12 percent of all families.[3]

Land Reform as Political Management

Despite its success, however, the land reform was limited by a perspective that eventually produced a crisis in agriculture and eroded the KMT–small farmer alliance. As in Korea, the reform was carried out not for the welfare of the farmers and the agricultural economy, but to stabilize the countryside politically and to secure the hegemony of the KMT. Learning from its disastrous experience on the Chinese mainland, the KMT sought to use land reform to blunt the appeal of Communism among the peasantry as well as eliminate the Taiwanese landlord class as a competing elite.[4] With the emergence of the small farmers as the dominant class, the KMT, in Michael Hsiao's words, "turned the rural sector from a potential source of political unrest into a fundamentally conservative social base."[5]

But the creation of a KMT–small farmer coalition was only one dimension of land reform.[6] The other dimension was less benign: the replacement of the landlord class by the KMT as the exploiter of the rural population.[7] State power was no longer mediated by landlords but reached directly to each villager via two key institutions: the police and the so-called Farmers' Associations. The policeman was described by one KMT official as "the most important resource person of all for community development on the island," while the Farmers' Associations were more critically painted by two agricultural experts as "much more agencies assisting the penetration of state power into the countryside ... than vehicles for village-level mobilization or participation."[8]

The new relationship was immediately employed by the KMT to secure part of the rice harvest "at a low price to distribute to its large number of soldiers and bureaucrats" who had fled the mainland on the eve of the Communist takeover.[9] In the next few years, the KMT government's policy was to effect a net transfer of resources from the countryside to the KMT's city-based supporters. This was accomplished through the forced sale of part of the rice harvest via the so-called rice-fertilizer barter. In this system of unequal exchange the government, which virtually monopolized fertilizer production, added a substantial marketing fee to the cost of fertilizer upon delivering it to the farmer in exchange for rice, making a large profit from the transaction.

In addition to the forced sale of part of the harvest, farmers were required to pay a land tax, a water fee, and other taxes, some of which were payable in rice and all of which took a substantial chunk of the farmer's remaining production.[10]

While government propagandists painted an image of a contented peasantry that now controlled the land, some village studies revealed simmering peasant discontent with the transfer of resources that was going on. For instance, in the village of Fu Kuei in central Taiwan, Wang Sung-Hsing and Raymond Apthorpe found that,

> After land reform, the farmers were freed of exploi-
> tation by a landlord and were incorporated into the
> national society, but they have had to pay more to the
> Government, though the amount is less than the rent
> paid before land reform to the landlord. Villagers
> described the land reform conducted by the Govern-
> ment as a kind of business which paid well for the
> Government which invested not a single penny.[11]

Fu Kuei's villagers "would not be surprised if one day the Government should take the position of landlords....Some villagers even
said that in effect their land belongs to the nation and farmers are
just its cultivators."[12]

Subsidizing Export-Led Industrialization

As KMT control of the island was consolidated in the late 1950s,
the mechanisms of unequal exchange were employed not just to
feed the exiled mainlanders but also to generate the capital for the
state-operated industrial enterprises set up by the KMT to assure
its strategic control of the economy. And beginning in the mid-
1960s, the subordinate role of agriculture in the economy was
strengthened by the KMT's decision to emphasize the development of export-oriented industries. The maintenance of low prices
for farm commodities became the key mechanism of agriculture's
subsidizing the process of export-oriented industrialization. In the
words of one technocrat:

> Low-price policies for farm products have been ap-
> plied in Taiwan as a way to promote industrial
> development through providing cheaper food for in-
> dustrial workers in the hope of keeping relatively low
> wage levels and low production cost for industrial
> goods. Low prices also favor export markets to earn
> foreign exchange for capital formation.[13]

Although the rice-fertilizer barter scheme was abolished after
1972, compulsory rice sale and other mechanisms permitted the
government to gain control of 40 percent of marketable supply.[14]
Control of such a huge segment of the rice harvest practically
eliminated the free market in rice, since whenever the price went
too high, the Provincial Food Bureau would release its stock onto

the market until the price moved back to the level desired by the government.[15]

Agricultural production grew by an impressive 4.8 percent annually between 1953 and 1962, before slowing down to 4 percent annually between 1963 and 1972. The spin-off for industry was substantial. According to one estimate, in 1951–55 the net outflow of capital from agriculture was 14.2 percent of the net national product and 74.8 percent of total capital formation. Between 1956 and 1960, the net outflow came to 8.6 percent of the net national product and 39.7 percent of total capital formation.[16] This was capital extraction on a massive scale.

Price policy was, in fact, used not simply to feed the labor force for export-oriented industries but to create it. "The government has intentionally held down the peasants' income," admitted Lee Teng-Hui, a leading agricultural policymaker before he became president of Taiwan in 1988, "so as to transfer these people—who originally engaged in agriculture—into industries."[17]

Demise of the Farm Economy

Terms of trade unfavorable to agriculture gradually but surely eroded the economic status of farmers. Their incomes rose in absolute terms, but dropped from about 70 percent of the income of the urban work force in 1966 to 60 percent in 1970, before recovering weakly to 66 percent in 1980 (see table 11.1).[18] "Apparently," noted one observer, "while affluence was becoming more homogenized in the urban sector, increasing poverty in the rural areas was becoming more equally shared."[19]

Labor-intensive production combined with liberal applications of fertilizer and pesticides was the key to the rapid growth of agricultural production in the 1950s and 1960s. However, the subordination of agriculture to industrial development siphoned off an estimated 1 million farm people to the cities between 1950 and 1965, and another 860,000 between 1965 and 1982.[20] Those leaving have mainly been the young and able-bodied, "leaving an agrarian population of mostly aging farmers."[21] Of those left behind, 58 percent were over thirty, and nearly 50 percent were women farmers earning only 60 percent of what their male counterparts would earn.[22] Moreover, many of those left behind have increasingly turned to more profitable pursuits than farming to make a go of it. Today only 11 percent of Taiwan's 1.2 million farmers are full-time farmers, and 69 percent of them earn the

Table 11.1

Per Capita Farm Family Income as Percentage of Non–Farm Family Income, 1966–1982

1966 %	1968 %	1970 %	1972 %	1974 %
69.8	57.9	60.2	66.5	68.4

1976 %	1978 %	1980 %	1982 %
67.7	64.0	66.4	67.9

Source: Chen Hsing-Yu, "Family Farms, Integrated Rural Development, and Multipurpose Cooperatives in Taiwan," *Economic Review* (Taipei), no. 222 (November–December 1984), p. 14.

major portion of their income from nonagricultural pursuits, like employment in rural industries.[23] As one analyst remarked, "Farming has become the real 'sideline' for most farm families."[24] (See table 11.2 for comparison of full- vs. part-time status of farm households in selected Asian countries.) Many families, in fact, are subsidized by remittances sent from daughters and sons working in urban industries.[25]

With rapid out-migration, the countryside was hit by a severe shortage of labor, which saw agricultural wages increase tenfold, in nominal terms, from NT$40.3 per day in 1964 to NT$473.5 per day in 1981.[26] This dynamic propelled a growing differentiation of the social landscape, as an itinerant seasonal labor force emerged, moving from village to village to offer its services.[27] A rural proletariat was being born in the midst of crisis.

Unfavorable terms of trade eventually contributed to eroding the productivity of agriculture. Using 1952 as a base of 100, the agricultural production index rose to 172 in the thirteen years from 1952 to 1965, but advanced to only 201 in the next nineteen years, 1965 to 1984.[28] The multiple cropping index (MCI)—a measure of the intensiveness of production—dropped from 189 in 1965 to 144 in 1984, a figure even below the MCI of 174 in 1952.[29] And the island's self-sufficiency in food, measured in calories, dropped

Table 11.2

Full- vs. Part-time Farm Households in Selected East Asian Societies

	Japan[a]	Taiwan	South Korea
		(% of farm households)	
Full-time	12.5	8.9	82.1
Part-time	87.5	91.1	17.9

Source: Michael (Hsin-Huang) Hsiao, "State and Small Farmers in East Asia with Special Reference to Taiwan" (Paper presented at Conference on Directions and Strategies of Agricultural Development in the Asia-Pacific Region, Academia Sinica, Taipei, January 5–7, 1988).

[a] Japan data from 1978; Taiwan data from 1980; South Korea data from 1979.

from virtually 100 percent in the early 1960s to 70 percent by the mid-1980s.[30]

Crisis Management

To defuse the farmers' growing discontent and shore up the KMT-peasant alliance, the government responded with two programs. One was to subsidize the production of rice; the other was to promote mechanization.

Initially, in the early 1970s, the government guaranteed rice farmers unlimited purchase of their rice at a price 20 percent higher than the cost of production. This proved too expensive, prompting a revision in 1977 whereby the government guaranteed the purchase of about 25 percent of each hectare of rice production.[31] But the benefits from this arrangement were very limited, since much of the rest of the crop was purchased at a low price by exploitative middlemen, uncontrolled by the state, who then proceeded to sell it at a high price to urban consumers.[32]

The rice subsidy program propped up rice production; 2.2 to 2.5 million metric tons are now produced annually. However, given their rising incomes, Taiwan's urban consumers have been diversifying their tastes to include more meat, fish, vegetables, and other grains in their diet, resulting in an annual rice consumption that has fallen below 2 million metric tons. An expensive rice surplus thus accumulated, which could only be disposed of at a loss in export markets, and at the risk of incurring retaliation from the United States, which has charged Taiwan with dumping and undercutting U.S. rice exports.[33] Diversification of production was an obvious solution, but an aggressive U.S. trade policy was also blocking off this alternative, with its effort to open up the Taiwanese market to U.S. meat, grain, and fruit imports.

The government's second response has been, as in Korea, to promote the American route to higher agricultural productivity and more efficient production: mechanization. Effective mechanization, however, requires economies of scale: that is, increased farm size, beyond the average landholding size of 1.17 hectares. To achieve this, the government is, for all intents and purposes, promoting reverse land reform, hoping to get marginal farmers to sell out, thus reducing the rural labor force from 1.3 million in the mid-1980s to 610,000 by the year 2000.[34] This would translate to "less than 10 percent" of the work force, down from the current 20 percent.[35] The vanguard of agricultural production would be 80,000 full-time farming households operating relatively large farms—about 10 hectares in size, in the view of some technocrats.[36]

There was, however, one hitch to the fulfillment of this vision of land reconcentration in the name of efficiency: farmers' refusal to either sell or lease their land "for fear of losing social and economic security."[37] Others refused to sell at the low price offered for agricultural land. Frustrated at the resistance of small farmers to turn their land into cash, one technocrat complained: "You know, in the U.S., the productivity of agriculture continually increased because of the enlargement of the size of the farm; but in Taiwan, the size of the farm shows no sign of increasing."[38] The culprit was identified as "the overprotection of tenants and the strict restrictions on the transfer of farmland after land reform, [which] have resulted in a rigid land tenure system which cannot provide an effective mechanism for enlarging farm size."[39]

In the opinion of others, however, the American solution is misguided. According to Michael Hsiao, one of Taiwan's most prominent social critics, it would mean displacing nine out of ten households. Either the aging work force continues as a farming class, or it is pushed into the cities, where most of its members will be misfits in the urban labor force. "If you're moving from labor-intensive production to high tech, which is the proclaimed policy, you're going to have problems absorbing this largely unskilled work force," Hsiao argues. "You're merely tranferring an agrarian problem to an urban and industrial setting."[40]

It is understandable, however, that the American solution is preferred by Taiwan's agricultural technocrats; being part of the KMT apparatus, they have never regarded the well-being of the farming community as an end in itself, but have always seen the countryside as a political or economic problem to be managed in the interests of KMT rule.[41] As in Korea, a thriving rural society and agriculture was not an integral part of the technocrats' vision of national economic development. Farmers were considered at the very least, as problems, and at most, as obstacles that needed to be weeded away in the interest of development or pacified in the pursuit of political stability.

The American Threat

With such a perspective, the technocrats were hardly the farmers' best defenders when the United States stepped up its efforts to open up Taiwan's agricultural market in the mid-1980s. Aside from pushing the government to crack down on clone makers and other copyright and patent violators, the United States sought to dismantle all barriers to the entry of its agricultural goods, the commodities in which it was still competitive following its loss of manufacturing supremacy to Japan. It soon became clear to technocrats and farmers alike that underlying the American campaign was an implicit trade-off: to keep the U.S. market open to Taiwan's manufactured exports, the KMT had to agree to eliminate all barriers to the flood of American agricultural imports. The aggressive American campaign was carried out under the rubric of free trade; to Taiwan's farmers, however, free trade translated into the extinction of Taiwan's agriculture.

To the Taiwanese, the U.S. trade offensive was merely the latest phase of a long-standing, relentless American drive to dominate the island's agricultural economy. The first phase had been the dumping of cheap surplus commodities like cotton, soybean, and corn via the PL (Public Law)–480 program in the 1950s. This effort, which the KMT government supported, ruined postwar Taiwan's diversified agricultural economy, which had produced not only rice and sugar but also soybeans, wheat, barley, corn, and many other grains.[42] Two hundred eighty-one million dollars worth of wheat and flour imports and $125 million worth of soybeans were unloaded on Taiwan in the period 1951–68 by the PL-480 pro-

Table 11.3

U.S. Share of Agricultural Imports, 1986–1987 (%)

Agricultural Import	%
High quality beef	100
Wheat	95
Soybeans	95
Coarse grains	86
Wine	56
Cotton	13
All agricultural imports	41
U.S. agricultural trade balance with Taiwan	$1.07 (1987)

Source: Robert Goldstein, *U.S. Agricultural Trade Opportunities with Pacific Rim Nations* (Washington, D.C.: Congressional Research Service, 1989), pp. 55–60.

gram.[43] As this was going on, production of nonrice common crops, including wheat and soybeans, declined from 13.5 percent of total agricultural production in 1951–55 to 8.1 percent in 1976–79.[44] Events in the 1970s enlarged U.S. penetration of the island's agricultural market. To buy American protection at a time that the U.S. economy was moving towards diplomatic recognition of Taiwan's rival, the People's Republic of China, the government basically allowed increased dumping of U.S. surpluses onto the island. Today, Taiwan is totally dependent on imports of wheat and produces only 1 percent of its soybean needs.[45] Eighty-five to 95 percent of the island's wheat imports and 95 percent of its soybean imports come from the United States, as do 86 percent of its imports of coarse grains, 100 percent of high-quality beef, and 56 percent of wine. All in all, the United States accounts for over 40 percent of Taiwan's agricultural imports, and the U.S. Department of Agriculture predicts that the island will eventually become the second leading market in the world for American agricultural commodities, behind Japan and ahead of Canada (see table 11.3).[46]

To fulfill that prophecy, Washington demanded in 1987 that Taiwan lift the tariff barriers protecting fruit producers and the chicken and turkey industry. This turned out to be the straw that broke the camel's back, for the fruit-poultry issue brought home to farmers the mess that agricultural policy had become under the KMT. On the one hand, to reduce the rice surplus, the government was encouraging farmers to diversify into such activities as fruit and poultry raising. Labor-intensive fruit-farming emphasizing high-quality, higher-value-added products was, in fact, the government's new policy, given the failure of the effort to promote large-scale mechanized production.[47] On the other hand, by caving in to U.S. pressure and dismantling trade barriers, the KMT government was making it impossible for farmers to compete in these very products.

The case of apples is illustrative. A decade ago, Taiwanese farmers dominated the industry. Under U.S. pressure, however, a ban on apple imports was lifted and tariffs were gradually reduced to 40 percent. By 1988, due to foreign competition and the appreciation of the Taiwanese currency, the price of a box of Taiwanese apples had fallen from $75 to $7, and foreign apples had captured 80 percent of the market.[48]

Resisting Extinction

Acquisition of farmland for nonfarming uses is the third of a triad of problems threatening agriculture, in addition to antirural government policies and U.S. trade pressure.

In the last decade, more and more farmland has passed into the hands of financiers, speculators, and corporations. Already, government and private corporations are said to hold 8 percent of farmland.[49] In the early 1980s, the government estimated that 4,000 hectares of new land would be needed each year for industrial and urban expansion.[50] In fact, according to one estimate, since the late 1970s an average of 10,000 hectares of farmland annually have been converted to residential areas, industrial zones, golf courses, and other nonagricultural uses, leaving just 650,000 hectares for farming, out of the 890,000 hectares that are officially classed as under cultivation.[51]

Facing extinction by a loose alliance of urban-industrial interests, U.S. trade interests, and government technocrats, the farmers took to the streets late in 1987. The protest against the KMT's caving in to U.S. trade pressure became the medium for expressing a broader discontent, with demonstrations also demanding "farmers' health insurance, agricultural funds, control over agricultural land use, prices of fertilizers and pesticides, farmers' education,...limit on the outflow of rural youth population, more participation of the farmers in the government's agricultural policymaking process."[52]

The farmers' demands drew widespread support from the population. The May 20, 1988, farmer's demonstration, in fact, turned into a national protest against the KMT in which students, workers, and middle-class people participated, provoking violent suppression by the authorities. Perhaps underlying this unity was a sense that the agricultural crisis was really but one dimension of a national crisis overtaking Taiwanese society. For as George Kuo has eloquently put it, the agrarian crisis is not only one of

> food price versus export economy but what form of balance [there should be] between food production, human value, economic growth, sustainable agriculture, and environmental integrity....
>
> As...agriculture deteriorates and the number of family farms decreases, the entire fabric of rural society is undermined. At the most personal and family level, foreclosure of a family farm is even more stressful than losing a job. At the next level, the rural community and cultural value of rural life are under siege. The loss of rural community means the loss of the rural patriarch to embrace the urban prodigal in the event of debacle in the industries. The rural crisis is affecting urban Taiwan as well. The destruction of the family farm system, whose values are inherent in the country's moral and ethical history, also affects the base on which urban centers are built. At the national level, the disappearance of food self-reliance and indigenous commodities would be a great loss for a country with a strong tradition of culinary art. The decline of agriculture, whose values are especially critical in this humid, tropical milieu, also affects the natural ecosystems on which the whole nation is based.[53]

12

The Making of an
Environmental Nightmare

As Taiwan's high-speed export-oriented growth enters its third decade, many Taiwanese are beginning to seriously ask themselves if it has all been worth it. For despite government's and business's constant self-congratulations on creating an economic miracle, the evidence is accumulating that the other face of high-speed growth is an environmental tragedy of massive proportions. Taiwan's landscape continues to be as enchantingly green as it was to the Portuguese seamen who christened it Formosa, or Beautiful Island. But beneath the greenery is poisoned soil. Beside the greenery flows polluted water. And increasingly, the green itself is toxic grain.

Deforestation

In some areas of Taiwan, the greenery is being stripped away irrevocably in the interest of more development. As industrial and residential developments encroach on fertile rice fields, the government has encouraged the clearing of forested land for agriculture. Not only have the virgin broadleaf forests that once covered the entire eastern coast been almost completely destroyed, but the second-growth broadleaf forests decreased by 20 percent between 1956 and 1977.[1] This development also threatens fauna since these shrinking forests themselves serve as the natural habitat for many endangered species, including the clouded leopard, which may still exist but which has not been sighted in the wild for years.

Much of what passes for forest conservation has, in fact, been the conversion of hardwood forests into profitable monocultural plantations of fast-growing conifers, such as *Cryptomeria japonica*. Not surprisingly, the replacement of what the Forestry Bureau disdainfully calls "messy vegetation" with more economically valuable trees has vastly simplified what were once diverse natural habitats.[2] Such forest monocultures have been found to support only 15 percent as many birds as are found in adjacent natural forests.[3]

A vast network of industrial roads has been built to open up the forests to logging, agriculture, and development. Predictably, the result has been serious soil erosion. Two-thirds of Taiwan slopes 10 percent or more, with about half of the island sloping more than 40 percent, making erosion from the destruction of mountain forests a nationwide problem. Whole slopes of bare soil are reported to have slid away.[4] To slow the filling of water reservoirs by erosion, some 1,385 check dams have been built, but these dams, not surprisingly, have themselves created an ecological crisis. "The design of these check dams rarely considered the needs of the fish that live in these streams," notes the *Taiwan 2000* report, prepared by a prestigious group of academics and environmentalists. Thus, "the habitat for all the freshwater fish has been seriously damaged already, and many species are isolated in small sections of a river."[5]

The Aborigines

Another species endangered by the lowlanders' assault on the mountain fastnesses of the island is Taiwan's aboriginal people, who make up 2 percent of the population. Confined to mountain reserves under Japanese colonial rule and continuing under KMT rule, the aboriginal communities tried to survive off the land, but their traditional economies and culture have been undermined by pollution, logging, and road building, which have caused declining crop yields, scarcity of game animals, and disappearance of fish from many rivers.

Much aboriginal land was taken over by government monopolies, including the powerful Taiwan Sugar Corporation. In addition, the KMT changed the reserve policy in 1987 to allow private development companies to buy tribal land "in order to fully utilize the land's potential."[6] The entry of developers has seriously destabilized not only the aborigines' economic life but also disrupted their cultural mores. For instance, in March 1987 the Nantou County government gave the go-ahead for the construction of a hotel within the Bunan Tribal Reservation without obtaining the permission of the tribal people. The hotel was sited on a tribal cemetery, and "without consulting the villagers, the county government began digging up bodies, in violation of Bunan cultural taboos"[7]—a move that provoked angry protest from the aborigines.

With their economic base swiftly eroding, there has been a great exodus of young aborigines to the coastal cities, many of them enticed to leave by labor recruiters with promises of good jobs and a better life. Instead, they are tracked into the lowest-paying jobs in the most dangerous and degrading working conditions. For example, aborigines make up the majority of Taiwan's deep-sea fishermen. Thousands of them have been detained in foreign ports—often for as long as six months or even years—for following their captain's order to stray into foreign territorial waters.[8]

Young aborigines have also been herded into prostitution in Taipei and other major cities. A recent study revealed that one-third of young aborigine women have worked as prostitutes.[9] The trafficking in girls as young as thirteen is very profitable; the girls sell for around $5,000. The youngest girls are given breast implants and hormone shots so that their bodies mature faster. To prevent escapes, women are told that if they try to leave, their sisters will be kidnapped to replace them.[10] Many aborigines view this whole process—the assault on their tribal land base and the miserable plight of tribals who move to cities—as nothing short of genocide.[11]

Toxic Grain

Environmental degradation pervades both the highlands and the lowlands. High rates of agricultural production in the lowlands were achieved through dependence on liberal applications of chemical fertilizers and pesticides. The costs of four decades of squeezing more productivity out of the land via more chemical inputs have now overtaken Taiwanese agriculture, to the distress of both farmers and consumers.

Taiwan's farmers' use of fertilizers tripled between 1952 and 1980, from 458,000 to 1,360,000 metric tons (see table 12.1). Since cultivated area increased by only about 3.5 percent during this period—from 876,100 to 907,353 hectares[12]—land was seeded very intensively with fertilizer. Taiwan is currently among the top users of chemical fertilizers per square inch in the world.[13] Undoubtedly this distressing development is connected to the fact that for a long time, the government was greatly dependent for its

Table 12.1

Trends in Fertilizer Use in Taiwan, 1952–1981

	1952	1955	1960	1965
Metric tons	458.37	562.56	664.87	797.45
Percentage increase		22.7	18.2	19.9

	1970	1975	1980	1981
Metric tons	678.58	1,240.83	1,359.81	1,244.76
Percentage increase	-14.9	82.9	9.6	-8.5

Source: Joseph Martellaro, "The Post-War Development of Taiwanese Agriculture," *Asian Economies* 45 (1983), p. 31.

revenues on the sale of fertilizers to farmers under the rice-fertilizer barter scheme.

The impact of fertilizer overuse has become better understood in the last few years. Heavy use of most nitrogen-source and other chemical fertilizers contributes to soil acidification, zinc losses, and decline in soil fertility. Fertilizer overuse is a major contributor to water pollution, specifically in the form of nitrogen and phosphorus, according to the U.S. National Research Council. Carried by water or by sediment, nutrient loading caused by nitrogen and phosphorus has devastating effects on surface waters, like rivers, lakes, and streams. It stimulates the growth of algae that speed up the natural process of eutrophication or oxygen loss, leading to the death of animal life.[14] Fertilizer runoffs also contaminate groundwater, which is the source of drinking water for many Taiwanese.

Fertilizer overuse has gone hand in hand with pesticide overdose. Today Taiwan is one of the top users of pesticides in the world, with an average of four kilos applied per hectare. The island's farmers now use close to 1 percent of the world's pesticide.[15]

Pesticides are a major source of contamination of Taiwan's surface water and groundwater. For farmers and farmworkers, constant exposure to pesticide substantially increases the risk of cancer, while pesticide residues in food not only increase the risk of cancer but may also have "behavioral effects, alter immune system function, cause allergic reactions, and affect the body in other ways."[16] Sociologist Michael Hsiao reports, "There are many cases of sudden death among farmers, and this is often attributed to pesticides."[17] The spraying of fruit orchards is said to have caused many cases of arsenic poisoning.[18]

Pesticide abuse is encouraged by the aggressive marketing tactics of private companies and the absence of effective government regulation of the trade. With some 280 brands of pesticides available,[19] even some government bureaucrats are provoked to exasperation. "There are so many different brand names," according to Yu-Kang Mao, director of the Land Reform Training Institute, "that farmers get confused. To make sure they have the proper dosage, they often end up overspraying."[20] When overspraying is combined with the multicropping practiced to take advantage of Taiwan's lush climate, then inch for inch, Taiwan's land is perhaps more chemically battered than the United States' monocrop agricultural land.

Among the pesticides that have been used are DDTR, dieldrin, aldrin, lindane, and heplactho. In the 1970s, the average soil sample contained 11.4 ppb (parts per billion) of pesticide; in some areas, DDTR was as high as 960 ppb. According to the annual report of the Plant Protection Center, twenty-three pesticides have been identified as discharging pollutants, with ten of these pesticides destroying rice seedlings.[21] Water pollution from pesticide runoff has been severe. Richard Kagan points out that "duck eggs reveal DDTR residues that are 30 times greater than DDTR in soil content."[22] Eight percent of irrigation channels have also been contaminated.[23]

Considering that the government has only nineteen field scouts and twelve field workers to monitor 1 million farmers,[24] it is unlikely that, even were tough laws suddenly to materialize, the toxic assault on the Taiwanese soil can be repelled in the next few years.

Though government and the agro-input businesses have hooked them into a chemical dependency, Taiwan's farmers are intensely aware of the limits and dangers of fertilizers and pesticides. For instance, Wang and Apthorpe were told by the farmers of Fu Kuei village that "chemical fertilizer...is like western medicine which is efficient and quick but not enduring. Farmyard manure is like Chinese medicine, slow but sure and enriching."[25] One way that farmers cope with pesticides is described by Hsiao: "Many farmers don't eat what they sell on the market. They grow another crop without using pesticides and that's what they consume."[26] In the meantime, consumers see insects and insect bites in vegetables as a sign that they are "clean."[27]

Fear of pesticides has altered the production process in some farming communities, as Huang and Apthorpe's detailed account of farming practices in Fu Kuei village makes clear:

> Insecticide is considered to be a very dangerous material. It has been known to be used for suicide in rural Taiwan. Some villagers would not like to spray insecticides themselves, though they have their own hand-dusters. They hire laborers to do it. Three professional sprayers, a wage-earning class, in the village, are described as more or less "no good" men.[28]

One of Fu Kuei's sprayers was crippled, and his account of his work provides a graphic example of how agriculture in Taiwan has evolved into a hazardous occupation:

> Because people are afraid of being poisoned, they ask me to spray their farms. This is so-called "paying money and let others die." I can only work four or five hours a day. Otherwise, I would be poisoned. If I had a headache, I stop spraying immediately and go to the clinic for an injection. The antidote is provided free of charge by the insecticide shop. Once I was almost going to die. At six o'clock I felt unwell. I went to the clinic. The doctor was so unwilling to wake up because he received only five NT$ each time. He looked at me askance and started to rinse his mouth slowly. I couldn't bear it. I walked back home. When I arrived there I collapsed. My wife sent me to Changhua Christian Hospital. They saved me from death. The sprayers in the neighbour village are considered useless men too. One of them liked money so much that finally he was poisoned and died in the field.[29]

Fear of pesticides is one of the reasons for the increasing agitation for medical insurance by farmers and their families. And it might be noted that medical insurance was one of the main demands of the May 20, 1988, farmers' demonstration that exploded into a riot.

Industrialization and Toxification

Overuse of fertilizer and pesticides is not the only cause of the poisoning of the countryside. Taiwan's formula for balanced growth is, ironically, now a major culprit. To prevent the concentration of industries in a few urban areas and to spread employment opportunities Taiwan's planners launched, in the 1960s, an aggressive policy of encouraging manufacturers to set up shop in the countryside. The result was a substantial number of the island's 90,000 factories locating on rice fields, along waterways, and beside residences. To check the helter-skelter character of the process, the government enacted token zoning legislation in 1981 barring firms from setting up in agricultural fields. The policy, however, remained largely unenforced: of new firms established in 1984, for instance, only 2,568 out of 4,259, or about 60 percent, were located in the correct zone.[30] With three factories per square kilometer, Taiwan's rate of industrial density is 75 times that of the U.S.[31] Thus jobs may have spread out a bit more equitably, but at the price of exposing rural communities and ecosystems to uncontrolled airborne and waterborne pollution.

With their profits dependent on reducing as much cost as possible, small and medium-size establishments have largely disregarded the government's weak waste-disposal regulations and dumped industrial waste into the nearest body of water,[32] placing it directly in the food chain. Twenty percent of farm land, the government admits, is now polluted by industrial waste water.[33] Thus it is hardly surprising that, according to Edgar Lin, one of Taiwan's leading environmentalists, 30 percent of the rice grown in Taiwan is contaminated with heavy metals, including mercury, arsenic, and cadmium.[34] Tracking and isolating such poisoned stocks of grain has become a near-impossible task, a fact underlined by the disappearance in the market of twenty tons of cadmium-contaminated rice in 1988.[35]

The poisoning of waterways through the unregulated dumping of industrial waste has been compounded by the dumping of human waste, only 1 percent of which receives even primary treatment.[36] Much of this sewage flushes into the rivers, providing nutrients for the unchecked growth of microorganisms, which outcompete fish for the oxygen available in the water. This untreated sewage is probably also responsible for the fact that Taiwan has the world's highest rate of hepatitis infection.[37]

Industrial poison and human muck have severely polluted the lower reaches of virtually all of Taiwan's major rivers (see figure 12.1).[38] Like the Keelung River in northern Taiwan, many of the island's rivers are little more than flowing cesspools, devoid of fish, almost completely dead. One writer with a penchant for understatement describes the Er-Jen River as "no longer scenic." One sees "carcasses of pigs instead of fish, black oily water and yellow foul-smelling smoke rising from the stream."[39] In addition, the river is known to be contaminated with mercury and copper.[40] In Hou Jin, a small town outside the city of Kaohsiung, forty years of pollution by the Taiwan Petroleum Company has made the water not only unfit to drink but also combustible.[41]

The water pollution situation is extremely serious, yet its real magnitude will be unknown for decades. There are almost no records of the types and quantities of toxic effluents dumped into waterways during the past thirty years. Testing for contamination is difficult, as there are hundreds of possible toxic substances, some of which are dangerous to human health at minute levels. Dioxin, for example, is considered carcinogenic in parts per trillion; no labs exist in Taiwan that can measure such small quantities. Yet it can safely be assumed that the volume of toxic chemicals dumped into waterways is high, considering the industries that exist in Taiwan, which include the most heavily polluting types like leather tanning, plastics, chemicals, petroleum refining, and pesticides—and also considering that there was a total lack even of discussion of regulation of disposal practices until the 1980s, and that the Environmental Protection Administration did not come into being until 1983.

It is thus quite understandable that, surveying the situation, Shih Shin-Minh, a noted ecologist, raised the possibility that efforts to save the environment "may be too late."[42] It is also understandable that cancer, Taiwan's leading cause of death, has doubled over the last 30 years.[43]

The Lethal Loop: The Case of Aquaculture

Water pollution has become so severe that it has not only degraded the environment but it is now threatening the productive capacity of the export-oriented economy as well.

Aquaculture provides a tragic example of the self-destructive logic of unrestrained export-oriented growth. Hailed as "the success story which every country in the business is scrambling

Figure 12.1

Pollution of Rivers in Taiwan

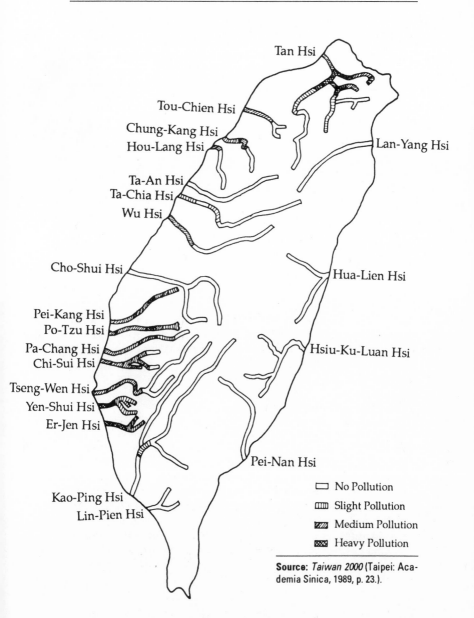

Tan Hsi

Tou-Chien Hsi

Chung-Kang Hsi
Hou-Lang Hsi

Lan-Yang Hsi

Ta-An Hsi
Ta-Chia Hsi
Wu Hsi

Cho-Shui Hsi

Hua-Lien Hsi

Pei-Kang Hsi
Po-Tzu Hsi

Pa-Chang Hsi
Chi-Sui Hsi

Hsiu-Ku-Luan Hsi

Tseng-Wen Hsi
Yen-Shui Hsi
Er-Jen Hsi

Pei-Nan Hsi

Kao-Ping Hsi
Lin-Pien Hsi

☐ No Pollution
▥ Slight Pollution
▨ Medium Pollution
▩ Heavy Pollution

Source: *Taiwan 2000* (Taipei: Academia Sinica, 1989, p. 23.).

to emulate,"[44] Taiwanese aquaculture has achieved fantastic growth rates, with prawn production, for example, increasing forty-five times in just ten years.[45] Like other industries in Taiwan, aquaculture is made up of thousands of small specialized producers dispersed throughout the country, most of them in coastal areas. These producers are precariously dependent on rivers and wells for clean, fresh water, which is fast becoming a scarce commodity. Thus, the outflow of toxic chemical wastes from upstream industries regularly results in mass deaths of shrimp and fish.

According to the *Taiwan 2000* report, "Many incidents of contamination that caused large-scale death of fish, shrimps, and oysters had been reported in 1986 and 1987. Even the lives of some consumers were threatened in some of the cases."[46] In the infamous "green oysters" incident, millions of New Taiwan dollars' worth of cultivated oysters had to be destroyed after they turned green. Local newspapers traced the contamination to upstream scrap-cable- and wire-processing factories that apparently did not have wastewater-treatment equipment.[47]

But aquaculture is both a victim and a victimizer. Intensive exploitation of groundwater has already caused severe land subsidence, in which the surface level of land actually sinks. Rice farmers from Tungkang complain that saltwater seepage into their lands from nearby aquaculture farms (which mix sea water and fresh water) reduces their yields, while other farmers complain that there is just not enough water left for their crops.[48] Aquaculture, in short, is caught in the middle of a lethal loop, destabilizing downstream ecosystems while being ravaged by upstream polluters.

Choking on Air

Taipei's air, like Seoul's, is contaminated by high levels of sulfur dioxide and nitrous dioxide. In fact, it is considered officially harmful 17 percent of the year by lenient Taiwanese standards.[49] While a pollution standard index (PSI) level of 140 to 150 is considered harmful by U.S. standards—and calls for warnings to stay indoors—the permissible level in Taiwan is PSI 170. Readings of 200 and even 300 are common, and only a reading of 400 or higher rates as hazardous.[50] Thus, it is hardly surprising that asthma cases among Taiwanese children have quadrupled over the last 10 years.[51]

Unlike in Seoul, where industries account for most pollution, 60 to 80 percent of Taipei's pollution comes from cars and motorcycles. Six thousand new cars are added to Taipei's already clogged roads each month. In fact, in June 1989 alone, 34,000 new cars and 153,000 new motorbikes came onto the roads.[52] Yet the government does not plan to require catalytic converters to filter emissions until 1994.[53] The ubiquitous motorcyclist wearing a surgical mask weaving in and out of Taipei's gridlock is becoming emblematic of the quality of life in one of the more prosperous NICs, in much the same fashion as the soldier with the gas mask symbolized life on the Western front during the First World War.

Pollution of Taiwan's air by the thousands of industrial enterprises must not, however, be underestimated. "In certain industrial zones," notes one writer, "the air is so toxic that nearby residents have grown used to living with frequent headaches, vomiting, and other painful side-effects of breathing air. No one wants to contemplate the long-term effects."[54]

The Nuclear Question

Without doubt, the greatest potential threat to the environment in Taiwan is nuclear power. Nuclear energy is seen by technocrats as an essential element in their program of high-speed growth. Taiwan now has three nuclear power plants in operation (see table 12.2). And if the technocrats had had their way, the island would have been inflicted with a plan to build twenty by the year 2000. Rising public opposition, however, has stymied the government's plans to build a fourth plant, and the growing space for democratic discussion has pushed the public to take a more critical view of the whole nuclear power program.

Nuclear Interest Groups

The same powerful nuclear interest groups that pushed through the development of nuclear energy in Korea are at work in Taiwan, notably the foreign vendors, the government–big business coalition, the technocrats, and the military. Like Korea, Taiwan proved to be a lifesaver for a U.S. nuclear industry threatened with extinction as a result of the loss of its domestic market in the late 1970s and the 1980s. With tight repression by the KMT curbing antinuclear sentiment, the nuclear monopolies were able to carve up the Taiwanese energy market. This "gentlemen's agreement" is clear from the pattern of contracts: General Electric supplied the

Table 12.2

Nuclear Power Plants in Taiwan

Power Plant	Site	Net Electricity Generated (megawatts)	Reactor Type	Reactor Supplier
Chinshan	Shihmin Hsiang			
Reactor 1		604	BWR	GE
Reactor 2		604	BWR	GE
Kuosheng	Kuosheng			
Reactor 1		948	BWR	GE
Reactor 2		948	BWR	GE
Maanshang	Maanshang			
Reactor 1		890	PWR	W
Reactor 2		890	PWR	W

Power Plant	Generator Supplier	Architect/ Engineer	Construc- tor	Initial Date of Operation
Chinshan				
Reactor 1	W	Ebasco	TPC	12/78
Reactor 2	W	Ebasco	TPC	7/79
Kuosheng				
Reactor 1	W	Bechtel	TPC	12/81
Reactor 2	W	Bechtel	TPC	3/81
Maanshang				
Reactor 1	GE	Bechtel	TPC	7/84
Reactor 2	GE	Bechtel	TPC	5/85

Source: Lien San-Lang, "On Decommissioning Nuclear Power Plants," *NATPA Bulletin* 7, no. 1 (February 1988), p. 46.

Note: BWR = boiling water reactor; PWR = pressurized water reactor; GE = General Electric (United States); W = Westinghouse (United States); TPC = Taiwan Power Company.

reactors for plants one and two, the Shihmin Hsiang and Kuo-sheng sites outside Taipei, and the generators for plant three at Maanshan. Competitor Westinghouse, meanwhile, provided the reactor for plant three and the generators for plants one and two. The San Francisco–based Bechtel Corporation provided the architectural and engineering services for plants two and three.[55]

Realpolitik entered Taiwan's nuclear equation in the fallout of the U.S. decision to cut off diplomatic relations with Taiwan and recognize the People's Republic of China. Seeking to replace severed diplomatic ties with tighter economic ones, the KMT–big-business coalition saw nuclear energy development as a way to induce prestigious U.S. corporations to increase their economic interests in Taiwan. With the nuclear vendors and other U.S. firms securely anchored in Taiwan, the KMT reasoned, the U.S. government would hesitate to cut off all military and political ties. They were right.

Taiwan's technocrats are also a natural constituency for nuclear power. Nuclear plants provide an opportunity for centralized bureaucratic control unmatched by any other energy technology: already, just three nuclear plants supply over 53 percent of the energy generated on the island. The centralization of Taiwan's energy supply is conducive to the technocrats' visions of state-guided high-speed growth. And centralized power production concentrates more economic and political power in their hands.

The commitment of Taiwan's energy technocrats to a nuclear future was underlined by Yen Chen-Hsing, chairman of the Atomic Energy Commission of the Executive Yuan, in December 1988, when he announced the long-term goal of developing small "self-made nuclear reactors." These light-water reactors, which would have one-third to one-half the power-generation capacity of imported plants, were projected as part of an effort to reduce dependence on U.S. energy multinationals through a program of "self-sufficiency in nuclear energy."[56]

The opportunity to reprocess spent fuel from reactors to make weapons-grade plutonium also made Taiwan's military, which is in perpetual competition with the Chinese Communists, a natural ally of the nuclear energy program. Two controversial incidents have highlighted the link between the "peaceful" nuclear power program and the nuclear weapons option. The most recent was the defection to the United States in 1988 of a Taiwanese colonel, Chang Hsien-Yi, who served as deputy director of the Nuclear Energy Research Institute (NERI) of the Chungshan Institute of

Science and Technology, the top military research center that is part of the Defense Ministry.[57] Identified as a CIA informant, Chang is said to have divulged information that led to U.S. pressure to demand the demolition of a secret nuclear research facility in 1987.[58] A similar incident occurred ten years earlier, when NERI was forced to destroy its nuclear waste program after a researcher provided documents to the United States.[59]

The Safety Question

Safety issues are of special concern to Taiwan because it is, together with Bangladesh, at the top of the list of the most densely populated countries in the world. Taiwanese nuclear power experts argue that the greatest threat to nuclear safety in Taiwan is not human error—the cause of both the Three Mile Island and Chernobyl disasters—but external events, such as earthquakes and typhoons.[60] Whether or not this assessment is true, the threat from natural disasters is itself strong grounds for questioning the soundness of the nuclear energy program, since Taiwan is regularly battered by typhoons, and the island lies along the so-called Pacific Fire Belt, a ring of intense tectonic and volcanic activity. Indeed, the Shihmin Hsiang and Kuosheng power plants twelve miles from Taipei are situated at the edge of the active Ta-Tun volcano group amid a maze of earthquake fault lines, according to the Center for Development Policy.[61] (See table 12.3 for information on population density around Shihmin Hsiang.)

But typhoons and earthquakes are not the only problems. The arrogant insistence by Taipower, the state energy monopoly, that no problems ever have or ever will exist at any of its plants contrasts sharply with widely published accounts of radiation leakages, accidents, and cover-ups. In July 1985 a fire at nuclear power plant number three forced the suspension of operations for fifteen months and caused $300 million in damages.[62] So alarmed were local residents that they organized meetings and rallies to demand safer emergency and evacuation plans as well as compensation for surrounding communities. The residents' actions apparently had little impact on plant officials, since another fire broke out at the same plant in August 1987.[63]

Plant number three is not the only accident-prone plant. According to one report, Taipower tried to cover up a major radiation leak at plant number one in January 1986.[64] This was apparently the second accident within a year. As one caustic account noted:

Table 12.3

Population Distribution around Nuclear Plants at Shihmin Hsiang (Chinshan 1 and 2)

Distance from Site (km)	Population within Radial Distance of Site (1973 data)	(1993 projected data)
1	215	226
2	1,756	2,147
3	4,832	5,991
4	6,182	7,679
5	11,129	13,864
10	43,781	56,515
20	282,473	453,470
30	2,785,904	3,876,840
40	3,599,731	4,991,167

Source: North American Taiwanese Professors' Association Task Force on Taiwan Nuclear Power Plant, "A Review of Probabilistic Risk Assessment and Reactor Safety in Taiwan," *NATPA Bulletin* 7, no. 1 (February 1988), p. 17.

Over 1985 and 1986, Taipower's No. 1 nuclear plant set a world record for continuous operation, 418 days without a shutdown....In March of this year local newspapers accused No. 1 plant of setting another world record, 56 days of continuous radiation leakage outside plant—from September 3 to October 28, 1985. Taipower denied the charge, but Taipower's credibility is at a low ebb right now.[65]

And the list goes on. In February 1988 a generator at the number one plant shut down automatically for unknown reasons, later discovered to be a computer error.[66] Two fuel pellets were stolen from the number three plant, then found a few days later.[67] Plant repair logs are sometimes incomplete or missing altogether.[68] Perhaps not unrelated to these mishaps is the inadequate training of plant personnel: 40 percent of Taipower's nuclear plant operators are reported to be unlicensed.[69] In the meantime, many of the best-trained nuclear operators are said to be recruited by U.S. firms and transferred to the United States.[70]

Most reports of plant safety violations are reported by nuclear plant workers who are upset by the dangerous working conditions. In May 1988 two hundred maintenance workers at plant number one walked through a puddle of radioactive water that the plant manager knew was there.[71] One Taipower engineer filed a lawsuit charging that exposure to radiation made him ill, but lost the case because pertinent records were found missing.[72]

There is a surreal quality to Taipower's record and plans in the area of radioactive waste disposal. Children in Taoyuan, near Taipei, played for weeks on a pile of scrap metal near their elementary school before it was discovered that it was radioactive.[73] Parts of nuclear power plants exposed to intense radiation that were replaced were said to have been sold as scrap metal, then recycled into metal for new buildings.[74] To store low-level waste, Taipower built an underground low-level waste depository on Lan Yu, or Orchid Island, which lies forty miles from Taiwan's southeast tip. Lan Yu, it so happens, lies on an earthquake fault line. Despite protests by the Yami aborigines who inhabit the place, Taipower plans to build a second low-level waste dump on the lush nine-square-mile island—plus a 247-acre national park above the dump, including a hall with exhibits for tourists extolling the virtues of nuclear energy.[75]

Long-term storage of spent fuel is even more problematic. Currently, spent fuel is stored at the reactor sites. But this is only temporary; a location must be found that can hold the materials for the hundreds of thousands of years that they emit deadly radiation. No viable solution, except perhaps shipping the waste out of Taiwan, may ever be found, if we are to believe one expert:

> Taiwan is an extremely densely populated island. It is virtually impossible to find a site which would be remote enough that a long-lived radio-nuclide can be isolated from the human environment. In addition, because Taiwan is a small island, marine life is a vital part of human resource. Therefore, the ocean surrounding Taiwan and all the nearby small islands are virtually an integral part of human environment. In other words, small islands outside of Taiwan, no matter how small their present population, cannot be considered "remote."...Due to its extremely active tectonics, Taiwan has a very complex geology. It is difficult to find a basaltic or shale formation that is continuous, homogeneous, stable, and big enough to

accommodate high-level wastes. Last, but not least, Taiwan's subtropical weather conditions call for special attention on studying hydrological (both surface and underground) problems.[76]

The Growth of the Environmental Movement

The stubborn effort of Taiwan's technocrats to ram through the building of more nuclear plants, despite Chernobyl and Three Mile Island, has unwittingly spawned a strong antinuclear movement. A key event was a well-publicized seminar sponsored by the Consumers' Foundation in April 1985, which brought together a number of scholars and intellectuals opposed to the building of the fourth nuclear power plant. The fledgling antinuclear sentiment sparked by this meeting was boosted shortly thereafter by the July 1985 fire at plant number three and the Chernobyl meltdown in April 1986. A grass roots anti–nuclear power movement was born, evolving much along the decentralized pattern of antinuclear movements in the advanced industrial countries. This network of antinuclear self-help associations has so far successfully stymied the construction of plant number four, leading a frustrated Taipower to hire the British public relations firm Ogilvy and Mather to promote nuclear power to an increasingly skeptical public.

The antinuclear movement, however, is just one prong of a broader environmental movement. Aside from forcing the suspension of the fourth nuclear power plant, this decentralized but increasingly powerful movement has stopped the construction of a $160 million titanium dioxide plant by Du Pont Corporation and forced the closing of a major petrochemical plant owned by the British ICI Corporation, which fishermen had accused of dumping acid waste in their fishing grounds.[77] Averaging one antipollution demonstration per day during 1987–88,[78] the movement represents the rejection by increasing numbers of Taiwanese of the KMT's technocratic pursuit of growth at any cost.

The main outlets for public outrage have been demonstrations and civil disobedience, since no institutional framework exists within the government for citizen participation in environmental planning and decision making. Even the formation of special-interest groups was effectively outlawed by the martial law decree of 1949, which included the formidably named Law Governing the Organization of Civic Bodies during the Extraordinary Period.

This law remained in effect until January 20, 1989,[79] even though martial law itself ended in the summer of 1987.

Hemmed in by tough political restrictions, it is not surprising that the environmental movement began in the early 1980s as a conservation movement stressing the preservation of wilderness areas and beautiful or spectacular natural sites. Made up of a loose alliance of concerned scholars, journalists, and government officials, the conservation movement was able to stir public consciousness through the press, which reported on its activities with more freedom than it did on explicitly antigovernment political events.[80] Surprisingly, victories were registered, like halting a planned cross-highland highway that would have opened up one of Taiwan's few remaining wilderness areas and stopping the planned damming of Toroko Gorge, "a geological wonder of world class proportions."[81]

Even before the July 1987 lifting of martial law, however, the movement was moving from conservation to confrontation. In 1986, citizens in Taichung spontaneously formed a committee to shut down a chemical plant that was polluting the county. They succeeded, providing inspiration for the citizens of neighboring Changhua County, who sought to stop a stronger foe, Du Pont, from pushing through a plan to build a titanium dioxide plant. Surprisingly, the Changhua Anti-Pollution Association was able to suspend what would have been the single largest foreign-investment venture in Taiwan's history, one which enjoyed the full backing of the KMT government.[82]

Since the lifting of martial law, neighborhood antipollution committees have proliferated. Targeting mainly the pollution-intensive petrochemical industry, grass roots environmentalists have employed confrontational tactics and direct action, with notable success. For instance, when negotiations failed to persuade management to stop dumping hazardous waste that was killing their fishing industry, 2,000 residents of villages near the Linyuan Petrochemical Industrial Zone occupied the complex, shutting down all eighteen factories. Faced with losses of NT$800 million a day, management agreed to the residents' demands for clean-up and compensation.[83]

In response to the popular protests, the government set up the Environmental Protection Administration (EPA) in 1987. It soon became clear, however, that the 900-person EPA had no teeth. In no case was this more evident than in that of the Chungchou waste treatment plant in Kaohsiung. A chlorine leak in March 1990 sent

1,400 people to the hospital. But it was only after 400 residents stormed the facility a few weeks later that the authorities moved—not to shut down the plant but to levy a small fine of $5,800.[84] In another instance, the authorities allowed a battery-recycling firm to stay open for months, even after a study discovered that half of its employees had contracted lead poisoning and kindergarten children nearby had developed mental disorders. In ten years, only ten plants have been shut down. Those that receive citations from the EPA often ignore the fine and go on polluting.[85]

Given this dismal history of enforcement, it is not surprising that many Taiwanese increasingly feel that only direct action brings results. As Michael Hsiao notes:

> People in Taiwan have learned that protesting brings results; most of the actions for which we could find out the results had achieved their objectives. The polluting factories were either forced to make immediate improvement of the conditions or pay compensation to the victims. Some factories were even forced to shut down or move to another location. A few preventive actions have even succeeded in forcing prospective plants to withdraw from their planned construction.[86]

Environment versus Growth

This decentralized, multiclass, grass roots movement has thus evolved as the most effective challenger to the model of high-speed, export-oriented growth espoused by the KMT and business elite. And while spontaneous in their origins, many environmental groups are allied with the opposition Democratic Progressive party (DPP), which chose green as its party color, linking the issues of democracy and the environment. Lately this cleavage has been expressed most sharply in the controversy over the construction of petrochemical plants, particularly the fifth and sixth naphtha crackers, which would provide petrochemical feedstocks to 30,000 downstream factories.[87]

Government and business propaganda painted the factories as essential to meet a 10 percent shortfall in petrochemical raw materials in the near term, which could increase to 30 percent if one of the plants was not built according to schedule. Relocating the naphtha crackers abroad, went the KMT-business line, would reduce Taiwan's economic growth by 1 percent per year, with

many midstream petrochemical processors forced to move overseas as well.[88]

Such arguments were beginning to sound less and less credible
to citizens. A 1985 survey showed that 59 percent of respondents
favored environmental protection over economic growth.[89]
Stymied by continuing citizen protests, the petrochemical companies have begun to locate elsewhere: Formosa Plastics is considering China as the site for its naphtha cracker; USI Far East has
chosen the Philippines; and Du Pont is setting up its titanium
dioxide plant in Korea, after some strong-arming of the government there by Washington.

Through its militant mass actions, the environmental movement is bringing home the message that a radical transformation
of Taiwan's priorities is in order. Such token measures as the
establishment of an Environmental Protection Administration are
no longer sufficient, say the critics. The economic growth rate must
be radically lowered. The controversial *Taiwan 2000* report asserts
that even if the annual rate of Taiwan's GNP growth were cut to
6.5 percent, stresses on Taiwan's already fragile environment
would double by the year 2000.[90]

Will this perilous prospect prove ultimately persuasive to the
KMT technocrats? Some Taiwanese environmentalists are skeptical, for they feel that there is more to the conflict than the clash of
contrasting visions of Taiwan's future between the largely
Taiwanese environmentalists and the largely mainlander KMT
elite. According to Hsu Shen-Shu, founder of the New Housewives Association, which has forged links between the emerging
feminist and environmental movements:

> Current policymakers do not love this place as their
> home since they still operate under the myth of re-
> turning to the Mainland and have not changed their
> basic opinion of Taiwan as a temporary stop, a hotel
> of sorts. After benefitting from the exploitation of the
> island, they send their children to the States because
> it's too polluted here in Taiwan.[91]

13

The Challenge from Labor

A s in Korea, cheap labor has been the secret of the successful export-oriented industrialization in Taiwan. Labor continues to provide Taiwan's competitive edge. The problem, from the point of view of the state-business elite, is that Taiwanese labor is no longer cheap. Taiwan and South Korea are running neck and neck in terms of labor cost in strategic industries. While the average hourly wage of Korean electronics workers in 1989 was $2.45, compared with Taiwanese workers' $2.31, Taiwanese textile workers were making $3.56 an hour to their Korean counterparts' $2.87.[1]

Nor does Taiwanese labor remain docile. While Taiwanese workers do not yet display the insurgent behavior of the Koreans, their behavior of late appears to be motivated more by class resentments than Confucian deference to capital.

Female Labor and Competitive Advantage

When Taiwan turned from a domestic market–directed, import-substitution industrial program to an export-oriented manufacturing strategy in the mid-1960s, cheap labor provided the edge, even among the NICs. Thus in 1972, the wages for unskilled labor were $45 a month in Taiwan, $68 in South Korea, $60 in Singapore, $82 in Hong Kong, and $120 in Japan. For skilled workers, the wage rates were, respectively, $73, $102, $183, $122, and $272.[2]

A big portion of this labor force was recruited from the 2 million people, mainly young women and men, that flooded the cities in the period 1952–85. Indeed, about 47 percent of the increase in the manufacturing labor force from the 1950s to the 1970s is attributed to the rural exodus.[3]

As in Korea, a key characteristic of the rapid industrialization process in Taiwan was women's high rate of participation in the formal work force. The doubling of the work force between the early 1950s and the early 1970s was due to the "rapid entry of females into the labor force at the same time males remained in school for longer periods and entered the labor force at an older age."[4] In just three years, the female participation rate rose from 35 percent in 1971 to 40 percent in 1974.[5]

Women workers, most of them fifteen to twenty-four years old, were tracked particularly into the export-processing zones established to attract foreign investment with tariff exemptions, tax holidays, and above all cheap labor. In the early 1980s, 85 percent of the work force in Taiwan's three export-processing zones (EPZs) was female.[6]

Low wages were, of course, the prime attraction of female labor. Thus, in the 1970s—the takeoff years of Taiwan's labor-intensive manufacturing industry—the average female wage was 62 percent of the average male wage, though men and women worked largely the same hours.[7] According to the *Investors' Guide* published by the EPZ administration in the early 1980s, the salaries of women workers were fixed at a rate 10 to 20 percent lower than salaries of men workers doing comparable work.[8]

Factors besides low wages contributed to the attraction of the female labor force. Among other reasons cited by employers were that women were more temperamentally suited to tedious, repetitive work than men; that women had the manual dexterity or nimble fingers required for textile work and electronics assembly; and that women were less likely to rebel than men. As one personnel manager of an electronics-assembly plant in the Kaohsiung Export Processing Zone commented, "This job was done by boys two or three years ago. But we found that girls do the job as well and don't make trouble like the boys. They're obedient and pay attention to orders. So our policy is to hire all girls."[9] Other zone managers told one researcher that men "lack the manual dexterity of women, and are often a source of trouble in the factory."[10] Thus while there were "extremely high" unemployment rates for men with blue-collar qualifications, thousands of low-wage, "manageable" young women were being tracked into the export-oriented industries.[11]

Low wages, achieved through reliance on female labor, provided the margin of profit that made investment in Taiwan so attractive to the multinational firms: between 1953 and 1973, average labor productivity went up by 8 percent per year, while real wages increased by only 4 percent annually.[12]

As in South Korea, proletarianization—more rapid than that which had taken place in many countries that industrialized earlier—was painful. Perhaps the best description of the quality of labor-management relations comes from analyst George Fitting:

> Inadequate and unenforced labor laws have led to the flourishing of a system in which the worker is exploited. The wage structure of the factories makes performance bonuses an important part of the salary, but bonuses can be withheld for the slightest infraction of factory rules. This gives management substantial leverage over workers. In addition, the bonus system has been manipulated by management to provide a means of reducing labor costs when business is slow. During lull periods, management often "docks pay on any available occasion in order to adjust expenditures on labor inputs."[13]

To cut wage costs even further, a favorite tactic of employers was to lay off workers just before they were due for end-of-the-year bonuses or retirement pay.[14]

Low wages and insecure employment were accompanied by hazardous working conditions. In the late 1970s, Taiwan had the highest rate of workers killed in factory accidents in the world—0.26 per 1,000 workers,[15] and insurance against occupational injuries was nonexistent. In the electronics-assembly factories, eye ailments and deteriorating eyesight were a byproduct of intense microscope work. Women endured literally sweatshop conditions, as the following account at an asbestos-weaving factory at Kaohsiung reveals:

> The company has a two-shift system. We work at day one week, at night the next. I don't feel well during the night shift, so I keep getting thinner and thinner. We must wear caps over our hair, cotton face masks, and uniforms. Your whole body gets covered with asbestos fluff all the same. There is no air conditioning, and in the summer you are sweaty and sticky over your whole body. The company says they can't put in air conditioning because the fiber is too damp and the air conditioners would get clogged anyway. There are a few vacuum tubes around the machines to remove

the fiber dust, but not enough. Working in a weaving factory is really unpleasant.[16]

Near the export-processing zones, women workers lived in barracks that were euphemistically called dormitories. As one analyst commented, "the dormitories remind one of the living conditions in 19th century Manchester." He continued:

One dorm contains 1000 girls. Each room accommo- dates 14 people and is outfitted with a little desk, a chair, and a narrow formica platform on which to sleep. The dorm, like the factory, does not have central air conditioning or heating, even though the summers reach a humid 100°F and winters drop to near freez- ing. Drinking water is not provided.[17]

As in Korea, a system of production evolved in which a male managerial hierarchy and white-collar aristocracy lorded over a female blue-collar work force. Among other things, this created a social situation ripe for sexual exploitation. Competition for scarce male partners was a source of tension among the women.[18] But even more tragic was the way the situation encouraged prostitu- tion. As one Presbyterian minister told Richard Kagan, at the Kaohsiung Export Processing Zone, "every evening foremen and managers from the EPZ, along with many shopkeepers and busi- nessmen from town, will drive up to the dorms in cars and motorcycles and pick up a bored, lonely, and overworked woman for an evening of pleasure."[19] In the late 1970s, alongside photo- graphy shops and pharmacies across the street from the women's dormitory in Kaohsiung there were abortion clinics—grim re- minders of the perils of what passed for social life at the EPZ.[20]

For many, in fact, work became a trap in more than a physical sense. Uprooted from their families and alone in the big cities, female workers were seen as somehow immoral and loose by a society that defined the role of women in terms of marriage and family. But the irony was that family pressure itself contributed to the women's being stuck on the treadmill. Linda Arrigo found that 20 percent of the women workers she was studying reported being pressured by their families to postpone marriage in order to keep contributing to the family finances.[21] Family pressure combined with the lack of a normal setting for meeting men to push many beyond the so-called marriageable age and into a forlorn future:

This sense of passing time with nothing to show for it is prevalent...among women who have reached the age of 26 or so but have no marriage prospects. Especially for the latter, the future in industrial employment is inevitable and bleak. Their income is not sufficient for a comfortable single life, and they are increasingly alienated from their natal families as time passes.

From the life histories...it is apparent that industrial employment partially liberates young women from paternalistic control and provides a refuge of sorts for those women disadvantaged in the traditional society, e.g., adopted daughters and divorced women. But the traditional society does not provide a social role for the growing numbers of unmarried women past customary marriage age, and it is likely they will continue to pass their personal lives isolated and hidden in dormitories and rented rooms, but continually subject to social censure.[22]

Barriers to Class Consciousness

Despite intense exploitation, the spread of working-class consciousness and the growth of organized labor was not rapid in the first two decades of high-speed industrialization. Several factors of a structural, cultural, and political character stood in the way of effective labor organizing.

For one thing, the bulk of labor was dispersed throughout Taiwan's small industries. More than 90 percent of Taiwan's 90,000 industrial enterprises were companies with fewer than thirty employees,[23] and an estimated 80 percent of the labor population was found in such firms.[24] Another structural factor that diluted working-class consciousness was the spread of rural industries, especially during the 1970s, which created "part-time proletarians," workers who held part-time industrial jobs while still earning part of their income as small farmers.

Also slowing down labor organizing were the strong familial relationships that cut across the class cleavage. In Taiwan and in Chinese society as a whole, family and kinship networks, assert Kuo Tai-Chun and Ramon Myers, "perform diverse functions and depend on highly personal ties of trust and reciprocity in which favors and assistance are mutually bestowed and received in local as well as broad spatial settings."[25] The family firm, for instance, is the predominant form of enterprise organization, accounting for an estimated 97.4 percent of all Taiwanese-owned firms.[26] What this meant was that, in a broad sense, a large sector of Taiwan's industrial workers "did not constitute a self-producing class, but were the daughters and sons of small farm-firm families."[27] The salience of the community and family network was further revealed in the fact that some 70–75 percent of migrants to Taiwan's urban areas found their jobs through relatives and friends, while new factories in rural areas typically relied on neighborhood labor.[28]

Aside from fostering strong dependency ties between employer and employee, family entrepreneurship provided an alternative goal for workers to aspire to. Reflecting on his experience in a small Taiwan factory, anthropologist Richard Stites asserts that many of his coworkers viewed factory work as "a temporary part in a career and a means to eventual entrepreneurship," leading them to have "little interest in unions" and to be "less likely to see matters exclusively from a workers' perspective."[29]

Even in the big-factory, transnational-dominated sector, the strong bonds of kinship contributed to slowing the development of working-class consciousness, especially among the young female labor on which this sector was highly dependent. Aside from their socialization to submissiveness, women workers were prevented from militant action by the heavy responsibilities they bore as breadwinners for their families of origin. As Susan Greenhalgh noted:

> Far from being the nucleus of the dynamic, affluent, influential transnational kernel...these women are relatively impotent members of the male-controlled families which are the units of income accumulation in Taiwan society. For these women, "worker" is a brief transitional role in their individual life cycles which intervenes between the roles of student, and wife and mother. Female factory labor is a strategy not for individual, but for family advancement, and female factory incomes belong to the family.[30]

But no matter how influential these factors were in slowing down the emergence of class solidarity, still the main barriers to the rise of working-class consciousness and organization were strong employer resistance and the KMT.

Until just a few years ago, government surveillance and the strong threat of repression were central mechanisms employed for labor control. For instance, in transnational corporations, management worked directly with the security offices, or branches of government security agencies within the factories. A big foreign corporation, researcher Linda Arrigo found out, was required to provide the salaries and offices for four to five security officers, virtually all of whom "are mainland Chinese and are loyal, not merely nominal, members of the ruling party."[31]

Employers have thwarted working-class organization in other ways. One of the most common has been preemptive unionizing, which means organizing a management-controlled union before an independent union can come into being. This makes it impossible for an independent union to emerge, since the law allows only one union per enterprise. If the emergence of an independent union cannot be prevented, notes Hsu Cheng-Kuang,

> The employer can use any excuse to discharge the active union organizer or to transfer the organizer to a job which is always worse than the original one. Furthermore, the employer often intervenes in the union election process in order to establish a union board dominated by management representatives. Finally, the employer can regulate the union activities by donating...to the union revenue.[32]

The most effective medium of control, however, is the KMT. Unlike the situation in South Korea, there exists in Taiwan a grass roots political machine that is able both to dominate the working class and to incorporate it into the structure of power. A monopoly on political power enabled the KMT to impose severe restrictions on organizing, like the Labor Union Law, which prohibits unions in workplaces with fewer than thirty employees—or almost 80 percent of the work force. Strikes, which were banned under martial law, continue to be illegal despite some revision of the Labor Disputes Law.[33]

The KMT state is a corporatist state—that is, it has prevented the emergence of independent communal and sectoral organizations by integrating the various interest groups into centrally controlled and vertically structured associations. Rather than oppose unionism frontally, the KMT set up a structure of formal union representation that served essentially as a means of tight control from the top, a system that labor expert Wu Nai-Teh labels "exclusionary corporatism."[34] This system consists of a three-tiered national union structure. Only one union is allowed at one enterprise, and all enterprise unions are combined into a provincial federation. The provincial federations are then linked together at the national-level Chinese Federation of Labor. Direct horizontal ties across enterprises, trades, and areas are banned.[35]

KMT control over the unions begins at a very basic level: formation of a union must have the approval of both the local labor department of the government and the local KMT committee. Moreover, the KMT decides who can be selected and appointed a union officer. A succinct account of the dynamics of this system of demobilization is provided by Hsu Cheng-Kuang:

> A carefully controlled system of cooptation is designed to reward "cooperative" union leaders selectively. The KMT party organization not only controls the access to the union posts, they can also easily send their nominated labor candidates to the seats in the legislature and national assembly through the sector constituency seats in the national election. Since the KMT see the labor organization as part of the state system, passive individuals who support the government labor policy are most likely to be appointed and selected as union officers.[36]

To deflect working-class energy from militant unionism, the KMT has channelled unions into such activities as providing social and recreational services for their members; setting up vocational education programs; assisting KMT efforts to dispel its bad international image as a violator of labor rights; mobilizing workers to vote for KMT candidates in local and national elections; and drafting labor legislation that amounted to mere window dressing.[37]

The KMT-business alliance was able to ensure that as of 1987, there existed only 2,471 unions, covering of 1.9 million workers, or a scant 23 percent of the labor force.[38] In 1984, according to one account, there were only 282 collective agreements between workers and employees, and these "were only documents consisting of restatements of employees' rights provided by present laws."[39] A fair summary of the ineffectiveness of unions is unwittingly presented by the official publication *Industry of Free China*:

> In a survey conducted...in 1979, no [sic] one employer in the sample acknowledged any impact of collective agreement on his/her personnel practices such as recruiting, training, promotion, wage determination,

and reduction of workforce. Unions were not active in grievance handling either. A study showed that of the 120 unions in the export processing zones...less than half (47.6 percent) of the unions handled the cases on behalf of their members. Thirty-eight percent would get involved only if employees had failed to reach a settlement through their own effort. Others just referred the cases to government officers for handling....Another survey showed that employers handled 71 percent of employees' grievances themselves; unions were involved in 11 percent of the cases, and the rest were settled by government officers....Other labor relations activities, such as the functioning of a factory council (i.e., workers' council), which is required by Chapter 10 of the Factory Law, were found in only 7 percent of the unions in the export processing zones.[40]

Where workers did persist in pushing their case, they could theoretically place disputes under arbitration by the county government. However, as one account put it, "Labor representatives may go into negotiations with the best of intentions, but their bargaining position is not strong. The fact that military police and Taiwan Garrison Command representatives are frequently present does little to steel their spirits."[41]

A Rude Awakening

Managed unionism and outright repression have, however, failed to quell Taiwan's workers. The number of labor disputes admitted by the government rose from 15 in 1965 to 485 in 1975 and 1,622 in 1985 (see table 13.1).[42] Between 1985 and 1987—that is, even before the lifting of martial law in July 1987— over 4,540 labor disputes went into arbitration in district courts.[43]

Behind such figures were courageous instances of organizing in the teeth of a martial law ban on strikes in one of the world's most effective police states. In 1974 workers went on strike at the U.S. firm General Instruments; identified by the union leadership and secret police, the leaders of the strike were dismissed.[44] But there were successful cases of defiance by bold leadership. In 1977, independent candidates won the union elections at the Far East Textile Company, giving birth to Taiwan's first free union.[45] In the early 1980s unions independent of the KMT successfully blocked

Table 13.1

Labor Disputes in Taiwan, 1965–1986

Cause of Dispute	1965	1975	1980	1984	1985	1986
Dismissals	1	150	122	263	447	234
Severance	9	79	93	273	375	47
Wages	0	97	184	278	328	972
Injuries	2	42	105	90	111	138
Other	3	90	197	250	361	194
Total number of disputes	15	485	700	1,154	1,622	1,458
Overall number of persons involved	295	16,809	6,065	9,761	16,517	11,308

Source: Hsu Cheng-Kuang, "Political Change and the Labor Movement in Taiwan" (Paper prepared for the Eighty-fourth Annual Meeting of the American Sociological Association, San Francisco, August 9–13, 1989), p. 14.

management plans to lay off workers and change work rules at such U.S.-owned firms as Timex, Waring, and Warner Electronics.[46] In another case in the early 1980s, laid-off workers of a large U.S. petrochemical firm staged a sit-in at the company headquarters (unheard-of behavior till then), confronted the chairman of the corporation, and eventually won severance pay considerably in excess of the legal minimum that the company initially offered.[47] But perhaps the most successful workers' actions were those that hit Columbia Electronics in 1981 and the Hsinchu Glass Works in 1985. At the U.S.-owned Columbia plant, the owners' plan to divest provoked 1,000 workers to take over the plant; they turned it over to local shareholders only after they received back pay and got firm assurances that the plant would remain open under new management.[48]

At the Hsinchu Glass Works, which was threatened with bankruptcy on account of embezzlement by its owners, workers took over management, ousted the old company union, and—in the face of KMT-backed efforts by the new board of directors to retake the company—have run the firm since 1985.[49] Learning from previous examples of direct action, the Hsinchu workers marched to the prime minister's office in Taipei and successfully obtained the cabinet's permission to elect a temporary management committee, which has run the firm at a profit since then.[50]

In 1984 the KMT government decreed a number of sweeping changes in the Labor Standards Law, which stipulated, among other things, an eight-hour working day, fixed overtime payments, year-end bonuses, severance pay, and medical insurance coverage for workers and their families. Great on paper, these reforms were not designed to be seriously enforced. Moreover, they were not enough to elect the KMT candidates to the seats reserved for labor in the National Assembly and the legislative Yuan in the elections of December 1986. The stunning victories of DPP candidates served notice to the KMT that labor was entering a new, more independent phase.

Several developments in the 1980s contributed to labor's growing clout.

First, with export-oriented growth continuing at some 8 to 10 percent annually and the surplus of rural labor drying up, a labor shortage gathered in severity in the late 1970s and early 1980s. Indeed, a 1977 survey revealed that labor turnover was almost 50 percent, and the most common reason given for leaving a position was change of job.[51] The ability of workers to vote with their feet made employers more receptive to workers' demands for higher wages, greater autonomy in organizing, and more respect. By the late 1970s, labor costs were rising at 15–20 percent per year.[52]

Second, there had emerged what Michael Hsiao calls the "second generation of workingclass."[53] "This new proletariat," claimed one labor specialist, was "no longer of recent rural origins and with conservative and rural values. They have had longer urban-industrial life and higher educational backgrounds. With these backgrounds, they are more conscious of their legitimate rights and tend to be active in employing collective actions to protest the unfair practices in the workplace and the government policies."[54]

Third, there was a growing sense among workers that while businessmen were making money hand over fist, they were missing out on Taiwan's wealth. As Ford union director Liu Hsing-Hung complained, "Look, we work hard for nine hours a day, but housewives make much more money than we do by playing the stock market. Why shouldn't we get a share of the profits?"[55]

These feelings in fact reflected objective realities. In the 1980s the growth of manufacturing wages failed to keep pace with the growth of other incomes. This was reflected in worsening income distribution: in 1978 the lowest-paid 40 percent of the population received 22.6 percent of the national income; by 1986 this was down to 21.8 percent. The top 20 percent, on the other hand, increased their share from 37.1 percent of income to 38.2 percent (see table 13.2).[56] As upsetting to the public as growing inequality was the concentration of income at the top. Two researchers discovered that "five Taiwan billionaires have more net wealth in total than 11 billionaires in Japan." The richest Taiwanese family, they pointed out, had three times the net wealth of the richest Japanese billionaire.[57]

A growing housing problem was one of the manifestations of the growing social crisis, as uncontrolled speculation on land by the rich drove up housing prices. "Many ordinary people," noted the *Financial Times*, "can no longer afford to buy a home unless they play the markets successfully. A state bank employee on a salary of NT$70,000 [US$2,592] a month would not earn enough in a lifetime to buy one of the new two-bedroom apartments selling for NT$40 million [US$148,148] in eastern Taipei."[58] Indeed, it is reported that a three-bedroom apartment with less than 1,000 square feet can easily come to US$400,000[59]—considerably above the current rates in San Francisco, California. As a result, the 1980s property boom is said to have placed home ownership beyond the reach of an estimated 21 percent of the population.[60]

Fourth, labor benefited from the political liberalization that gathered steam from the mid-1980s on, and from synergistic interaction with the political opposition, the consumers' movement, and the powerful environmental movement. Moreover, to counter the appeal to labor from the opposition Democratic Progressive Party and the Labor Party, sectors within the KMT pushed the party to establish a greater distance from the employers, allowing workers to take advantage of growing fissures within the government party to push through their demands for wage raises and other benefits.

Not to be discounted was a fifth factor: the international pressure exerted by the AFL-CIO and labor rights organizations in Washington, which successfully lobbied Congress for a law that would require the administration to drop tariff privileges accorded under the General System of Preferences (GSP) for countries that violate the rights of their workers. While the AFL-CIO's aim was hardly altruistic—it sought to prevent the further loss of

Table 13.2

Income Distribution, 1978–1986

Income Group	Share of Income (%)		
	1978	1982	1986
Lowest 20%	8.89	8.69	8.30
Second-lowest 20%	13.71	13.80	13.51
Middle 20%	17.53	17.56	17.38
Mid-upper 20%	22.70	22.68	22.65
Upper 20%	37.17	37.27	38.16
Ratio of highest to lowest group	4.18	4.29	4.60

Source: Simon Long, *Taiwan to 1993: Politics Versus Prosperity,* Special Report No. 1159 (London: Economist Intelligence Unit, 1989), p. 54.

U.S. manufacturing jobs by capital flight to low-wage areas like Taiwan—the annual AFL-CIO testimony at the office of the U.S. Trade Representative helped focus world attention on the condition of Taiwanese workers and elicited strong pressures worldwide on the KMT.

Accumulated resentments finally broke out after the lifting of the 38-year-old martial law in the summer of 1987. Over 2,900 labor disputes were registered in 1987 and 1988, involving close to 39,000 workers.[61] The struggle for year-end bonuses—essential for Chinese New Year festivities—became the focus of strike activity in the winter of 1987-88. Employees in thirty-two companies launched "quickie" strikes for higher bonuses, making the point that Taiwan's entrepreneurs were rolling in cash. Labor's potential power was demonstrated in two events that followed. On Labor Day (May 1) of 1988, eighteen hundred members of the independent Railroad Engineers' Association walked off their jobs and shut down the island's entire railroad system for one whole day. And in August 1988 the bus drivers of Miaoli staged a twenty-three-day strike. Since strikes were still technically illegal, the railroad engineers called their action a "mass vacation" and the Miaoli drivers labeled theirs an "extended union meeting."[62]

Independent unionism was boosted when the independent Labor Union Alliance won 70 percent of official positions, at the expense of the KMT candidates, at the strategic Taiwan Petroleum Workers' Union in March 1988.[63] Many independent candidates also won in elections at the key Nan-Ya Plastics Company, Taiwan Electric Company, and Postal Workers' Union.[64] Another milestone towards independent unionism was achieved with the formation in May 1988 of the Federation of Independent Labor Unions by twelve key independent unions representing about 12,000 workers.[65]

An even greater upsurge of labor militance occurred at the end of 1988, when 156 disputes over bonuses were registered. These were but a prelude to a year of bitter strikes: 300 workers closed down Nestle's Taiwan subsidiary in Hsinchu and barricaded the foreign managers in their offices overnight after the company shut down a coffee plant. One of the largest chemical suppliers of Taiwan's plastics industry, Taita Chemical, was struck by its 200 workers and brought to court for violation of the Labor Standards Law.[66] Wildcat strikes at Ford Motor Company's Taiwan subsidiary forced Ford to turn over a bonus amounting to 5 percent of profits—a fixed percentage that was reportedly included in the first collective agreement that the company concluded with union members.[67]

In the struggles against the firms, the workers followed a sophisticated strategy of justifying strikes as a means to compel firms to live up to the provisions of the 1984 Labor Standards Law. As Lou Mei-Wen, one of the country's most respected organizers, put it, "The capitalists themselves violate the law. But the courts cannot punish them. So by going on strike we compel them to follow the law. Strikes are reasonable."[68] By taking this stand, workers were able to increasingly drive a wedge in the once-solid KMT-employer alliance. The fact that local officials were delegated by a new law to arbitrate and decide labor disputes gave even more leverage to workers, since with the liberalization of the political system, local officials now depended on workers' votes to get elected. Thus in two of Taiwan's recent major labor conflicts, the government was forced into either a neutral role or a pro-labor role at critical points. When Nestle's foreign managers were barricaded by workers in Hsinchu, goes one account, "the managers' pleas to the authorities to rescue them elicited little response."[69] At the bitter strike at Taita Chemical Company, management in fact accused the government of "taking a pro-labor attitude."[70]

Nonetheless, workers were keeping up the pressure on the authorities to liberalize the Labor Standards Law. "Unions are still repressed by the existing law," asserted Lou Mei-Wen. "There are too many conditions placed on the right to strike and the law does not give government officials the power to punish capitalists who violate the law."[71] This pressure created even greater conflict in the ranks of the KMT. For instance, the KMT government's Council for Labor Affairs proposed to legalize strikes if half the workers agreed to the action, but the Ministry of Economic Affairs, backing the employers, refused the move.

Greater worker militance pushed manufacturing wages up by 60 percent between 1986 and 1989.[72] However, the KMT and management were more alarmed by the fact that labor's concerns went beyond wage issues. Indeed, as in Korea, the thrust of labor activism has been to challenge the economic and political foundations of the regime itself:

> First, labor's demands were far-ranging, calling not only for wage increases but also for union autonomy, fair labor practices, reform of current labor laws, and liberalization of management's authoritarian style. While the demonstrations initially began in the large industries, they increasingly spread to smaller companies, implying that the problems were not simply bread and butter issues, but went to the heart of the corporatist regime and authoritarian paternalism which has characterized Taiwan's industrial relations over the past decades.
>
> Second, union democracy became an overwhelmingly dominant issue in the recent strife. In most cases, the more independent union members challenged the representativeness and legitimacy of the union leaders, by accusing the latter of being controlled by the company, and [being an] "outer force" from the KMT. This basic "democracy" problem was a result of long-term interference of the management and the KMT in the union activities, by using the union simply as an instrument for facilitating industrial peace and political stability rather than as an autonomous representative organization of the working class.[73]

Conclusion

Though less spectacular than Korea's labor upsurge in the same period, Taiwan's working class was following a militant course after being excluded for so long from meaningful control of their life-chances. Having been excluded from the process of determining the direction of economic development, workers did not feel they had a stake in the future of high-speed export-oriented growth. Government and business exhortations to temper wage demands to preserve export competitiveness were regarded by workers as simply another trick to deprive them of what was rightfully due to them after thirty years of exploitation, deprivation, and repression. And as democratization unfolded, public debate did not dwell on how to keep up the dynamism of an economic model that was entering into crisis but focused on how the benefits of past growth would be distributed among competing social groups.

Despite all the academic talk about familism in labor-management relations and workers' Confucian deference to their superiors, the political decompression since 1987 has clearly revealed that the main bond between workers and management during Taiwan's growth decades was essentially the repressive one: KMT control. Given this past, creating a new relationship built on consensus and negotiation will be very difficult. "Unions here are either going to be going the Korean way or the Japanese way," asserted a Ford labor-relations specialist. "We and many other companies would like to see them go the Japanese way."[74] But contrary to the hopes of the Taiwan's business elite, the Taiwanese workers were apparently choosing the Korean way.

14

The Triple Alliance in Taiwan

Although their cheap labor provided the foundation of the export-oriented Taiwanese economy, the benefits of high-speed growth did not redound to the workers but accrued mainly to a formidable triple alliance of the state elite, domestic capitalists, and foreign investors.

Like all power blocs, the "triple alliance" in Taiwan was one that involved the partners in both complementary and competitive relationships. Playing the leading role, state technocrats successfully pushed domestic businesses to adopt an export orientation, but local entrepreneurs complained about the way the KMT state and party enterprises dominated the domestic market. Transnational corporations readily embraced the cheap labor and investment incentives that the KMT state offered, but they consistently thwarted its attempts to get them to transfer technology and resisted its policies to limit their penetration of the domestic market. Yet so long as the two pillars of the economic paradigm held—expanding export markets and cheap labor—these differences were not allowed to disrupt a highly profitable relationship.

The State and the Economy

Within the triple alliance, it is clearly the state that has exercised the dominant role. The image of Taiwan being a beehive of small producers is accurate, if one does not leave out of the picture the formidable queen that dominates the hive—the state sector. Indeed, while the Korean state is often pictured as more interventionist, in the sense of exercising more hands-on guidance of the direction of private enterprise, the Taiwanese state has more classical, quasi-socialistic aspects—most notably, the domination of a massive segment of the economy by state-owned firms and party-owned enterprises.

The government, for one, is the island's biggest landowner, having title to an estimated 70 percent of Taiwan's land. More consequential, of course, is the KMT state's presence in the financial and industrial sectors. The assets of the twelve state-owned institutions make up 92.5 percent of the total assets of the top fifty financial institutions.[1] The central state institution is the Central Bank of China, which controls the flow of credit to industry through its power to set interest rates. State domination of the financial sector is guaranteed by the fact that practically all the commercial banks, whose lending operations conform closely to the rates set by the Central Bank, are owned by the state.[2]

The bulk of state credit—more than three-quarters in the early 1980s—has gone to big corporations, both private and public. Accounting for 30 percent of all bank loans in 1983 were government enterprises.

Taiwan's public sector originated with the Nationalist government's takeover of enterprises belonging to the Japanese *zaibatsu* and the Japanese colonial government after the Second World War. In the early 1950s, state enterprises accounted for close to 57 percent of industrial production. At the end of the phase of import-substitution industrialization, which saw several big private enterprises emerge with state assistance, the figure stood at some 40 percent. Since the early 1970s, the share of state enterprises has stabilized at about 20 percent of industrial production.[3]

These figures, however, give an inaccurate impression of the actual weight of the state sector in industry. By the mid-1980s, this sector was made up of about fifty-nine large enterprises, which exercised the dominant role in such strategic sectors as petroleum, steel, railways, electric power, tobacco and spirits, shipbuilding, and telecommunications.[4] Ranked according to sales, seven of the ten top enterprises were state-owned; and the top-ranked private firm, Nan-Ya Plastics, was outstripped by four state firms. At the top of the heap was China Petroleum Corporation, which was in eighty-first place of the world's 500 largest corporations outside the United States, with sales worth NT$210,074 million ($7.8 million) and assets worth NT$137,464 million ($5.1 million) in 1983.[5]

Adding to the weight of the state sector was the network of around fifty companies owned wholly or partly by the KMT.[6] These ranged from communications empires like the Central

News Agency, to petrochemical firms like the Orient Union Chemical Corporation, to financial institutions like the Central Investment and Trust Corporation.[7] Also in this network are small firms like bus companies and service companies geared to employ retired soldiers.[8] According to estimates made by the political opposition, about half of the total assets of Taiwan's corporations—about NT$380 billion—are controlled directly or indirectly by the government and the KMT.[9]

The state's presence in the economy must be evaluated not only in quantitative terms but in terms of its qualitative relationship to the rest of the economy. The tremendous influence of the state sector stems from the fact that it controls the "commanding heights of the economy," to use Lenin's terms, either by monopolizing public utilities or by occupying the leading positions in key oligopolistic sectors. State control of strategic industries, combined with state control of the financial system and KMT party control of a wide range of enterprises, creates what Huang Chi in his excellent study describes as "the potential to form a relatively closed system through internal exchanges and through vertical and horizontal integration."[10] Concentrated government control in the context of relatively dispersed private ownership creates a situation whereby private enterprises "depend more heavily on the public sector than the other way around."[11]

Heavy private-sector reliance on government inputs is indicated by the fact that the state was the sole producer of 36 of 304 major industrial products, according to a listing from the Industrial Bureau in 1982.[12] "From gasoline for cars to raw materials for the clothes we wear, everything is more or less under the Nationalist [KMT] control," asserts one opposition expert on state-KMT holdings."[13]

Even enterprises that developed with little overt government support, such as those in the petrochemical sector, owe much of their success to the pricing policies for the government's monopolized inputs. As Lin Chung-Chen has noted, "The rise to power of the petrochemical industry has less connection to government power than the textile and cement industries, and its efficiency has been admirable. But the intermediate products of the petrochemical industry have often benefited from the low price policy for raw materials."[14]

In recent years the share of state enterprises in production has been declining. But this statistical trend apparently has not affected the essentially subordinate role of private enterprise. As one journal of the petrochemical industry complained: "The CPC [China Petroleum Corporation] plays such an important role in the petrochemical industry that each step it takes may affect us in a significant way. But our words and deeds carry little weight in the CPC's destinies."[15]

American advisers to the KMT government in the 1950s and 1960s inveighed regularly against what they feared was the socialist potential of a large state-owned sector. Their fears were misplaced. For while the KMT's economic philosophy initially had some socialist inspiration, it was hardly inclined to serve socialist ends.

The KMT's creation of a large state sector found its initial justification in the original ideology of the Kuomintang, as articulated by its founder Sun Yat-Sen. Sun's Principle of the People's Livelihood proposed the development of "state capital" in order to "establish a developmental state capable of initiating...economic development and preventing capitalist domination."[16] Moreover,

> The state should own monopolistic sectors and set up needed industries that are too large or too risky for private capitals. With a potent state capable of regulating and checking capital for the service of people's livelihood, Sun foresaw cooperative relationships among state, local, and foreign private capitals. Viewing poverty rather than inequity as China's foremost economic problem, Sun considered it possible to prevent capitalist domination by equalizing land rights and developing state capital.[17]

But for the corrupt, counterrevolutionary KMT state that saw Taiwan as a temporary refuge and a springboard for retaking the mainland, ideology was far less important than interests. Like its control over agricultural production via the unequal fertilizer-rice exchange policy, control over strategic sectors of the economy was mainly geared to safeguard the political domination exercised by the KMT and its 1.5-million-member retinue of soldiers, bureaucrats, party faithfuls, business people, and family dependents from the mainland. The state sector served as a mainlander economic preserve, which, among other things, served to counter and control a private sector which, for the most part, was dominated by indigenous Taiwanese. As Denis Simon notes in his superb analysis of Taiwan in the 1970s:

Most local businessmen claim that state control is politically motivated—that is, since the government lacks a widespread economic base, the state has strategically chosen to remain active in key industries where it can exert more influence over the economy in general, and the private sector in particular. Most government enterprises are staffed primarily by Mainlanders, especially in the areas of upper management. This makes at least partially credible views about the "political" character of government-operated firms.[18]

KMT Politics and Big Business

Ambivalence has characterized the KMT relationship to private capital since the 1950s. The ambivalence is not so much rooted in an ideological contradiction between state and private enterprise as in fears that letting private enterprise flourish without state controls would erode the KMT's ability to control events in Taiwan. Entrepreneurs were welcome—so long as their businesses not only brought profit to themselves but also added to the power of their patrons in the KMT bureaucracy. "Bureaucratic capitalism," asserts Alice Amsden, is the appropriate term for the KMT's relationship to private interest groups, which has prevailed over the past forty years:

Under bureaucratic capitalism, public office (or office in public corporations) provided a source of private gain, and private enterprise was profitable only in close alliance with the state. Initially, the Jiang Jie-she [Chiang Kai-Shek] regime in Taiwan took a direct role in realizing surplus value for the dominant Mainlander bureaucratic capitalist class. Later, the Nationalist Government appropriated the surplus value produced by the peasantry and proletariat for the benefit of the increasingly dominant industrial capitalist class (by now composed of Mainlanders as well as Taiwanese and foreign firms).[19]

A privileged circle of entrepreneurs well connected with the KMT have, in fact, exercised close control of the island's industrial economy together with the state technocratic elite. These industrial groups emerged during the period of import-substitution industrialization (ISI), when the KMT, through tariffs and import restrictions, sought to create a self-sufficient industrial sector through the production of a variety of commodities ranging from textiles and garments to petrochemical products. The industrial groups' fortunes were built—and continue to depend—on monopolistic or oligopolistic domination of Taiwan's protected domestic market.

To be sure, the opening up of the industrial economy to entrepreneurial groups did not stem only from the KMT's desire to reward loyal mainlander elites but also from other factors, like the desire to jump start the economy out of stagnation in the early 1950s and—not to be underestimated—the stance of U.S. officials, who wielded their veto power over aid funds to press the KMT to give private enterprise a greater role in the economy.[20] But private enterprise was manipulated to assure, rather than contradict, the KMT's command of the economy.

U.S. aid was, in fact, used to advance the interests of KMT-linked mainlander entrepreneurs, as was evident in the beginnings of the operations of the textile industry. Key mainlander families from Shanghai and Shantung that came to Taiwan with Chiang Kai-Shek were the beneficiaries of the import-substitution policies. Aside from imposing import restrictions and other protective measures, the KMT supported the mainland entrepreneurs directly through the entrustment policy. Under this program,

> the government distributed raw cotton, which was provided under the U.S aid program, to spinning mills and then bought the yarn back at a set price. Thus the responsibility of the mill was limited to spinning only and everything else was taken care of by the government.[21]

With profits guaranteed by a closed market and many costs subsidized, the production of cotton tripled from 1950 to 1953, and by 1954 textiles had been established as the leading manufacturing industry in Taiwan.[22] Their dominance in textiles assured, the mainlander entrepreneurs plowed their profits into other industries. Thus Hsu Yu-Hsiang, a Kiangsunese who founded the Far Eastern Textile Company, diversified his investment into cement and department stores. Another mainlander, Yen Ching-Ling, owner of Tai Yuen Textile Company, used over $3 million in U.S. grant money to establish Yue Loong motors in 1953.[23] With technical assistance from Willys and Nissan, Yue Loong monopolized the assembly of automobiles for the protected domestic market until the late 1960s. Another mainlander with a textile background also founded the auto assembler Lio Ho, which teamed up with Ford in 1974 to create Ford–Lio Ho, one of Taiwan's biggest manufacturers.

It is thus not surprising that with KMT patronage, mainland entrepreneurial groups became ensconced at the upper levels of the economic power structure. Among the top ten business groups in 1981, three were mainlander-controlled: Far Eastern (number three), Yue Loong (number seven), and Pacific Electric Wire (number ten).[24] Of the top twenty-one mainlander-led business groups, fifteen were started in the period prior to 1960, "when government was most concerned about resettlement of the Mainlander minority, and government protection was rather extensive."[25]

But mainlander entrepreneurs were not the only ones showered with favoritism by the KMT. Taiwanese "comprador" families, as they were called by their critics, were integrated into the structure of bureaucrat capitalism. Most of these were large landlord families—the Big Five Taiwanese families, to use a common characterization[26]—who had forged strong political ties to the KMT in the period right after World War II, when the KMT occupied Taiwan. When land was expropriated during the agrarian reform, the landlords were compensated with shares in four large public enterprises producing cement, paper, mineral, and forestry products. Eventually, the Big Five Taiwanese families were able to secure control of the four enterprises, thanks largely to their links to the KMT.[27] Some of them, like the current chief executive officers of Taiwan Cement and Tatung, two of Taiwan's top ten private businesses, were also awarded seats in the KMT's Central Standing Committee.[28]

Another grouping of Taiwanese industrialists had less traditional ties to the KMT but were quick to respond to opportunities presented by the state's industrial priorities, and they were benefited by the insistence of USAID that industrial projects be opened up to a wider set of entrepreneurs. Y. C. Wang, a lumberyard owner, agreed to manufacture polyvinyl chloride (PVC) in a plant established by USAID and proceeded to turn Formosa Plastics and its subsidiaries "into the island's most successful and best integrated conglomerate."[29] USAID's lending policies, in fact, had major social consequences, as Huang Chi notes in his excellent study:

> The aid funds that went to private enterprises had a catalytic effect on new industries such as glass, syn-

thetic fibers, polyvinyl plastics and many others. Since most private enterprises were owned by local Taiwanese, encouraging private enterprises implied dispersing economic power and creating a new power center in society.[30]

Thus, it was not surprising that it was towards this latter group that the KMT state was most ambivalent, since over time most of the most dynamic big businesses were headed by Taiwanese. By 1983, of the ten leading business groups, seven were headed by Taiwanese (see table 14.1).[31] While these business groups were, in varying degrees, dependent on state policies—for instance, relatively cheap oil from the KMT state-controlled China Petroleum Corporation made the Taiwanese-dominated petrochemical industry profitable—there were fears on the part of the state of the Taiwanese ambitions for self-sufficiency and independence. These fears sometimes translated into controversial policy decisions: when Y. C. Wang of Formosa Plastics applied to build a naphtha cracker for his own plastics firm in the late 1960s, the government rejected his proposal and decided that such a facility should be set up and owned by the state. It was likely that the KMT feared that Wang, who had remained somewhat aloof from the government, might become even more independent of state patronage.[32]

The Formosa Plastics case was not unique. The pattern of state intervention in the economy has in fact been influenced by this struggle between the mainlander and indigenous Taiwanese economic interests. Power was apparently a major consideration when the KMT government arrogated to itself the spearhead role during the second state import-substitution program in the 1970s, which saw the launching of ten major industrial projects, including the state-owned Kaohsiung Shipyards, government-owned China Steel's integrated cold rolling mill, and state-owned China Petroleum's petrochemical project, including both upstream naphtha-cracking facilities and downstream petrochemical production. The technocratic rationale for state-enterprise leadership was that private capital did not have the capability of making the huge investments needed to support accelerated industrial expansion in Taiwan. However, state control was at least partly a front for the mainlanders' efforts to continue to exercise strategic direction of the economy vis-à-vis the up-and-coming Taiwanese business class.

Because Taiwanese big business perceives the KMT government as placing obstacles in the way of their success, business's support

Table 14.1

Top Ten Business Groups in Taiwan

Group	Ownership[a]	Assets (in millions of NT$[b])	Rank According to Assets	Sales (in millions of NT$[b])
Formosa Plastics	T	63,608	1	59,576
Cathay Trust	T	42,088	2	8,501
Far Eastern	M	36,694	3	27,276
Taiwan Spinning	T	29,267	4	26,301
Tatung	T	28,330	5	19,873
Shin Kong	T	27,600	6	18,054
Yue Loong	M	26,497	7	27,878
Linden International	T	25,449	8	19,512
Taiwan Cement	T	14,842	9	13,918
Pacific Electric Wire	M	14,700	10	10,162

Group	Rank According to Sales	Number of Employees	Rank According to Number of Employees	Number of Member Firms
Formosa Plastics	1	30,006	1	10
Cathay Trust	13	5,207	18	17
Far Eastern	3	15,984	4	21
Taiwan Spinning	4	16,039	3	27
Tatung	5	24,692	2	33
Shin Kong	7	8,612	9	18
Yue Loong	2	11,792	5	9
Linden International	6	8,979	7	10
Taiwan Cement	9	3,639	22	7
Pacific Electric Wire	10	4,892	19	6

Source: Huang Chi, "The State and Foreign Capital: A Case Study of Taiwan" (Ph.D. dissertation, Indiana University, 1986), p. 149.
[a] T = Taiwanese; M = Mainlander.
[b] NT$ = New Taiwan dollars.

for the KMT government is qualified. Indeed, Simon claims that "instead of resting upon a coalition between the state and big business, the current regime has only a limited amount of direct political support among a select group of businessmen of Taiwanese extraction."[33]

Despite such contradictions, however, there are likely to be more common interests than there is conflict among the big business groups and between these groups and the state. While distinct from the mainlander business groups, the fifteen heavily inter-locked groups that form the inner circle of Taiwanese big business, the anthropologist Ichiro Namazaki discovered, were linked with their mainlander counterparts through positions in the governing boards of trade associations and other business organizations.[34] These business linkages were complemented by political ties to the KMT: close to half of the fifteen groups had core managers who had held elected office (see figure 14.1).[35] In fact, since the death of Chiang Kai-Shek in 1975, many of the sons of Taiwanese capi-talists have been recruited by the KMT to run for political office, including the legislature, in a calculated effort to cement the ties between the KMT and the Taiwanese elite.[36]

Given these evolving ties, says Namazaki, the potential is there for the inner circle of the Taiwanese business elite "to dominate Taiwan's corporate economy, allied with mainlander counterparts and foreign multinationals supporting and perhaps supported by the policies of the Nationalist government."[37]

Viewing the situation from another angle, Simon suggests that a rough congruence of interests has been effected by the common benefits derived from the framework of export-oriented growth:

> The nature of the KMT-directed economic program generally has reflected the state's particular needs to strengthen and expand its economic base, as well as the position of the Mainlanders within the economy; the program has also reflected the successful use of economic policy to win political support. Basically, even though Taiwanese and Mainlanders remain divided at the central political level, for the most part, they share an interest in and have shared the benefits of pursuing an export-led model of development with visible levels of TNC [transnational corporation] par-ticipation.[38]

The State and Small and Medium Capital

There are an estimated 260,000 business enterprises in Taiwan, and 98 percent of them are considered small businesses.[39] In 1981 these small and medium enterprises produced 55 percent of

Figure 14.1

Relations among Different Sectors of Taiwan's Business Class

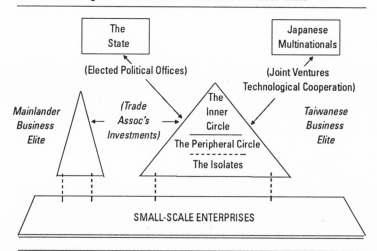

Source: Ichiro Namazaki, "Networks of Taiwanese Big Business: A Preliminary Analysis," *Modern China* 12, no. 4 (October 1986), p. 521.

Taiwan's nonagricultural output and employed 70 percent of all employees. They were also the backbone of the island's trading economy, accounting for 65 percent of exports.[40]

The source of the dynamism of small businesses is their link to the international economy. The decisive development that forged this link was the reorientation of economic policy in the mid-1960s from an import-substitution strategy directed at the domestic market towards export-led growth. Without this external connection, small and medium businesses would have been mired in stagnation, since, as Lin Chung-Chen writes, they "have no space to grow in the domestic market, which is controlled by enterprise blocs."[41]

Perhaps the key mechanism that promoted the dynamism of the small and medium entrepreneurs was the ingenious tariff and tax rebate system. Under the system, exporters were qualified to gain refunds on customs duties and other taxes for those inputs they imported; or the local producer of these inputs could sell inputs to the exporter at the lower world price and was then entitled to claim the amount of tariff duties and other taxes that the exporter would have paid had he imported instead.[42] This had the effect of encouraging Taiwan's exporters to be internationally competitive while protecting domestic input producers.[43]

It is doubtful, however, that Taiwan's small entrepreneurs were able to take advantage of bank credit, which went mainly to the big enterprises. The statistics bear out this observation: more than three-quarters of all loans and discounts issued by the Taiwanese banking system have been in large amounts (more than NT$1 million) and have gone to big corporations.[44] As a result, a massive curbside, or informal, money market arose alongside the formal banking system to service the financial needs of Taiwan's small and medium entrepreneurs. The role of this informal financial network was underlined by the fact that in the early 1970s an estimated 82 percent of the financial requirements of private firms had to be raised in the informal money market.[45] The curbside money market was critical to small and medium entrepreneurs but it was also costly. For instance, in April 1977, at a time that the rate of interest on the Bank of Taiwan's export loan program (for which few exporters were qualified) was set at 6.5 per year and the lowest rate for secured bank loans was 11 percent per year, the rate for the cheapest loans on the curbside money market in Taipei stood at 23.1 percent.[46]

Thus, Taiwan's small and medium entrepreneurs achieved their export successes despite state credit policies that favored state and big private capital. They also achieved the world's highest rate of savings, which the KMT then channeled into its banks. But rather than being rechanneled as reasonably priced credit to assist small and medium exporters, these savings were used to finance the operations of state enterprises, KMT enterprises, and big private firms. As Chu Yun-Han notes, "Monetary policy did not inhibit growth, but neither was monetary expansion used to finance industrial plans."[47]

Inability to obtain credit was not the only complaint of small Taiwanese entrepreneurs. The government, said one disgruntled small businessman, "doesn't supply us with information on trends in international trade, and we have to pay more than the bigger firms to buy materials from big or state-run companies."[48]

Indeed, though lauded as quick and nimble in their response to world market trends, life for Taiwan's small entrepreneurs was not easy even in the heyday of export-led growth. A 1973 report by the consulting firm Arthur D. Little Corporation enumerated several problems: "(1) lack of financing, especially from private banking institutions who seem to prefer the larger firms; (2) low productivity; (3) low efficiency due to poor economies of scale; (4) deficient management practices; and (5) lack of marketing information and techniques."[49] This situation has not appreciably changed.

Lack of receptiveness on the part of state agencies and traditional Taiwanese distrust of the KMT state led small entrepreneurs to forge marketing links with foreign corporations. Foreign corporations, in turn, discovered the advantages of having Taiwanese firms, with their cheap labor, produce under contract. Thus, the spread of the OEM (original equipment manufacturer) arrangement. Small and medium-size Taiwanese firms churned out cheap products that were marketed under well-known brand names by foreign buyers, like K mart, Sears, J. C. Penney, Hewlett-Packard, Texas Instruments, IBM, Schwinn Bicycle Company, Wilson Sporting Goods, and General Electric, Taiwan's biggest exporter.[50] Even the bigger exporters, like the electronics firm Tatung, found the OEM arrangement indispensable: in 1984, Tatung exported $210 million worth of products, but only $49.5 million, or 23.5 percent, was under its own brand name.[51]

Subcontracting is so institutionalized that one foreign executive remarked, "You really can't consider Taiwan an exporting nation. Taiwan is simply a collection of international subcontractors for the American market."[52]

But beyond lack of brand-name recognition in world markets, this arrangement exacts a high price: severe dependence and low profits. "How much of the exports from Taiwan is arranged by the Japanese multinational enterprise bloc is still undetermined," asserts Lin Chung-Chen, "but Taiwan's exporters believe that the proportion is considerable. In other words, the smaller Taiwanese enterprises, due to the absence of an independent sales network, may be controlled by a small number of U.S., Japanese, and big domestic enterprise blocs, and their profits are limited."[53] In fact, according to Huang Chi, the Japanese marketing firms were estimated to control 50 percent of Taiwan's exports, even to the United

States.[54] Another estimate put it at as high as 70 percent.[55] A large portion of this was handled by the eleven major Japanese trading firms operating in Taiwan, including Mitsubishi, Marubeni, Mitsui, and Beisei Trading Company.[56] The profits of the American buyers and the Japanese middlemen can be gleaned from the low export price of many Taiwanese commodities, said to come to only 10 to 20 percent of their retail price in the United States.[57]

Not only do the foreign marketing firms determine the profits of their Taiwanese subcontractors, but the Japanese also "tend to use their status as major customers to push local firms to buy their capital goods. This practice worsens the chronic trade deficit between Taiwan and Japan and allows the latter to penetrate even more deeply into Taiwanese enterprises by controlling their technology."[58]

Glorified as the dynamo of Taiwan's economy, the small and medium-size enterprises are in fact skating on thin ice, largely unsupported by government credit and exploited by transnational corporate buyers. What government propaganda and academic treatises do not mention is the high rate of bankruptcy in this sector.

The State and Foreign Investment

Prior to the mid-1980s, Taiwan had the reputation of being a paradise for foreign investors. Between 1951 and the end of 1985, about $5.16 billion worth of foreign investments entered Taiwan, 77 percent of which, or $3.99 billion, came from non-Chinese sources.[59] While seemingly minor in terms of their contribution to total GNP, foreign investors actually had a substantial presence in the most dynamic and modern sectors of the Taiwanese economy: they accounted in the late 1970s for 54.7 percent of total production in electronics, 35.5 percent in machinery, 27.9 percent in nonmetals, and 17.9 percent in chemicals.[60] Certainly, when compared to the situation in Korea, foreign investment has had a much larger impact on the Taiwanese economy.

Among foreign investors, Americans were clearly dominant in terms of volume of investment. From 1951 to 1985, 43 percent of non–overseas Chinese investment came from the United States, 28 percent from Japan, 13 percent from Europe, and 16 percent from other countries (see table 14.2).[61] The relatively high level of foreign investment that streamed into Taiwan in the last three decades was largely a reflection of the fact that the island was a

Table 14.2

Foreign Investment in Taiwan, 1951–1985

Investor Nation	Amount Invested (in billions U.S. $)	Percentage of Total Foreign Investment
United States	1.72	43
Japan	1.13	28
Europe	0.53	13
Others	0.61	16
Total	3.99	

Source: John Ni, "Foreign Investment Policy and Export Promotion: A Case Study of the Republic of China," in Seiji Naya et al., *Direct Foreign Investment and Export Promotion: Policies and Experiences in Asia* (Honolulu: Resource Systems Institute, University of Hawaii, 1987), p. 260.

Note: Data does not include investments by overseas Chinese, which came to $1.17 billion for the period.

battleground of intense competition between U.S. and Japanese industry. To offset the flood of cheap Japanese imports, particularly in electronics, to the U.S. market, many U.S. firms relocated their assembly operations to Taiwan and other third world countries.[62] The incentives were mainly two: cheap labor, and items 806.30 and 807.00 of the U.S. tariff code. The latter allowed the duty-free entry of U.S. components sent abroad for assembly or reprocessing, then reexported back to the United States; only the value added by foreign labor was subject to tariffs. By the late 1960s, "roughly half of U.S. imports came in under tariff item 807, most of them from the factories of U.S. firms in Mexico and Taiwan."[63]

As quotas were placed on Japanese imports and U.S. firms threatened to gain a competitive edge by relocating to Taiwan, Japanese firms sought to regain advantage by moving their own assembly operations to Taiwan. Thus, according to Thomas Gold, "Taiwan...became vital to the global production structures of corporations from two different core economies."[64] The Japanese government encouraged this migration, in line with its policy of moving polluting, labor-intensive, and low-technology firms overseas and reserving the home islands for high-tech, higher-value-added industries. Thus Taiwan "functioned as a receptacle for declining Japanese industries in Japan's global strategy to restructure its industry."[65]

The KMT state actively played the crucial role in linking cheap Taiwanese labor to foreign capital. In the 1960s, state policy was guided by the need to keep economic growth going after the exhaustion of the import-substitution industrialization of the 1950s. In the 1970s and 1980s, however, especially as development technocrats achieved strong influence at the Ministry of Economic Affairs, a major concern of the state became expanding the infrastructure for growth and facilitating transfer of technology from foreign to Taiwanese firms. The state made special efforts to pair foreign corporations with domestic producers to generate the massive investments needed by the projects as well as to prevent the foreign corporations from achieving hegemony over local production. And all throughout, economic considerations were intertwined with strategic ones: attracting foreign capital was seen as a way to enmesh foreign interests with the interests of Taiwan, making it more difficult for the People's Republic of China to isolate Taiwan internationally.[66]

The state devised an elaborate incentive system to encourage foreign investors. Of course, the main incentive was the cost of labor, which was kept cheap by a combination of state surveillance and repression, KMT-managed unionism, and paternalistic management practices. There were other attractions, however, which were contained in three basic laws governing foreign investment. Liberalized over the years, the foreign investment code carries incentives such as tax holidays, limits on income taxes and income-tax deductions for exports, unlimited repatriation of profits, and shortened periods before capital could be repatriated.

But perhaps the most attractive package came in the form of the export processing zones (EPZs), three of which were in operation by the late 1970s. In addition to giving investors the advantages of nonunionized labor and the incentives already contained in the basic foreign investment statutes, locating in an EPZ entitled an investor to

> (1) exemption from import duties and dues on imported machinery, raw materials, fuels, semi-finished products, and other commodities for processing; (2) exemption from commodity tax payments on raw materials and semi-finished products imported for self-use; (3) a remarkable cutback in red tape as-

sociated with applications for and licensing of investment, plant establishment, export, import, inward and outward remittances; (4) provision of standard factory buildings by the EPZ administration for immediate occupation with a 70 per cent loan to be paid back on a 10-year installment basis.[67]

By normal, narrow economic standards, the Kaohsiung sanctuary and other EPZs were a success: by the end of 1984, aggregate committed investment in the three zones came to $417.5 million, employment came to 85,000, and the EPZs enjoyed a surplus of nearly $1 billion in foreign trade.[68]

In the early 1980s, another type of zone meant to attract foreign investors was established, mainly to attract high-tech investment: the Hsinchu Industrial Park, also known as the Silicon Valley of Taiwan. While offering the same duty-free access to imported inputs and a five-year income tax holiday, the Hsinchu Industrial Park also offered the intellectual infrastructure of three of Taiwan's leading technology institutes (Tsinghua University, Chiaotung University, and the Industrial Technology Research Institute). By 1989 there were more than eighty high-tech companies established at Hsinchu.[69]

Relations among foreign investors, the KMT state, and domestic big business were not, however, always harmonious. Subtle conflicts pervaded these dealings. Both the KMT state and the big-business class as a whole would have preferred it if the Japanese had concentrated their investments on export enterprises rather than also seeking to gain a foothold in the local market. The government, for instance, discouraged Japanese firms from the petrochemical industry, because of fears that the Japanese had already penetrated too deeply into Taiwan's economy. American investors like Union Carbide, however, were encouraged to participate in the development of the industry.[70]

Joint ventures also reflected the historical divisions in Taiwan's political and economic elites. The close relationships of mainlander bureaucrats with U.S. aid agencies from the 1950s and 1960s led to a pattern of mainlander bureaucrats becoming mediators between mainlander capitalists and U.S. investors, in contrast to Taiwanese businessmen, who preferred to deal with the Japanese firms on account of previous colonial ties. This subtle competition is captured by Huang Chi:

The state tends to forge close relations between some local capitalists and U.S. firms as part of the strategy to counterbalance the Japanese influence on Taiwan's economy and those Taiwanese businessmen closely linked with Japanese firms. Therefore, the cleavage between Taiwanese and mainlanders is also an important social origin of the KMT state's policies toward foreign investment.[71]

Preferences, however, were never allowed to get to a point where they would harm the climate for foreign investment. While the technocrats complained of Japanese tightfistedness in technology transfers or subtly steered joint ventures in some areas to the Americans, Japanese investment was largely unobstructed and, indeed, barely regulated. So long as the state, big business, and foreign capital derived substantial benefits from high-speed export-oriented growth, conflicts within the triple alliance of the state, local big business, and foreign investors (American or Japanese) could be contained and defused.

Fissures in the Alliance

It was precisely the gradual disappearance of the key conditions for the success of export-oriented industrialization in the late 1980s that began to create fissures in the coalition. The growing fragility of the structure of interests around export-oriented growth were manifested in various ways.

The appreciation of the New Taiwan dollar and the rise in labor costs owing to labor's new militance were ending Taiwan's viability as an export manufacturing base. Thus many Japanese and U.S. investors who had come to Taiwan to take advantage of cheap labor were either leaving or planning to leave. This did not mean a decrease in foreign investment inflows. However, many of the new investments, like foreign banking operations, were geared not at producing exports to the United States but at penetrating the local economy to take advantage of Taiwan's new prosperity. These were precisely the investments that were perceived as threatening the interests of the local enterprise blocs that had traditionally controlled the domestic market.

Both foreign and local businesses were increasingly disappointed at the KMT state's inability to control rising labor unrest and the hard-hitting environmental movement. As pressures for democratization spread, many KMT elements realized that the old hard-line repression against labor would no longer work, and that now it was necessary to court the working class if the KMT were to maintain its power in the long run. The effort of some KMT officials to project themselves as mediators rather than as partisans in labor conflicts led many business people to doubt the reliability of the KMT apparatus as a defender of management's interests.[72] For foreign corporate executives, the environmental movement's successful campaigns to stop Du Pont from building a titanium dioxide plant and force the British Imperial Chemical Industries decision to shut down a polluting plant in southern Taiwan were indications that the KMT state could no longer be counted on to deliver on its promises to foreign investors.

As political liberalization spread, many of Taiwan's small and medium entrepreneurs began to change their stance towards the KMT from wariness to active opposition, with many casting not only their ballots but also their financial support to the opposition Democratic Progressive Party.[73] In other words, the economic cleavage between the Taiwanese small business strata and the KMT-connected economic power elite threatened to become a political division as well. Whether or not this would actually come about depended greatly in the position of two swing groups: the Taiwanese big business groups and the Taiwanese members of the KMT leadership. By early 1990, it was becoming clear to President Lee Teng-Hui and other KMT leaders that to survive in the long run, the KMT had to "Taiwanize" not only its leadership but also its program.

True, these were still only fissures in the coalition of interests around export-oriented growth. But it was certain that they would widen as the three-decades-old strategy ran out of steam.

15

The Structural Squeeze

I n 1989 the average wage of a Taiwanese textile worker was over thirteen times that of his or her counterpart in Sri Lanka.[1] Clearly, trying to base Taiwan's competitive advantage on cheap labor was a losing battle. But like their colleagues in Korea, many of Taiwan's technocrats had a panacea for the island's looming difficulties: high technology.

Ever since the 1970s, in fact, Taiwan's technocrats had projected the transformation of the island's industrial base from labor-intensive industries to high-tech and other capital-intensive industries. Like the heavy and chemical industry (HCI) program in Korea, the second-stage import-substitution strategy launched in the early 1970s was meant to set up the infrastructure of basic, or upstream, industries that would support the establishment of more technologically sophisticated downstream firms. Ten major projects, including petrochemical facilities and China Steel's integrated cold rolling mill, were put in motion between 1973 and 1980. Fourteen more massive investments were declared for the 1980s, including the modernization of the telecommunications network and more naptha-cracking facilities for the petrochemical sector.

Beyond establishing the infrastructure for a technologically upgraded industrial sector, the KMT state actively promoted the transfer of technology from foreign investors. The foreign-investment statutes were revised to establish preferences for investment in pioneer areas. For example, in 1977 the government extended the period during which the tax holiday would be in effect for capital- or technology-intensive investments. Incentives were complemented by sanctions: for instance, mandatory export levels for Japanese investors were often set higher because of their "notorious" reluctance to transfer advanced technology.[2]

Incentives were also created to encourage both foreign and local firms to engage in research-and-development activity in Taiwan, with the hope that this would speed up the diffusion of advanced technology. Perhaps the best-known product of this effort is the Hsinchu Industrial Park. The establishment of the park was especially aimed at bringing in expatriate Taiwanese and other overseas Chinese high-tech entrepreneurs and capital, by offering them advantages that came with locating in export processing zones. These included access to generous long-term loans with low interest rates; the provision of state equity contribution that could go as high as 49 percent of capitalization; and proximity to three of Taiwan's leading universities, eight specialized national research labs, and a large computer facility.[3] By 1989 the government had been able to attract more than eighty companies to Hsinchu, forty-seven of them start-up ventures founded by Taiwanese returnees from the United States.[4]

Foreign Investors and Technology Transfer

After nearly two decades, how successful has Taiwan been in its effort to technologically upgrade its industrial base? The news has been filled with stories about the computer wizardry of a local firm made good such as Acer, about plans to set up more wafer-fabricating plants to mass-manufacture memory chips, or DRAMs, and about the purchase of the Silicon Valley powerhouse Wyse Technology by a Taiwanese consortium. For the most part, however, the government's technology upgrading and acquisition policies have so far yielded very few substantive results.

True, some technology transfer has been spurred by government regulations on local procurement of parts. For instance, when Singer Sewing Machine Company invested in Taiwan in 1963, the government required that the company try to procure 83 percent of the parts needed for production from local suppliers. By 1967 Singer was using nothing but locally made parts except for the needles for its straight-stitch model, having spawned in the process a brood of suppliers.[5] Similarly, in the electronics industry local parts suppliers by 1978 were said to be providing 70.7 percent of all components purchased by local firms, 59 percent in the case of joint ventures, and 33 percent in the case of wholly owned subsidiaries.[6] And in the auto-parts industry, some 2,300 firms employing some 92,000 people arose to service the local assemblers and joint ventures.

Undoubtedly, then, some backward linkages did take place. But for the most part, the upstream firms that arose were mainly small labor-intensive, relatively low-tech operations. Indeed, in the auto-parts industry, as one account put it, "87 percent of the firms in the industry hire less than 50 people and 65 percent of the firms have a registered capital less than US$15,000, in 1986."[7]

This situation reflected the technological status of the bulk of Taiwan's industry. As a 1989 report of the Economist Intelligence Unit puts it, "The private sector has proved relatively slow...to upgrade and modernize. Rather, the response of the labour-intensive industries has tended to try to adapt existing production methods by seeking to keep costs down. The predominance of small and medium sized enterprises has inhibited large capital expenditures on new plants."[8]

After almost three decades of promoting direct technology transfers from foreign firms, Taiwan had little to show for it by the end of the 1980s. At the export processing zones, local technicians "complain of the unwillingness of foreign supervisors, especially those in Japanese firms, to allow them to gain a comprehensive understanding of the production process."[9] Indeed, Japan "still tends to invest in lower technology assembly operations, and faces mounting criticism in Taiwan, as on the mainland and elsewhere in the region, for its reluctance to transfer technology."[10] This reluctance is reflected in the fact that although the number of cases of Japanese investments were nearly double those of the United States as of 1983, 840 compared with 422, the value of Japanese investments was only about 75 percent of the value of U.S. investments.[11]

Perhaps the case of the Japanese multinational giant Hitachi best exemplifies the difficulties associated with technology transfer from the Japanese. Lower labor costs and backward integration contributed to improving the firm's overall competitiveness in the U.S. market. Yet, as Denis Simon makes clear, Hitachi's contribution to Taiwan's economy, especially in the area of technology transfer, was questionable on a number of points:

> All marketing and sourcing decisions were (and still are) made by the parent firm in Japan. There is very little room for decision-making flexibility. Secondly, upper level management and control over technology rests in the hands of the Japanese....Last, the technological contributions of the firm were also limited, and

there appeared to be very little spillover into the local economy, even in the area of worker training.[12]

Some backward integration was sparked by the Japanese giants, but often it was not local suppliers that benefited. Many electronics firms, for instance, have sourced their parts mainly from Japanese-invested firms, and the latter, in turn, "tend to purchase only a minimum of their needed raw materials and supplies from local suppliers."[13]

Indeed, instead of transferring technology, Japanese firms encouraged technological dependence. Japanese trading firms were notorious for pushing their capital goods on local firms, notes Huang Chi, enabling them "to penetrate even more deeply into Taiwanese enterprises by controlling their production technology."[14]

But lest we get the impression that it was only the Japanese that were stingy in transferring technology and wary of local sourcing, many American firms were just as guilty of limiting technological diffusion or fostering technological dependence. In the 1970s a number of major U.S. firms set up shop in Taiwan to service the needs of other firms manufacturing final products, thus limiting technological transfer that could have come if backward linkages had been established with Taiwanese suppliers instead. Among these firms were Ampex, which made parts and assemblies for tape recorders; Bendix, which manufactured printed circuit boards; General Instruments, which produced electronic components; and Corning Glass, which turned out television picture tubes.[15] The dynamics of what was a nearly closed system of U.S. manufacturers and suppliers was exemplified by the American firm Zenith. According to Simon,

> About 65 percent of the components and raw materials used in the firm's finished products are sourced from within Taiwan, and 35 percent are imported. Although this would seem to indicate that Zenith does purchase a substantial portion of its parts locally, this is not necessarily the case. Approximately 69 percent of the parts purchased locally are sourced from foreign-invested firms in Taiwan, 54 percent from U.S. companies and 15 percent from Japanese-invested firms. An examination of the U.S. firms that serve as suppliers for Zenith indicates that each of these firms came to Taiwan with the expressed pur-

pose of acting as a supplier to other foreign- invested companies producing final products. Only 20 percent of total sourcing derives from purchases from local firms. The Zenith plant manager noted that local firms tend to be unreliable about the quality and quantity of parts supplied to Zenith, and thus the company has found it necessary to arrange for purchases from a number of local firms and has not been willing to develop a more extensive relationship with any one particular firm. As of late 1978, Zenith had relations with over 50 satellite factories.[16]

In short, while some foreign firms did spawn Taiwanese suppliers, key foreign firms preferred to buy from the subsidiaries of their traditional Japanese or U.S. suppliers. Moreover, local Taiwanese suppliers tended to be low-tech and low-profit operators who were engaged in furious competition with one another. The Japanese pattern of long-term supplier arrangements failed to take hold, resulting not only in limited technological diffusion to suppliers but also in chronic instability, a very limited capital base, and very limited opportunities for growth. By the end of the 1970s there were still only 175 companies in Taiwan registered as large. While 87 percent of all factories were locally owned, 57 percent of the large firms were wholly or partly foreign owned.[17]

Managed Improvisation

How then do we reconcile this reality—limited technology transfer to technology-short local firms—with the image of Taiwan's entrepreneurs producing a thousand and one imitation products, from fake Rolexes to IBM PC clones? The answer appears to be ingenious imitation engineering that blends low-tech production processes with some engineering skills and some high-tech processes: in short, managed improvisation. Wenlee Ting provides a succinct description of this process:

The reality behind the low technological facade of the NICs involves a production function in which capital and labor, especially the latter, operate under a system of multiple uses. The interactive uses of capital and labor are actually a kind of "managed improvisation" in which multiskilled workers and technicians are actively interchangable in most stages of the production process.... In the multiple uses of capital, the same piece of equipment is usually applicable to different functions and operations at the various stages of the manufacturing process. As a result, the production and assembly line of NIC firms are less continuous and more intermittent in workflow than that of U.S. and Japanese systems.[18]

However, managed improvisation is limited in its possibilities. It relies principally on product modification, or minor changes in the design and features of a product, to respond to changes in the market. This means adding more bells and whistles rather than transforming a product through innovation. "Process innovation," notes Ting, "the forte of the Japanese, still seems to escape the capability of NIC firms." This is precarious in a world of high-speed technological change, since modification and even product improvement "are still essentially technologically dependent postures in which the firm reacts to rather than anticipates the emerging market dynamics."[19]

In short, Taiwan and the other NICs still have to cross the technological divide that lies between cloning and innovation.

The Demise of Textiles and Garments

Taiwan, it is becoming clear, is stuck in this netherworld between low tech and high tech. The consequences of this unenviable situation of being outstripped by lower-cost producers in labor-intensive industries yet still being incapable of making the leap to high tech are best illustrated by developments in the textile and garments industries.

Textiles and garments were the *wunderkind* of Taiwanese industry in the 1960s, being the cutting edge of the program of export-oriented industrialization. Textile and garment exports increased twentyfold over the decade, so that by 1970 textile and garment exports accounted for $470 million, or close to 32 percent of all export earnings.[20]

Cheap and low- or medium-quality products, produced under OEM contracts with Japanese or American trading firms, were the backbone of the export surge. The golden sixties and early 1970s, however, gave way to the industry's time of troubles beginning in the late 1970s, as the industry confronted the challenges of protectionism, rising wages, currency appreciation, and, most critically, sharp competition from both lower-wage developing

countries and firms in the advanced economies that were rein-
vigorated by automation.

The textile industry became a target of protectionist pressures
as early as 1963, when the United States limited imports of Taiwan-
made cotton textiles.[21] Like the Koreans, however, the Taiwanese
had cleverly anticipated the move and shifted heavily to synthetic
fibers. Throughout the 1970s synthetic fiber goods, production of
which was boosted enormously by the development of Taiwan's
petrochemical industry, became the main source of profits. But the
protectionist threat could not be warded off, and in 1971 the
United States also imposed a quota on imports of Taiwanese-made
synthetic goods, followed by the European Community (EC) in
1975. Whether bilaterally negotiated, as in the case of the United
States, or unilaterally imposed, as in Europe, quotas have been a
significant constraint on Taiwanese textile and garment exports
since then. As of 1985, for instance, 92.1 percent of Taiwan's textile
exports to the United States and 84 percent of its exports to the EC
were subject to quota restrictions.[22]

The second development that made life difficult for the industry
was the rising wages of workers. Even without effective unionism,
wages for factory workers in Taiwan doubled, and between 1983
and 1988 manufacturing wages rose by about 55 percent.[23] The
main reason for the rise in wages was a labor shortage created by
the drying up of the surplus labor force from the rural areas.
Forced by this situation to compete for workers with other, higher-
paying industries, the clothing industry had to upgrade wages.
Still it did not fare well in the competition: from a peak of 334,000
workers in 1971, the labor force in textiles plunged to 258,000 in
1980.[24]

When a third element was added—the appreciation of the New
Taiwan dollar by almost 40 percent between 1985 and 1988 vis-à-
vis the U.S. dollar, due to U.S. trade pressure—then the very
survival of the industry was at stake. Together these three forces
produced the bankruptcy of some 480 textile and garment firms
in just two years, 1987 and 1988.[25] This was reflective of a broader
trend throughout the export industries: 9,000 factories, or nearly
10 percent of the total number of export manufacturers in Taiwan,
folded in the period from 1987 to the middle of 1989.[26]

These three forces made Taiwan's position extremely precarious
in international competition. Like their counterparts in Korea,
Taiwanese textile and garment makers found their position deteriorating rapidly, squeezed between the growing edge in cheap

labor costs attained by the other developing countries and advances in cost-competitive labor-saving technology in the advanced countries. With the average wage in Taiwan's textile industry being ten times that in China, thirteen times that in Sri Lanka, and five times that in Thailand,[27] there was no way that the Taiwanese could beat the other third world textile powers in the mass production of low- or medium-quality textiles and garments (see table 15.1).

At the same time, the development of open-end spinning and shuttleless weaving systems and the application of microelectronic technology to the production process enabled firms in Europe and the United States to pull ahead in high-fashion commodities. The threat from the revitalized textile and garment producers of advanced countries was captured by the following account:

> There is almost a race against time to substitute machinery for departing workers. It now takes four times as many workers in a mill in Taiwan to produce a bale of yarn (440 lb) as it does in Japan. And it takes 1.75 man-hours to manufacture a dozen men's dress shirts in a U.S. garment factory; in Taiwan it takes 2.7 hours. The major difference lies in the extent of automation.[28]

That was 1981. Many technocrats saw the salvation of the industry in technological upgrading and focusing on upscale fashion commodities. As in Korea, however, exhortations to automate and produce high-quality garments fell flat in the absence of government backing and in the face of the Taiwanese producers' continuing addiction to the cheap-labor solution and their continuing affliction with a subcontractor mentality. As two observers noted more recently:

> Outdated technology and skill have hindered progress in bleaching and dyeing. Success in producing fashionable textiles requires a sensitive response to shifts in consumer preferences, ability to produce in small lots with very tight delivery schedules, and precise quality controls. These are not easy tasks.[29]

As the escalating bankruptcies showed, being small—and thus without the capital resources for automation—was leading to what the president of one of Taiwan's largest firms described as the "survival of the fittest in the apparel industry."[30] The grim

Table 15.1

Comparative Labor Costs in the Textile Industry, Spring 1989

Country	Average cost per operator hour (in US$)	Ratio to U.S. cost per operator hour (%)
NICs		
Hong Kong	2.44	25
South Korea	2.87	30
Taiwan	3.56	37
Selected developing countries		
China	0.40	4
India	0.65	7
Indonesia	0.23	2
Philippines	0.64	7
Sri Lanka	0.26	3
Thailand	0.68	7
Selected industrial countries		
Japan	13.98	144
United States	9.71	—

Source: Werner International, "Spinning and Weaving Labor Cost Comparisons" (New York, Spring 1989).

prospects for the industry that had made Taiwan into an exporting power were summed up by the Economist Intelligence Unit:

> The government's reluctance to...formalizing the im-migration of cheaper labor will push more and more of the labor intensive employers into overseas invest-ment, or into contracting out arrangements with cheaper labor centers. This, combined with slower world trade growth in 1990, will add impetus to the trend of corporate failure among the smaller textiles, footwear and toy manufacturers, who are unable to make the economies of scale needed to finance foreign investment or automation.[31]

The Auto Industry: The End of Ambition

As in Korea, the automobile industry, with the range of forward and backward linkages that it offers, has been seen in Taiwan as a strategic industry—one that could pull the economy across the high-tech barrier. But the evolution of the Taiwanese automobile industry provides a good case study of the severe constraints that handicap even the most determined third world government when it seeks to develop a self-sustaining technological capability in an extremely competitive international industry marked by rapid innovation.

The Taiwanese automobile industry was born in 1953, with the founding of the Yue Loong Motor Company. Under heavy protection, Yue Loong assembled Willys Jeeps, then Nissan vehicles, for the domestic market. With heavy protection assuring high profits and low-volume production, four other companies were formed in the 1960s: San-Fu, Sanyang, Lio Ho, and China Motor. Little technological upgrading, however, occurred during this period, though a requirement that companies obtain 60 percent of their products from local sources helped stimulate the growth of a parts and components industry. Instead, like Yue Loong, the four new car companies took the easy way out: hooking up with Japanese partners to assemble their cars. Thus by the end of the 1960s, "the emerging production structure became increasingly similar to the competition among the Japanese auto producers in their home markets."[32] In other words, the local assemblers were merely serving as instruments for Japanese penetration of the local market. This was, of course, an ironic development, inasmuch as the government banned the entry of already assembled Japanese cars and imposed high tariffs and high taxes on assembled American and European cars precisely to develop a technologically dynamic domestic auto industry.[33]

According to a 1972 report by the Industrial Development Board, almost all of the automobile assemblers and parts producers acquired their technology and production know-how under license from foreign sources, in most cases from Japan.[34] It did not seem, however, that significant backward linkages were created or that substantial technology transfer took place. For instance, in the case of Yue Loong:

> Local content for the Nissan-licensed sedans has increased from 35 percent in 1960 to about 60 percent in 1975. However, the most critical parts are still sourced

from Japan. Moreover, all designs are still under the strict control of the parent company. According to the agreement, Yue Loong is not allowed to export the vehicles produced under the agreement. Production is only for the local market.[35]

Low-volume production, high domestic prices (sometimes double the international price of a similar model), dependence on foreign technology, and a short-term profit orientation on the part of the assemblers characterized the industry until the late 1970s. Though the producers were stagnant, however, the market was profitable, as indicated by Ford's enthusiastic purchase of 70 percent of the equity of Lio Ho in 1972, when Toyota severed its tie to the Taiwanese firm in order to set foot on the mainland.

One of the problems was that with tariff rates on imported automobiles set so high, the automobile manufacturers could simply raise their prices to fulfill local content requirements and still sell their cars. As Kuo points out, "If the price [of a car] is $1000 and the value of imported parts is $500, the ratio of domestic value added is 50 percent. However, if the price is $2000 and the value of imported parts is still $500, the ratio will become 75 percent."[36]

Indeed, despite talk about a vibrant auto-parts industry, severe technological stagnation in manufacturing processes was plaguing the industry. Among both the assemblers and the auto-parts makers, product quality was hampered by continued dependence on manual production methods, backwardness in precision processing, and virtual absence of design capabilities for automobiles and automobile components.[37] A list of basic deficiencies shared by the Taiwanese and Korean auto industries was laid out by Konomi Tomisawa:

> In press metal mold, for instance, metal mold with rigidity and strength for mass production has not been produced to now because small volume production was sufficient. They are also weak in metal molds which require precision processing both in designing and processing. The related industries also do not have lightweight material and processing technology for parts and components used in automobile engines that can endure high output and high speed rotation. Nor do they have any high quality plastic which does not change in color or get deformed after long hours of use. They also have to depend on Japanese products

if they try to mass produce or improve processing precision in their facilities.[38]

What all this showed was that market incentives alone were not enough to create an industry. In contrast to its counterpart in Korea, Taiwanese big business was cautious. But then the Taiwanese did not have the guaranteed access to credit that might have overcome their propensity towards short-term profit-making and encouraged risk-taking. They were saddled with a government that was one of the most conservative in the world in the management of state finances. Moreover, the absence of a heavy industrial base to provide key inputs was a major constraint, and this base could not simply be called into existence by demand from downstream, or consumer goods, industries but had to be created through massive, targeted investment.

Thus, in the late 1970s, frustrated government officials designated the automobile industry as one of the strategic industries. Perhaps a key factor influencing their decision was Hyundai's successful Pony, which was seeking entry into the Taiwanese automobile market in the late 1970s.[39] To put teeth into its efforts, the government raised the local-content ratio to 70 percent on most vehicles and set up the Automobile Industry Technology Research Team. In August 1979 the government passed the Automobile Industry Promotion Act, which contained the following goals: establishment of a plant to manufacture civilian and military trucks; setting up of an export-oriented automobile plant with an annual capacity of 200,000 units; development of advanced and high-quality parts manufacture; and advancing research-and-development capabilities.[40]

In implementing the new guidelines, the state practically left the six domestic and joint-venture automakers behind and brought in two state enterprises to manage the truck and export-car projects, Taiwan Machinery and China Steel. The rationale apparently was that through vertical integration, that is, combining the heavy industrial base of these two enterprises with motor vehicle production, economies of scale would result, lowering costs, reducing supply bottlenecks, and facilitating technological upgrading.

The truck project, worked out with General Motors, turned out to be a financial fiasco. China Steel, on the other hand, was able to reach tentative agreement with Toyota for a joint car venture with the following points: annual production of 300,000 units; achievement of 90 percent domestic content in five years; and reaching a 50 percent export target in eight years.[41] This was an ambitious plan to force technology transfer and develop significant backward and forward linkages via a partnership between a state enterprise and the most advanced world manufacturer. But the deal fell through, partly as a result of Toyota's unwillingness to agree to a fairly rigid government schedule that specified a strictly enforceable year-by-year plan for reaching domestic-content and export-ratio targets, partly by moves on the part of Yue Loong and Ford Lio Ho to sabotage the deal.[42]

But a more important reason for the demise of the Big Auto Plant project was internecine bureaucratic conflict between two paradigms for the development of the auto industry. This conflict politicized the whole process and made it difficult for Taiwan's technocrats to act as one and effectively negotiate with Toyota. On one side were technocrats at the Council for Economic Planning and Development (CEPD), whose formula for upgrading consisted of rapid technology transfer via the Big Auto Plant project, accelerated liberalization of the auto industry, and swift development of the automotive-parts industry. This approach put less stress on protecting existing assemblers than on rapid upgrading of the industry as a whole, not only to service the domestic economy but also to compete internationally. On the other side were leading technocrats at the Ministry of Economic Affairs, who espoused a more traditional approach that emphasized "continuation of Taiwan's import substitution policy, a high local content requirement in automobile production, maintaining a generally protectionist import policy, and, finally, controlling the importation of foreign automotive technology."[43]

The scrapping of the Big Auto Plant project turned out to be the divided technocrats' final attempt to force technology transfer from abroad in order to eventually produce Taiwanese-designed automobiles manufactured by Taiwanese assemblers with Taiwanese components. In 1985, the government made an about face, gave up the goal of a domestic industry–dominated car market, and sought instead the integration of Taiwanese capabilities into the emerging international division of labor in the automobile industry. The Automobile Industry Development Act passed in 1985 contained the following drastic measures: reduction of the tariff on imported cars from 65 percent in 1985 to 30 percent in 1990; reduction of the local content ratio from 70 percent in 1985 to 50 percent in 1988; abolition of the local-content ratio for exported cars; and no regulation on the entry and amount of foreign capital destined for parts production or export-car production.[44]

One immediate effect was to step up the denationalization of the industry in the name of efficiency and competitiveness. In addition to Ford Lio Ho, which is owned 70 percent by Ford, and Sanyang, which is owned 14 percent by Honda, new equity links were forged. Nissan took a 25 percent stake in Yue Loong in 1987. In the following year, Toyota bought 22 percent of truck manufacturer Kuo Zui; Mitsubishi bought 25 percent of China Motor; and Fuji Heavy Industries bought 45 percent of Ta Ching Motors.[45]

As one government official saw it, "The goal is to be part of the international division of labor rather than developing a fully integrated industry."[46] Another underlined: "We have to make ourselves an indispensable part of multinational corporations' worldwide strategy."[47] In this effort, Taiwan would serve mainly as an assembly point for American, Japanese, or American-Japanese multinational car ventures. For instance, Ford Lio Ho plans to engage in the knockdown production of Mazda automobiles not only for the domestic market but also for export to the United States. (For more on tie-ups between the Taiwanese auto industry and foreign corporations see figure 15.1.)

Unlike the Koreans, the Taiwanese were gearing their goal away from competition to complementary production within a Japanese-imposed division of labor. Says one Japanese analyst, using words reminiscent of wartime Japan's economic vision, "China-Taiwan aims for coexistence and coprosperity with Japan by producing the items that are not economically suitable for Japan."[48] However, the Japanese-imposed division of labor "is not an equal division of labor as seen among the EC countries, but a vertical one within the automobile industry as a whole. In other words, it will mostly be inter-product division of labor on low-price compact cars which have fewer parts and a higher percentage of labor in the entire process."[49] Taiwan's main contribution in the grand scheme remained, in short, its manufacturing capability based on cheap labor. Needless to say, this was a fragile asset in the face of competition for the investments of the auto multinationals from other countries with lower labor costs, especially at a time when Taiwanese wages were inexorably on the rise.

Figure 15.1:

Tie-ins between Taiwanese Automobile Manufacturers and Foreign Corporations

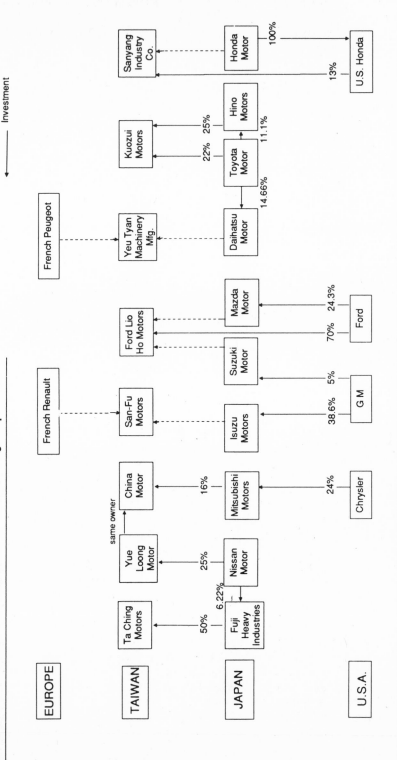

Source: Konomi Tomisawa, "Development and Future Outlook for an International Division of Labor in the Automobile Industries of Asian Nics" (Briefing paper for the First Policy Forum of the International Motor Vehicle Program, May 5, 1987), p.13.

Electronics: Beyond Cloning?

Currently the workhorse of the Taiwanese export machine, electronics is an industry worth more than $8 billion. While consumer electronics still garners most revenues, Taiwan has also developed a strong computer industry and a semiconductor industry. It shipped more than 2 million personal computers in 1988, accounting for 10 percent of all personal computers produced worldwide.[50]

But despite its seemingly stunning achievements, Taiwan's industry is built on sand, in terms of technology.

The electronics industry in Taiwan began with foreign investors looking for cheap labor sites beginning in the mid-1960s. U.S., European, and Japanese and firms, such as Zenith, RCA, Philips, and Matsushita, came to Taiwan in the 1960s and 1970s and set up assembly lines designed to produce television sets and other consumer commodities for export to the United States. Many Taiwanese companies arose to service these big foreign producers, making capacitors, resistors, transformers, tuners, antennas, and picture tubes. Much of this was accomplished by low-tech imitative strategies, sometimes with foreign supervision, more often through elementary reverse-engineering of components, embodying what Ashoka Mody describes as "elementary technology."[51]

Domestic firms that relied principally on cheap assembly labor branched out from producing components and parts for black-and-white and color television in the 1970s to producing computer peripherals on an original equipment manufacturer (OEM) basis for mainly U.S. firms. As Morris Crawford notes,

> Segments of Taiwan's computer industry began in its consumer electronics firms. Initially, these companies supplied export markets with products or simple components that could be made with relatively little change in their factories.[52]

Computer peripherals and personal computers, as well as consumer electronics items like VCRs, are what Mody calls "medium technology" products, characterized by low-medium technological requirements in both design and manufacturing.[53] Indeed, many skeptics point out that most of these products "do not possess any more high technology than the products [low-cost television components] that preceded them."[54] Be that as it may, it was on the basis of these products that Taiwan established itself as an electronics powerhouse. By the late 1980s terminals, disk drives, printers, and monitors accounted for 70 percent of Taiwan's electronics output.[55] Seventy-five percent of that output went to U.S. computer firms, who were mainly looking for low-cost products made by cheap labor rather than innovative, high-tech, design-intensive items.

Achieving such skill at making low-tech or low-medium tech items was not easy. As Mody points out, "There is considerable anecdotal evidence which suggests that the Japanese have restrained the technological development of their collaborators."[56] Indeed, in contrast to Korea, "the hangover of the Japanese connection is such that even when components are available locally they are often imported from Japan."[57]

Computers: From Cloning to Innovation?

Contrary to the popular impression, cloning computers—an activity in which Taiwan has excelled—is not a high-tech affair. As in Korea, it was the 8-bit Apple II personal computer that gave Taiwan's cloners their start, because it was relatively easy to reverse-engineer and assemble from commercially available, off-the-shelf components. Taiwanese copycats, with some ingenuity, some engineering skills, and a lot of cheap labor turned out products with brand names like Orange and Pineapple.[58] Says one account: "The Apple II was an especially easy model to copy; almost any electronics shop in Taiwan could use off-the-shelf parts to duplicate the circuit board at the computer's heart."[59]

Having gained experience with the Apple, Taiwan's cloners turned to the IBM PC in 1982. Like the Apple, the IBM PC had open architecture; indeed, IBM made its PC easy to copy and encouraged the proliferation of PC clones to "gain market penetration in its battle with Apple."[60] Many Taiwanese entrepreneurs were more than happy to take the invitation, and few of them had high-tech capabilities. One cloner, for instance, simply shifted his small factory from producing switches for video games to making exact replicas of the IBM PC, with the help of a few engineers. With the demand for clones in China and Japan, his business grew rapidly.[61]

Many more small entrepreneurs jumped into the business when U.S. companies like Chips and Technologies managed to pack more processing power into fewer chips and sold the chips sets, with IBM-compatible circuitry, in the open market.[62] In fact, these chip sets provided a means by which "scores of companies could produce [PC] AT clones faster, cheaper, better, and more reliable than IBM's."[63]

Taiwan's computer industry is really a glorified title for the mass cloning of easy-to-copy IBM models. Fourteen percent of the world's IBM PC clones are made by Taiwanese manufacturers.[64] According to one observer it is not innovative capability that accounts for Taiwan's international strength in computers but "sheer volume."[65] In 1989 the Taiwanese were expected to sell 3 million finished PCs, as well as 3 million system boards—the core of PCs assembled by small manufacturers around the world.[66]

While a handful of Taiwanese firms developed some design and innovation capability, for the most part clever imitation was at the heart of the Taiwanese computer industry. As Stan Shih, the much-admired president of Acer (Taiwan's premier computer firm, which had revenues of about $500 million in 1988), admitted, "Although we are not a global technological leader, we endeavor to be a quick follower of global technological developments. For instance, we are the second firm in the world to produce both the 80386 [Intel micropocessor-based] computer and the IBM PS/2 compatible."[67]

What distinguishes Acer, however, from other Taiwanese producers is that like the Korean conglomerates it appears to have mastered manufacturing efficiencies—that is, it has managed to efficiently assemble imported computer parts on a massive scale, using a combination of imported high technology and low-wage labor. A revealing account of Acer's capabilities is provided by David Sanger:

> Visitors to Acer's new plant in the Government-supported science and industry park here, an hour from Taipei, might be forgiven for thinking that they were in one of the computer manufacturing plants of the International Business Machines Corporation or the Compaq Computer Corporation. Like I.B.M. and Compaq, Acer now assembles personal computers on moving 'pallets' designed to test each freshly assembled machine automatically. Robots move around, stacking inventory and sending computers that fail quality-control tests back for repair.
>
> In fact, the use of basically the same parts— Panasonic disk drives, Oki chips and Chips and Technologies chip sets—in machines sold under different

labels has allowed economies of scale that are crucial to the company's phenomenal growth.

Taiwan's low wages are a big factor, too. The rows of young women who spend endless hours pressing tiny chips onto circuit boards—the grinding, monotonous work that makes up the least glamorous side of the industry—get about $350 a month, a fraction of the wages in Silicon Valley.[68]

This account suggests several things about Acer and the other leading-edge Taiwanese cloners:

First, Taiwan's computer industry still largely consists of assembling imported parts and components, although it is probably less dependent on imported parts than the Korean computer industry. As a representative from Acer's main rival, Mitac Corporation, stated, "Half the parts of our machines, including the more complex chips, come from the U.S. and Japan."[69] For instance, key chips used in legal copies of IBM PCs are supplied by the U.S. firm Phoenix Technologies, which gets up to 20 percent of its $65 million in annual revenues from Taiwan.[70]

Second, like its Korean counterparts, Acer's edge appears to lie in its efficient organization of a production process that still relies to a great extent on cheap labor. The Acer factory, in fact, appears to be a prime example of the discontinuous process of managed improvisation described by Wenlee Ting, in which some automated high-tech processes are interspersed with classic labor-intensive production lines.[71] This makes for efficient cloning, but hardly indicates a capacity for self-sustaining product innovation.

Third, Taiwan's skill at mass manufacturing with low labor costs is merely an upgrading of its traditional role as a supplier on an OEM basis for foreign firms using licensed technology. For instance, Acer makes not only IBM PC compatibles and the IBM PS/2 but also, using licensed, borrowed technology, Unisys's most advanced PC, powered by an Intel 80386 microprocessor; Canon PCs for the Japanese electronics maker; and Philips PCs for the European market.[72] IBM's competitor, Sun Microsystems of Mountain View, California, recently licensed two big Taiwanese electronics manufacturers, Datatech Enterprises and Tatung, to produce low-end desktop computers based on Sun's Sparc microprocessor design and its software. This was part of Sun's strategy to "make the combination of Sparc hardware and Unix operating software as popular as IBM-compatible personal computers."[73] The Japanese giant Toshiba has also licensed its technology to the

Taiwanese as part of its own strategy to make its PCs an industry standard.[74]

In short, the attractiveness of Taiwan as a contractor continues to be its efficient organization of cheap labor. And this time, in addition to cheap, unskilled female labor, the multinationals are making use of cheap skilled labor. Competent engineers trained in Taiwan's universities can be hired at $10,000 a year[75]—far less than the standard rates for engineers in the United States. But as in textiles and the automobile industry, cheap labor is a fragile asset, as third world countries with much lower wage costs for both unskilled and skilled labor than Taiwan's make determined bids to attract the electronics multinationals.

Moreover, producing under OEM contracts or under license has severe drawbacks, including low profit rates. Acer, for instance, plans to pay IBM between 2 and 4 percent for licensing rights to various PC technologies.[76] While this may be tolerable in good times, in bad times it severely limits profitability—as in the first half of 1989, when a slowdown in sales of older PCs cut Acer's profits by 54 percent.[77] Giants like Acer can absorb royalty payments, but royalties make life infinitely more difficult for the smaller manufacturers, for whom as little as 5 percent royalties—the amount initially proposed by IBM for its PS/2 model—would be devastating because of the already low profit margins.

The Chip Challenge

In semiconductors, Taiwan began as a haven for U.S. firms like Texas Instruments seeking cheap female labor for the labor-intensive operation of wiring together packaged chips in wafers shipped from high-tech wafer-fabrication labs in the United States. But with labor costs in Taiwan rising, many semiconductor firms have preferred to go to lower-wage areas like Malaysia and the Philippines instead. To avoid a ghost-town fate after the cheap-labor boom, the Taiwanese government took the lead in developing the front-end wafer fabrication, the high-valued-added and technology-intensive segment of the industry.

The government has taken a number of initiatives to make up for the private sector's caution or simple lack of capital. Among other things, it set up a high-tech research outfit, the Electronics Research and Service Organization (ERSO), to provide basic research and development for electronics companies. ERSO basically assembles groups of interested companies for collective

R&D, with the government throwing in a huge chunk of the project financing. Currently, the government funds almost half of electronics R&D in Taiwan.[78] ERSO has also supplied financing to launch chip manufacturers, like United Microelectronics Corporation (UMC), Taiwan's first manufacturer of integrated circuits.

Another government initiative was its provision of over 48 percent of the capital for the Taiwan Semiconductor Manufacturing Company (TSMC), a joint venture with the Dutch multinational Philips and private Taiwanese firms, to manufacture complex computer chips, many of them designed by ERSO's engineers. By 1989 TMSC was manufacturing some 12,000 chips a month.[79]

The government is not, however, directly involved as a participant in the most publicized joint venture, the one between Texas Instruments and Acer to produce DRAMs for Taiwan's computer industry.

Despite this flurry of joint ventures, it is still unlikely that the Taiwanese will be key players in front-end semiconductor fabrication, apart from the few successes like UMC and TSMC. Three factors handicap the Taiwanese semiconductor players: shortage of capital, low R&D, and lack of high-tech personnel.

Except for a few state-aided ventures, most Taiwanese firms do not have the capital resources for semiconductor competition. Advanced semiconductors require an initial investment of at least $100 million,[80] an amount that is beyond the capabilities of Taiwan's typically small- and medium-size firms. The conglomerate structure is the key difference between Korea's ability to manufacture the all-important DRAMs and Taiwan's hesitation to move in this direction. As Mody notes, "The Koreans have been, and will continue to be, more successful than the Taiwanese because the historical evolution of their organizational structure (specifically the growth of large firms) places them today in a position to undertake large and risky investments. In contrast, the Taiwanese firms are of a much smaller size, making them considerably more dependent on government support, and creating much stronger barriers to moving to successively new generations."[81]

The Taiwanese and the Koreans are in a savage competition in the electronics field, and the Koreans' ability to support their semiconductor operations with profits in other electronics areas has made a telling difference. As Mody describes it:

What the Taiwanese firms lack, in comparison with Korean conglomerates, is organizational economies of scale. In purchasing inputs and even more in international marketing, Korean firms have been able to do much better because they sell large volumes of individual products and they sell several products. For example, for a period of time, Taiwanese firms had larger exports of personal computer systems than Korean firms. However, in the past few years, Daewoo and Hyundai have begun marketing very large volumes of personal computers. "The Koreans have poured $100 million into new computer plants to improve efficiency and have been quoting prices that the Taiwanese are struggling to match. To keep up, the Taiwanese have cut prices, but the South Koreans can quickly outpace them by switching factories from TV and VCR production to computers if necessary." Similarly, Korean firms have begun marketing a number of products in the United States under their own brand names; Taiwanese firms, with minor exceptions, are a long way from that stage.[82]

Indeed, the incipient move to produce not memory chips but the customized application-specific logic processors is being dictated by competition from the organizationally superior South Korean firms. What Acer president Stan Shih said of the competition in computers applies just as well to semiconductors: "It is dangerous to stay in the low end of the computer market, an easy target for other companies along the Pacific Rim, especially the South Koreans."[83]

But if the Taiwanese might not be able to compete with the Koreans and the Japanese in the mass production of memory chips, can they succeed by cultivating niche markets, that is, by specializing in logic chips, or ASICs, that control a variety of specific functions? The Taiwanese may well succeed, for a time. The history of the U.S. microelectronics industry is full of examples of small-scale corporate innovators who successfully carved out niches in design-intensive areas of both hardware and software. But the problem, Mody points out, is that niche markets do not remain niches for long; when they become mass markets they become subject to economies of scale that favor the capital-rich Korean or Japanese giants:

There are some problems with the actual realization of...potential comparative advantage in design-oriented activities. The medium-size firms face problems of growth. As noted, they rely on niche markets. Over time, however, a niche market changes character: it either disappears or it grows into a mass market. If the latter happens, large firms with superior resources are attracted. The ensuing competition is usually very hard on the smaller firms.[84]

The second major obstacle hampering Taiwanese efforts in semiconductors is the still-low level of R&D activity. Acer is said to devote 5 percent of its revenues annually to R&D, but that is the exception rather than the rule. According to a recent survey by the National Science Council, Taiwan's firms on average spend just 0.44 percent of sales on R&D—far less than firms in most industrialized countries.[85] (See table 15.2 for data on combined public and private R&D expenditures.) Tom Wang, the expert on the Taiwanese electronics industry at Dataquest, claims that Taiwanese firms in fact spend proportionally less of their revenues on R&D than Korean firms, which are not noted for splurging on R&D.[86]

Part of the problem is apparently the sheer lack of capital of most electronic firms: one government report reveals that of Taiwan's 2,078 electronics firms, only 136 had sales of over $10 million per company; most of them had sales of less than $1 million.[87]

The vaunted Hsinchu Industrial Park, which hosts eighty high-tech companies, is in this context an island in a low-capital, labor-intensive sea. And as one account points out, "The state of technological advancement of Hsinchu [should] not be exaggerated. Its stress on computer software, microcomputers and peripherals, electronics and bioengineering, still leaves it as 'high value added' by Taiwan's standards, but low technology by comparison with even the lower range of industrialized countries."[88]

Low capability in R&D is due not only to low capital formation but also to a short-term profit mentality or the "absence of long-term business planning on the part of local suppliers, who sometimes jeopardize long-term partnerships for short-term windfalls."[89] This orientation towards the short term has in fact led many foreign electronics buyers to worry that "many local manufacturers, distracted by potentially lucrative speculation in Taiwan's overheated stock and real estate markets are reluctant to engage in vigorous investment activities, a phenomenon which

Table 15.2

Combined Government and Business Expenditures on Research and Development as Percentage of GNP

Country	R&D Expenditures as Percentage of GNP[a]
Taiwan	0.99
Korea	2.00
West Germany	3.00
Japan	3.00
United States	3.00

Source: Liang Kuo-Shu and Liang Ching-Ing Hou, "Trade Strategy and Industrial Policy in Taiwan," in Thornton Bradshaw et al., eds., *America's New Competitors* (Cambridge: Ballinger Publishing Co., 1988), p. 65.; John Wilson and Sheridan Tatsuno, "South Korea: Following the Leader," *Strategic Issues* (Dataquest), February 1989, p. 7.

[a] Taiwan data from 1984; all others from 1988.

threatens the future development of the island republic's information industry."[90] Nearly 20 percent of Taiwan's publicly traded firms now earn more than 50 percent of their pretax recurring profits from activities outside their principal operations—a sure sign of heavily playing the stock market.[91]

Taiwan has reached the point where the old methods of reverse engineering, no matter how ingenious, can no longer substitute for R&D that produces design and process innovations to match Japanese and American advances and outmaneuver the Koreans. As Crawford notes, reverse engineering is hardly a cheap way to acquire expensive know-how:

> Reverse engineering is by no means a simple route to technology, or a cheap way to get expensive know-how. Reverse engineering takes longer than licensing to get the technological knowledge, and may produce information that is obsolete by the time it can be used on the production line. The ERSO experience with its disk drives [that were obsolete by the time they were ready] is a case in point. Reverse engineering also may produce inaccurate results that lead to costly production errors. Many industrialists and business advisors

regard reverse engineering as an expensive, inadequate substitute for licensing.

The most difficult part of R&D, he continues, is in applying
technology to the production line, and here,

> reverse engineering and other forms of technology
> transfer can only give the manufacturer detailed in-
> formation. He must still apply the knowledge in his
> own manufacturing environment and do it in a way
> that will "cut production costs to the bone and still
> turn out a reliable product."[92]

Interestingly, Taiwan has a different problem from Korea when
it comes to R&D. Whereas excessive conglomerate power appeared to be a hindrance to innovation in Korea, in Taiwan the
cutthroat competition among the many small Taiwanese producers made profits so small that little was left over for R&D.

Related to the lack of R&D is the third major obstacle to developing the capacity of sustained innovation in microelectronics: the
insufficiency of technical personnel. Mody points out that it may
be incorrect to assume that the potential pool of skilled technical
manpower in Taiwan and other NICs is very large. Expanding the
hardware and software design sector will involve "manpower
requirements [that] will be very high and it is not obvious that the
supply will keep pace."[93]

Indeed, the supply is not keeping pace in Taiwan. Dataquest's
Tom Wang bemoans the fact that Taiwan does not have a strong
engineering base because "not enough people are specializing in
technical fields."[94] Despite some well-known cases of "reverse
brain drain," such as F. C. Miau, one of the founders of a leading
electronics firm, Mitac, the island continues to suffer from a "serious brain-drain problem—20 percent of college graduates go
abroad to get higher degrees; only 20 percent return."[95] Tom Wang
claims that "the best students are educated in American universities, then work for U.S. companies."[96] One recent estimate of the
number of Taiwanese scientists and engineers in the United States
puts it at 30,000.[97]

Perhaps the most cogent assessment of the island's future in
electronics was provided by a high-level engineer from Sun Microsystems with extensive experience in Taiwan:

> Taiwan will be very competitive mainly at the low
> tech tier of the industry, producing the capacitors,
> resistors, transistors, and cables, all the low-cost com-

ponents that people elsewhere don't want to produce anymore. But Taiwan isn't Korea. Without significant government support and involvement, it won't be able to really compete at the higher, high-tech tiers, where you can't simply depend on cloning anymore but you need constant innovation.[98]

Conclusion

As Taiwan's competitive advantage in labor costs was eroding in the face of severe wage competition from other third world countries, its technocrats offered the vision of a high-tech future. That vision, however, is turning out to be an illusion, as significant obstacles stand in the way of the structural transformation of the Taiwanese economy.

Japanese and U.S. corporations resisted significant transfer of advanced technologies, and their preference for their traditional suppliers limited the backward-linkage effects of their investments in Taiwan.

A close look at three key industries reveals the difficulties Taiwan encounters in making the technological transition.

In textiles and garments, continuing reliance on cheap labor and the lack of capital to upgrade and automate machinery have placed the industry between a rock and a hard place, threatened from below by third world manufacturers with much lower labor costs, but unable to compete in upscale, high-fashion items against the highly automated production processes and greater sophistication of producers in the advanced countries.

In automobiles, the enormous capital and technological requirements of competing successfully with the giants of the international automobile industry have forced the KMT government to retreat from its initial ambition of making Taiwan an independent producer with a self-sustaining technological capability. Instead it has had to accept a subordinate role in whatever division of labor is designed by the big Japanese, American, and European assemblers.

In the strategic area of electronics, Taiwan is finding it difficult to graduate from mass cloning based on the efficient organization of cheap labor and managed improvisation in the production process. Lack of capital resources, little R&D by firms that oftentimes preferred to play the stock market, and a still very limited base of technical personnel pose major obstacles to self-sustaining innovation in high technology.

In sum, despite its increasingly middle-class affluence in comparison with other third world countries, Taiwan's economy continues to be essentially founded on cheap labor. And this has been an increasingly fragile asset.

16

Taiwan's Dilemmas

The realization that transforming Taiwan's economy into a high-tech, R&D-based economy may not be a realistic option appears to be spreading among KMT technocrats. A gap is actually developing between rhetoric and reality, says social policy critic Michael Hsiao: "Moving up to more value-added, capital-intensive production is the stated policy, but reliance on labor-intensive production remains the operative policy."[1]

Sticking to Cheap Labor

The technocrats have no choice, for the response of Taiwanese businesses and foreign investors to the upward pressure on wages has not been to move to automate or shift their investments to high-tech areas. Instead they have chosen to transfer capital to China and other low-wage countries in Southeast Asia and the Caribbean and to bring in foreign workers to fill the labor shortage and depress wage rates.

In 1988 and the first eight months of 1989 alone, an estimated $3.3 billion was invested abroad by Taiwanese businessmen. A favorite target for the island's investors was Southeast Asia, where wages stood at one-third to one-half of wages in Taiwan. Thailand, known for its stability, accounted for some $2 billion in 1988 alone. Also in 1988, Indonesia drew $913 million from Taiwan, Malaysia $307 million, and the Philippines $105 million.[2] Another popular area, particularly for textile and garment manufacturers, was the Caribbean, which offered not only cheap labor but also special access to the U.S. market under some provisions of the Caribbean Basin Initiative.

China, however, promised to develop as Taiwan's strategic reserve for cheap labor. With wages in China as low as one-twentieth of wages on the island, investors have flocked across the

Taiwan Straits to invest an estimated $1 billion in China, disregarding the formal political hostility that still marks the relations between the two nations.[3] The migrant companies include electronics assemblers, as well as shoe and textile and garment operations. Two hundred twenty-five enterprises, a huge chunk of Taiwan's shoemaking industry, have settled across the straits.[4]

But it was not only local entrepreneurs that were dismantling, or seriously considering dismantling, their local operations, but also some big Taiwan businesses. Formosa Plastics, the island's biggest private business group, publicly stated that it was no longer sure about continuing to invest in Taiwan and was actively looking for an alternative site to build a naphtha cracker.[5] Foreign investors were also not heeding the government's policy to upgrade their production technology, many of them preferring to move instead. For instance, Crown Corporation, a Japanese audio equipment maker, shifted most of its manufacturing operations from Taiwan to the Shenzen Economic Zone in China. Another Japanese firm, telecommunications manufacturer Uniden, transferred its main factories from Taiwan and Hong Kong to the Philippines and China. The rationale articulated by Sakari Suya, president of one of the Uniden affiliates, confirmed much past Taiwanese criticism about the Japanese not wanting to move up to high-tech production: "The starting salary of women employees is typically 1900 pesos—roughly one-third that in Taiwan. It is easier to recruit qualified employees in the Philippines, and since very few people quit their jobs, it is very advantageous to makers such as ours, which require workers to perform repetitive tasks."[6]

The other route to cheap labor is importing foreign workers. There is no agreed-upon estimate of the number of foreign workers in Taiwan, but according to the Economist Intelligence Unit, as of mid-1988, "10,000 such workers were legally employed in Taiwan, and a further 50,000–80,000 were guessed to be working illegally."[7]

Whatever the dispute on their numbers, the workers have become a central fact of Taiwanese economic life. Whole factories are now said to be run mainly on foreign labor.[8] The workers are concentrated "in the industrial Taipei suburb of Taoyuan and in central Taiwan. Both have a preponderance of small to medium-sized factories."[9]

Most of the workers are Filipinos, Thais, Indonesians, and Malaysians. Their average wage rates were reported at around

$250 a month, or less than half the average monthly earnings of workers in manufacturing.[10] Illegal workers smuggled in from China were in even worse shape: construction workers from the mainland, who had slipped into Taiwan on fake foreign passports or jumped from fishing boats, received less than one-third of the wage paid to local laborers.[11]

Apart from their low wages, illegal workers live very difficult lives. By employing workers outside the jurisdiction of the Labor Standards Law, firms are under no obligation to provide them any benefits, such as health insurance, vacation time, severance pay, or pension.[12] Also, employers often confiscate their workers' passports, so that even illegal aliens who originally entered Taiwan on tourist visas find it difficult to return home.[13] Placement agents are particularly a scourge on illegal workers. As one account of the lives of Filipina maids, or *amahs*, observed:

> All the Filipinas agreed that working through a placement agency is undesirable. This is because the threat of deportation is often used by agencies to ensure complicity and obedience on the part of the amahs. An agency may pay for one's flight from the Philippines, help with official paperwork at both ends, provide a lump sum in advance to one's family at home (as much as US$1000, a huge amount by current Filipino standards), and guarantee a position upon arrival in Taiwan. Of course, the amah is expected to repay all this, and is also charged a commission. As a result, the amah may only get half of her earnings for a year or more, and she is locked into the job provided her, regardless of conditions there. In order to prevent an amah from running, agencies will confiscate her passport immediately upon arrival, making escape all but impossible.[14]

And of course there is the constant threat of deportation by the state, which is exercised arbitrarily. For while working in Taiwan with a tourist visa may not be legal, "it is not exactly illegal either. Article 15 of the Foreign Visa Regulations states that the holder of a visa shall not do anything besides the 'purpose' stated in the application, though there is no prescribed punishment for any breach. The only possible sanctions are the requirements to pay undeclared taxes and possible difficulty when applying for reentry."[15]

There are reasons for the government's ambiguous posture. One is clearly to dampen the wage demands of the labor force and keep unions weak with the threat of covertly encouraging the growth of an illegal labor force or even legalizing it. Another purpose served by the government's studied ambiguity is to keep the Taiwanese business community off balance in the interest of assuring the dominance of the mainlander elite. Many small- and medium-size Taiwanese capitalists fear a KMT-labor understanding that would tighten restrictions on the movement and employment of foreign labor and impose sanctions on firms that employed illegal workers.

Be that as it may, what we now see is the development of a labor system similar to that which developed in Europe in the 1960s and 1970s: a two-tier labor force composed of poorly paid, unorganized guest workers and better-paid, organized indigenous workers. The presence of foreign workers dampens the wage demands of the local labor force, while chauvinism is encouraged to keep foreign workers in their place. The bargain is Faustian in the classical sense, for Taiwan may well be able to slow down its loss of competitiveness in wage costs, but only at the price of provoking destabilizing social conflicts.

Taiwan's Crisis

The dilemma of losing the cheap-labor advantage to other third world producers but being unable to make the transition to a high-tech, skill-intensive economy is but one dimension of a larger crisis overtaking the Taiwanese route to development. Like Korea, Taiwan faces the problem of a late democratization that comes on the heels of high-speed late industrialization. By excluding the working class so forcefully from the decision-making process, the KMT created an opposition force that felt it had no strong stake in the continuing success of the KMT's chosen path of economic growth. One of the tragic legacies of late democratization is profound alienation; and while the Taiwanese working class still has to attain the level of militance of Korean workers, it is only a matter of time before that combative consciousness is attained. Late democratization ensures that politics in the era of political decompression will focus not on achieving consensus on the strategic direction of the economy but on the battle for the fair distribution of the benefits of high-speed growth, which workers feel have been long denied them.

The costs of the couplet of late industrialization and late democratization include one of the world's most serious environmental crises and the profound erosion of the agrarian economy. Certainly, ordinary citizens and farmers were aware, even at the period of takeoff, of the deterious effects of pesticides, fertilizers, toxic wastes, and unrestricted air pollution. Yet they found no political outlet to express their concerns, which were swamped by the KMT's overwhelming emphasis on growth at any cost. As a result, what took centuries to accomplish in the West—the destruction of vital dimensions of the environment— has been telescoped into three decades in Taiwan. Ironically, one of the boasts of Taiwan's technocrats—that industrialization is dispersed through the rural areas—has became a major cause of the environmental disaster. Growth imposed from above, with no democratic controls, has produced an ecological mess that some environmentalists fear might be too late to rectify.

With no political outlets for protest, farmers were rendered quiescent as agricultural development was subordinated to export-oriented industrialization, the countryside was depopulated, and those who remained were reduced to deriving most of their income from nonagricultural pursuits. When a weak-kneed KMT caved in to U.S. demands to open up the domestic market to U.S. agricultural surpluses, the farmers finally took to the streets to try to stop the looming extinction of much of Taiwanese agriculture. Among other things, the explosion ended the so-called KMT– small farmer alliance that had been built on the land reform carried out in the now-distant past. This left the KMT with one less bulwark to place against the emergence of an independent-minded working class, the rise of a vigorous environmental movement, and the increasing dissatisfaction of Taiwan's small entrepreneurs.

In the face of these challenges, the capability of the KMT-business elite to continue imposing a policy of high-speed, export-oriented, and cheap-labor-dependent industrialization has been weakened by frictions in the ruling coalitions of mainlander politicians and businesses and Taiwanese capitalists, and of the KMT regime and the mass of Taiwanese small- and medium-size entrepreneurs who see themselves as being systematically discriminated against. Increasing support from these sources for the opposition Democratic Progressive party threatens to translate an economic contradiction into a political one as well.

Taiwan, then, is headed not only for major structural difficulties in its economy but also for decades of social and political instability. A belated attempt to introduce democratic competition and grant labor a new status may indeed be too late to save both KMT hegemony and the paradigm of export-oriented growth.

Towards an Alternative Economic Program

But is there a viable alternative to the thirty-year-old model of growth? As in Korea, no coherent alternative program has yet emerged, but different elements are emerging in the public debate on the deepening political and economic crisis. Perhaps foremost is the need to end the extreme dependence on volatile export markets by making domestic demand and domestic needs the main engine of growth. Although the absolute rise of incomes has created a viable domestic market, sustaining and expanding this market will demand social measures correcting the increasingly unequal distribution of national income and, especially, the lopsided difference in urban and rural incomes.

Taiwan must also propel a massive investment program to save agriculture and the environment. Such an enterprise would not only fulfill urgent social needs, but create new stimuli for domestic-driven economic growth. A revitalized agrarian economy based on small farms and cooperatives could complement urban demand, while an environmental rescue program would stimulate the emergence of a new industry producing anti-pollution equipment. While an environmentally benign, domestic demand–driven strategy might result in lower growth rates in the long term, its impact would be a more viable economy with healthier long-term prospects produced by radically reducing the heavy costs imposed by strip-mine high-speed industrialization.

In its relations with external economies, Taiwan might forge equitable agreements on trade, technology transfer, and investments with neighboring countries, particularly in Southeast Asia. Rather than create the lopsided division of labor and unequal patterns of trade characteristic of Japanese and U.S. corporate expansion, Taiwan, together with Korea, could promote regional arrangements in which technological advances would be diffused more evenly, the benefits from trade spread out more evenly, and the negative impacts of foreign investments limited more effectively. It would be important to forge regional and international investment codes to make the runaway shop option less attractive by preventing government and corporations from undercutting the welfare of different countries by offering cut-rate prices for labor.

Needless to say, the KMT is too tied to the old political and economic order to be the agent of such an economic transformation, despite its corporatist rhetoric and the ongoing "Taiwanization" of its formerly mainlander-dominated leadership. A new progressive economic program can only come into being on the shoulders of a new coalition in power, a coalition whose main pillars will be labor, farmers, and the multiclass environmental movement.

The China question will, of course, figure in all this, but how China will fit into a new economic agenda is up to the people of Taiwan to decide.

PART III

Singapore Adrift

Introduction to Part III

Here is a Third World country that went overnight from slums to skyscrapers," writes one of Singapore's admirers. "It shows how quickly a nation can leap, even in a time of maximum world competition."[1]

Until the recession of 1985–86, this 235-square-mile island with 2.6 million people was touted by many economists and corporate executives as the most successful of the newly industrializing countries. Undoubtedly, the statistics are impressive. Growth averaged over 10 percent per year from 1965 to 1980, topping South Korea, Hong Kong, and Taiwan. By the mid-1980s, Singapore's per capita income, at $7,410, was the highest in Asia after Japan's; at a par with New Zealand's; and significantly higher than that of Spain, which is considered Europe's "hottest" economy. And by 1995, if the current growth rate persists, Singapore will be richer in per capita terms than Great Britain, its former colonizer.[2]

Singapore's landscape confirms the numbers. Not only do skyscrapers glitter in the tropical sun, but the shopping malls along Orchard Road rival the opulence of those in Beverly Hills. Slums are nonexistent, as over 80 percent of the island's population has been relocated to government-subsidized high-rise housing.[3] Though one might encounter a few beggars—denounced as being "more in need of discipline than care" by a high government official[4]—poverty has become largely invisible. And everywhere one finds the stamp of efficient technocratic planning—in the impressive road and traffic system, in the newly constructed underground MRT (Mass Rapid Transit), which equals in precision and efficiency the subway systems in Tokyo and Washington, D.C.

But all is not well in the city at the Straits. Though hidden from the foreign eye, poverty is present. Inequality is increasing. Political discontent lies just beneath the surface of this authoritarian society. And the accoutrements of prosperity barely conceal the technocrats' apprehensions that the old formula for Singapore's record-breaking pace of economic growth has run out of steam.

Everywhere there is a sense of the fragility of it all, and no one captures this mood more than the *jefe maximo* himself, Lee Kwan-Yew and his son, and, in the opinion of many, heir apparent, Lee Hsien-Loong, who warns that "overnight, an oasis can become a desert."[5]

17

The Making of
a Transnational Haven

Becoming a desert island seemed to be the fate that awaited Singapore at the time of the disastrous separation from the Federation of Malaysia in 1965. In their plan to upgrade Singapore from a center of entrepôt trade to an industrial metropolis, Prime Minister Lee Kwan-Yew and the leadership of the People's Action party had envisioned the Federation as the protected market for Singapore's industrial goods. With the loss of this market, PAP technocrats dumped the accompanying strategy of import-substitution industrialization and in desperation adopted the new approach of export-oriented industrialization. The world became a substitute market for Malaysia, and the motor of the new strategy became not local entrepreneurs but an alliance between the PAP state elite and foreign capital.

Attracting the Multinationals

Export markets, foreign capital, and cheap labor were the essential ingredients of the new approach, and the PAP government pioneered among third world governments in devising packages of incentives that would attract the multinationals. The main attraction was, of course, low-cost labor, the supply of which the government ensured by decapitating and thus destroying the independent labor movement. But there were other incentives as well, including a genuinely free trade regime with scarcely any tariffs on imports and exports, unrestricted repatriation of profits and investments, and 100 percent foreign ownership of firms. In addition, the government offered sites in industrial estates, efficient supporting infrastructure, and a variety of tax incentives.

In its effort to diversify Singapore's economy from manufacturing, the government has in recent years offered multinationals that

Table 17.1

Tax Incentives Available to Foreign Investors in Singapore

1. Pioneer status for approved manufacturing and service activities—exemption of tax on profits; tax relief period of five to ten years.
2. Expansion incentive for approved manufacturing and service activities—exemption of tax on profits in excess of preexpansion level; tax relief period of up to five years.
3. Approved foreign loan scheme for manufacturing and service activities–exemption of withholding tax on interest.
4. Approved royalties for approved manufacturing and service activities—half or full exemption of withholding tax on royalties.
5. Export incentive for approved export activities—90 percent tax concession on approved export profits.
6. Double tax deduction for expenses on export promotion and development.
7. Double tax deduction for expenses on research and development.
8. Accelerated depreciation allowance.
9. Investment allowance for approved manufacturing and service activities, approved research and development activities, approved construction operations, and approved projects for reducing consumption of potable water.
10. Postpioneer incentive for approved companies enjoying pioneer status or export incentive as a follow-up to pioneer incentive—corporate tax rate of not less than 10 percent for up to five years upon expiry of pioneer or export incentive.
11. 10 percent concessionary tax on income of Asian Currency Units, offshore income of insurance companies and income from offshore gold transactions.
12. Tax exemption on income from approved syndicated loans and syndicated credit facilities.
13. Tax exemption on income of Singapore-registered ships.
14. 50 percent tax concession on export income of approved warehousing, technical, or engineering services.
15. 50 percent tax concession on export income of approved consultancy services.
16. 50 percent tax concession on export income of approved international trading companies.
17. Concessionary 10 percent tax on income from approved headquarter operations.
18. Venture capital incentive for investment by eligible companies and individuals in approved new technology projects—losses incurred from the sale of shares, up to 100 percent of equity invested, can be set off against in the investors' other taxable income.

Source: Lim Chong-Yah *et al.*, *Policy Options for the Singapore Economy* (Singapore: McGraw-Hill Book Co., 1988), p. 258.

set up research and development facilities or locate their regional headquarters in Singapore additional incentives, such as double tax deductions for R&D expenses and a concessionary 10 percent tax on income from approved headquarter operations (see table 17.1). Another incentive—not to be underestimated—was the aura of stability projected by the authoritarian regime. In fact, a 1985 study of manufacturing firms showed that 69 percent of the sixty-seven wholly owned foreign firms surveyed listed political stability as their main reason for investing in Singapore.[1]

This variety of incentives raised the stock of foreign equity investment in Singapore nearly tenfold in just eleven years from $1.7 billion in 1970 to $16.8 billion in 1981.[2] U.S. multinationals led the list of foreign investors, having placed almost $4 billion by 1985. The Japanese were second, with almost $3 billion; but for the first time, in 1986, they outstripped the United States in new investment commitments, as Japanese firms relocated many of their manufacturing operations to Singapore to escape the high costs of domestic production brought about by the appreciation of the yen.[3]

Whether American, Japanese, or European, most investors have not been disappointed by the benefits accorded by the PAP state's foreign investment regime. For instance, even under the conditions of industrial restructuring unfavorable to multinationals from 1979 to 1984, the average annual rate of return for U.S. investment in Singapore averaged 35.4 percent, compared to 16.9 percent for investment in Hong Kong, 18.4 percent for Taiwan, and 15.2 percent for Korea (see table 17.2).[4]

The predictable result of PAP policies was the overwhelming domination of the economy by multinational firms. In 1981, for instance, wholly or majority-owned foreign firms numbered 4,303, or 20 percent of over 21,000 companies operating in Singapore.[5] But in the mid-1980s these foreign companies accounted for 70 percent of the gross output in the manufacturing sector, over 50 percent of employment, and 82 percent of direct exports.[6] That the price for superficial prosperity was indeed costly was underlined by one prominent local economist:

> Reliance on foreign investment has not been without cost, although often the price which has been paid goes unnoticed in the euphoria of success...the profits of a foreign subsidiary ultimately belong to foreigners, and not to the domestic population. The foreign share of Singapore's GDP must be one of the highest

Table 17.2

Comparative Rates of Return on U.S. Direct Foreign Investment in Manufacturing in Selected Countries, 1979–1984

Country	1979 %	1980 %	1981 %	1982 %	1983 %	1984 %
NICs						
Hong Kong	22.6	15.8	15.4	18.9	15.9	13.0
Singapore	34.4	37.5	40.2	25.6	40.2	34.7
South Korea	18.8	—[a]	-18.0	11.2	38.0	41.2
Taiwan	26.2	19.0	14.4	11.7	17.3	21.8
ASEAN Members						
Indonesia	20.4	22.9	—	76.3	na	9.9
Malaysia	27.5	31.3	—	26.5	32.8	15.4
Philippines	15.8	13.4	11.0	3.6	-6.1	—
Thailand	20.0	16.1	26.9	-4.8	97.1	—

Source: *Business International,* November 29, 1985, reproduced in Lim Chong-Yah *et al., Policy Options for the Singapore Economy* (Singapore: McGraw-Hill Book Co., 1988), p. 262.

[a] Loss reported for South Korea, 1980. Exact figure not available.

in the world, rising from 10 percent in 1966–67 to a high of 28 percent in 1979/80....In other words, only about three quarters of Singapore's GDP is what the official publications call "indigenous GDP." Unlike the other Asian NICs, this is a major price to pay for rapid growth.[7]

Marginalizing the Local Entrepreneur

Multinational domination translated into the severe marginalization of the local entrepreneurial class. In 1985 wholly or majority–locally owned firms in manufacturing accounted for less than 30 percent of gross output, less than 47 percent of employment, and less than 18 percent of direct exports.[8]

Without the protection enjoyed by domestic producers in Taiwan and South Korea, the failure rate for local entrepreneurs was quite high. As Lee Kwan-Yew himself pointed out in a speech in 1978, about 38 percent of wholly owned Singaporean enterprises established since 1960 had gone under.[9] Indeed, as economist Koh Ai-Tee and Lee (Tsao) Yuan put it, "the successful local entrepreneur is a scarce and precious resource in Singapore today."[10] The blame was laid squarely at the doorstep of government policy in a 1986 report by a body of small businessmen: "Singaporeans have been traditionally entrepreneurial. But an economic policy which stresses the role of foreign investment in manufacturing inevitably forces the local entrepreneur into a lesser role."[11]

That sense of a lesser role was expressed, with some bitterness, by the executive of a medium-size Singaporean firm: "There's nothing in the middle. You have the MNCs [multinational corporations] on top and the rest below. What you have is a polarized economy. The chances for medium- or small-medium-size companies like us to grow are being cut out. You're competing with multinational salary scales."[12]

When it opted for a strategy of making multinationals the engine of growth, the PAP technocratic elite envisioned a situation in which the foreign corporations would stimulate the growth of the local industries that would service them. This has clearly not happened. At least as of the mid-1980s, subcontracting was not substantial, with foreign firms sourcing no more than 25 percent of their input from local establishments.[13] When multinationals did establish complementary relations with local entrepreneurs, it often ended up with the former dominating and eventually buying up the latter. One top-level Singaporean manager explained the process in this fashion:

> We've invited everybody to come in and start a business. The Japanese have taken us at our word. They tell us, "You be my agent. You build up my market. You carry it out and you make a little bit of money." Then they come in on the eleventh year and say, "Look, I don't like the way you're running things. So we'll buy 50 percent of the company." By year three you have the Japanese managers running everything. So now they say, "We don't mind giving you a percentage, but it's now 75 percent for us." We've given up even our own market. So what happens is that that fellow is a rich man because he is still getting his income from that 25 percent. His son will drive a BMW and probably settle in Australia.[14]

Indeed, the multinationals not only failed to serve as a locomotive for the growth of local businesses but they "competed with domestic entrepreneurs for the small Singapore market," being able to enjoy advantages of brand name and access to the parent companies' resources in the areas of technology, finance, management, and marketing expertise.[15] This unequal battle, claimed a small businessmen's group, led to local enterprises being snuffed out by foreign competitors "through predatory pricing launched from protected home bases."[16] Local construction and retail companies, adds one prominent economist, have had to contend with "the entry of large Japanese and Korean companies which have the ability to bid competitively and withstand short-run losses in order to gain market share."[17]

Local businesses resent not only the lack of protection in their home market but also the fact that government incentives have actively discriminated in favor of the multinationals. For instance, the requirement that pioneer enterprises have investments of over $1 million to be entitled to tax breaks automatically cuts out most local firms since only a handful can reach that level of capitalization. More broadly, policies supportive of foreign investors were enacted well before policies supportive of small businesses: foreign investment policy was enacted in the early 1960s, while measures directed at assisting small local firms, like the Small Industries Finance plan, were adopted only ten to fifteen years later.[18]

In explaining the marginal character of the local business community, the PAP elite has resorted to all explanations except the obvious. One government favorite has been the alleged "absence of the entrepreneurial spirit" among Singaporeans. As local entrepreneurs note, this is a strange charge since the Singaporean Chinese helped build Singapore as a trading entrepôt. The PAP's riposte is that "the entrepreneurship required in an entrepôt economy is not the same required in a modern, industrialized, and diversified economy."[19] But this is a difficult proposition to defend since Chinese merchants made the transition from commerce to industry in places like the Philippines, Thailand, Taiwan, and Hong Kong.

Clearly, the crowding out of domestic entrepreneurs by the multinationals is the main reason for the lack of dynamism of local business. According to one Singaporean businessman, under conditions where multinational capital is favored, encouraging one's children not to become entrepreneurs may actually be rational:

"So the Asian businessman tells his son, go become a lawyer, be an engineer, or a doctor, but for God's sake, don't become a businessman. Don't you know how hard it's been for me."[20]

Indeed, given the uncongenial atmosphere at home, notes economist Koh Ai-Tee, Singaporean businesses may have "found it attractive to relocate to Malaysia, Indonesia, Philippines, and Thailand because factor endowments there accord well with the labor-intensive nature of their operations, and also because these industries were given special treatment under the import-substitution industrialization pursued by these countries."[21] Though statistics are sketchy, fragmentary evidence suggests that Singaporeans "may have substantial overseas investments in a number of countries in the Asia Pacific region...in real estate, manufacturing, and service activities."[22] As one top Singaporean executive put it, "They're being squeezed out at home. They're running to Malaysia and Thailand. It's inevitable."[23]

Failure of a Revolution

For a long time, the PAP state–multinational capital relationship was viewed as a partnership of equals. Yet in reality foreign capital was the undisputed senior partner in the alliance, as underlined by the dismal results of the PAP state's ambitious effort to upgrade Singapore's industrial structure from labor-intensive to high-tech manufacturing in the 1980–85 period.

This Second Industrial Revolution was intended as a preemptive response to the same forces that pushed the Taiwanese and Koreans to emphasize technological upgrading of their production processes: the loss of the cheap-labor advantage. Beginning in 1979 the PAP government adopted a series of policies designed to transform the island into a base for higher-value-added, high-tech industries. Central to the strategy was a wage correction policy, consisting of raising wages for local workers while at the same time phasing out cheap foreign labor. The strategy, which raised unit labor costs by 40 percent over six years, was designed to move Singapore out of direct competition with other countries that could offer lower wage rates in labor-intensive industries and enhance the productivity of higher-paid labor through capital- and skill-intensive production processes. "Without any apology," notes analyst Gary Rodan, "the PAP tried to force lower value-added, labor-intensive industries to upgrade operations or close operations in Singapore altogether. It remained fundamentally important that Singapore offer *lower* labor costs, the lure for higher-value-added investments, but not the lowest labor cost per se."[24]

The Second Industrial Revolution was the supreme attempt at technocratic manipulation. But the multinationals did not follow the script laid out by PAP economists. The technological upgrading of production processes hardly took place, as indicated by the fact that wages accounted for 50 percent of value added in manufacturing by 1984.[25] Instead of upgrading their investments, the Japanese, for instance, substantially reduced their new investment commitments, with the 1980 figure falling by 56 percent of the previous year's.[26] For a time Japan redirected much of its low-value-added investment to Hong Kong without significant increases in higher-value-added production in Singapore.[27]

The Second Industrial Revolution sought not only to upgrade production processes and promote investments in more technologically intensive products but also to encourage multinationals to locate the R&D phases of their operations in Singapore. The results were dismal: only 59 out of some 4,300 wholly or majority-owned foreign firms engaged in R&D in Singapore in 1981–82, and the number increased by only one firm in 1984–85.[28] The problem was illustrated in the computer industry. Investments in computer hardware rose sharply in the early 1980s, with a substantial chunk —some $2 billion—devoted to the manufacture of disk drives. But despite the fact that Singapore now manufactures more disk drives than any other country in the world,[29] hardly any R&D is done on the island by top major foreign disk-drive firms. Moreover, these investments, as Rodan points out, "involved the assembly and testing of disk drives rather than any more complete or skilled manufacturing process."[30]

The crisis that followed the wage-correction policy forced government technocrats to confront the fact that because cheap labor continued to be Singapore's main asset in the multinationals' eyes, it could be tinkered with only at great risk. One consultant to the multinationals presented their perspective:

> The EDB [Economic Development Board] people explained that they'd misunderstood why companies had come to Singapore. Good infrastructure was important, but it wasn't the main driver. Cheap wages were. Multinational companies, faced with the decree, didn't see the point in giving two-dollar-an-hour paychecks to unskilled Singaporeans when

Malaysian, Thai, or even Mexican workers could do
the same jobs for under one dollar. On top of that, all
those countries had begun offering their own incentives to lure industry. So the Singapore shortcut was
backfiring. Companies being courted went elsewhere.
Some already stopped investing. And a few got ready
to pull out.[31]

The combination of a 40 percent decline in investment and
weakening international demand for key manufactures brought
about the city-state's most serious recession in twenty years in
1985, as gross domestic product declined by almost 2 percent.

The downturn underlined, among other things, the tragic consequences of a policy of not extending preferential treatment to
local entrepreneurs and not protecting the domestic market. Had
a differential wage-correction policy been applied, local entrepreneurs could have moved into labor-intensive areas being va-
cated by the multinationals. And had they enjoyed a protected
domestic market, local producers could have prospered by responding to the increased demand brought about by higher wages
in the multinational sector. In other words, the international recession and decline in foreign investments in the export sector could
have been counteracted by a booming domestic economy. As it
turned out, the local entrepreneurs were visited with the worst of
all possible worlds. "All you did with high-wage policies," remarked one local executive, "was kill off a few more Singapore
businesses that couldn't keep up."[32]

Instead of creative Keynesian policies, the government insti-
tuted a series of draconian measures to get the economy out of the
recession, including a freeze on wages in 1986 and 1987, a 15
percent reduction in the employers' contribution to the Central
Provident Fund (a system of forced savings), and lowering of
corporate taxes from 40 to 30 percent.[33]

By February 1986 the government appeared to have reversed
the earlier policy of stressing high-technology investment in favor
of "all forms of investment which can make profits."[34] Hard labor
instead of high productivity became, for a time, the government's
rhetorical response to the crisis. As Minister of Trade and Industry
Lee Hsien-Loong, Lee Kwan-Yew's son, asserted in a 1986 pep
talk, Singapore could become competitive by getting workers "to
work 44 hours a week, where others will only work 38…to do third
shifts and keep plants open 24 hours per day."[35]

Instead of being phased out, as originally intended, cheap foreign workers were brought in at a record rate of 2,000 to 3,000 a month, raising the foreign labor force from 100,000 in 1985 to 150,000 in 1988.[36]

Among those attracted again to Singapore by the prospects of cheap labor were Japanese companies, who were being pushed out of Japan by the higher production costs brought about by the rapid appreciation of the yen. It was Japanese investment, totaling close to $1 billion between 1986 and 1988, that enabled Singapore to snap out of the recession. And clearly cheap labor for low-value-added, labor-intensive production was the magnet that attracted capital back: a 1988 survey showed that value added per worker in Japanese-owned manufacturing companies stood at $40,254, compared to $77,182 in U.S. firms.[37]

But despite the wave of investments from Japan, Singapore's technocrats realized that its multinational-dependent export-oriented economy was more than ever in a precarious position.

On the one hand, its neighbors were widening their labor cost advantage—a threat underlined in 1988 by the cost-cutting moves of Seagate, the U.S. disk-drive manufacturer that is the island's biggest employer. While cutting 800 workers from its 10,000-strong Singapore work force, Seagate transferred some of its production to Bangkok. The move to Bangkok was matched by two of Seagate's rivals, Micropolis Corporation and Maxtor Corporation, which planned to set up plants in Bangkok and Penang (Malaysia), respectively.[38] These developments were ominous, for electronics made up a good third of Singapore's manufacturing sector.[39]

On the other hand, with the failure of the Second Industrial Revolution to attract R&D facilities and other high-tech investments, the PAP technocrats worried that the window of opportunity for high-tech migration might be closing. As a 1986 report from the Economic Committee (a blue-ribbon government commission) warned, "With increasing automation, productivity will go up, and the developed countries, despite their higher labor costs, will become more attractive locations to site factories."[40] In short, like Taiwan and Korea, Singapore was undergoing a structural squeeze, threatened at one end by lower-cost labor in other third world countries but unable to make the transition to high-tech production.

Facing this dilemma, Singapore's technocrats began to talk less about making the island a center of high-tech manufacturing and more about plans to develop it as Southeast Asia's financial and service center. This meant displacing Hong Kong as the regional banking center and stock market, and doubling efforts to get corporations to make Singapore their regional headquarters, or the staging area for their manufacturing and marketing forays into the other countries of the Association for Southeast Asian Nations.

Will this effort to carve out a new niche in the world economy as a regional financial and management-control center succeed? Two developments stand in the way. One is the tremendous progress in telecommunications, which is likely to lead multinationals to dispense with regional intermediaries and hook up directly with their subsidiaries in the different Southeast Asian countries. The second is the emergence of Tokyo as the financial center of Asia, if not the world. As Lawrence Krause remarks:

> In the future, the more serious competition for both Singapore and Hong Kong will come from Tokyo. Japan is in the midst of deregulating its financial business, thereby improving the international competitiveness of its institutions....The overwhelming strength of Tokyo comes from the existence of a huge pool of savings in Japan, which financial institutions, with government encouragement, are willing to invest abroad. The factor is so important that Tokyo is unlikely to be rivalled in the long-term capital market. In the short-term market, other banking centers can compete—but only by finding niches and trading on thin advantages.[41]

Despite its seeming prosperity, Singapore in 1990 is trapped in the treadmill of the export-oriented economics that it once so enthusiastically embraced. Having so completely opened itself up to the world market and the multinationals with the illusion that it could influence the former and manipulate the latter, the PAP technocrats now see that their policies have reduced Singapore's economy to a mere service economy, the fate of which is totally dependent on the calculations and whims of the multinationals, especially the powerful Japanese. As one local executive saw it,

> You've turned Singapore into a pure service economy. What you're saying is look, Mr. Multinational, I'll look after you, I'll cloth you, I'll feed you, I'll look after your kids. But I don't know how to do business. I'll leave

that to you because it's not intrinsic to me. All I am is a servicing agent.[42]

18

Controlling the Labor Force

W ithout natural resources and without an agrarian economy, Singapore's chief asset has been its labor force. As in Korea and Taiwan, Singapore's rulers realized that to succeed in their chosen strategy of export-oriented manufacturing, they needed a labor force that could be molded and manipulated to meet technocratic targets. Of the three newly industrializing countries, Singapore has been the most successful at subjugating labor, an "achievement" underlined by the astounding fact that only one strike took place between 1978 and 1989.[1]

In the service of the multinationals, the PAP state developed a labor policy with three central elements: the demobilization of local labor and its incorporation into an authoritarian corporatist state structure; the use of foreign labor to meet labor shortages, fill the worst-paid jobs, control the wage rates of the local working class, and buffer local labor in hard times; and finally, the incorporation of women into the labor force to serve a variety of functions, including filling low-paid "feminized" positions in the occupational structure, easing the labor shortage in boom times, and buffering the male labor force in times of recession.

Demobilizing Labor

Singapore has one of the world's most docile working classes. Yet it was not always so. Trade unions played a key role in the struggle for independence; indeed, it was the strategic employment of strikes by progressive unions that brought Lee Kwan-Yew's People's Action Party to power in the late 1950s.

But after taking power, the PAP turned on its erstwhile allies. The most important instruments it used to repress the labor movement were union deregistration and the Internal Security Act of

1960, which enabled the government to detain indefinitely anyone suspected of subversion. The climax of the confrontation between the leftist labor movement and the PAP-dominated government was the infamous Operation Cold Store in February 1963, which netted more than 100 trade unionists and other oppositionists. Cold Store's aftermath was a 90 percent decline in work stoppages between 1963 and 1964.[2] With anti-PAP unions suffering wholesale, arbitrary deregistration, the pro-PAP National Trade Union Congress (NTUC) became organized labor's sole voice.

Repression was followed by the passage in 1968 of two brazenly promanagement bills: the Employment Act, which reduced a whole range of workers' benefits and the Industrial Relations Act, which downgraded collective bargaining and gave management full discretionary power over dismissals, promotions, transfers, and other vital issues in labor-management relations.

This legislation—which deprived labor of many of the gains it had achieved in the anticolonial struggle[3]—took place in the context of an ideological redefinition of the role of labor in the PAP-dominated society. In a key 1969 policy speech, one of the regime's chief ideologists, S. Rajaretnam, set forth that Singapore had no room for the "old-style trade unionist" whose goal "was to inject a corresponding degree of militancy into a docile and disorganized working class."[4] In modern-day Singapore, he contended, modernization and economic development were the overriding considerations, and economic modernization was to be "a joint effort by government, entrepreneurs, and workers." Under these conditions, the old-style trade unionist motivated by class interests had to give way to the "new-style trade unionist," one of whose functions was "to think out ways and means of how workers can get a greater share of the growing cake without slowing down the rate of development."

Ideological redefinition and repressive legislation were accompanied by a wholesale restructuring of the institutional context of labor-management relations. What some observers described as a system of "authoritarian corporatism" was consolidated with the 1972 creation of the National Wages Council (NWC), a tripartite body composed of representatives of labor, government, and management that was mandated to formulate national wages guidelines. In effect, the NWC became a key institution for centrally organizing and controlling labor to serve the PAP's technocratic development objectives.

The statistics reflected this destruction of class solidarity and atomization of the work force. Work stoppages fell from eighty-eight in 1962 to five in 1973 to one in 1977. No strikes took place between 1978 and 1986[5]—probably a record for a country outside the Communist bloc. And the atrophy of genuine unionism is seen in other figures, as well: union membership dropped from close to 250,000 in 1979 to 211,000 in 1988;[6] as a percentage of the active work force, those unionized dropped from 20 percent to 16 percent in the same period.[7] This trend evoked a classic Aesopian comment from one labor expert writing for a state-controlled think tank:

> Singapore has a strong trade union movement, but the function of the trade unions has been redefined. In its new definition, the objective of a trade union has changed "from an organization whose main objects were to impose restrictive conditions on the conduct of trade or business or to promote, organize or finance strikes or lock-outs" to that of an organization "that seeks, among other things, to promote good industrial relations and raise productivity for the benefit of employees, employers and the economy of the Nation."...However, as is evident from the data on trade union membership...the membership has been declining in the 1980s. One may wonder whether this decline is attributable to the redefinition of the trade union function.[8]

Indeed, withdrawal from the system of corporatist unionism did not mean that workers ceased pressing their demands. It indicated that workers might have tried to achieve their interests through means other than controlled unionism. This interpretation receives some support from the fact that whereas unionized trade disputes declined from over 1,100 in 1972 to slightly over 300 in 1982, non-unionized trade disputes rose from slightly over 1,000 in 1972 to close to 1,590 in 1982.[9]

The total conversion of organized labor into an arm of the PAP state came in the late 1970s, when the NTUC charter was revamped to open up senior leadership posts to nonunion representatives. Up to half of the Central Committee and one-third of triennial delegates could now come from nonunion ranks—especially from the ranks of technocrats and PAP party people. These changes paved the way for the prime minister to appoint non-union persons to the secretary-generalship.[10]

Filling in key posts with nonunion PAP members was the government's response to resistance within the ranks to its determined effort to convert the labor movement into a pliant instrument. Indeed, shortly after the reorganization of the NTUC, Lee Kwan-Yew warned labor of the omnipotence of the PAP government: "If the union leadership challenges the political leadership, the political leadership must triumph, if necessary by changing the ground rules to thwart the challenge, using legislative and administrative powers, and when necessary, backed by the mandate of the electorate."[11] By the 1980s, independent unionism was a dead letter, allowing Lee Kwan-Yew to boast that labor's perspective had been technocratized: "One reason why we don't have many industrial disputes is because our unions know that their opponent or adversary is not the boss....It's some other factory some place else that's manufacturing that product and if you can't match that quality, you're out."[12]

Perhaps more than any other government leader anywhere, Lee could justly claim that he had created the ideal labor force for capitalism.

Women in the Work Force

With cheap labor continuing to be a prime motivation for multinationals' decision to locate or stay in Singapore, the PAP authorities increasingly resorted to two labor reserves in their desperate effort to keep Singapore competitive in wage costs: women and foreign labor.

The proportion of Singaporean women in the labor force rose from 17 percent in the late 1960s to almost 48 percent in 1988.[13] Aside from meeting an absolute labor shortage, the surge of women into the labor force was encouraged by the technocrats to provide employers with an alternative to high-cost male employees; to track Singaporean women into certain occupations where foreign corporations preferred female personnel; and to buffer the male labor force during periods of slow growth.

In 1984 the average woman worker earned S$511 while the average male worker earned S$703, which put women's wages at around 73 percent of men's wages (US$1.00=S$1.97 in May 1989).[14] The lower wage costs for women made a big difference to employers, especially for the lower and middle positions in the occupational hierarchy. But even within the skilled occupations where average educational levels tend to be more equal, women's wages have been lower than men's.[15] For instance, in 1984, among professional and technical personnel, women's wages were 47 percent of men's, and among administrative and management personnel, women's wages were 71 percent of men's (see table 18.1).[16]

Women have been channeled primarily into areas where stereotypically feminine characteristics like beauty, willingness to serve, docility, and intellectual passivity are valued by employers. Thus, the lower rung, white-collar, clerical positions have been increasingly "feminized."[17] At the same time, the new labor-intensive jobs in electronics and textiles created in the 1970s were mainly filled with women for much the same reasons as in Taiwan and Korea. As Aline Wong has written, "In Singapore...foreign corporate managers consider women workers to have special

Table 18.1

Wage Differentials, by Occupation and Sex, 1984

| | Median Gross Monthly Income (in S$)[a] | | Women's Wages as Percentage of Men's Wages |
	Female	Male	
Professional/technical	1,221	1,659	47
Administrative/management	1,692	2,375	71
Clerical	605	705	86
Sales	466	752	62
Service	356	563	63
Production	390	619	63
Total	511	703	73

Source: *Report of Labor Force Survey of Singapore 1984*, reproduced in Lai Ah-Eng, "Economic Restructuring in Singapore and the Impact of the New Technology on Women Workers," in Cecilia Ng, *Technology and Gender* (Kuala Lumpur: Women Studies Unit, Universiti Pertanien Malaysia and Malaysian Social Science Association, 1987), p. 118.

[a] S$ = Singapore dollars. (S$2.17=US$1.00.)

qualities—docility, diligence, and the 'swift fingers' and tolerance for repetitive tasks—that make them especially suitable for unskilled work in the export-processing industries."[18]

The evidence also suggests that like the foreign work force, women act as an elastic reserve army of labor that can expand in boom times and absorb the main blows during recessions. Perhaps the most cogent technocratic expression of this function came from S. Dhanabalan, a top cabinet minister, who said in 1975 that recessions would be "tempered by the outflow of foreign workers and by the outflow of female workers from the labor force."[19] This was borne out during the slowdown of 1974, when 79 percent of the 16,900 workers thrown out of work were women, and during the milder slowdown of 1980 which "again brought about massive layoffs of female electronic workers in large U.S. firms."[20]

In boom times, in contrast, the government has gone all-out to push women into the labor force. For instance, reflecting the government's approach to the 1988 labor shortage, the *Straits Times* urged employers to "tap the pool of 30,000 economically inactive Singaporeans, mainly housewives, who are willing to work."[21]

But despite their critical role in the labor force, Singaporean women continue to be regarded by PAP technocrats as an adjunct to the male labor force. Thus no active effort has been made to redress current inequalities. Not only have wage and income levels been unequal, but women have not been represented in top positions. According to a 1983 survey, only 4 percent of managers, 22 percent of clerical supervisors, and 11 percent of executive officers were women.[22] Moreover, the support services that would make women's participation more consistent have been scarce. For instance, 51 percent of the women who left the labor force in 1984 did so because of housework and childcare responsibilities.[23] As Lai Ah-Eng notes:

> Government attitudes toward childcare and other problems of women's participation in the labor force is best summed up as follows: Women's work has never been regarded by the government (nor by society) at large as a matter of women's equal right to work as men. Rather, women's work is considered to be dispensable when the economy requires it, or supplementary to men's work at best....Historically, therefore, the government's position regarding childcare provision has been characterized by reluctance

and lack of initiative. Skills training for women has consequently also not received serious attention.[24]

Labor-force data in the late 1970s showed that a large percentage—50 percent—of the female work force in manufacturing belongs to unions.[25] But this hardly meant anything since most workers are automatically made union members when recruited. Perhaps more indicative of women's real power is the fact that although membership in textile and electronics unions in Singapore is 80 percent female it was not until 1984 that the first woman was appointed as executive secretary of an industrial union.

While the lot of the Singaporean woman worker is superior to that of the foreign worker, both male and female, it remains substantially below that of the Singaporean male worker. But one of the main mechanisms for improvement—a strong, independent union movement—is nonexistent. Even more distressing, employer discrimination in hiring, promotion, and training was legally taken out of the sphere of the already emasculated unions by the 1968 labor reforms, and defined as falling under "employers' prerogative."[26]

Foreign Workers: The Reserve Army of Labor

Early in 1989 the Singapore government decreed that overstaying foreign workers who did not surface before March 31 would face jail terms of at least three months and three lashes of the cane. The move caused a diplomatic crisis with surrounding countries, especially Thailand, whose prime minister was reported to have mused at one cabinet meeting that "instead of sending [transport] ships, we should send warships to Singapore."[27] Twelve thousand overstaying workers were deported, but even before the year ended, many of those same workers were back in Singapore. Among them was Somkid Kamjan, who became the center of international controversy as the first Thai sentenced to be caned and jailed[28]—an episode that illustrates the PAP technocrats' ambivalent relationship with foreign workers. Try as it might the government would like to be rid of them but can't afford to.

Foreign workers have long been central to the functioning of the Singapore economy. And instead of diminishing over time, as the PAP technocrats would prefer, they have become even more critical, following the failure of the technocrats' Second Industrial Revolution to wean the multinationals—especially Japanese firms—from valuing Singapore mainly as a site for labor-intensive operations.

The statistics tell the story: between 1970 and 1980 foreign workers jumped from being 2 percent to 11 percent of the work force. Between 1980 and 1984 more than half of the growth of the work force was accounted for by "guest workers."[29] Conservative estimates place their current number at 150,000, or about 12.5 percent of the current work force of 1.2 million.[30] Foreigners make up nearly a quarter of the work force in manufacturing and about half the labor force in the textile industry, the second biggest employer in the country.[31]

Broadly speaking, foreign workers fulfill four key functions for the Singapore economy. First, as noted earlier, they serve as a source of cheap labor, which continues to be the mainstay of the economy, despite government efforts to reduce their role. Foreign workers are paid much less than local workers; domestics, for instance, are paid one-fourth to one-half the average hourly wage of the Singapore worker. Second, foreign workers are used to fill household, construction, and unskilled manufacturing jobs that are spurned by Singaporeans, who prefer the higher paying and more skilled positions in the electronics and service sectors. By bringing in foreign workers the PAP state can check local workers' ability to raise relative wages for these undesirable jobs.[32] Third, foreign labor acts as a shock absorber during times of economic crisis, thus preserving political stability. As one government official put it, "The foreign workers act as a buffer for the Singapore labor force, to help even out the more extreme fluctuations of the …labor force."[33] At no time was this buffering function more evident than during the 1985–86 recession: 90,000 jobs were lost, 60,000 of them held by foreigners.[34] And finally, foreign workers, because they are transient, save the state many essential social expenditures. The Singapore government does not have to pay for their education—a not unimportant saving given the fact that a substantial number of foreign workers, like Filipino domestics, are relatively well educated. Nor does the state have to worry about old-age social security expenditures, since most will be forced to return to their home country after their prime laboring years.

If the government cannot get rid of foreign workers, it nevertheless seems determined to make their sojourn in Singapore unpleasant. Thai workers, for instance, live in communal rooms in tin shacks, evoking the following comment from a visiting Thai official: "My pet dogs live better."[35] Most are paid $8 a day, after tax, and much of their wages goes to paying off the debt incurred to pay the $1,500 that is usually charged by labor contractors for getting them a job in Singapore.[36] Moreover, living and working in Singapore can be dangerous: more than 200 Thai workers have died from mysterious causes since 1983.[37]

Workers are also subjected to a regime of strict legal controls designed to make it impossible for them to settle in Singapore—most of them, that is. The technocrats run a class-biased labor and immigration policy. Foreign workers are divided into two groups, those who earn over S$1,500 per month, the employment pass holders, and those who earn less than S$1,500, who are issued work permits. There is a world of difference between the two: employment pass holders, most of whom are executives with multinational firms, are the richest segment of the Singaporean work force and are encouraged to settle in Singapore. Work permit holders, on the other hand, especially women, are at the bottom of the income hierarchy and are hemmed in by tough restrictions governing their presence in Singapore. As Pang Eng Fong and Linda Lim put it, "Whereas foreign male workers, especially the self-employed, constitute an 'aristocracy' among the Singapore workforce, foreign female employees belong to its 'underclass.'"[38]

The class dimension in guest labor policy is accompanied by a racial dimension. Since the early 1980s the government's policy has been to phase out or drastically reduce the foreign labor force from the "nontraditional sources," except in construction, ship-building, and domestic service. This term is actually a euphemism for a policy of racial discrimination since a great number of workers from Malaysia, the "traditional source," has been, like the vast majority of Singaporeans, Chinese. Nontraditional sources were Indonesia, Thailand, Sri Lanka, India, Bangladesh, and the Philippines. At the same time, foreign workers from "new sources"—South Korea, Hong Kong, Macau, and Taiwan—were allowed in "ostensibly because, being of Chinese or close to Chinese descent, they might blend better into the society."[39] Recently, the government offered to take in 100,000 Hong Kongers who wish to emigrate before China takes over the colony in 1997.

Foreign workers live under a web of onerous restrictions designed to keep them constantly off balance. They are contracted for short durations, with no guarantee of automatic renewal. The government is, in fact, moving to institute a "revolving pool of foreign workers on short-term work permits."[40] Foreign workers are subjected to tight surveillance by immigration authorities.

Given the insatiable demand for cheap labor, companies hire undocumented labor, tempting many workers to either enter illegally or remain after their permits have expired. This leads to a perilous game of hide-and-seek with efficient immigration authorities, who now conduct about one hundred raids a month. And in a small island the chances of getting caught are quite high: 16 percent of all jail inmates are undocumented workers.[41]

Work permit holders are also prevented from bringing their families to Singapore and strongly discouraged from marrying or even having relationships with Singaporeans. It is in the area of marriage relations between Singaporeans and people on work permits that the repressive nature of Singapore's policy towards foreign workers comes out most clearly. While there is nothing in the letter of the law that would prevent a Singaporean from marrying a foreign worker, the strict requirements make such unions extremely difficult. Workers on temporary permits need to apply to the comptroller of labor if they plan to marry a Singaporean—something not required of expatriates or employment pass holders. Marrying without obtaining permission brings about immediate cancellation of the foreigner's work permit, his or her deportation, and a permanent ban on entry to Singapore.[42]

In the late 1970s permission to marry was made contingent on the couple's agreement to sign a sterilization bond stipulating that both husband and wife would undergo voluntary sterilization after the birth of their second child. This requirement led to instances of forced separation and broken families "when the Singaporean partner, usually the man, reneged upon his undertaking to undergo sterilization after his wife had honoured hers. In the event, her work permit would be cancelled by the Commissioner for Employment and she would be compelled to leave, abandon her children behind and forbidden to return to Singapore."[43]

More recently, the government's operative policy has been to deny residence in Singapore to non-citizens married to Singaporeans. The public, in fact, assumes that such unions are impossible to legalize. This popular perception and its tragic consequences for many is expressed, poignantly, by Song Jiang, a character in one of the Singaporean novelist Philip Jeyaretnam's stories:

> A Singaporean has no right to marry a foreigner and
> expect her to be allowed to live in Singapore. Only
> recently I read in the papers about a Singaporean who

committed suicide after his Indonesian wife was deported. It does not matter how genuine the marriage is. Everything is discretionary. A privilege is not a right. But what gives the state the right to say that all those important things, who I marry, where I live, are privileges, not rights?[44]

Indeed, government policing extends beyond questions of marriage to the sex lives of women workers, who have made up close to 30 percent of the foreign labor force. A female work permit holder is required, by law, to undergo a pregnancy test once every six months. If she is found pregnant, she is repatriated and her employer forfeits the bond taken out on her.[45]

Domestics: A Case Study of a Foreign Work Force

Regulations on marriage and sex have become increasingly important as the demand for female foreign workers, particularly domestics or maids, has risen in recent years. Foreign domestics have grown in importance as the government pushes Singaporean women to become active in the labor force to fill the shortage of labor caused by the conjunction of multinational demand and the island's low population growth. One economist has estimated that "20,000 Singapore women would have to quit jobs and return to the home without the domestic help."[46] Clearly, domestics are a segment of the foreign work force that the PAP will not be able to phase out.

Precise statistics on the number of domestics are difficult to obtain, but it is estimated that Filipino domestics alone numbered 30,000 in 1988, or three-quarters of the total of foreign domestics and about 20 percent of the estimated 150,000 foreign workers.[47]

Domestics are at the bottom of the economic hierarchy—a fact that became very clear in interviews we conducted in the summer of 1988. The Filipino domestics, according to those interviewed, made from S$250.00 to S$300.00 a month.[48] This works out to an hourly rate of S$1.45—or far less than the average hourly rate of S$3.50 for Singapore's production workers. Moreover, this is using a nine-hour workday as a basis for comparison. The typical domestic, said the interviewees, starts work at 5 a.m. and does not stop till 11 p.m.—a total of seventeen hours. That this was not unique to Filipino domestics is indicated by an account of the training of Sri Lankan domestics bound for Singapore: "We put them through the pressure cooker to see if they have any shortcomings. Training starts at 4:30 a.m. They may not get back to sleep until 11 p.m."[49]

Being a cog in a tightly regulated labor force, the Filipino domestic is allowed to stay for four years, though under certain circumstances, her stay can be extended to six years. During that period, she cannot do part-time domestic work for another employer, nor is she allowed to take on service work like waitressing or office work. With a substantial number of them having some college education, Filipinas are chafing at the no part-time work rule. The consequences are severe if caught: expulsion from Singapore for the Filipina, and forfeiture of the bond and other penalties for the employer. Already deprived of means to supplement her domestic-work income, the domestic is also vulnerable to abuse from employers who "lend" her to friends and relatives—an illegal act but one Singapore authorities say is common.[50]

The oppressiveness of the work situation is compounded by Singapore's strict laws on pregnancy. The employer stands to lose the S$5,000 bond posted for the domestic should she get pregnant. Money has become such an important incentive for the preservation of virginity that many employers keep close track of the whereabouts of their maids. Some of them have even resorted to locking up the domestics at home during the day when they are not present. On the other hand, the loss of both maid and bond money does not deter some employers from sexually harassing their household help—a common complaint in the interviews.

In their efforts to cope with these various problems, domestics are basically alone, for they are forbidden to form unions. Any incipient organizing effort is immediately quashed by the authorities. For instance, one of the factors that led the government to crack down on a network of Christian activists in 1987 was their establishment of the Gaelang Center to provide counseling and other forms of support to Filipinas and other domestics.

Like other foreign workers, the Filipino domestics suffer from the Singapore government's manipulation of the different national labor markets to achieve the lowest wage costs. Thus pressure from Filipino domestics to raise wages—backed by the Philippine government—has led the government to increasingly resort to Sri Lankan and Indonesian domestics, who are said to be willing to work for less than S$150, or half of what many Filipino domestics make.[51] What is currently happening to Filipino domestics is merely a repetition of what happened a few years earlier to Filipino construction workers who played a central role in building the MRT rapid transit system: their pressure for higher wages was defused with the government's importation of Thai workers who were willing to accept lower wages than the Filipinos.[52]

Foreign workers have, for the most part, meekly submitted to the restrictions and rules imposed on them. But in the few instances of militant action, the government has moved decisively and swiftly. When female workers struck at an American-owned plastics factory in May 1973 and marched to the U.S. Embassy with posters urging Americans to "go home to your villages," eighty-four of the women, who were migrant workers from Malaysia, were accused of leading the strike and deported as "undesirable elements."[53] The lesson was apparently not lost on the foreign work force.

The tragic lot of the foreign worker in Singapore is perhaps best exemplified in the odyssey of Somkid Kamjan, who, as previously mentioned, was the first Thai worker to be sentenced to a three-month jail term and three lashes at the cane. Thrown out of Singapore in 1989, he was back a few months later with a work permit. By the time he returned, however, his Filipino girlfriend, a domestic, had been sent home by her employer. "My heart, very pain," Somkid told a reporter upon learning that the system had, after all, triumphed in the end.[54]

19

Brave New Isle

One of the central problems confronting the ruling People's Action party has been how to get the population to accept its permanent supremacy and its development strategy of yoking Singapore's human resources to the investment plans of transnational corporations. Its solution has been to create a party-state apparatus that combines ideological domination, demobilization, and repression to achieve a pervasive technocratic control of all sectors of society. Merely describing the Singapore state as repressive does not do justice to the complex process of social control and social engineering put into motion by the PAP elite. Perhaps more appropriate is Manuel Castells's description of the Singapore state as a hegemonic state that promotes "social reform, social organization, and social control, to actually achieve at the same time political legitimation and political domination."[1]

The Ideology of Domination

To legitimize its rule, the PAP has elaborated an ideology of technocratic pragmatism. At the core of this ideology are several themes, one being the idea of survival.[2] The central image cultivated by the authorities is that of a small island-state, surrounded by big hostile states. The implicit image is that of a Chinese outpost surrounded by an unsympathetic Malay sea. The theme of survival in a hostile world is especially sounded in times of rising domestic discontent, and no one has mastered the rhetoric of survival more than Lee Kwan-Yew. "My deepest concern," the iron-willed prime minister has asserted, "is how to make the young conscious of security. By security I mean defense against threats to our survival, whether the threats are external or internal....Civilization is fragile. It is especially so for an island-state."[3]

Survival, however, must be secured not only against external enemies but also against internal ones—in short, the Communists. And the key to survival is economic growth. As Lee put it, "Higher wages as productivity increases, and workers educated by their own leaders in the realities of our economic situation will...produce a solid and secure situation which the communists cannot easily exploit."[4] The economy, therefore, has come to take on "a symbolic rather than empirical meaning and significance," observes John Clammer. "In the Singapore case, 'economics'...is what the system is really all about."[5]

This leads to the third element in the ideological formula: the notion of a trade-off between economic progress and political rights. To secure unhampered progress, people must be willing to have their freedoms limited by a benign elite. In formal, constitutional terms, citizens' rights and preferences are upheld, but "in substance," claims Chua Beng-Huat, "one's private sphere is a shrinking realm thoroughly encroached by administrative interventions."[6] Again, Lee Kwan-Yew provides the most candid rationale for the limitation of individual freedom. "I am often accused of interfering in the private lives of citizens," he told a National Day Rally in April 1987. "Yes, if I did not, had I not done that, we wouldn't be here today. And I say without the slightest remorse, that we wouldn't be here, we would not have made economic progress, if we had not intervened on very personal matters—who your neighbor is, how you live, the noise you make, how you spit...or what language you use." He concluded: "We decide what is right. Never mind what the people think. That's another problem."[7]

A corollary of this notion of a trade-off between prosperity and political rights is the idea that Western-style democratic processes are inappropriate for Singapore. As Deputy Prime Minister Goh Chok-Tong put it in a remarkably frank speech at the Fletcher International School of Law and Diplomacy in 1985:

> Imagine the fate of the country if the outcome of every election were a cliff-hanger. Picture to yourself the frenzied supporters, the jostling for power, the excitement, the uncertainty, the catastrophe. There would be total chaos....In Singapore, we have not worked a two-party system. Many people believe that such a two-party system, with two parties of equal but opposing strength, is a necessary feature of democracy....Unlike the United States, our political

talent pool is just too small for us to share equally
between two parties. Better for us to concentrate our
limited talents in the main party and have it represent
the broad majority of the population. It does not make
sense to keep half of our best people in opposition all
the time. That is why we regularly comb the length
and breadth of the country for suitable candidates to
stand on the governing party ticket. We even coopt
those who disagree with us on certain policies, provided they share our core values.[8]

Goh ended by invoking an image of disaster, a favorite PAP
rhetorical device: "For a small country like Singapore, we always
worry about freak election results. A demagogue, or a honey-
combed politician, can cause an election upset....If he cannot
follow up his victory with effective government, disaster will
befall the country. Once the country has a great fall, we cannot
possibly stick Humpty Dumpty together again."[9]

Coupled with the rejection of Western democratic ideology and
practices as inappropriate for Singapore has been a recent effort
to enshrine Confucianism as the center of national ideology.
"Western ideals emphasize the rights and privileges of the individual over the group, and particularly over the state," asserts
Lee Hsien-Loong, son of Lee Kwan-Yew. But Eastern societies
"believe in individuals fulfilling themselves through the greater
identity of the group." He went on to say:

The Chinese call it sacrificing the smaller self to
achieve the greater self. This emphasis on other-
directed values—communitarian values— on duties
above rights—is one of the distinguishing features of
the NICs, and in the view of many sociologists, a key
factor in their success.

I am not suggesting that Westerners are incapable
of selfless service to others, or that there are no selfish
people in the Orient. But there is a real difference
between East and West....

We are in this respect an Oriental society, and we
should remain one. If we swing to the other extreme,
and accept uncritically the more unrestrained Western views of the absolute supremacy of individual
rights and liberties—views which are challenged
even in the West, we will be ruined.[10]

Father and son argue that the new emphasis on Confucianism is an attempt to endow the new generation of Singaporeans with a psychological or moral ballast,[11] but others perceive a more sinister political purpose. As one opposition politician noted rhetorically, "What better idea than to link the Eastern values to a national ideology, get the whole population to support it and gradually shift support for the national ideology into support for the government and the PAP?"[12] Perhaps the most pithy comment of the new Confucianism is, not surprisingly, uttered by a fictional character in Philip Jeyaretnam's novel *First Loves*: "What I hate is the way we're told we're Asians and therefore liberal democracy is not for us....And my own heritage is denied. Chinese culture is reduced to Confucianism. And Confucianism is simplified to endorse totalitarianism."[13]

To the Malays and Indians, who compose 15 percent and 6.5 percent, respectively, of the island's population, the effort to make the Confucian culture of the Chinese majority the cornerstone of the Singaporean ideology is, of course, positively threatening. As one Malay member of parliament warned: "It is one thing for the people to dress in the national constumes of others or to partake of other culinary traditions, but to adopt from elsewhere and call one's own something as personal, deep, and powerful as a value is a different and more serious exercise altogether."[14]

Finally, PAP ideology is unabashedly elitist,[15] and probably the most disturbing manifestation of elitism is what the prominent oppositionist Francis Seow has called the "eugenics prejudice of the government."[16] The poorer and less-educated citizens of Singapore were systematically discouraged in the 1970s and early 1980s from having more children. With his usual candor, Lee offered the following rationale during the third reading of the abortion bill in December 1969:

> Free education and subsidized housing lead to a situation where the less economically productive people in the community are reproducing themselves at rates higher than the rest. This will increase the total population of less productive people.
>
> Our problem is how to devise a system of disincentives, so that the irresponsible, the social delinquents, do not believe that all they have to do is to produce their children and the government then owes them and their children sufficient food, medicine, housing, education, and jobs.[17]

A birth control policy was put into effect that was probably more explicitly class oriented than programs elsewhere. Non–university graduate women were discouraged from having more than two children, while university graduates were encouraged to do so through tax incentives. In addition, a university-graduate mother was given priority to register her third child in the school of her choice, while the non–university graduate mother could register the third and subsequent child only when and where a place was found (although the child was never formally denied a place).[18] To avoid the various disincentives to having more than two children, recalcitrant couples had the option of volunteering one or the other spouses for sterilization.[19]

Not only was the population policy elitist. It was objectively—though not explicitly—racist since the Malay community was poorer and much less educated than the Chinese population. The racist or Chinese chauvinist element was also evident in the stringent laws governing marriage between a Singaporean and a foreign worker. To obtain permission for the marriage in the latter part of the 1970s, as previously noted, a couple had to sign a sterilization bond stipulating that both husband and wife would undergo voluntary sterilization after the birth of the second child.[20] The main targets of this law were domestics, most of whom were Filipinos, Indonesians, or Sri Lankans.

The racist population policy went against the proclaimed multiracialism of the PAP, and much of it stemmed from the personal beliefs of Lee Kwan-Yew. To Lee's way of thinking, according to his biographer James Minchin,

> The advantage of the overseas Chinese is that they are uprooted, amenable to modernisation, while being robust and having cultural "ballast." Lee aims at engineering a transfer of the ordered values and literary riches of Chinese tradition, with their bestowal of identity under the mandate of heaven, into the more adaptable and technologically oriented mould of a modern English-language society. He believes that the overseas Chinese, unlike the Malays, have been able to jettison just enough of their inherited baggage to remain trim but stable for the voyage across the ocean towards the harbour of rationality.[21]

That is the intellectual rationale. There is apparently a more visceral one that emerges in Lee's personal opposition to interracial marriage: "grandparents like to see grandchildren in their own likeness."[22]

The government's population control policy succeeded only too well, with annual average population growth dropping to less than 2 percent annually between 1986 and 1985 and expected to drop even lower to about 1.5 percent in the 1990s. But the success was not exactly to the government's liking. Since 1980 there has been a continuous decline in fertility among the Chinese, whereas there was an upward trend among the Indians and the Malays.[23] In 1986, for instance, the output of babies among Chinese Singaporeans fell short by 15,000 of what the government deemed desirable for racial balance purposes.[24] In typical fashion, Lee Kwan-Yew called attention to the "crisis" created by the "lopsided procreation pattern" and forced a 180 degree turn in population policy. The PAP invoked the specter of a graying population, with the poor breeding faster than the rich, greater dependence on foreign labor, and the depletion of the talent pool because "educated mothers do not procreate sufficiently to meet national needs."[25] The unstated apprehension was pointed out by James Clad: "Living adjacent to fast-breeding Malaysia and Indonesia, the racial arithmetic looked troublesome to some. Singapore's minority Malays, who comprise 15 percent of the population, also have a higher rate of reproduction than the majority Chinese."[26]

Thus zero population growth was replaced by a new goal, with the accompanying slogan, "At least two. Better three. Four if you can afford it." The 1987 and 1989 budgets extended tax rebates of about US$10,000 for third and fourth children.[27] The 1990 budget contained an even sweeter "financial aphrodisiac": a tax rebate of US$10,600, good for seven years, for couples who have a second child before the mother is twenty-eight.[28]

But the population policy's traditional class bias was retained in the new incentive structure. For instance, a cash grant of S$10,000 was instituted in 1984 as an incentive for lower-educated women to volunteer for sterilization after attaining the desired family norm for their status.[29] Also, "plans were drafted to enable better-educated foreigners to marry Singaporeans while rules designed to prevent Singaporeans from marrying migrant workers or domestic helpers were tightened."[30]

Women's social emancipation through better education and increased participation in the work force, it became clear, had become the fly in the technocratic ointment. Women college graduates were, in particular, the targets of the aging male Lee

Kwan-Yew's ire. But they ignored his admonition that they marry their educational inferiors, though the population experts warned that such an attitude would result in two-thirds of them remaining spinsters.[31] And they did not flock to the Social Development Unit's "love boat" ocean cruises, which sought to match educated women with men who were their academic equals or were slightly inferior.[32] These enterprises may not have yielded many children, but they did bring, according to one observer, "a little tragi-comic relief to the community at large."[33]

Demobilization and Technocratic Reintegration: Public Housing

To gain legitimacy, the PAP did deliver the goods, but in the process it also moved to demobilize and convert the population into a pliable mass by destroying class, communal, and residential solidarities and "reintegrating" people into officially sanctioned and controlled collectivities.

The demobilization and reintegration of labor into an authoritarian corporatist state structure is one example of this process. But perhaps the most interesting—and successful—case of how the government has used a combination of dominance and integration is the public housing program.

In the early 1960s close to a third of Singapore's population was living in the *kampong*, the dense and discontented lower-class residential areas.[34] At the same time, the geographical compartmentalization of ethno-cultural communities was regarded as a recipe for communal conflict and a significant obstacle to the PAP's building of a mass base.

Two decades later, the PAP had finished implementing one of the most successful ventures in public housing in the world. By 1984, 81 percent of the population was housed in government-financed flats, 74 percent of which were owner occupied.[35] In the process, both the slum and kampong communities that had provided the base of lower-class Chinese resistance to the PAP and the Malay communities were forcibly dissolved, and residential patterns were reconstituted to facilitate technocratic control. In James Minchin's insightful description,

> The HDB [Housing Development Board] has been Lee's effective instrument in altering the political demography of Singapore—breaking up natural communities based on affinity of race, clan, religion,

language, and dialect or on generations of friendly contact and shared work, and transferring the fragments into compact areas that are easy to monitor and easy to isolate should the need arise.[36]

Breaking up the Malay communities, which the PAP feared Malaysia would use as bases of subversion, was a major government concern. The government's hope, observed Stanley Bedlington, was that "the removal of Malays from the solidary motifs of the urban ghetto into ethnically integrated public housing will result in new psychological configurations, in which Malays will no longer have to glance backward over their shoulders, fearful of the approbation of their peers and neighbors should they wish to break away from parochially defined norms of behavior."[37]

But the social costs, from the perspective of the Malay community, have been high. Again, the comments of Bedlington, a CIA intelligence officer, are perceptive:

> Many Malays feel sadly out of place in the anonymous concrete corridors of the housing estates. Their new flats are too small to accommodate the ritual and ceremony integral to their culture, they have been taken out of an extended family setting into a nuclear setting, and, most important, there are no mosques or Malay coffee shops through which to express their Malay identity.[38]

Moreover, the economic costs have been high, since the Malays cannot rear the ducks and chickens and grow the vegetables that filled a large portion of subsistence needs in the slums. To sustain the higher expenses of high-rise living, many parents herded into the flats have "let their children drop out of school to earn money for the family's upkeep, and so the back-breaking wheel of poverty goes on."[39] This condition is, of course, one that the Malays share with lower-income Chinese and Indian families, who "may be able to pay their monthly mortgage by using their forced savings in the Central Provident Fund (CPF), yet...must tighten their belts for other consumer necessities, including food."[40] Indeed, John Clammer claims that the percentage of the population living in poverty has risen in the past few decades, thanks largely to the Housing Development Board:

> In the 1950's and 1960's most low-income families...could manage in the kampong environment on very little rent, employment in nearby cottage in-

dustries, and communal facilities. Today, the same family faces HDB rent, high utilities cost, rising transportation costs, and the usual expenses for food, clothing, medicine, and so on. A family that could survive on [S]$400 a month in the kampong, would find it very hard to do so in the HDB estates, as the rising number of rent-arrears families indicates.[41]

Two decades of public housing have produced nothing to replace the lost solidarity of the kampong. Indeed, the minister of housing warned in 1983 that "this conglomerate of different social groups must be quickly welded into a cohesive community if we are to avoid turning our public housing estates into soulless monstrosities."[42]

Of course, the old forms of communal and community solidarity could not be completely eradicated, to the chagrin of the authorities. Thus, after taking pride in breaking up the kampong, Lee Kwan-Yew complained that Malays still apparently preferred to live together on the same floor in the HDB high rises.[43] More ominous to some government officials was the possible recreation of communal ghettoes, since many Chinese and Malays tended to apply for housing in their old communal areas and were "willing to wait as long as necessary to get an apartment in the area of their choice."[44] This return to the source had to be nipped "in the bud before it becomes serious," advocated the minister of national development.[45]

To create a new integrated community, the HDB initiated the formation of Residents' Committees and Citizens' Consultative Committees to promote "neighborliness, ethnic harmony, and community cohesiveness."[46] They were also intended to function as a medium of dialogue between people and government on key social, economic, and political issues. In practice, however, control overshadowed the goals of creating community and facilitating dialogue. As one observer saw it,

> Ideally, the [citizens' consultative] committees are supposed to act like a New England town meeting, but in reality they are nominated by and are responsible to the PAP leadership....The committees also serve as a channel of recruitment within the PAP, and young political activists are often absorbed therein as apprentices for future political roles. Tech-

nically designed to be above partisan politics, in fact they are tightly controlled by the PAP.[47]

Having turned into partisan groupings, it is no surprise that the Residents' and Consultative Committees have by and large failed to mitigate the insensitive approach that HDB technocrats brought to the housing program. As a result, assert Manuel Castells and Lee Goh in their comprehensive study of the housing program, "While the general population recognizes the commendable achievements of the HDB in producing decent housing for the people, they are wary of its role as an overwhelmingly insensitive landlord and as a powerful social control agent of the People's Action Party government."[48] The relationship between the HDB and the residents is described as "one of distrust and immense tension," but the fact that "there are few, if any, alternative housing options for the people...subjects them to all the Draconian practices, rules, and regulations of the HDB."[49]

The quality of the relationship between the housing authority and the people was, indeed, reflective of the quality of the broader relationship between PAP and the people of Singapore.

The Repressive Dimension

The PAP does not depend solely on the manufacture of consent to remain in power and push through its political economy of transnational hegemony. It has also not hesitated to employ repression to remove what it considers obstacles to its policies. That the PAP must not be fearful of repressing for the social good is a lesson that Lee Kwan-Yew has drilled into the hearts of the second-generation leadership of the PAP.

The PAP's success in monopolizing political power cannot be understood without calling attention to its periodic employment of the Internal Security Act (ISA), which allows the government to detain suspected subversives for as long as two years at a time. There were three periods in Singapore's history when the ISA was employed extensively with telling effect: once, to destroy the left-wing leadership of the labor movement via Operation Cold Store in 1963; then, for another wave of arrests in the late 1970s; and again in the summer of 1987 to round up twenty-two Christian activists on charges of being part of a "Marxist conspiracy."

Preventive detention, claims Amnesty International, is central to the staying power of the government: "Although the numbers of persons held in preventive detention may seem small in comparison with many Asian countries, the Singapore authorities have used preventive detention ever since independence on a selective basis as a means of repressing and discouraging legitimate, nonviolent opposition in Singapore. When the government has felt that it faced growing criticism from influential circles, such as lawyers, journalists, or students, it has often reacted by arresting or harassing individuals prominent in those fields, and has reduced them to the role of acquiescent observers."[50]

The ISA is not the only drastic instrument of repression that the government has used to squelch independent opposition. The government has used tax and business laws to harass prominent oppositionists, as when it drove J. B. Jeyaretnam out of office and intimidated Francis Seow from reentering the country. It has also engaged in the politically motivated exercise of the constitutional provisions to ban noncitizens from Singapore or deprive citizens of their citizenship under certain legally specified conditions.[51]

The government, moreover, has sharply curtailed freedom of the press with the "gazetting" (that is, the official declaration of restrictions on circulation) of foreign publications, which often provide the only avenue for opposition groups to reach the public given the self-censorship and progovernment bias of the local press. Under a 1986 amendment to the Newspaper and Printing Presses Act, the government can declare any newspaper or periodical published outside Singapore as interfering in the domestic politics of Singapore. Gazetted publications may not be sold or distributed without the prior approval of the government, and at one time or another the ban has hit the *Far Eastern Economic Review, Asiaweek, Time,* and the *Asian Wall Street Journal.*

Local newspapers, like the *Singapore Straits Times,* censor themselves, and woe to the journalist who falls afoul of the government line.[52]

The absence of genuine freedom of speech was brought home to us during our field work in Singapore in 1988, when none of our respondents, except for known oppositionists Francis Seow and J. B. Jeyaretnam, agreed to be identified in print. "You must understand," one respondent implored, "I have a business to look after, and those people are rather vindictive."[53]

Despite its strong effort to cultivate legitimacy by delivering economic prosperity, the Singapore state is essentially a one-party state. While many of Lee's other admirers hesitate to use the word, Milton Friedman gets right to the point when he says that in Singapore, "you have the forms of democracy, but the reality is dictatorship."[54] What many others would dispute is Friedman's characterization of Lee's dictatorship as "benevolent."[55]

Lee is sometimes described as the primus inter pares among Singapore's founding fathers, the others being the former economic czar Goh Keng-Swee, former PAP chairman Toh Chin-Chye, former foreign minister Sinnathamby Rajaratnam, and former president Devan Nair. But the notion of collective leadership does not match reality. True, Lee allowed Goh much leeway in formulating the economic policies that promoted high-speed growth, but this was possible only because Goh always acknowledged Lee's supremacy. In practically all areas of political life, key initiatives have been Lee's personal decisions: the split with the Communists in the early 1960s, Operation Cold Store in 1963, Singapore's withdrawal from Malaysia in 1965, the savage crackdown on dissent in the late 1970s and again in 1987. Those in the inner circle who crossed swords with Lee or earned his enmity were quickly banished to the party's periphery, as was the case with Toh Chin-Chye and Devan Nair.

The dynamics of succession to his position illustrate the aging prime minister's near absolute power. Lee has not hidden from the press and the world at large that Goh Chok-Tong, now the deputy prime minister, will only be assured of the top job if he measures up to Lee's expectations. Shortly before the September 1988 elections, Lee said that to become prime minister Goh "needs to improve by 100 percent."[56] Lee also declared that even after he retired, he would be ready to take back control should the need arise.[57] For his part, Goh has played the role of the sycophant in public, claiming that "Prime Minister Lee Kwan-Yew has given Singapore political stability. He has made democracy work, not just in the sense of holding elections honestly and regularly, but in the real sense of building a nation from scratch and giving its people a better life."[58]

Lee is nevertheless skeptical of the capabilities of the PAP's second generation to govern—and especially as to whether they can exercise the iron hand of repression. The arrest of twenty-two young Christian activists for subversion in the summer of 1987, which came like a thunderbolt on a clear day, is interpreted by some Singaporeans as having been engineered by Lee to test the mettle of the second generation of PAP leaders, some of whom are suspected of being "closet liberals." The arrest, claimed one prominent businessman after asking us to shut off our tape recorder, "bore the signature of Lee Kwan-Yew." It was to remind the younger PAP leaders that repression was an essential pillar of continued PAP domination of Singapore's politics. "This man, after all, once said that 'repression is like making love. It's easier the second time around.' "[59]

Lee Kwan-Yew may be puritanical in his emphasis on hard work, clean politics, and technocratic efficiency, but he is, when all is said and done, a dictator—a man who inspires fear and elicits grudging respect but never evokes the affection that would go to a more benevolent statesman. In *The Prince*, Machiavelli asks whether is it better for a prince to be loved or feared and proceeds to answer that it is better to be feared. Lee has clearly learned his Machiavelli. But it is doubtful that Machiavelli provides a sound guide to the crisis that is gradually overtaking Singapore's politics and economy.

20

Uncertain Future

As the 1980s drew to a close, Singapore's spectacular growth seemed to have resumed after the recession at mid-decade. In 1989 the gross domestic product rose by some 8.5 percent after shooting up by 11 percent in 1988. Government rhetoric was upbeat, with technocrats proclaiming that their target to exceed Switzerland's per capita GNP by the end of the century was within reach.[1]

But the official rhetoric masked very real problems that had overtaken the "miracle economy."

Poverty and Inequality

Poverty was hidden, but it existed. According to one estimate, it was probable that over 30 percent of Singapore's households were below the poverty line, thanks to HDB policies that had unwittingly promoted "shelter poverty," that is, poverty brought about when households had to deprive themselves of nonshelter basic necessities in order to meet the high costs of housing.[2]

Moreover, after declining in the late 1960s and the early 1970s, inequality was on the rise. Between 1979 and 1983, income inequality widened between workers in different occupations and between workers with different educational qualifications. By 1983 the average earnings of administrative and managerial personnel were five times more than those of production and service personnel.[3]

Growth: A Testament to Failure

While appearing upbeat, PAP technocrats were in fact ambivalent about the growth rate for it was, paradoxically, a testament to the failure of the Second Industrial Revolution. After refusing to cooperate with the PAP government's efforts to move them en masse into more high-tech production, foreign interests began investing massively again when the PAP technocrats reversed their high-wage policy. True, some investments were showcase high-tech operations, like R&D centers set up by Hewlett Packard, Matsushita, and Apple.[4] But most were destined for labor-intensive manufacturing. Moreover, instead of being phased out, foreign workers were imported at a record rate of 2,000 to 3,000 a month as the economy recovered from the depression of 1985–86, raising the official estimate of the foreign labor force from 100,000 in 1985 to 150,000 in 1988.[5]

PAP's great frustration with its inability to move manufacturing into more value-added, skill-intensive production manifested itself in a contradictory policy towards work permit holders. Domestics were characterized as imposing social costs on Singapore,[6] yet government economists also acknowledged that without domestics, it would prove impossible to carry out their preferred policy of meeting the labor shortage by pushing Singaporean women in large numbers into the labor force. More workers were imported, but the levy that employers were charged for each foreign worker was raised from S$175–200 to S$250 a month.[7] The government flushed out and deported some 12,000 illegal workers, mainly from India and Thailand, early in 1989, but allowed most of them back legally by the end of the year. Their absence had made itself felt in delays in big construction projects.[8]

While technocrats could not officially express apprehensions over the quality of growth, such apprehension was articulated by business figures close to official circles. For instance, one business leader told the ASEAN-Japan Economic Council that unless Japan upgraded the quality of its investments in Singapore, the island's increasing dependence on Japan for direct investments "could have ominous consequences for Singapore's economic prospects, leading to a substantially slower growth and even a drop in living standards."[9]

Voting With One's Feet

In the view of some technocrats, the high-wage policy failed because the transnationals were not willing to pay more money for a largely unskilled or semiskilled work force. The solution was therefore to upgrade the skills of a nation where the college-educated came to only 12 to 13 percent of the population, compared to 32 percent in South Korea and 20 percent in Thailand.[10] A grand scheme for skills upgrading was formulated, but the strategy threatened to founder against a worrisome development: a sharply increased rate of emigration among skilled personnel.

Emigration from Singapore was negligible in the 1960s, rose to 2,000 families a year in the mid-1980s, then jumped to 4,700 families (16,000 people) in 1989.[11] For a population of 2.3 million, this figure was fairly significant. Proportionally speaking, one account pointed out, "the exodus from Singapore, which faces no threat from China, was not far below the flight from Hong Kong" that same year.[12] Indeed, many businessmen regarded the actual emigration rate as much higher than the official figure.[13] And it was even more significant if one considered that those leaving tended to be the young skilled professionals. In just one year, for instance, Singapore Airlines lost fifty-two employees, including aircraft engineers, flight engineers, cabin crew, and general staff[14]—precisely the people that PAP technocrats had envisioned as the core of Singapore's future work force.

Lee Kwan-Yew condemned those departing as "washouts" in his annual National Day Rally speech in August 1989 and invoked the specter of a Singapore that was being "creamed off."[15] Lee affected great distress, provoking the *Economist* to write that "leaving is perhaps the cruelest of opposition gestures."[16] For what the prime minister conveniently failed to see was that although some migrants were undoubtedly motivated by economic reasons, others were fleeing the PAP's all-pervasive technocratic supervision of daily life. As one Singaporean told a newspaper reporter, "People just get tired of living in the sixth form [the equivalent of twelfth grade in the U.S. educational system] the whole of their lives."[17] A lawyer explained his decision to leave saying: "This man [Lee Kwan-Yew] is giving people like me no choice. People demand more democracy, they want honest-to-goodness opposition, and if they cannot get it, they will vote with their feet and leave."[18]

The migrants' decision to leave expressed what some analysts see as a basic incompatibility between economic and technological creativity and political authoritarianism. As one prominent expatriate economist put it,

> There is a link between political and economic liberalization, between individual freedom and the intellectual creativity which goes with high tech success. The Singapore government must have more confidence in the people's ability to operate both a more

market-oriented economy and a more democratic
policy. Many Singaporeans have this confidence; and
it would be good if the government would have the
same confidence in its people that they have in themselves.[19]

The sudden rise in emigration in the late 1980s probably reflected
the fact that Singapore's middle class was giving up hope that
prosperity would somehow make Lee Kwan-Yew and the PAP
more amenable to loosening political controls.

Towards an Alternative Economic Strategy

Unable to make the transition to a high-tech productive base
because of a lack of cooperation on the part of the multinationals,
Singapore's economy, it was becoming clear, was also strait-
jacketed by the PAP's suffocating control. Once the pillar of high-
speed export-oriented industrialization, the hegemonic
partnership between foreign capital and the PAP had become
anachronistic.

Despite the veneer of technocratic confidence, economic policy
in Singapore is adrift. Forward movement, however, can no longer
come from mere readjustments of the old paradigm; it will require
more fundamental changes not only in the strategy of growth but
in the very structure of power. A more viable strategy of development would first of all include greater democratization. The PAP
state, it must be emphasized, is one of the dwindling number of
one-party dictatorships. As in Eastern Europe, moving towards a
new stage of economic development in Singapore would require
thoroughgoing political liberalization and democratization. Beyond a certain point, technological and economic creativity cannot
coexist with political disenfranchisement. That point has been
reached in Singapore. As in Taiwan and South Korea, the people
are alienated from an "economic miracle" built on their backs.
Only through democratic participation in political and economic
decision making would the citizenry develop an enduring stake
in the national economic enterprise.

The second element of a new economic paradigm would be to
favor local business—not transnational corporations. The recession of 1985–86 underlined the fact that these corporations have
little interest in Singapore beyond its ability to provide low wages
and political stability, yet the difference between famine and
plenty in Singapore continues to lie in their investment decisions.

The local business class has a more all-sided and more solid interest in Singapore. As many Singaporean economists have urged, it is time to build up the local business class to reduce the country's unhealthy overdependence on foreign capital. A healthy, competitive domestic business class would also mean that more of Singapore's wealth could be retained in the economy instead of being siphoned off as multinational profits—a figure that now comes to about 28 percent of GDP.

Building up local business would involve sharply reversing the incentive system that has favored the transnationals in the past three decades. It could mean giving local businesses easier access to credit, granting them subsidies selectively, and instituting a measure of protection for the domestic market. It could also involve partnerships between the government and local business to speed up technology transfer from transnational corporations and foreign research institutions.

Third, an element of a new development strategy would be to build a more dynamic internal market. The 1985–86 recession underlined the importance of having an expanding domestic market that can counter recessionary conditions in the export sector. Consolidating a domestic market would involve measures that also promote equity, notably programs to end shelter poverty and raise the incomes of the 30 percent of the population now living under the poverty line, and efforts to reverse the growing inequality in personal incomes.

The new strategy would also involve a new deal for labor. Greater democracy and a more dynamic internal market are linked to the emergence of a free labor movement that could negotiate with foreign and local capital to set wage levels without the repressive mediation of the PAP. A new deal for labor would not be discriminatory, but would instead promote equality in wage rates, equal rights for women workers, and move to gradually incorporate foreign workers as full-fledged members of Singapore's work force, with rights to unionize, strike, marry Singaporeans, and, after meeting residency requirements, settle in Singapore. In short, the artificial stratification of the Singaporean work force is an anachronism that must go the same way as the authoritarian corporatism of the PAP.

Given its size, the Singapore market, no matter how dynamic, cannot serve as the main pillar of sustained development. Thus the final element of a new paradigm is a new relationship with Southeast Asia. Singapore's development in the past thirty years has integrated its economy more tightly with the advanced industrial countries than with the Southeast Asian region. Over 40 percent of both exports and imports are with the advanced countries belonging to the Organization for Economic Cooperation and Development (OECD). Moreover, in its relation to Southeast Asia, Singapore has traditionally been a convenient point of entry for Western and Japanese capital seeking to penetrate Southeast Asian markets. The PAP's master plan for the 1990s, which is to make Singapore the financial hub and regional headquarters for multinationals operating in Southeast Asia, would merely deepen this unhealthy relationship.

As the world trading system splits up into techno-protectionist trading blocs in the 1990s, Singapore risks marginalization by sticking to its original role. The future lies in regional techno-trading blocs marked by equitable agreements on trade, capital movements, and technology transfer. The framework for a dynamic regional market now exists in the form of the Association of Southeast Asian Nations. The challenge of the 1990s is to give ASEAN substance and, specifically, to give Singapore a place in a vibrant regional division of labor.

In short, even as it restructures its domestic economy, Singapore must transform its relationship to the outside world. It can choose to maintain itself as a world city, a role appropriate to a period when the world economy was largely guided by free trade, or it can become a truly Southeast Asian metropolis in a post–free trade era.

Conclusion

The NICs, the Future, and the Third World

The past few years have seen the end of the unique conjunction of external and internal factors that allowed a few countries limited ascent within the capitalist world system. In this survey of South Korea, Taiwan, and Singapore, one thing became very clear: the old strategy of high-speed, export-oriented growth will not get the NICs through the 1990s. The strategy of development needs drastic, if not fundamental, revision to avoid the scenario of the NICs falling back to the third world.

There is currently active discussion of economic reform in all three countries. In Singapore, local business is demanding an end to the preferential treatment of foreign investors. In Taiwan, the environmental movement is seeking to subordinate growth to ecological equilibrium. In Korea, even some government technocrats have conceded that income redistribution and the domestic market must be the centerpiece of an alternative economic program.

The debate, however, has not yet yielded a comprehensive and coherent new vision of an alternative mode of development. Nonetheless, as we examined the social conflicts and structural contradictions in the three countries, it became increasingly clear that although the crisis has a unique configuration in each country, the NICs have fundamentally similar problems that call for a similar strategic response. It also became evident that economic models that pit efficiency against equity and economic growth against ecological equilibrium are obsolete. Instead at this stage the NICs may find that the imperatives of economic effectiveness, ecological stability, equity, and democracy may be more complementary than competitive. Indeed, it is possible to discern the contours of a comprehensive alternative paradigm.

The Domestic Market, Growth, and Equity

Clearly, viable export markets are unlikely to grow significantly in an age of protectionism. The domestic market, in short, must now serve again as the main engine of growth, as it did in the 1950s. This is especially true in Korea and Taiwan; while in Singapore, the domestic market must be cultivated hand-in-hand with the regional Southeast Asian market. Income levels have risen significantly in all three countries to make domestic market-driven growth a viable strategy. Indeed, in Korea the workers' push for higher wages created a boom in domestic demand that compensated for the severe slowdown of export growth in 1989. While Korea's car exports dropped to almost 30 percent in the first half of 1988, domestic sales jumped up by 58 percent. Ironically, had they not been saved by the higher incomes brought about by worker militance, Hyundai Motors and Daewoo Motors, two of Korea's most aggressively antiunion firms, would have had a severe crisis of overproduction on their hands.

Growth will not, however, be sustained unless measures are taken to correct the worsening distribution of income in all three NICs. Concretely, this means decisive policies that will hurt the now dominant groups. For instance, in Singapore, it will require keeping more of the value of Singapore's production in the country in the form of income for its population rather than as profits to be repatriated by the multinational firms. In Korea income redistribution will necessarily have to be tied to dismantling the chaebol or at least ending their stranglehold on national resources. And in both Taiwan and Korea, a dynamic internal market cannot emerge unless there is something like a massive Marshall Plan to save the agrarian economy and a reversal of the tacit policy of withdrawing protection from agricultural commodities to preserve the urban manufacturers' access to the U.S. market.

Sustainable Development

Further environmental degradation can no longer be an acceptable trade-off for double-digit growth rates. But making environmental preservation a priority need not mean an end to growth. It may mean lower growth rates, but the main impact of an environmentally sensitive development policy will be to channel the quality of economic growth onto an ecologically sustainable path. For instance, restricting the growth of the petrochemical industry can be counterbalanced by a large-scale investment program to save the environment, which may in turn spawn a whole manufacturing subsector devoted to making antipollution equipment, waste-treatment facilities, and other environmental protection systems. To be successful, such an effort must, of course, include a government-led restructuring of technical education to produce large numbers of environmental engineers, scientists, and monitors, and the formulation of an attractive package of financial and moral incentives for such technical personnel to remain in Taiwan and Korea.

Also, a shift away from chemically dependent agriculture to organic farming would mean turning to more labor-intensive yet higher-value-added production. Most likely, the consumers' growing demand for uncontaminated products would serve as a strong incentive for paying more for safe grain, produce, and meat. Organic farming, with its high demand for labor-intensive care, could help reverse the depopulation of the countryside and spark a resurrection of agriculture.[1]

A Selective Export Policy

Making the domestic market the engine of growth does not imply an end to exports as a key component of economic strategy. But instead of chasing evanescent markets all over the world, Korean, Taiwanese, and Singaporean entrepreneurs could focus on selected markets, like Southeast Asia. And instead of competing with the Japanese on a whole range of commodities, from low tech to medium tech to high tech products, they can focus on a narrower band of manufactured exports for which they can build a more solid base of intermediate and basic industries.

For example, rather than try to build supertrains and upscale cars for export to advanced country markets, the Taiwanese and Korean auto industries could shift a significant portion of their resources to producing energy-efficient and non-polluting public transportation vehicles and systems for third world markets. Instead of wasting resources competing with Japan and the United States in the frontiers of biotechnology, the NICs could focus on developing versatile electro-mechanical implements for labor-intensive organic farming. Rather than rush into developing workstations powered by state-of-the-art RISC microprocessors and 4-megabit memory chips, the Taiwanese and Koreans could concentrate on producing simple, user-friendly PCs for use in third world educational and work settings. In other words, the NICs could fill the massive need for cheap medium-tech items designed for use in third world tropical settings.

Developing Equitable Regional Associations

The 1990s are likely to see the hastening of the breakup of the liberal postwar international trade regime. The creation of the U.S.-Canada Free Trade Area is likely to be the first step in the United States' gradual retreat to Fortess America, just as the creation of a single European market in 1992 is certain to lead to a more protectionist European Community. The relevant question is, will the Asia-Pacific area be able to avoid being turned into a Japanese-dominated economic zone?

The future of the Pacific depends greatly on the NICs. They can either remain economic and technological dependencies of Japan, or they can work with their less-developed neighbors in Southeast Asia and the Pacific to create a regional counterweight to Japanese economic colonization. Such an economic bloc could be built on very different relationships than those characteristic of both U.S. and Japanese economic expansion, which has traditionally been marked by a lopsided division of labor, technological monopoly, unequal transfers of capital, chronic trade deficits, and environmental degradation. In contrast, the NICs, ASEAN, Indochina and the Pacific countries could fashion institutions and agreements that would, among other things, ensure that divisions of labor that facilitate trade do not congeal into permanent cleavages, that technological know-how is spread around systematically, and that foreign investment develops an economy integrally instead of simply creating cheap labor enclaves.

Economic ventures could build on the initial technological strengths of the NICs and their less-developed neighbors. To take just one example, the Philippines produces many skilled computer programmers and engineers, who cannot find jobs in the local economy. Korea, in contrast, is strong in computer hardware but weak in software development. In the past, U.S. firms have taken advantage of Philippine software specialists' low wages to design advanced programs at a fraction of the price they would pay U.S.-based software companies. Instead of serving as cheap labor for American bargain hunters, Filipino and other Southeast Asian programmers could be designing programs for Korean computer hardware as part of a comprehensive, long-term agreement that would include the exchange of software and hardware know-how between the ASEAN countries and the NICs.

Handled creatively, joint ventures could also be a conduit of technological exchange between the NICs and their less-developed neighbors in construction, agriculture, shipbuilding, motor vehicles, consumer electronics, and the environmental protection industry.

While facilitating positive exchange, such arrangements must also do away with the currently negative dimensions of the NIC-ASEAN relationship, especially in the areas of environment and foreign investment. A regional environmental code should make it impossible for runaway polluters from Taiwan and South Korea to site their production facilities in the Philippines, Malaysia, or Indonesia. Similarly, a regional labor code would make the runaway shop option less attractive by preventing cutthroat competition in the price of labor offered to Japanese, NIC, and other foreign investors by the ASEAN or Indochinese authorities.

Rectifying the grossly unequal relationship with Japan must also be high in the NIC-ASEAN agenda. A unified front presented by eleven countries would provide powerful leverage to force Japan to transfer selected high technologies, reduce its chronic trade surplus with the NICs and Southeast Asia, and terminate its rapid destruction of tropical rain forests.

The obstacles in the way of regional cooperation must not be underestimated. One has only to look at ASEAN to appreciate how distrust among neighbors can sabotage the process. Twenty-five years after its founding, ASEAN remains largely an anti-Communist alliance, with the bulk of the trade and investment activities of its member countries still oriented outside the Southeast Asian region. Nor can one brush off the likely responses from Japan and the United States. Efforts to regulate trade and investment are likely to elicit a frontal retaliatory attack from the United States and a more sophisticated divide-and-conquer response from the Japanese.

Will the NICs see their interest as lying in such a federation? One thing is certain: unless they participate in such a techno-trading bloc for cooperative economic development and collective economic defense, they will become mere satellites of the Japanese juggernaut.

Democracy and Economic Strategy

To be successful in the long term, strategies for growth can no longer be imposed from above by state technocratic elites. Command economics, whether of the capitalist or socialist variety, is obsolete: that is the message of the concurrent social upheavals in Eastern Europe, Korea, and Taiwan. That is also the meaning of the spectacular rise in the number of people leaving Singapore. More than ever, people want an active say in economic policy, and unless it is based on a rough consensus forged by democratic means that policy will ultimately founder. Democracy, one might say, has become a factor of production.

Democracy, however, is no longer simply seen as limited to the formal task of voting for one's policy preferences and for one's representatives. The definition of democracy is being expanded to include equality in access to resources and the ability to make decisions at the workplace. In Korea, this expanded meaning of democracy is now expressed in efforts to curtail the power of the chaebol, if not dismantle them. Within the Korean enterprise, it is manifested in the campaign to end militarist management and gain for workers a greater say not only in the conditions of work but also in making decisions governing investment. Democracy may make forging consensus at the national, local, and enterprise levels more difficult and complex, but it also ensures that once arrived at, strategies for development are solidly endowed with legitimacy.

Just as the state was decisive in moving the NICs along high-speed, export-oriented growth, so will it be the key factor in the process of breaking with the past and moving in a new economic direction. However, the authoritarian political requirements of the strategy of high-speed, export-oriented growth have led the current state elites to develop strong vested interests in the obsolete paradigm. Thus, it is unlikely that they can be counted on to preside over the creation of a new, more democratic political framework to nurture the new strategies. Whether the Lee Kwan-Yew government in Singapore, the KMT in Taiwan, or the Roh Tae-Woo government in South Korea, the old state elites are irretrievably bound up with the old economic regime. The break with export-oriented growth can only be made if a new coalition of forces comes to political power, a coalition based on those sectors of society that have the greatest stake in a new strategy of development: the farmers, small and medium businesses, workers, and environmentalists.

The NICs and the Third World

Since the NICs are often set up as a model for the rest of the third world, this book would be incomplete without some reexamination of the lessons that they bear for countries seeking to escape from underdevelopment.

Thoughout Africa, Asia, and Latin America, the IMF and the World Bank are today supervising over thirty structural adjustment loans that are, in part, geared to create conditions for successful passage to NICdom. Third world governments everywhere are delivered the same missive: devalue the currency and cut wages to make your exports competitive; reduce social expenditures and eliminate government budget deficits; dismantle your tariff and nontariff barriers to imports; and promote a positive climate for foreign investment. For the technocrats at the World Bank and the International Monetary Fund, structural adjustment programs bring together, in happy harmony, three goals: making "spendthrift" third world governments live within their means, enabling them to pay their debts to the commercial banks, and creating the conditions by which they can become future NICs.

The NIC experience does have tremendous relevance for the third world, but this is not to be found in the World Bank–IMF injunctions to pursue the strategy of export-oriented growth, stifle the domestic market through draconian income-slashing measures, and completely open up the domestic economy to foreign investment and manufactured imports from the advanced industrial countries. Not only do these prescriptions distort the NIC experience, they lead to disaster in an increasingly protectionist world economy. Indeed, nowhere is the intellectual bankruptcy of such agencies as the IMF and the World Bank more evident than in their crusade to bring down protective mechanisms in third world economies even as the West enacts a thousand and one tariff and nontariff barriers to the free flow of goods from the third world and the NICs.

The lessons of the NICs for the third world are elsewhere. One of the most important is, undoubtedly, the critical role played by land reform in setting the stage for economic takeoff. While later agricultural policy in Taiwan and Korea ended up betraying the peasantry, it started off on the right foot, with a comprehensive redistribution of land. Land reform in Taiwan and Korea was decisive, compared to the weak, half-way reform in places like the Philippines and most of Latin America. In Taiwan and Korea land reform eliminated the politically reactionary landlord class, freed up resources for investment in industry, and created a market of rural consumers with effective demand that served as the main stimulus for economic growth in the first decade of development. The lesson for Latin America, the Philippines, India, Brazil and other states that hesitate to take on their entrenched landlord classes is that land reform is the *conditio sine qua non* for national development.

Other lessons—both positive and negative—are to be found in the role of the state in the NICs.

Contrary to the ideology of Western free marketeers, the need in most parts of the third world is for more state, not less. The problem is that in places like the Philippines and many parts of Latin America, the state is too enmeshed in civil society, being, in many ways, the private property of economic interest groups. And in areas where traditional economic elites are weak, as in most of Africa, the state has been treated as an instrument of repression or as a treasury to be plundered by political elites. Planning often-times is merely paper pushing—a necessary exercise to get aid from the World Bank and Western governments.

In the NICs the state was able to achieve a degree of independence not only from domestic economic elites but also from foreign agencies. The Korean state is a very interesting study of pragmatic, as opposed to ideological, economic nationalism. While mouthing anti-Communist, antisocialist, and pro–free market slogans, it set out in practice to protect its domestic market and created one of the world's most stringent foreign investment regimes. While receiving massive amounts of IMF and World Bank assistance as a preferred anti-Communist client, the state launched, in the face of opposition from the two agencies, the heavy and chemical industry drive that spurred the creation of a more-solid heavy and intermediate industrial base. While there were major problems associated with the strategy of export-oriented development, one cannot say that the Korean state was lacking in either the vision or the will to create a more independent national industrial economy.

But while one can applaud the governments for being able to whip the dominant interests of civil society into line, the fact is that these same governments also repressed their own people.

Which brings up the question: Was authoritarianism necessary to lay the foundations of a strong developmental state? Samuel Huntington has probably made the strongest case for the affirmative in his 1968 book, *Political Order in Changing Societies*, which argues that creating order must precede the exercise of democracy. What is interesting though is that, with the exception of South Korea, hardly any of Huntington's examples of modernizing authoritarian elites in the third world—whether military or Communist—were ultimately able to successfully guide their countries in the transition from underdevelopment. And recent history is littered with examples of repressive regimes that failed as modernizers, from Brazil's military junta to Nigeria's soldiers to Ferdinand Marcos' executive-military dictatorship in the Philippines. Given this history, one cannot dismiss the confident contention of one opposition parliamentarian that had democracy come sooner "Taiwan would still have grown, but its development would have been more balanced and more healthy."[2]

The issue is critical, but it is one that will probably not be settled for a long time since not only facts but also fundamental political values are at issue. What is not likely to be disputed, however, is that the NIC state elites made a tragic mistake in identifying the consolidation of a strong developmental state with the institutionalization of authoritarian rule. Interestingly, this was the same error made by those running the Communist countries of Eastern Europe. While there were significant differences between the NIC and the Eastern European economies, notably the complete absence of the market in the latter, they also had their instructive similarities. Like the NICs, the Eastern European economies racked up high industrial growth rates in their first decades of development after World War II.[3] In both types of command economy, the costs piled up, mainly in the form of deep alienation among workers and other social groups that felt they were being run over by the locomotive of high-speed growth and had no power to stop it. Environmental destruction was partly a product of development from above, since there were no channels for feedback from the grass roots on the ecological impact of various policies, like the tragic intensification of chemical agricultural methods and the benign treatment of polluters in the forefront of economic growth.

When the NIC governments, like their counterpart command regimes in Eastern Europe, were finally forced to democratize, the legacy of years of accumulated resentment and distrust guaranteed that democratic processes would center not on forging a new consensus on economic strategy but on waging a bitter struggle to redistribute economic and political power. Late democratization, while infinitely better than authoritarian rule, is nevertheless very costly from the perspective of long-term economic development.

Authoritarianism, then, ultimately weakens state leadership, whereas democratic accountability, no matter how messy initially, ultimately strengthens it. This paradox is arguably one of the most valuable lessons that the third world can derive from the NICs. To be ultimately successful, a strategy for economic development must be democratically chosen, democratically planned, democratically implemented, and democratically modified.

Notes

Introduction: The Rise and Crisis of the Dragon Economies

1. Personal interview with Lee So-Sun by Walden Bello, Seoul, May 20, 1988.

2. John Naisbitt, "Asian Economies to be Giants of 21st Century," *Japan Economic Journal*, December 30, 1989 – January 6, 1990, p. 9.

3. We did not include Hong Kong in our study because so many of its recent, present, and future economic and political trends have been greatly influenced by increasingly tight economic relations with China and by one apocalyptic event: the colony's devolution to China in 1997.

4. Ramon Myers, "The Economic Development of the Republic of China on Taiwan, 1965-1981," in Lawrence Lau and Lawrence Klein, eds., *Models of Development: A Comparative Study of Economic Growth in South Korea and Taiwan* (San Francisco: Institute for Contemporary Studies, 1986), p. 47.

5. Jon Halliday, "The Economies of North and South Korea," in John Sullivan and Roberta Foss, eds., *Two Koreas—One Future?* (Lanham, Md.: University Press of America, 1987), p. 36.

6. *Ibid.*

7. Thomas Gold, *State and Society in the Taiwanese Miracle* (Armonk, N.Y.: M. E. Sharpe, 1986), pp. 86–87.

8. Ahn Junghyo, *White Badge* (New York: Soho Press, 1989), p. 40.

9. Gavan McCormack, "The South Korean Economy: GNP versus the People," in Gavan McCormack and Mark Selden, eds., *Korea North and South: The Deepening Crisis* (New York: Monthly Review Press, 1978), p. 101.

10. Akio Morita and Shintaro Ishihara, *The Japan That Can Say "No"* (Tokyo: Kobunsha Kappa-Holmes, 1989), unauthorized translation by Japanese-American Joint Leadership Foundation, p. 73.

11. See, among others, Bruce Cumings, "The Origins and Development of the Northeast Asian Political Economy: Industrial Sectors, Product Cycles, and Political Consequences," *International Organization* 38, no. 1 (Winter 1984), pp. 1–40.

12. Huang Chi, "The State and Foreign Capital: A Case Study of Taiwan," Ph.D. Dissertation, Dept. of Political Science, Indiana University, Feb. 1986, p. 189; Denis Simon, "Taiwan, Technology Transfer, and Transnationals: The Political Management of Dependency," Ph.D. Dissertation, University of California at Berkeley, 1980, p. 350.

13. Kim Kwang-Doo and Lee Sang-Ho, "The Role of the Korean Government in Technology Import," in Lee C.H. and Ippei Yamazawa, eds., *The Economic Development of Japan and Korea* (New York: Praeger, 1990), p. 93.

14. Kent Calder, "The North Pacific Triangle: Sources of Economic and Political Transformation," *Journal of Northeast Asian Studies*, 7, no. 2 (Summer 1989), p. 5.

15. Quoted in Foreign Policy Association, "Third World Development: Old

Problems, New Strategies," *Great Decisions '86*.

16. Alice Amsden, "Late Industrialization in South Korea: The General Properties of Expansion Through Learning," Manuscript, Boston, 1988, p. 6-2. This excellent manuscript has since been published as *Asia's Next Giant: South Korea and Late Industrialization* (New York: Oxford University Press, 1989).

17. The influential role of the Singaporean state in depressing wages below their market value was openly admitted in the late 1970's, when the government issued the "corrective wage policy," which wil be discussed in detail in the Singapore section. What is important to note here is that the government "argued that the policy has been necessary to restore wages to their market value." As Gary Rodan has commented, "The very notion of a 'corrective' wage policy is an indictment on the freedom of labor as a factor of production. It is an open admission of the government's control over a key aspect of the economy. For this reason alone, it is hard to accept uncritically the notion of comparative advantage in labor costs as having any meaning in isolation from...the state's role in helping to define these costs. The 'advantage' is thus anything but natural or given." "Industrialization and the Singapore State in the Context of the New International Division of Labor," in Richard Higgott and Richard Robison, eds., *Southeast Asia: Essays in the Political Economy of Structural Change* (London: Routledge and Kegan Paul, 1985), p. 179.

18. David Mulford, "Remarks before the Asia-Pacific Capital Markets Conference," San Francisco, November 17, 1987.

19. Interview with Y.C. Park, senior manager, Tae Heung, Ltd., by Walden Bello, Seoul, May 23, 1988.

20. So threatened was Taiwan by the American offensive that in 1988 it took to importing large quantities of gold from the United States to reduce the trade surplus, which it did again in 1989. Even without the gold imports, however, the impact of the American pressure on Taiwan is seen in the fact that the surplus fell by 30 percent between 1987 and 1989, from $16 billion to $12 billion. See "Annoying Big Brother," *Economist*, January 13, 1990, p. 68.

21. Peter Montagnon, "Wanted: A Truly Free Market," *Financial Times*, April 2, 1990, sec. 3, p. v.

22. "Most People Here Put Environmental Protection Before Economic Growth," *China News* (Taipei), May 5, 1985. See also Michael Hsiao and Lester Milbrath, "The Environmental Movement in Taiwan," Paper prepared for the Sino-U.S. Binational Conference on Environmental Protection and Social Development, Taipei, August 20-23, 1989, table 7, p. 23.

23. "Sympathy for South Korea," *Financial Times*, March 22, 1990.

24. Kim Sam-O, "Better Labor Conditions Creep into NICs," *Electronics Korea*, December 1989, p. 38.

25. Gregory Moulton, "Future Newly Industrializing Countries: More Competition," *Confidential*, Office of Global Issues, Central Intelligence Agency, Washington, D.C., March 1984, p. 8.

Korea: A Model Unravels
Introduction to Part I

1. Robert Delfs, "Intellectuals Advocate Strongman before Democracy: Little

Dragons Model," *Far Eastern Economic Review*, March 9, 1989, p. 12.

2. Quoted in *Ibid.*

3. Stefan Wagstyl, "South Korean Finance and Industry: Turmoil of Transition," *Financial Times*, November 27, 1989, sec. 3, p. i.

4. Quoted in "Roh Blames Labor for Stumbling Economy," *Asian Wall Street Journal*, January 11, 1990, p. 3.

5. Quoted in *Korea Times*, November 1, 1989, reproduced in *Foreign Broadcast Information Service Daily Report: East Asia* (hereafter to be referred to as FBIS) November 2, 1989, p. 27.

Chapter 1. The Making of an Insurrectionary Working Class

1. Even Tibor Scitovsky, a conservative economist who admires the Taiwan and Korean models, admits that "one is tempted to add the two countries' very long working week as a further manifestation of the work ethic, but in view of the very limited bargaining strength of their unions, it is hard to tell to what extent those long working hours are voluntary and to what extent they are imposed." Scitovsky, "Economic Development in Taiwan and South Korea, 1965–81," in Lawrence Lau, ed., *Models of Development: A Comparative Study of Economic Growth in South Korea and Taiwan* (San Francisco: Institute for Contemporary Studies Press, 1986), p. 140.

2. Economic Planning Board, cited in Hagen Koo, "Dependency Issues, Class Inequality, and Social Conflict in Korean Development," in Kim Kyong-Dong, ed., *Dependency Issues in Korean Development* (Seoul: Seoul National University Press, 1987), p. 377.

3. "South Korea's Miracle," *Economist*, March 4, 1989, p. 77.

4. International Labor Office (ILO), cited in Choi Young-Il, "Distribution of Wealth: A Critical Issue in South Korea," *Korea Report* (Washington, D.C.), September–October 1987, p. 7.

5. Interview with key executive of wood-processing factory in Inchon who wished to remain anonymous, by Walden Bello, Inchon, May 18, 1988.

6. International Labor Office, cited in *South Korea's New Trade Unions* (Hong Kong: Asia Monitor Resource Center, 1987), p. 8.

7. "South Korea's Miracle," *Economist*, March 4, 1989, p. 77.

8. Lee Keum-Hyun, "Ours Is Not to Question Why," *Business Korea Electronics*, September 1988, p. 51.

9. Barry Renfrew, "Korea's Growth Take Its Toll on Workers," *Asian Wall Street Journal*, January 9, 1989, p. 11.

10. Lee Keum-Hyun, p. 51.

11. Tony Michell, "From LDC to NIC: The Republic of Korea: Employment, Industrialization and Trade, 1961–1982," Unpublished manuscript, Seoul, 1988, p. 134.

12. *Ibid.*

13. Michael Launius, "The State and Industrial Labor in South Korea," *Bulletin of Concerned Asian Scholars* 16, no. 4, p. 10.

14. Alice Amsden, "Late Industrialization in South Korea: The General Prop-

erties of Expansion through Learning," Unpublished manuscript, Boston, 1989, p. 8-2. This manuscript has since been published with the title *Asia's Next Giant: South Korea and Late Industrialization* (New York: Oxford University Press, 1989).

15. Korea Federation of Labor Unions, cited in Choi Young-Il, p. 7.

16. *Ibid.*, p. 8.

17. You Jong-Il, "Capital-Labor Relations of the Newly Industrializing Regime in South Korea: Past, Present, and Future," Unpublished paper, April 1989, p. 12.

18. Lee Jeong-Taik, "Dynamics of Labor Control and Labor Protest in the Process of Export-Oriented Industrialization in South Korea," *Asian Perspective* (Korea) 12, no. 1 (Spring–Summer 1988), p. 146.

19. *Ibid.*, p. 145.

20. "Workers' Wages and Rights: A Battle for Survival and Dignity," *Business Korea Electronics*, December 1988, p. 49.

21. Michell, p. 134.

22. Song Byung-Nak, "The Korean Economy," Unpublished manuscript, Seoul, 1989, p. 27.

23. *Ibid.*

24. Choi Jang-Jip, "Interest Control and Political Control in South Korea: A Study of the Labor Unions in Manufacturing Industries, 1961–1980," Ph.D. dissertation, Department of Political Science, University of Chicago, August 1983, pp. 270–271.

25. Song Byung-Nak, p. 274.

26. *Ibid.*

27. You Jong-Il, p. 32.

28. *Ibid.*, pp. 32-33.

29. "Hyundai Group: Tough Time for Tough Management," *Business Korea*, July 1988, p. 29.

30. *Lost Victory: An Overview of the Korean People's Struggle for Democracy in 1987* (Seoul: Christian Institute for the Study of Justice and Development, 1988), p. 237.

31. See "When the 'Have-Nots' Rise Up," *Korea Business World*, May 1989, p. 17.

32. John Gittelsohn, "Shattering Glass," *Korea Business World*, May 1989, p. 18.

33. Hong Won-Tack, "Export-Oriented Growth of Korea: A Possible Path to Advanced Economy," Seminar Paper no. 382, Institute for International Economic Studies, Stockholm, June 1987, p. 36.

34. Quoted in Michell, p. 139.

35. *Ibid.*, pp. 139–140.

36. Choi Jang-Jip, pp. 139–140.

37. Quoted in Launius, p. 7.

38. "Samsung Heavy Ind.: Striking over the Right to Unite," *Business Korea* (January 1989), p. 29.

39. Choi Jang-Jip, p. 293.

40. You Jong-Il, p. 35.

41. Choi Jang-Jip, p. 339.

42. *Ibid.*, pp. 246–247.

43. Cited in Michell, p. 142.

44. Ronald Rodgers, "Labor Relations Law and Labor Control in the Republic of Korea," *Korea Scope*, 1984, no. 4, p. 13.

45. Lee Jeong-Taik, p. 152.

46. Kim Seung-Kuk, "Class Formation and Labor Process in Korea: With Special Reference to Working Class Consciousness," in Kim Kyong-Dong, ed. *Dependency Issues in Korean Development*, p. 407.

47. Michell, p. 170.

48. Much of the following account of the union struggles of the 1970s is drawn from Choi Jang-Jip's excellent study.

49. Choi Jang-Jip, p. 204.

50. You Jong-Il, p. 35.

51. Kim Dong-Wan, "A Reflection on the Recent Labor Movement in Korea," in *International Consultation on Development in Korea Report (Revised)* (Seoul: Christian Institute for the Study of Justice and Development, 1982), pp. 25–30.

52. Interview with brother of Jeon Tae-Il, Seoul, May 20, 1988.

53. Choi Jang-Jip, p. 220.

54. You Jong-Il, p. 41.

55. *Ibid.*, p. 19.

56. Lee Jeong-Taik, p. 143.

57. Liz McGregor, "The Poor Are with Us," *Korea Business World*, April 1989, p. 34.

58. Song Byung-Nak, p. 241.

59. *Ibid.*, p. 244.

60. Economic Planning Board, cited in Choi Young-Il, p. 8.

61. Michell, p. 147.

62. *Ibid.*

63. "Local Anaesthetic," *Far Eastern Economic Review*, August 17, 1989, p. 63.

64. "Realigning Korea's National Priorities for Economic Progress: The Presidential Commission Report on Economic Restructuring," *Korea's Economy 5*, no. 1 (July 1989), pp. 22–23.

65. "Land Tax Reform: Can the Circle Be Broken?," *Business Korea*, November 1989, p. 27.

66. Catholic Institute for International Relations, *Disposable People: Forced Evictions in South Korea* (London: Catholic Institute for International Relations, 1988), p. 9.

67. Asian Coalition for Housing Rights, "Evictions in Seoul, South Korea," *Environment and Urbanization* (London), April 1989, p. 90.

68. Michael Prowse, "Unequal Society Rethinking Its Priorities," *Financial*

Times, sec. 3, June 15, 1989, p. xii.

69. Asian Coalition, p. 90.

70. McGregor, p. 37.

71. Cited in *ibid.*

72. S. Santhamah, "Seoul Evicts Its Poor to Make Way for Olympics," *Third World Network Features*, March 1988.

73. "Land to the Dweller," *Economist*, September 16, 1989, p. 36.

74. Maggie Ford, "Seoul in Twist Over Top 30," *Financial Times*, June 15, 1989. The comparison to San Francisco Bay Area prices is provided by the authors.

75. "Land Tax Reform: Can the Circle be Broken?," *Financial Times*, June 15, 1980.

76. Quoted in Mark Clifford, "Seoul Plans Swinging Taxes on Real-Estate Profits: Landed in Trouble," *Far Eastern Economic Review*, September 14, 1989, p. 72.

77. You Jong-Il, p. 51.

78. *Ibid.*, p. 36; also "A Quick Lesson in Labor Relations," *South*, September 1989, p. 61.

79. Kim Tae-Sik, "Yonhap Wraps Up Year's Labor Developments," December 13, 1989, reproduced in *FBIS*, December 13, 1989, p. 29.

80. "Chung Ju-Jung: Corporate Leader in Class of His Own," *Financial Times*, sec. 3, June 15, 1989, p. ix.

81. *Ibid.*

82. Gittelsohn, p. 18.

83. Personal interview with Lee So-Sun by Walden Bello, Seoul, May 20, 1988.

84. Personal interview by Walden Bello with worker who prefers to remain anonymous, Inchon, May 18, 1989.

85. Lho Joo-Hyoung, "Workers' Power," *Korea Business World*, June 1989, p. 28; see also Kim Tae-Sik, p. 29.

86. Kim Tae-Sik, p. 29.

87. Damon Darlin, "Spring Offensive: Korea's Long-Suppressed Unions Adopt Confrontational Style in Fight for Rights," *Asian Wall Street Journal Weekly*, April 17, 1989, p. 2.

88. Quoted in David Easter, "South Korea Blames Labor for Economic Woes," *Guardian* (New York), April 4, 1990, p. 17.

89. *Ibid.*

Chapter 2. The Rise of Command Capitalism

1. Quoted in Foreign Policy Association, "Third World Development: Old Problems, New Strategies," *Great Decisions '86*.

2. Quoted in Alice Amsden, "Late Industrialization in South Korea: The General Properties of Expansion through Learning," Unpublished manuscript, Boston, 1989, pp. 2-36. This manuscript has since been published with the title *Asia's Next Giant: South Korea and Late Industrialization* (New York: Oxford University Press, 1989).

3. Quoted in Song Byung-Nak, "The Korean Economy," Unpublished manuscript, Seoul, 1989, p. 125.

4. *Ibid.*, p. 124.

5. Quoted in Alice Amsden, "Private Enterprise: The Issue of Business-Government Control," *Columbia Journal of World Business* 23, no. 1 (Spring 1988).

6. Quoted in Amsden, "Late Industrialization," pp. 2–38.

7. Song Byung-Nak, p. 126.

8. *Ibid.*, p. 195.

9. *Ibid.*, p. 126.

10. *Ibid.*, p. 336.

11. Tony Michell, "From LDC to NIC: The Republic of Korea: Employment, Industrialization, and Trade, 1961–62," Unpublished manuscript, Seoul, 1988, p. 83.

12. Amsden, "Late Industrialization," pp. 4–12.

13. Quoted in Kim Jin-Moon, "Kukje in Court: Fighting to Regain an Empire," *Business Korea*, May 1988, p. 22.

14. Lyuba Zarsky, "State-Led Growth: Rapid Industrialization in the Republic of Korea, 1963-1979," Unpublished paper, University of Massachusetts, Amherst, 1987, p. 21.

15. Richard Leudde-Neurath, *Import Controls and Export-Oriented Development: A Reassessment of the South Korean Case* (Boulder: West View Press, 1986), p. 143.

16. Hong Won-Tack, "Export-Oriented Growth of Korea: A Possible Path to Advanced Economy," Seminar Paper no. 382, Institute for International Economic Studies, Stockholm, 1987, p. 25.

17. Song Byung-Nak, p. 133.

18. *Ibid.*, pp. 203–204.

19. Koo Bon-Ho and Bark Tae-Ho, "Government Policies, Recent Trends, and the Economic Impact of Direct Foreign Investment in Korea," *Korea's Economy* (Washington, D.C.), December 1988, p. 3.

20. Koo Bohn-Young, "The Role of Direct Foreign Investment in Korea's Recent Economic Growth," in Kim Joong-Woong, *Financial Development Policies and Issues* (Seoul: Korea Development Institute, 1986), p. 232.

21. Koo Bon-Ho and Bark Tae-Ho, p. 7.

22. Richard Leudde-Neurath, "State Intervention and Foreign Direct Investment in South Korea," *Institute for Development Studies Bulletin* (Sussex) 15, no. 2 (1984), p. 21.

23. *Ibid.*, p. 22.

24. Figure for Korea from Koo Bon-Ho and Bark Tae-Ho, p. 4; figure for Singapore from Lim Chong Yah et al., *Policy Options for the Singapore Economy* (Singapore: McGraw-Hill Book Co., 1988), p. 247.

25. Michell, p. 75.

26. *Ibid.*, p. 79.

27. Choi Byung-Sun, "Institutionalizing a Liberal Economic Order in Korea: The Strategic Management of Economic Change," Ph.D. dissertation, Harvard

University, Cambridge, Massachusetts, 1987, p. 350.

28. Kim Byung-Kook, "Bringing and Managing Socioeconomic Change: The State in Korea and Mexico," Ph.D. dissertation, Harvard University, Cambridge, Massachusetts, 1987.

29. Chu Yun-Han, "Authoritarian Regimes under Stress: The Political Economy of Adjustment in the East Asian Newly Industrializing Countries," Ph.D. dissertation, University of Minnesota, 1987 (distributed by University Microfilms International Dissertation Information Service), pp. 82–83.

30. *Ibid.*, p. 83.

31. Moon Chung-In, "South Korea: Between Security and Vulnerability," in James Everett Katz, ed., *The Implications of Third World Military Industrialization* (Lexington, Mass.: Lexington Books, 1986), p. 246.

32. *Ibid.*

33. Chu Yun-Han, p. 83.

34. Song Byung-Nak, p. 167.

35. Chu Yun-Han, p. 88.

36. Moon Chung-In, pp. 249–50.

37. Chu Yun-Han, pp. 103–104.

38. Michell, p. 63.

39. Shim Sung-Won, "Pohang Iron and Steel Co.: Vicissitudes: The Days of the Steel Giant," *Business Korea*, April 1988, p. 49.

40. Michell, p. 66.

41. John Bennett, "Trade—The Key to Korea's Growth," in *Korea's Economy* (Washington, D.C.: Korea Economic Institute of America, 1990), p. 14.

42. Song Byung-Nak, p. 174.

Chapter 3. From Command Capitalism to the Chaebol Republic

1. *The Rise of Korea in the Electronics Market*, Executive Summary (Toronto: Domicity, 1989), p. 1.

2. Lee Kyu-Ok and Lee Chae-Hong, "Economic Integration and Economic Power Concentration," *Korea Development Review*, Spring 1985, p. 49, cited in *Social Justice Indicators in Korea* (Seoul: Christian Institute for the Study of Justice and Development, 1987), p. 16.

3. Alice Amsden, "Late Industrialization in Korea: The General Properties of Expansion through Learning," Unpublished manuscript, Boston, Massachusetts, pp. 5-44. This manuscript has since been published with the title *Asia's Next Giant: South Korea and Late Industrialization* (New York: Oxford University Press, 1989).

4. Leroy Jones, quoted in Song Byung-Nak, *The Korean Economy*, Unpublished mansucript, Seoul, 1989, p. 157.

5. Two of the top ten industrial companies in *Fortune's* list of the 150 largest industrial companies in the Pacific Rim are Korean: Samsung (no. 5) and Daewoo (no. 9). "Pacific Rim 1989," special issue, *Fortune*, 1989, p. 125.

6. "South Korea's Conglomerates: Do or Be Done For," *Economist*, December 9, 1989, p. 74.

7. Asia Monitor Resource Center, *South Korea's New Trade Unions* (Hong Kong: Asia Monitor Resource Center, 1988), pp. 52-53.

8. See "In Retrospect: Trials and Tribulations," *Business Korea*, March 1988, p. 32; also Tony Michell, "From LDC to NIC: The Republic of Korea: Employment, Industrialization, and Trade, 1961–1982," Unpublished manuscript, Seoul, 1988, p. 121.

9. "In Retrospect," *Business Korea*, March 1989, p. 32.

10. *Ibid.*

11. *Ibid.*; also Song Byung-Nak, p. 184.

12. Kim Jin-Moon, "Chaebol Under Fire: Debt Builds, Performance Sputters," *Business Korea*, November 1989, p. 22.

13. Chu Yun-Han, "Authoritarian Regimes under Stress:The Political Economy of Adjustment in the East Asian Newly Industrializing Countries," Ph.D. dissertation, University of Minnesota, 1987 (distributed by University Microfilms Dissertation Information Service),p. 108.

14. "A Man-made Miracle," *Economist* South Korea Survey, May 21, 1988, p. 16.

15. Laxmi Nakarmi, "Samsung Group: Lee Byung-Chull's New Challenges," *Business Korea*, June 1987, p. 28.

16. *Ibid.*, p. 27.

17. Ira Magaziner and Mark Patinkin, "Fast Heat: How Korea Won the Microwave War," *Harvard Business Review* (January-February 1989), p. 86.

18. *Ibid.*, p. 89.

19. Calculated from figures in *Social Justice Indicators in Korea*, p. 19. Hyundai and Samsung together accounted for 13.8 percent of total borrowing by 30 major chaebol.

20. Kim Jin-Moon, p. 22.

21. Amsden, pp. 5-36.

22. *Social Justice Indicators in Korea*, p. 21.

23. *Ibid.*

24. *Ibid.*

25. Kim Jin-Moon, p. 22.

26. *Ibid.*

27. *Ibid.*

28. Quoted in *ibid.*

29. Amsden, pp. 5-40.

30. Kim Jin-Moon, "Kukje in Court: Fighting to Regain an Empire," *Business Korea*, May 1988, p. 22.

31. See "Presidential Adviser Moon Hi-Gab: Aggressive, No Nonsense," *Business Korea*, November 1989, p. 28; also, "Investigation Findings: Putting Rumors to Rest?" *Business Korea*, November 1988, p. 35.

32. "Land Tax Reform: Can the Circle Be Broken?," *Business Korea*, November 1989, p. 28.

33. Maggie Ford, "Seoul in a Twist over Top 30," *Financial Times*, June 15, 1989.

34. "The Chaebol Draw Fire," *Business Korea*, June 1989, p. 7.

35. Stephen Haggard and Moon Chung-In, "Industrial Change and State Power: The Politics of Stabilization in Korea," Unpublished paper, Cambridge, Massachusetts, August 1986, p. 27.

36. Michell, p. 122.

37. World Bank, *Korea: Managing the Industrial Transition*, vol. 2 (Washington, D.C.: World Bank, 1986), p. 33.

38. *Ibid.*, vol. 1, p. 94.

39. "Ilhae Foundation: Glory Days on the Decline," *Business Korea*, June 1988, p. 14; Kim Jin-Moon, "Kukje in Court," p. 22.

40. Hong Won-Tack, "Export-Oriented Growth of Korea: A Possible Path to Advanced Economy," Seminar Paper no. 382, Institute for International Economic Studies, Stockholm, 1987, p. 40.

41. Kim Jin-Moon, "Economic Policymakers: Putting Theories into Practice," *Business Korea*, March 1989, p. 33.

42. "Interview with Moon Hi-Gab: Reform in the Age of Democracy," *Business Korea*, November 1989, p. 33.

43. *Yonhap*, December 29, 1989, reproduced in FBIS, January 4, 1990, p. 43.

44. Mark Clifford, "The Return of Korea Inc.," *Far Eastern Economic Review*, December 28, 1989, p. 41.

Chapter 4. Sacrificing Agriculture

1. Peter Leyden, "Acute Shortage of Wives for Korean Farmers," *San Francisco Chronicle*, June 19, 1989, p. A13.

2. "Loneliness Is Not the Farmers' Only Problem," *Far Eastern Economic Review*, July 18, 1985, p. 69; Sohn Jie-Ae, "Agricultural Policy: Tilling the Fields of Change," *Business Korea*, April 1989, p. 57.

3. Larry Burmeister, *Research, Realpolitik, and Development in Korea: The State and the Green Revolution* (Boulder: Westview Press, 1988), p. 36.

4. Bruce Cumings, "The Abortive Abertura: South Korea in the Light of Latin American Experience," *New Left Review*, no. 173, January–February 1989, p. 12.

5. *Ibid.*

6. Pak Ki-Hyuk, "Farmland Tenure in the Republic of Korea," in *Land Tenure and Small Farmers in Asia*, FFTC Book Series, no. 24 (Taiwan: FFTC, 1983), pp. 115–116.

7. *Ibid.*, p. 113.

8. *Ibid.*, pp. 115–116.

9. Tony Michell, "From LDC to NIC: The Republic of Korea: Employment, Industrialization, and Trade, 1961–1982," Unpublished manuscript, Seoul, 1988, p. 38.

10. Economic Planning Board, cited in Song Byung-Nak, "The Korean Economy," Unpublished manuscript, 1989, p. 244.

11. Michell, p. 38; Ban Sung-Hwan, Moon Pal-Yong, and Dwight Perkins, *Rural Development* (Cambridge, Mass.: Harvard University Press, 1980), p. 213.

12. Michell, *ibid.*

13. Burmeister, p. 68.

14. Song Byung-Nak, p. 244.

15. Burmeister, p. 73.

16. Phyllis Kim, "Saemaul Agriculture: South Korean Farmers Prop Up Export-Oriented Economy," part 2, *AMPO* (Japan-Asia Quarterly Review) 12, no. 3 (1980), pp. 57–58.

17. Robert Wade, "South Korea's Agricultural Development: The Myth of the Passive State," *Pacific Viewpoint* 24, no. 1 (May 1983), p. 13.

18. National Agricultural Cooperative Federation, in Ban Sung-Hwan *et al.*, p. 223.

19. Paul Ensor, "No More Padded Paddy," *Far Eastern Economic Review*, December 22, 1983, p. 87.

20. Kim, p. 62.

21. Quoted in *ibid*.

22. "National Report: South Korea," Paper prepared for Christian Conference of Asia-Urban Industrial Mission (CCA-URM) Consultation, September 8–13, 1987, p. 25.

23. Kim, p. 63.

24. *Agricultural Cooperative Yearbook 1979*, cited in table 61 of *Realities of the Korean Economy* (Seoul: Christian Institute for the Study of Justice and Development, 1981), p. 85.

25. *Ibid.*, table 60, p. 84.

26. David Johns, "(Im)politically Priced?," *Business Korea*, December 1987, p. 71.

27. Mick Moore, "Mobilization and Disillusion in Rural Korea: The Saemaul Movement in Retrospect," *Pacific Affairs*, Winter 1984–85, p. 589.

28. *Ibid.*

29. Vincent Brandt, quoted in Young Whan-Kihl, "Politics and Agrarian Change in South Korea: Rural Modernization by 'Induced' Mobilization," in Raymond Hopkins, Donald Puchala, and Ross Talbot, eds., *Food Politics and Agricultural Development: Case Studies in the Public Policy of Rural Modernization* (Boulder: Westview Press, 1979), p. 152.

30. Food and Agriculture Organization, *Village Forestry Development in the Republic of Korea: A Case Study* (Rome: FAO, 1982), p. 77.

31. Wade, p. 16.

32. Song Byung-Nak, p. 244.

33. Young Whan-Kihl, p. 161.

34. Park Chan-Hee, "The Reality of the Four Trillion Won Farm Household Debt" (in Korean), *Chosun*, March 1987.

35. Burmeister, p. 46.

36. Song Byung-Nak, p. 244.

37. Park Chan-Hee, "The Reality of Farm Debt,"; see also National Agricultural Cooperative Federation figures, cited in *Social Justice Indicators in Korea* (Seoul: Christian Institute for the Study of Justice and Development, 1987), figure

III.3.3, p. 94.

38. Park Chan-Hee, "The Reality of Farm Debt,"

39. "As Farm Debt Rises, Farm Population Plummets," *Sindong-A*, April 1989, reproduced in *FBIS: East Asia*, August 9, 1989, p. 40.

40. David Satterwhite, "Whither the Peasantry? Politics and Structural Transformation in the Republic of Korea," Unpublished paper, 1984, p. 13.

41. "Barley: Rice's Poor Cousin," *Business Korea*, December 1987, p. 72.

42. Kim Sam-O, "Agriculture: Buying the Farm," *Business Korea*, November 1989, p. 18.

43. "Open Agricultural Policy: A Controversial Issue in Korea," *Grassroots* (Seoul) 1 (Spring 1988), p. 6.

44. "Bilateral Positions: An Exchange of Views," *Business Korea*, April 1988, pp. 44–46.

45. Cho Soon, "The Korean Economy at a Crossroads: A Blueprint for Internationalization," *FYI* (For Your Information) (Washington, D.C.), January 27, 1989, p. 2; Kim Sam-O, p. 18.

46. Kim Sam-O, *ibid.*

47. *Ibid.*

48. Robert Goldstein, *U.S. Agricultural Trade Opportunities with Pacific Rim Nations*, 88-755 ENR (Washington, D.C.: Congressional Research Service, 1989), pp. 36–38.

49. Hwang Ui-Pong, "The Exploding Farmers Movement and Creation of Chonnongnyon," *Sindong-A*, April 1989, reproduced in *FBIS: East Asia*, August 7, 1989, p. 34.

50. *Ibid.*

51. Kim Sam-O, p. 18.

52. "Government Denies U.S. Claims on Beef Imports," *Yonhap*, March 24, 1990; reproduced in *FBIS: East Asia* March 27, 1990, p. 18.

53. Mark Clifford, "Cheap Foreign Beefs," *Far Eastern Economic Review*, July 21, 1988, p. 58.

54. Cho Soon, "Challenges Facing Korea Today and U.S.-Korea Economic Relations," *FYI* (*For Your Information*) (Washington, D.C.), May 4, 1989, p. 6.

55. Pak Ki-Hyuk, p. 116; 1985 figure from "Open Agricultural Policy: A Controversial Issue in Korea," *Grassroots* (Seoul) 1 (Spring 1988), p. 6.

56. Pak Ki-Hyuk, p. 116.

57. "As Farm Debt Rises, Farm Population Plummets," p. 40.

58. Suh Sang-Mok, "Rapid Democratization and New Challenges to Policy Makers in Korea," *FYI* (Washington, D.C.), July 10, 1989, p. 2.

59. Food and Agricultural Organization, p. 81.

60. "Saemaul Scandal: Decline of an Empire," *Business Korea*, April 1988, p. 17.

61. Hwang Ui-Pong, p. 26.

62. *Ibid.*

63. Quoted in "Addition to Article on Farmers Movement," *FBIS*, August 9,

1989, p. 42.

Chapter 5. The Toxic Trade-off

1. *Cooperative Energy Assessment* (Argonne, Illinois: Republic of Korea Ministry of Energy and U.S. Department of Energy, September 1981), p. 23.

2. *Cooperative Energy Assessment*, p. 23; figure for Thailand from Katshushiko Suetsugu, "Pollution Is Starting to Threaten Asian Growth," *Japan Economic Journal*, August 26, 1989, p. 9.

3. Food and Agriculture Organization, *Village Forestry Development in the Republic of Korea: A Case Study* (Rome: FAO, 1982), p. 22.

4. "National Report: South Korea," Paper prepared for the Christian Conference of Asia/Urban Industrial Mission Consultation, September 8–13, 1987, p. 29.

5. Phyllis Kim, "Saemaul Agriculture: South Korean Farmers Prop Up Export-Oriented Economy," part 1, *AMPO* (Japan-Asia Quarterly Review) 12, no. 1 (1980), p. 8.

6. David Steinberg et al., *Korean Agricultural Services: The Invisible Hand in the Iron Glove* (Washington, D.C.: U.S. Agency for International Development, 1984), p. B-21.

7. Chung Tae-Sung, "Holding the Reins of a Bureaucratic Economy," *Monthly Chungang* (Seoul), October 1978.

8. Phyllis Kim, "Saemaul Agriculture," part 2, *AMPO* 12, no. 3 (1980), p. 63.

9. Interview with Ahn Byong-Ok of Korean Anti-Pollution Organization, by Walden Bello, Seoul, May 5, 1988; see also Chung Tae-Sung, "Holding the Reins."

10. Kim Kyu-Eun, "Temperature Rising: Korea in Middle of Fight against Greenhouse Effect," *Korea Business World*, June 1989, p. 52. In contrast, it took 30 years, from 1950 to 1980, for global mean temperature to rise 0.4 degrees centigrade. (Bill McKibben, *The End of Nature* (New York: Random House, 1989), p. 25).

11. Sonya Hepinstall, "A Smell of Success in the Battle Against Pollution," *Far Eastern Economic Review*, July 18, 1985, p. 70.

12. "The Environment: A Survey," *Economist*, September 2, 1989, p. 7.

13. *Cooperative Energy Assessment*, p. 126.

14. Hepinstall, p. 70.

15. *Cooperative Energy Assessment*, p. 126.

16. Kim Sam-O, "Kamikaze Traffic Appalls Public," *Business Korea*, March 1990, pp. 32–33.

17. *Cooperative Energy Assessment*, p. 126.

18. Figures from Economic and Social Commission for the Asia Pacific (ESCAP)/United Nations Center for Transnational Corporations (UNTC) Joint Unit, cited in Vute Wangwacharakul, "Trade, Investment, and Sustained Development," Paper prepared for ESCAP/ADB (Asian Development Bank) Expert Meeting on Trade, Economics, and Environmental Sustainability, Oc-

tober 23–27, 1989, table 16, p. 48.

19. Chung Tae-Sung, p. 5.

20. Hepinstall, p. 71.

21. "Power Play: Korea Seeks to Diversify Generating Sources," *Korea Business World*, February 1989, p. 42.

22. Maggie Ford, "Breakneck Progress Turns South Korea Green," *Financial Times*, August 24, 1989, p. 4.

23. General Electric Company–Tempo, "Republic of Korea/U.S. Cooperative Energy Assessment, Phase I," Draft report, Washington, D.C., June 1980, p. 126.

24. *Cooperative Energy Assessment*, p. 126.

25. *Ibid.*

26. Kwon-Sook Pyo, quoted in Hepinstall, p. 72.

27. " 'Trillions of Won' Needed for Clean-Up," *Yonhap*, August 10, 1989, reproduced in *FBIS: East Asia*, August 10, 1989, pp. 26–27.

28. *Ibid.*

29. *Ibid.*

30. ESCAP/UNTC Joint Unit, cited in Wangwacharakul, table 9, p. 41.

31. Carl Goldstein, "Something Must Crack," *Far Eastern Economic Review*, November 30, 1989, p. 80.

32. "Du Pont Given Go-Ahead for Korean Plant," *Asian Wall Street Journal*, January 2, 1990, p. 4.

33. *Cooperative Energy Assessment*, p. 126.

34. Wangwacharakul, table 17, p. 49.

35. *Cooperative Energy Assessment*, p. 126.

36. *Ibid*, p. 127.

37. *Ibid.*

38. Lee Keum-Hyun, "Ours Is Not to Question Why?," *Business Korea Electronics*, September 1988, p. 51.

39. *Ibid.*

40. *Ibid.*

41. *Ibid.*

42. *Ibid.*, p. 52.

43. Ford, p. 4.

44. "KEPCO: Front-Runner in Nuclear Power Development," *Korea Business World*, May 1988, p. 43.

45. Peter Hayes and Lyuba Zarsky, "Nuclear Electric Futures in Developing Countries of Asia Pacific," Unpublished manuscript, Amherst, Mass., July 1984, p. 24.

46. Frank Nipkau, "South Korea: Dream Land for Nuclear Energy," Unpublished paper, 1988, p. 1; also Joseph Manguno, "Seoul Braced for Renewed Nuclear Furor," *Asian Wall Street Journal*, September 13, 1988.

47. Nipkau, p. 2.

48. Manguno, "Seoul Braced."

49. *Asian Wall Street Journal*, cited in "Public Joins the Debate," *Business Korea*, December 1989, p. 54.

50. Shim Sung-Won, "Nuclear Power: Bringing On a New Generation of Generators," *Business Korea*, July 1988, p. 77.

51. Mark Clifford, "Seoul's Nuclear Fallout," *Far Eastern Economic Review*, July 30, 1987, p. 46.

52. Shim Sung-Won, p. 76.

53. Robert Pahlke, quoted in *A Race Against Time* (Toronto: Royal Commission on Electric Power Planning, 1978), pp. 154–155.

54. Zalmay Khalilzad, quoted in Walden Bello, Peter Hayes, and Lyuba Zarsky, "500 Mile-Island: The Phillipine Nuclear Reactor Deal," *Pacific Research*, 10, no. 1, p. 29.

55. General Electric Company–Tempo, pp. 4–55, 4–56.

56. Ministry of Science and Technology, quoted in Peter Hayes, "South Korean Nuclear Trade," Unpublished paper, Amherst, Mass., 1988, p. 17.

57. *Ibid.*, p. 18.

58. *Ibid.*

59. John Fialka, "North Korea May Be Developing Ability to Build Nuclear Weapons," *Asian Wall Street Journal Weekly*, July 24, 1989, p. 5.

60. Patrick Tyler, "Pentagon Reportedly Says U.S. Could Cut Pacific Forces, Bases," *San Francisco Chronicle*, December 20, 1989, p. A17.

61. Lee Bong-Suh, quoted in "Preparedness: Key Word in Korean Energy Policy," *Korea Business World*, May 1988, p. 42.

62. "Residents Protest Nuclear Waste Disposal," *Korea Herald*, December 13, 1988, reproduced in *FBIS: East Asia*, December 14, 1988, p. 34.

63. "South Korea's Anti-Nuclear Power Movement Builds," *Nuke Info Tokyo*, no. 11 (May–June 1989), p. 6.

64. Ford, p. 4.

65. Philip Hilts, "Higher Cancer Risk Found in Low-Level Radiation," *New York Times*, December 20, 1989, p. A1.

66. Hayes, "South Korean Nuclear Trade," p. 16.

67. *Ibid.*

68. Noh Yang-Keun, "The Safety Problems of Nuclear Power Plants," *Korea Times*, October 30, 1988, p. 8.

69. *Ibid.*

70. "Nuclear Power Plant Breaks Down in Southeast," *Yonhap*, November 5, 1988, reproduced in *FBIS: East Asia*, November 8, 1988, p. 18.

71. Ford, p. 4.

72. Hilts, p. A1.

73. Quoted in Hayes and Zarsky, p. 51.

74. *Ibid.*, p. 50

75. Hayes, "South Korean Nuclear Trade," p. 4.

76. Manguno, "Seoul Braced."

77. Hayes and Zarsky, 1984, p. 47.

78. *Ibid.*

79. Noh Yang-Keun, p. 8.

80. "Korea Will Need 55 Nuclear Power Plants by Year 2031," *Korea Times*, June 1, 1989.

81. "South Korea's Anti-Nuclear Power Movement Builds," *Nuke Info Tokyo*, p. 6.

82. "Power Plant Construction: Preventing a Future Blackout," *Business Korea*, December 1988, p. 33.

83. "Public Joins Debate," p. 51.

Chapter 6. High Tech: Solution or Illusion?

1. "Plans for Massive Investment in High Tech," *Hanguk Kyongje Sinmun*, July 1, 1989, reproduced in *FBIS: East Asia*, August 23, 1989, pp. 32–33.

2. *Asiaweek*, August 11, 1989, p. 56.

3. "The Game is Just Beginning," *Electronics Korea*, March 1990, p. 101.

4. Kim Woo-Choong, "A Korean Perspective on the International Automobile Industry," *UMTRI Research Review* (University of Michigan Transportation Research Institute, Ann Arbor) 18, nos. 2 and 3 (November–December 1987), p. 19.

5. Lee Kye-Sik, senior official of Economic Planning Board, quoted in Stefan Wagstyl, "South Korean Industry and Finance: Turmoil of Transition," sec. 3, *Financial Times*, November 27, 1989, p. i. A recent report of the Korea Institute for Industrial Economics and Technology reveals that if the technological level of advanced countries is 100, Korea's level is 55 in primary alloying technology, 55 in chemical synthesizing and polymerization, 30 in machinery automation, 60 in machinery designing, 50 in electronic and electric designing, and 45 in the fiber dyeing technology. Yi Sok-Ku, "Domestic Technology Development 'A Pressing Need,' " *Chungang Ilbo*, March 7, 1990, reproduced in *FBIS: East Asia*, June 4, 1990, pp. 41–42.

6. Park Tai-Won, "Higher Education and Technological Innovation in Economic Development of Korea," *Pacific Focus* (Inha University, Inchon, Korea) 1, no. 2 (Fall 1986), p. 11.

7. "Royalty Payments Increase as Trademarks Sought," *Yonhap*, May 4, 1990; reproduced in *FBIS: East Asia*, May 4, 1990, p. 16.

8. According to Yi Kyong-Tae, industrial director of the Korea Institute of Economics and Technology. Quoted in "Small Company Technology Development Discussed," *Kyongje Sinmun*, November 24, 1989, p. 17; reproduced in *FBIS: East Asia*, February 1, 1990, p. 38.

9. Kim Sam-O, "A Blip in the Economy's Growth Prompts Concern," *Business Korea*, February 1990, p. 30.

10. John Naisbitt and Patricia Aburdene, *Megatrends 2000* (New York: William Morrow, 1990), p. 200.

11. Y. K. Sohn, Intel Korea manager, quoted in "Intel Korea: Eyeing Advanced

PC Environments," *Electronics Korea,* January 1989, p. 28.

12. Lee Kark-Bum, "International Division of Labor and Small-Scale Industry: The Case of the Korean Automobile Industry," in Kim Kyong-Dong, ed., *Dependency Issues in Korean Development* (Seoul: Seoul National University Press, 1987), p. 429.

13. "Promotion Law," *Korea Business World,* August 1988, p. 47.

14. According to Kwon Yong-Hu, president of O-Sung Chemical Company, in "Small Company Technology Development Discussed," p. 38.

15. Personal interview with Sheridan Tatsuno, Dataquest, by Walden Bello, San Jose, California, March 16, 1989.

16. John Wilson and Sheridan Tatsuno, "South Korea: Following the Leader," *Strategic Issues* (Dataquest), February 1989, p. 7.

17. Figures provided in Stephen Kreider Yoder, "Reverse 'Brain Drain' Benefits Asia but Robs U.S. of Scarce Talent," *Asian Wall Street Journal Weekly,* April 14, 1989, p. 25.

18. George Gilder, *Microcosm: The Quantum Revolution in Economics and Technology* (New York: Simon and Schuster, 1989), pp. 66, 322.

19. According to Kwon Yong-Hu, in "Small Company Technology Development Discussed," p. 38.

20. Kim Sam-O, p. 30.

21. "Plans for Massive Investment in High Tech," p. 33.

Chapter 7. Textile's Troubles

1. William Cline, *The Future of World Trade in Textiles and Apparel* (Washington, D.C.: Institute for International Economics, 1987), p. 12.

2. World Bank, *Korea: Managing the Industrial Transition,* vol. 3 (Washington, D.C.: World Bank, 1986), p. 18.

3. *Ibid.,* p. 20.

4. Chi Jung-Nam, "Coming of Age for Textiles in Korea," *Asian Business* 24, no. 2 (February 1988), p. 13.

5. Ministry of Trade and Industry, in World Bank, *Industrial Transition,* p. 32.

6. Tony Michell, "From LDC to NIC: The Republic of Korea: Employment, Industrialization, and Trade, 1961–82," Unpublished manuscript, Seoul, 1988, p. 165.

7. *Ibid.,* p. 167.

8. Chi Jung-Nam, p. 13.

9. Kim Byong-Kuk, *Kim Woo-Choong: Schumpeterian Entrepreneur* (Seoul: Bobmun Sa, 1988), p. 54.

10. *Ibid.,* p. 58.

11. *Ibid.,* pp. 66–67.

12. Michell, p. 170.

13. Cline, p. 12.

14. *Ibid.,* p. 16.

15. Asian Development Bank, *Korea: Study of the Manufacturing Sector with*

Special Reference to New Technology-Based Small and Medium Industries (Manila: Asian Development Bank, 1987), p. 39.

16. World Bank, *Industrial Transition, p.* 29.

17. Werner International, "Spinning and Weaving Labor Cost Comparisons," New York, Spring 1989.

18. World Bank, *Industrial Transition,* p. 24.

19. Cline, pp. 142–143.

20. World Bank, *Industrial Transition,* p. 24.

21. *Ibid.,* p. 25.

22. World Bank, *Korea's Development in a Global Context* (Washington, D.C.: World Bank, 1984), p. 63.

23. Ashoka Mody and David Wheeler, "Towards a Vanishing Middle: Competition in the World Garment Industry," *World Development* 15, no. 10–11 (1987), p. 1271.

24. See Joseph Grunwald and Kenneth Flamm, *The Global Factory: Foreign Assembly in International Trade* (Washington, D.C.: Brookings Institution, 1985), pp. 17–18.

25. World Bank, *Industrial Transition,* p. 32.

26. "Firms Moving to Caribbean Nations," *Korea Newsreview* (Seoul), November 18, 1989, p. 22.

27. World Bank, *Industrial Transition,* p. 30.

28. *Ibid.,* p. 31.

29. *Ibid.,* pp. 22–23.

30. "1990 Business Outlook," *Business Korea,* January 1990, p. 75.

31. *Ibid.*

32. World Bank, *Industrial Transition,* p. 11.

33. "1990 Business Outlook," p. 75.

34. Alice Rawsthorn, "A Structure Suited to Quality," *Financial Times,* September 8, 1989, p. 10.

35. Interview with Y. C. Park, top executive of Tae Heung, Seoul, by Walden Bello, May 23, 1988.

36. "Realigning Korea's National Priorities for Economic Progress: The Presidential Commission Report on Economic Restructuring," *Korea's Economy* 5, no. 1 (July 1989), p. 15.

Chapter 8. Ambition and Frustration in the Auto Industry

1. Kurt Hoffman and Ralph Kaplinsky, *Driving Force: The Global Restructuring of Technology, Labor, and Investment in the Automobile Industry* (Boulder: Westview Press, 1988), p. 76.

2. Hyun Young-Suk, "A Technology Strategy for the Korean Motor Industry," Paper prepared for International Motor Vehicles Project Forum, Acapulco, Mexico, May 1989, p. 12.

3. Kevin Done, "Ford Chief Warns of World Car Glut," *Financial Times,* January 9, 1990, p. 16.

4. Kim Byung-Kook, "Export-Promotion Strategy Reevaluated: Case Study of the Korean Automobile Industry," Ph.D. Dissertation, Harvard University, Cambridge, Mass., 1982, p. 215.

5. Hyun Young-Suk, p. 5.

6. Kim Byung-Kook, p. 27.

7. *Ibid.*, p. 29.

8. Yoon Ik-Soo, "South Korea's Industrial Environment," Report for University of Michigan Transporation Research Institute, Ann Arbor, Mich., 1985, sec. 4, p. 33.

9. "Auto Industry Poised for Greater Growth," Undated supplement on Korea in *Asian Wall Street Journal Weekly*, 1989, p. 5B.

10. See Louis Kraar, "Detroit's New Asian Car Strategy," *Fortune*, December 10, 1984, pp. 172–178.

11. Hyun Young-Suk, p. 7.

12. Kim Woo-Choong, "A Korean Perspective on the International Automotive Industry," *UMTRI Research Review* (University of Michigan Transportation Research Institute, Ann Arbnor, Michigan) 18, nos. 2 and 3 (September–October/November–December 1987), p. 19.

13. "Daewoo Motor: The End of the Road for GM?" *Business Korea*, October 1988, p. 48.

14. Kim Byung-Kook, p. 29.

15. "Daewoo Motor: The End of the Road for GM?," p. 48.

16. *Ibid.*

17. Hyun Young-Suk, p. 6.

18. *Ibid.*, p. 8.

19. *Ibid.*, p. 12.

20. *Ibid.*, p. 7.

21. Kim Byung-Kook, p. 29.

22. Mitsubishi representative in Orange Country, California, interviewed by Paula Fomby, December 1988.

23. Hyun Young-Suk, p. 13. Setting the technological levels of advanced countries at 100, a recent study by the Korea Institute for Industrial Economics and Technology evaluated Korea's status in a number of key car technologies thus: in the suspension system technology attaching the frame to the wheels, Korea's design level is 20–40 percent of the West German and Japanese level; in steering systems, the level is no more than 10 percent; in the automatic brake system, which prevents cars from skidding when the brakes are applied suddenly, Korea's technological level is 10–40 percent of the West German's, 40 percent in the electronic brake device, and 50 percent in the hydraulic device. Korea is only now embarking on the development of the twin cam engine (DOHC engine), which the United States, Japan, and West Germany developed in the 1970s. Yi Sok-Ku, "Domestic Technology Development 'A Pressing Need,' *Chungang Ilbo* (Seoul), March 7, 1990, reproduced in *FBIS: East Asia*, June 4, 1990, pp. 41–42.

24. Koichi Shimokawa, "Development of the Asian NICs Automobile Industry

and Future Prospect of the Global Division of Labor—Japan, ROK, China-Taiwan, and Thailand," Paper prepared for International Motor Vehicles Policy Forum, Acapulco, Mexico, May 1989, p. 10.

25. "Hyundai Cars in the U.S.: Ready for a Second Takeoff," *Business Korea,* September 1988, p. 56.

26. Mark Clifford, "Local Anaesthetic: Domestic Sales Buoy Up South Korean Car Makers," *Far Eastern Economic Review,* August 17, 1989, p. 64.

27. J. David Power, quoted in Richard Stevenson, "Sales Dip Deflates Hyundai Bubble," *New York Times,* October 31, 1989, p. C1.

28. See, among others, *Ibid.,* p. C7.

29. Clifford, p. 64.

30. "Fifth in the World in the Mid-1990s," *Korea Business World* (May 1989), p. 60.

31. Andrew Greaves, "Technology Challenges Facing the Motor Industry: Right and Wrong Strategies," Paper prepared for the International Motor Vehicle Program, Massachusetts Institute of Technology, Cambridge, Mass., September 1986, pp. 22-23.

32. Hyun Young-Suk, p. 11.

33. Hoffman and Kaplinsky, p. 135.

34. Lee Kark-Bum, "International Division of Labor and the Small-Scale Industry: The Case of the Korean Automobile-Parts Industry," in Kim Kyong-Dong, ed., *Dependency Issues in Korean Development* (Seoul: Seoul National University Press, 1987), p. 429.

35. Konomi Tomisawa, "Development of Future Outlook for an International Division of Labor in the Automobile Industries of Asian NICs," Briefing paper for First Policy Forum of the International Motor Vehicle Program, Cambridge, Mass., May 5, 1987, pp. 27, 29.

36. Stefan Wagstyl, "South Korean Finance and Industry: Turmoil of Transition," Section 3, *Financial Times,* November 27, 1989, p. I.

37. Mark Clifford, "The Engine Is Straining," *Far Eastern Economic Review,* January 18, 1990, p. 38.

38. Hyun, Young-Suk, p. 10.

39. "Labor Strife," *Korea Business World,* April 1989, p. 56.

40. "1990 Business Outlook," *Business Korea,* January 1990, p. 69.

41. Hyun Young-Suk, p. 13-14.

42. "First Half Domestic Sales," *Korea Business World,* August 1989, p. 44; "First Half Exports Down," *Korea Business World,* September 1989, p. 71.

43. Hoffman and Kaplinsky, p. 78.

44. Yoon Ik-Soo, p. 28.

45. *Ibid.,* p. 31.

46. Tomisawa, p. 17.

47. Done, p. 1.

48. Tomisawa, p. 17.

Chapter 9. Chaebol Dreams and Silicon Realities

1. "Parading a Canard," *Electronics Korea*, December 1989, p. 17.

2. John Wilson and Sheridan Tatsuno, "South Korea: Following the Leader," *Strategic Issues* (Dataquest, San Jose, Calif.), February 1989, p. 4.

3. *Ibid.*

4. Joo Dae-Young, "Milestones: Reflecting on Omens of 1988," *Electronics Korea*, March 1989, p. 13.

5. Lee Keum-Hyun, "Industry after Thirty Years: Painful Steps toward Maturity," *Business Korea Electronics*, August 1988, p. 48.

6. Tony Michell, "From LDC to NIC: The Republic of Korea: Employment, Industrialization, and Trade, 1961–1982," Unpublished manuscript, p. 176.

7. Ashoka Mody, "Alternative Strategies for Developing Information Industries," Paper prepared for Industry Development Division, Industry and Energy Dept., World Bank, Washington, D.C., October 1988, p. 16.

8. Morris Crawford, "Technology Transfer and the Computerization of South Korea and Taiwan: Part I: Developments in the Private Sector," *Information Age* 9, no. 1 (January 1987), p. 11.

9. Ashoka Mody, "Recent Evolution of Microelectronics in South Korea and Taiwan: An Institutional Approach to Comparative Advantage," Unpublished paper, Boston, Mass., 1985, p. 13.

10. Estimated from Shin Kyung-Mi, "Korea's Fabulous Fabs," *Business Korea Electronics*, October 1988, p. 22.

11. Geoff Crane, "Small and Medium Enterprises: Korea's Best Bet for the Future," *Electronics Korea*, January 1989, p. 11.

12. Domicity, *The Rise of Korea in the Electronics Market* (Toronto: Domicity, 1989), p. 1.

13. Lee Byung-Jong, "Technology Imports: A Shortcut to Building Know-How?," *Business Korea*, November 1987, p. 25.

14. *Ibid.*

15. "Joint Ventures: Building a Manufacturing Base for Japan," *Business Korea*, June 1988, p. 24.

16. "Quality Spells Profits and Problems," *Electronics Korea*, November 1989, p. 29.

17. "Joint Ventures," p. 24.

18. Stefan Wagstyl, "South Korean Finance and Industry: Turmoil of Transition," Section 3, *Financial Times*, November 27, 1989, p. i.

19. Electronics Industry Associations of Korea (EIAK), March 13, 1989, p. 19.

20. Jeong Man-Seok, "Korea's Star," *Korea Business World*, December 1988, p. 62.

21. "Localization Targets 760 Electronics Parts," *Korea Business World*, September 1988, p. 78.

22. Personal inteview with Michael Borrus, by Walden Bello, San Francisco, March 21, 1989.

23. Lee In-Duck, manager at Daewoo Electronics Audio Marketing Depart-

ment, quoted in "Imports: Caught between Competing Interests," *Electronics Korea,* June 1989, p. 22.

24. Lee Byung-Jon, "Exporting Electronics to Japan: Riding High on the NIC Boom," *Business Korea,* June 1988, p. 23.

25. Joseph Manguno, "Korea: VCR Firms Face Critical Test in the U.S. Market," *Asian Wall Street Journal Weekly,* April 3, 1989, p. 1; also Shin Kyung-Mi, "KFTA Report: Warning Signals Flash for Exports, *Eletronics Korea,* June 1989, p. 20.

26. Manguno, p. 1.

27. Geoff Crane, "Spoils of War," *Business Korea,* August 1989, p. 49.

28. "Heung Yang's HY-8050 VCR-TV: A Taste of Things to Come," *Electronics Korea,* February 1989, pp. 31–32.

29. Manguno, p. 25. On microwave ovens, Geoff Crane writes that "with Japanese manufacturers now regaining competitive clout through offshore manufacturing bases, the dilemma facing Samsung Electronics (SEC), Goldstar, and Daewoo Electronics is how to regain profitability without sacrificing market share." "Spoils of War," *Business Korea,* August 1989, p. 49. Motohiro Matsumoto writes that "today, it's the NICs that are on the run, at least in the Japanese market. And while the large consumer electronics makers are beginning to recapture the low end of the market, it's Japan's small and midsized firms that are mainly responsible for routing the NIE's manufacturers." "Electronics Giants Have NIEs on the Run," *Japan Economic Journal,* September 2, 1989, p. 2.

30. Geoff Crane, "Industry Review: Local FAX Managers Gear Up for Export," *Electronics Korea,* March 1989, pp. 27-28.

31. Ashoka Mody, *Korea's Computer Strategy,* Case 0-686-070 (Cambridge, Mass.: Harvard Business School, March 1986), p. 6.

32. *Ibid.*

33. Lenny Siegel, "PC Standards," *Global Electronics* (Mountain View), September 1988, p. 1.

34. *Ibid.*

35. "In the U.S., the Chips are Up," *Asiaweek,* March 10, 1989, p. 49.

36. John McCreadie, "Korean PC Firms Make Impressive Gains Here," *Electronic Business,* December 10, 1988, p. 146.

37. Domicity, p. 1-6.

38. Personal interview with Michael Borrus, San Francisco, March 21, 1989.

39. Y. K. Sohn, Intel Korea manager, quoted in "Intel Korea: Eyeing Advanced PC Environments," *Electronics Korea,* January 1989, p. 28.

40. Mody, *Korea's Computer Strategy,* p. 8.

41. Alden Hayashi, "Hyundai's Headache," *Electronic Business,* February 6, 1989.

42. Interview with Lenny Siegel by Jay Gonzalez, Mountain View, July 14, 1988.

43. Domicity, p. 1-7.

44. Choo Hoon, executive vice president of Hyundai Electronics' information-systems division, quoted in Hayashi, p. 28.

45. McReadie, p. 148.

46. "PC's: No Home Field Advantage against Taiwan," *Business Korea Electronics*, January 1988, p. 34.

47. "Promotion Law," *Korea Business World*, August 1988, p. 48.

48. Yi Sang-Won, "Software Industry: Hard Solutions for a Soft Problem," *Business Korea Electronics*, December 1988, p. 15.

49. *Ibid.*, p. 12.

50. "Promotion Law," p. 47.

51. George Gilder, *Microcosm: The Quantum Revolution in Economics and Technology* (New York: Simon and Schuster, 1989), pp. 323–324.

52. Morris Crawford, *Programming the Invisible Hand: The Computerization of Korea and Taiwan* (Cambridge, Mass.: Program on Information Resources Policy, Harvard University, 1986), p. 33.

53. *Ibid.*, pp. 33–34.

54. "Foreign Software Companies: Bringing Up the Korean Market," *Electronics Korea*, May 1989, p. 23.

55. Gilder, p. 324.

56. Domicity, p. 1-9.

57. Mody, "Recent Evolution of Microelectronics," p. 13.

58. Shin Kyung-Mi, "Dataquest Conference: Asian Chips in the Pacific Age," *Business Korea Electronics*, December 1988, p. 30.

59. Personal interview with Kenneth Flamm, Washington, D.C., March 7, 1989; see also Bob Johnstone, "South Korea Embarks on a Mass Memory Test," *Far Eastern Economic Review*, August 18, 1988, p. 84.

60. Johnstone, *ibid.*

61. Personal interview with Kenneth Flamm, by Walden Bello, Washington, D.C., March 7, 1989.

62. Johnstone, p. 84.

63. Domicity, p. 1-9.

64. Shin Kyung-Mi, "Semiconductors: Korea's Fabulous Fabs," *Business Korea Electronics*, October 1988, p. 23.

65. Personal interview with Michael Borrus, March 21, 1989.

66. David Sanger, "South Korea's High-Tech Miracle," *New York Times*, December 9, 1988, p. C4; also Jay Stowsky, "The Weakest Link: Semiconductor Equipment, Linkages, and the Limits to International Trade," BRIE Working Paper no. 27 (Berkeley, Calif.: Berkeley Roundtable on the International Economy, August 1987).

67. For account of U.S. dependence, see Sanger, p. c4.

68. Ashoka Mody and David Wheeler, "Technological Evolution of the Semiconductor Industry," Discussion Paper no. 37 (Boston, Mass.: Center for Asian Development Studies, Boston University, 1986), p. 2. With the Japanese increasingly cautious about providing Koreans with semiconductor manufacturing technology, the Koreans are increasingly edgy about developments in the U.S. microelectronics industry, their other source of semiconductor manufacturing

equipment. As one account notes, "In the United States...semiconductor makers and equipment makers are jointly producing manufacturing equipment for 16-megabit DRAM, raising fears that U.S. semiconductor makers might attempt to block the transfer of manufacturing equipment to head off our future competition...Should that happen, it could spell the end of our semiconductor industry that entirely relies on imports for manufacturing equipment." Yi So-Ku, "Domestic Technology Development 'A Pressing Need,' *Chungang Ilbo*, March 7, 1990 reproduced in *FBIS: East Asia*, June 4, 1990, p. 43.

69. John Wilson and Sheridan Tatsuno, p. 7.

70. Hayashi, p. 27.

71. Stefan Wagstyl, "Hitachi to Sell Chip Technology to South Korean Group," *Financial Times*, July 28, 1989.

72. "Technology Exports Reportedly Increasing," *Nihon Keizai Shimbun*, reproduced in *FBIS*, March 9, 1989, Annex, p. 5.

73. Jacob Schlesinger, "Hitachi Joins Goldstar in Plan for Chip Plant," *Asian Wall Street Journal*, July 31, 1989, p. 6.

74. Jacob Schlesinger, "Japanese Chip Producers Shift Strategy," *Asian Wall Street Journal*, January 10, 1990, p. 1.

75. Quoted in Jeffrey Henderson, *The Globalization of High Technology Production* (London: Routledge, 1989), p. 65. The author cites as source, K. Berney, "The Four Dragons Rush to Play Catch-Up Game," *Electronics Week*, May 6, 1985, pp. 48–52.

76. Gilder, p. 343.

77. Personal interview with Michael Borrus, March 21, 1989.

78. Yi Sang-Won, "Semiconductor Industry: 'Can Do' Spirit Isn't Enough," *Business Korea Electronics*, December 1987, p. 15.

79. Domicity, p. 1-11.

80. "TI's New Marketing and PR Strategies," *Business Korea Electronics*, July 1988, p. 38.

81. "ITC Rules Hyundai, U.S. Firms Infringed on Intel Chip Patent," *Asian Wall Street Journal Weekly*, March 27, 1989, p. 3.

82. Wilson and Tatsuno, p. 6.

83. Interview with Lenny Siegel by Jay Gonzalez, July 14, 1988.

84. This phenomenon of high-tech guerrillas was described by, among others, Kenneth Flamm. Personal interview with Kenneth Flamm, Washington, D.C., March 7, 1989.

85. "Manpower: A Critical Resource in Short Supply," *Electronics Korea*, April 1989, p. 17.

86. Quoted in "Another Japan? Korea's Success in Manufacturing Belies a Lack of Many Industrial Arts," *Asian Wall Street Journal*, supplement, November 14, 1988, p. 7.

87. Personal interview with Ashoka Mody, by Walden Bello, Washington, D.C., March 6, 1989.

Chapter 10. Korea's Economy at the Crossroads

1. Geoff Crane and Kim Kwang-Won, "Foreign Investment: A New Environment Emerges," *Electronics Korea*, July 1989, p. 13.

2. Jeong Man-Soek, "Korea Looks Abroad," *Korea Business World*, August 1988, p. 10.

3. "Overseas Investments Up," *Electronics Korea*, February 1989, p. 57.

4. "Footwear: Makers Go South," *Business Korea*, March 1988, p. 59.

5. "Plans for Massive Investment in High Tech," *Hanguk Kyongje Sinmun*, July 1, 1989, reproduced in *FBIS: East Asia*, August 23, 1989, pp. 32–33.

6. Yu Ul-Sang, "A Challenge to High Technologies—A Report on the 'Public Hearing to Determine National Policy-Level Research Priorities,' " *Tong-A Ilbo*, reproduced in *FBIS: East Asia*, November 29, 1989, pp. 44–45.

7. "Plans for Massive Investment," pp. 32–33.

8. " 'Trillions of Won' Needed for Clean-Up," *Yonhap*, August 10, 1989, reproduced in *FBIS: East Asia*, August 10, 1989, pp. 26–27.

9. Kim Kyung-Hee, "Unemployment: Emerging Problem," *Korea Business World*, July 1989, p. 25.

10. *Ibid.*, p. 25.

11. *Ibid*, p. 25.

12. *Ibid.*, p. 22.

13. "Electronic Firms Expand," *Korea Business World*, July 1989, p. 62; "Overseas Investment: Big Surge Ahead," *Business Korea*, March 1988, p. 52; "Overseas Investment Up," *Electronics Korea*, February 1989, p. 57; Jeong Man-Soek, p. 10.

14. Jeong Man-Soek, p. 11.

15. Stefan Wagstyl, "South Korean Finance and Industry: Turmoil of Transition," *Financial Times*, November 27, 1989, p. i.

16. Suh Sang-Mok, "Rapid Democratization and New Challenges to Policymakers in Korea, *FYI* (Washington, D.C.), July 10, 1989, p.2. The author is a member of the National Assembly and former vice president of the Korea Development Institute.

Taiwan in Trouble
Introduction to Part II

1. "Taiwan Survey," *Economist*, March 5, 1988, p. 4; see also *Christian Science Monitor*, May 29, 1987.

2. An exemplary analysis of the interaction of the cold war and economics in Northeast Asia is Bruce Cumings' "The Origins of the Northeast Asian Political Economy: Industrial Sectors, Product Cycles, and Political Consequences," *International Organization* 38, no. 1 (Winter 1984).

3. Thomas Gold, *State and Society in the Taiwan Miracle* (Armonk, New York: M. E. Sharpe, 1986), pp. 86–87.

4. Peter Wickenden, "Tight Money and Lax Law in Taiwan," *Financial Times*, June 20, 1990, p. 6.

5. Paul Mooney, "Taiwan Eager for New Policy Allowing Investment in China," *San Francisco Chronicle*, February 21, 1990, p. A13.

6. Yao Ming-Chia, "Watching and Waiting in Crisis: The Confidence Crisis of Entrepreneurs," *Tian Xia* (Taipei), May 1, 1988.

Chapter 11. Agriculture: The Road to Extinction

1. Shim Jae-Hoon, "Strains of Success," *Far Eastern Economic Review*, June 2, 1988, p. 16.

2. "Taipei Says Rioters Will Be Punished," *Sing Tao International*, May 23, 1988, p. 2.

3. Mao Yu-Kang, "Agricultural Development Policy and Performance in Taiwan, ROC," continued, *Industry of Free China*, December 1984, p. 20.

4. Stuart Thompson, "Taiwan: Rural Society," *China Quarterly*, no. 99 (1984), p. 558.

5. Michael (Hsing-Huang) Hsiao, "State and Small Farmers in East Asia with Special Reference to Taiwan," Paper presented at Conference on Directions and Strategies of Agricultural Development in the Asia-Pacific Region, Academia Sinica, Taipei, January 5–7, 1988, p. 8.

6. The concept of a KMT-farmer coalition comes from Chin Pei-Hsiung, "Housing and Development in Taiwan," Working Paper no. 483, Institute of Urban and Regional Development, University of California, Berkeley, June 1988, p. 80.

7. Thompson, p. 558.

8. Wang Sung-Hsing and Raymond Apthorpe, *Rice Farming in Taiwan: Three Village Studies* (Taipei: Academia Sinica, 1974), p. 11.

9. Huang Chi, "The State and Foreign Capital: A Case Study of Taiwan," Ph.D. dissertation, Dept. of Political Science, Indiana University, February 1986, p. 108.

10. Wang and Apthorpe, p. 148.

11. *Ibid.*, p. 147.

12. *Ibid.*, p. 148.

13. Hsu Wen-Fu, "Price and Pricing of Farm Products," p. 94.

14. *Ibid.*, p. 88.

15. *Ibid.*

16. Joseph Yager, *Transforming Agriculture in Taiwan* (Ithaca: Cornell University Press, 1988), p. 254.

17. Quoted in Richard Kagan, "The 'Miracle' of Taiwan," Unpublished manuscript, Institute for Food and Development Policy, San Francisco, 1982, p. 37.

18. Chen Hsing-Yiu, "Family Farms, Integrated Rural Development, and Multi-purpose Cooperatives in Taiwan," *Economic Review* (Taipei), no. 222 (November–December 1984), p. 14.

19. Denis Simon, "Taiwan, Technology Transfer, and Transnationalism: The Political Management of Dependency," Ph.D. dissertation, University of California, Berkeley, 1980, p. 388.

20. Thompson, p. 559; also calculated from figures provided in Chen Hsing-Yiu, p. 7.

21. Huang Shu-Min, "Agricultural Modernization in Rural Taiwan," *Journal of*

Asian-Pacific and World Perspectives 7, no. 1 (1983), p. 23.

22. George Kuo, "Not by Rice Alone: Hunger for Justice in Taiwan," *Food Symposium 88 Newsletter* (Tokyo), 1988, p. 8.

23. *Ibid.*

24. Jack Williams, "Vulnerability and Change in Taiwan's Agriculture," *Pacific Viewpoint* 29, no. 1 (1988), p. 29.

25. Personal communication from Linda Gail Arrigo, April 3, 1990.

26. Chen Hsing-Yiu, p. 15.

27. Personal interview with Michael Hsiao, Taipei, by Walden Bello, May 12, 1988.

28. Williams, p. 26.

29. *Ibid.*, p. 27.

30. *Ibid.*, p. 32.

31. *Ibid.*

32. Personal interview with Michael Hsiao, Taipei, May 12, 1988.

33. Williams, p. 32.

34. *Ibid.*, p. 34.

35. Personal interview with Mao Yu-Kang, director of Land Reform Training Institute, Taipei, May 10, 1988.

36. As recounted by Michael Hsiao, personal interview, Taipei, May 12, 1988.

37. Mao Yu-Kang, "Current Land Problems and Policies of Taiwan, the Republic of China," *Industry of Free China*, June 1987, p. 13.

38. Personal interview with Mao Yu-Kang, Taipei, May 10, 1988.

39. Mao Yu-Kang, "Current Land Problems," p. 13.

40. Personal interview with Michael Hsiao, Taipei, May 12, 1988.

41. See Donald Puchala and Jane Stavely, "The Political Economy of Taiwanese Agricultural Development," in Raymond Hopkins *et al.*, eds., *Food, Politics, and Agricultural Development: Case Studies in the Public Policy of Rural Modernization* (Boulder, Colo.: Westview Press, 1979), pp. 107–131.

42. Personal inteview with Michael Hsiao, Taipei, May 12, 1988.

43. Yager, p. 251.

44. *Ibid.*, p. 56.

45. Robert Goldstein, *U.S. Agricultural Trade Opportunities with Pacific Rim Nations*, (CRS report for Congress) (Washington, D.C.: Congressional Research Service, January 9, 1989), pp. 57, 58.

46. *Ibid.*, p. 56.

47. Personal interview with Mao Yu-Kang, Taipei, by Walden Bello, May 10, 1988.

48. James McGregor, "Many Taiwan Farmers Face Hard Times," *Asian Wall Street Journal*, November 21, 1988.

49. Kuo, p. 10.

50. Kagan, p. 46.

51. Kuo, pp. 10–11.

52. Hsiao, "State and Small Farmers," p. 3

53. Kuo, p. 14.

Chapter 12. The Making of an Environmental Nightmare

1. Academia Sinica, *Taiwan 2000: Balancing Economic Growth and Environmental Protection* (Taipei: Academia Sinica, 1989), p. 81.

2. Forestry Bureau, quoted in *Taiwan 2000*, p. 94.

3. *Ibid.*, p. 120.

4. *Ibid.*, p. 86.

5. *Ibid.*, p. 91.

6. "Another Roadside Attraction," *Occasional Bulletin: Taiwan Church News* (Taiwan) 4, no. 1 (1987), p. 10.

7. Marc Cohen, *Taiwan at the Crossroads* (Washington, D.C.: Asia Resource Center, 1989), p. 121.

8. "Fishermen's Service Center Reports Details of Detainment," *Occasional Bulletin: Taiwan Church News* 4, no. 2 (1987), p. 5.

9. "Concern about the Plight of Tribal Aborigines," *Occasional Bulletin: Taiwan Church News* 3, no. 1 (1986), p. 11.

10. "Demonstration against Prostitution in Taipei," *Occasional Bulletin: Taiwan Church News* 4, no. 2 (1987), p. 3; "The Rainbow Project's Report on Prostitution," *Occasional Bulletin: Taiwan Church News* 5, no. 3, p. 5.

11. Personal communication from Linda Gail Arrigo, March 20, 1990.

12. Statistics from Chen Hsing-Yiu, "Development of Agriculture and Agricultural Trade in the Republic of China on Taiwan," *Industry of Free China* 14, no. 2 (1985), p. 9.

13. "Are You Really Going to Eat That?" *Bang* (Taipei), March 1988, p. 13.

14. National Research Council, National Academy of Sciences, *Alternative Agriculture* (Washington, D.C.: National Academy of Sciences, 1989), pp. 99–100.

15. "Are Your Really Going to Eat That?" p. 13.

16. National Reasearch Council, p. 126.

17. Personal interview with Michael Hsiao, Taipei, May 12, 1988.

18. Richard Kagan, "The 'Miracle' of Taiwan," Unpublished manuscript, Institute for Food and Development Policy, San Francisco, 1982, p. 39.

19. *Ibid.*, p. 38.

20. Personal interview with Mao Yu-Kang, by Walden Bello, Taipei, May 10, 1988.

21. Kagan, p. 30.

22. *Ibid.*, p. 39.

23. *Ibid.*, p. 30.

24. "Are You Really Going to Eat That?" p. 13.

25. Wang Sung-Hsing and Raymond Apthorpe, *Rice Farming in Taiwan: Three*

Village Studies (Taipei: Academia Sinica, 1974), p. 168.

26. Personal interview with Michael Hsiao, Taipei, by Walden Bello, May 12, 1988.

27. *Ibid.*

28. Wang and Apthorpe, *p. 168.*

29. *Ibid.*, pp. 169–170.

30. Academia Sinica, *Taiwan 2000*, p. 298.

31. "Ground Water Contamination," *Simple Earth* (Taipei), 1, 2 (March 1990). This articles uses statistics drawn from *Environmental Indicators for 1989* (Taipei: Environmental Protection Administration, 1989).

32. Carl Goldstein, "Cash from Trash," *Far Eastern Economic Review*, September 21, 1989, p. 80.

33. George Kuo, "Not by Rice Alone: Hunger for Justice in Taiwan," *Food Symposium 88 Newsletter* (Tokyo), 1988, p. 11.

34. Neal Rudge, "Edgar Lin," *Bang*, March 1988, p. 12.

35. Kuo, p. 11.

36. Alison Maitland, "Anger Grows over Taiwan's Polluted Success Story," *Financial Times*, October 13, 1989.

37. Academia Sinica, *Taiwan 2000*, p. iv.

38. *Ibid.* p. 23.

39. "College Students Study Environmental Pollution," *Occasional Bulletin: Taiwan Church News* 4, no. 1 (1987), p. 10.

40. Academia Sinica, *Taiwan 2000*, p. 150.

41. Rudge, p. 12.

42. Interview with Shih Shin-Minh, Taipei, by Walden Bello, May 12, 1988.

43. "Victim of Its Own Success," *Newsweek*, June 4, 1990, p. 76.

44. "Quality in Quantity," *Far Eastern Economic Review*, August 20, 1987, p. 64.

45. *Ibid.*

46. Academia Sinica, *Taiwan 2000*, p. 318.

47. *Ibid.*

48. Anwar Nassir, "Pollution Leaves Bitter Taste," *Far Eastern Economic Review*, August 20, 1987, p. 64.

49. "Taiwan Survey," *Economist*, March 5, 1988.

50. Samuel Wu, "How Is the Government Helping You to Stay Healthy: Public Health in an Industrializing Nation," *Bang*, February 1989, p. 39; Yvonne Welton, "What's a PSI Anyway?," *Bang*, February 1989, p. 5.

51. "Victim of Its Own Success," p. 76.

52. Alison Maitland, "Green Factor Enters Center Stage in Run-Up to Election," *Financial Times*, October 10, 1989, Section 3, p. 6.

53. Rudge, p. 13.

54. "The Church Faces Taiwan's Environmental Problems," *Occasional Bulletin: Taiwan Church News* 3, no. 1 (1986), p. 2.

55. Lien San-Lang, "On Decommissioning Nuclear Power Plants," table 4, *NATPA (North American Taiwanese Professors' Association) Bulletin* 7, no. 1 (February 1988), p. 46.

56. "Taiwan to Develop Self-Made Nuclear Reactors," *Lien Ho Pao*, December 17, 1988, p. 1, reproduced in *Foreign Broadcast Information Service Daily Report* (hereafter referred to as *FBIS: China*), December 27, 1988, p. 57.

57. "Nuclear Scientists Reportedly Left with U.S. Help," *Agence France Presse*, March 24, 1988, reproduced in *FBIS: China*, March 24, 1988, p. 85.

58. "Paper Speculates on CIA Role," *Agence France Presse*, March 12, 1988, reproduced in *FBIS: China*, March 14, 1988, p. 57.

59. *Ibid.*, p. 58.

60. NATPA Task Force on Taiwan Nuclear Power Plants, "A Review of Probabilistic Risk Assessment and Reactor Safety in Taiwan," *NATPA Bulletin* 7, no. 1 (February 1988), p. 16.

61. "U.S. Has Ok'd Six Nuclear Reactors on Seismic and Volcanic Taiwan Sites," *Export Monitor* (Center for Development Policy), reproduced in *Asian Issues*, "Taiwan National Report," series 2, no. 2 (September 1980), p. 65.

62. T. Sen-Lee, "An Economic Review of Taipower Nuclear Program Electricity and Policy," *NATPA Bulletin* 7, no. 1 (February 1988), p. 50.

63. "Fire Reported at Nuclear Power Plant," *Agence France Presse*, August 29, 1987, reproduced in *FBIS: China*, August 31, 1987, pp. 27–28.

64. Jonathan Sprague, "Hot Plants Cool Fears," *Bang*, July 1988, p. 8.

65. *Ibid.*, p. 7.

66. *Ibid.*, p. 8.

67. *Ibid.*

68. *Ibid.*

69. *Ibid.*

70. Personal communication from Linda Gail Arrigo, March 20, 1990.

71. Sprague, p. 8.

72. *Ibid.*

73. *Ibid.*

74. Interview with Edgar Lin, by Walden Bello, Taichung, May 14, 1988.

75. Cohen, p. 356.

76. Lin Wunan, "Managing Nuclear Wastes in Taiwan, " *NATPA Bulletin* 7, no. 1 (February 1988), p. 38.

77. John Elliot, "ICI Closes Taiwan Chemical Plant after Protests," *Financial Times*, September 25, 1989.

78. Cohen, p. 103.

79. Sheldon Severinghaus, "The Emergence of an Environmental Consciousness in Taiwan," Paper prepared for the 1989 Annual Meeting of the Association for Asian Studies, Washington, D.C., March 17–19, 1989, p. 13.

80. Personal interview with Sheldon Severinghaus, Asia Foundation, San Francisco, by Walden Bello and Stephanie Rosenfeld, September 18, 1989.

81. Severinghaus, p. 11.

82. Cohen, p. 358.

83. "Pollution in Taiwan: Filthy Rich," *Economist*, July 15, 1989, p. 67; "Premier Yu on Environmental Protection, Protests," China News Agency, October 15, 1988, reproduced in *FBIS: China*, October 18, 1988, p. 70; "Linyuan Waste: People Fighting for a Cleaner Environment," *Bang*, December 1988, p. 35.

84. "Victim of Its Own Success," p. 76.

85. According to one high-level EPA official, not a single fine has been paid. See also "Environmental Mishaps Dampen Earth Day in Taiwan," *Occasional Bulletin: Taiwan Church News* (Tainan), vol. VII, no. 2 (March–April 1990), p. 5.

86. Michael Hsiao and Lester Milbrath, "The Environmental Movement in Taiwan," Paper prepared for the Sino-U.S. Binational Conference on Environmental Protection and Social Development, Taipei, August 20–25, 1989.

87. "Premier Yu on Environmental Protection, Protests," p. 70.

88. "Build Naphtha Crackers Here or Suffer Decline in Industry, Top Planner Says," *China News* (Taipei), August 6, 1988.

89. "Most People Here Put Environmental Protection before Economic Growth," *China News* (Taipei), May 5, 1985. See also Hsiao and Milbrath, table 7, p. 23.

90. Academia Sinica, p. 34.

91. Quoted in Lee Anne Simpson, "Hsu Shen-Shu of the NEHA," *Bang*, March 1988, p. 10.

Chapter 13. The Challenge from Labor

1. Werner International, "Spinning and Weaving Labor Cost Comparisons," New York, Spring 1989.

2. Thomas Gold, *State and Society in the Taiwanese Miracle* (Armonk, N.Y.: M. E. Sharpe, 1986), p. 79.

3. Hsu Cheng-Kuang, "From False Consciousness to Independence: The Characteristics and Tendencies of the Labor Movement in Taiwan," (in Chinese), Taipei, Academia Sinica, 1988.

4. Ramon Myers, "The Economic Development of the Republic of China: Taiwan, 1965–81," in Lawrence Lau and Lawrence Klein, eds., *Models of Development: A Comparative Study of Economic Growth in South Korea and Taiwan* (San Francisco, Calif.: Institute for Contemporary Studies, 1986), pp. 35-36.

5. Richard Kagan, "The 'Miracle' of Taiwan," Unpublished manuscript, Institute for Food and Development Policy, San Francisco, 1982, p. 63.

6. George Fitting, "Export Processing Zones in Taiwan and the Republic of China," *Asian Survey* 22, no. 8 (August 1982), p. 737.

7. Mark Cohen, *Taiwan at the Crossroads* (Washington, D.C.: Asia Resource Center, 1988), p. 108.

8. Fitting, p. 737.

9. Rebecca Cantwell *et al.*, *Made in Taiwan: A Human Rights Investigation* (New York: Clergy and Laity Concerned, 1978), quoted in Kagan, p. 67.

10. Denis Simon, "Taiwan, Technology Transfer, and Transnationalism: The

Political Management of Dependency," Ph.D. dissertation, University of California at Berkeley, 1980, p. 389.

11. *Ibid.*

12. Hou Chi-Ming and Hsu Yu-Chu, quoted in Kagan, p. 72.

13. Fitting, p. 738.

14. Andrew Tanzer, "Taiwan's Work Force Stirs," *Far Eastern Economic Review*, February 26, 1982, p. 78.

15. *Ibid.*

16. Linda Gail Arrigo, "The Industrial Work Force of Young Women in Taiwan," *Bulletin of Concerned Asian Scholars* 12, no. 2 (April–June 1980), p. 31.

17. Kagan, p. 67.

18. Fitting, p. 738.

19. Kagan, p. 68.

20. *Ibid.*

21. Arrigo, p. 29.

22. *Ibid.*, p. 34.

23. Hsu Cheng-Kuang, p. 8.

24. Wu Nai-Te, "The Labor Movement—Where To?," *United Daily* (Taipei), May 1, 1988.

25. Kuo Tai-Chun and Ramon Myers, "The Great Transition: Political Change and the Prospects for Democracy in the Republic of China on Taiwan," *Asian Affairs: An American Review*, February 1988, p. 118.

26. Susan Greenhalgh, "Microsocial Processes in the Distribution of Income," Paper presented at the Taiwan Political Economy Workshop, East Asia Institute, Columbia University, December 18–20, 1980, p. 13.

27. Chin Pei-Hsiung, *Housing and Economic Development in Taiwan*, Working Paper no. 483 (Berkeley: Institute of Urban and Regional Development, June 1988), p. 110.

28. Chin Pei-Hsiung, pp. 109–110. Chin cites in support the work of Susan Greenhalgh and Richard Stites.

29. Richard Stites, quoted in Chin Pei-Hsiung, pp. 109–110.

30. Greenhalgh, p. 9.

31. Linda Gail Arrigo, "Economic and Political Control of Women Workers in Multinational Electronics Factories in Taiwan: Martial Law Coercion and World Market Uncertainty," *Contemporary Marxism*, no. 11 (Fall 1985), p. 83.

32. Hsu Cheng-Kuang, "Political Change and the Labor Movement in Taiwan," Paper presented at the 84th Annual Meeting of the American Sociological Association, San Francisco, August 9–13, 1989, p. 6.

33. Marc Cohen, *Taiwan at the Crossroads: Human Rights, Political Development, and Social Change on the Beautiful Island* (Washington, D.C.: Asia Resource Center, 1988), p. 129.

34. Wu Nai-Te, "Can't Be Cut, Can't Be Tied—What's Next? How Political Parties Face the Labor Movement," *China Quarterly*, February 6, 1988 (in Chinese).

35. Hsu Cheng-Kuang, p. 4.

36. *Ibid.*, p. 5.

37. Joseph Lee, "Labor Relations and the Stages of Economic Development," *Industry of Free China*, April 1989, p. 22.

38. *Ibid.*, p. 18.

39. *Ibid.*, p. 22.

40. *Ibid.*, pp. 22–23.

41. Tanzer, p. 78.

42. Hsu Cheng-Kuang, "Political Change...", p. 14.

43. Simon Long, *Taiwan to 1993: Politics versus Prosperity*, Special Report no. 1159 (London: Economist Intelligence Unit, 1989), p. 53.

44. Linda Gail Arrigo, personal communication, April 3, 1990; see also Marc Cohen, draft of section of labor of report on Taiwan, Washington, D.C., undated, p. 2.

45. Ho Shuet-Ying, *Taiwan—After a Long Silence* (Hong Kong: Asia Monitor Research Center, 1990), p. 16.

46. Cohen, *Taiwan at the Crossroads*, p. 133.

47. Tanzer, p. 78.

48. Cohen, draft, p. 3.

49. *Ibid.*

50. *Ibid.*, p. 7.

51. Cited in Simon, p. 365.

52. *Ibid.*

53. Michael Hsiao, "Development Strategies and Class Transformation in Taiwan and South Korea: Origins and Consequences," *Bulletin of the Institute of Ethnology, Academia Sinica* (Taipei), no. 61 (Spring 1986), p. 210.

54. Hsu Cheng-Kuang, p. 8.

55. James McGregor, "Growing Clout of Taiwan's Work Force Is Giving New Shape to Labor Relations," *Asian Wall Street Journal Weekly*, April 10, 1989, p. 2.

56. Long, p. 54.

57. Cited by Fan Liang-Shing, "Taiwan's International Reserve Accumulation: Causes and Effects," Paper delivered at Conference on Taiwan Economy and Trade, Washington, D.C., April 18–20, 1990, p. 14.

58. Alison Maitland, "Unpalatable Price of Success," *Financial Times*, October 10, 1989, sec. 3, p. iii.

59. Fan Liang-Shing, p. 10.

60. Lincoln Kaye, "Sleep-in for Housing," *Far Eastern Economic Review*, September 7, 1989, p. 42.

61. Ho Shuet-Ying, p. 63.

62. Lee, p. 25; Cohen, *Taiwan at the Crossroads*, p. 129.

63. Lee, p. 25.

64. Hsu Cheng-Kuang, p. 8.

65. Interview with Lin Hsien-Kui, official of the Provincial Federation of Labor, by Walden Bello, Taipei, May 5, 1988.

66. McGregor, p. 2.

67. John Elliott, "A Watershed in Labour Relations," *Financial Times*, October 10, 1989, sec. 3, p. vi.

68. Personal interview with Lou Mei-Wen, by Walden Bello, Taipei, May 8, 1988.

69. McGregor, p. 2.

70. *Ibid.*

71. Personal interview with Lou Mei-Wen, Taipei, May 8, 1988.

72. "Labor Disputes Create Major Problems for Country," Central News Agency, February 2, 1989, reproduced in *FBIS: China*, February 2, 1989, p. 76.

73. Hsu Cheng-Kuang, p. 10.

74. Quoted in McGregor, p. 2.

Chapter 14. The Triple Alliance in Taiwan

1. Huang Chi, "The State and Foreign Capital: A Case Study of Taiwan," Ph.D. dissertation, Dept. of Political Science, Indiana University, February 1986 (distributed by University Microfilms Dissertation Information Service), pp. 124, 126. This work is extremely useful, both for its analysis and its information.

2. *Ibid.*, p. 124.

3. *Ibid.*, p. 140.

4. "Taipei Moves to Trim Business Empires, but the KMT's Critics Aren't Appeased," *Asian Wall Street Journal Weekly*, October 9, 1989, p. 17.

5. Huang Chi, pp. 132, 137.

6. "Taipei Moves to Trim Business Empires," p. 17.

7. *Ibid.*; also Huang Chi, pp. 135–136.

8. Personal communication from Linda Gail Arrigo, April 3, 1990.

9. "Taipei Moves to Trim Business Empires," p. 17.

10. Huang Chi, p. 137.

11. *Ibid.*, p. 138.

12. Lin Chung-Cheng, "The Relations of Structure and Government Role to Income Distribution—A Preliminary Study," Translated from Chinese, Academia Sinica, 1988.

13. Quoted in "Taipei Moves to Trim Business Empires," p. 17.

14. Lin Chung-Cheng.

15. Quoted in Huang Chi, p. 138.

16. Chin Pei-Hsiung, *Housing and Economic Development in Taiwan*, Working Paper no. 483 (Berkeley: Institute of Urban and Regional Development, June 1988), p. 84.

17. *Ibid.*

18. Denis Simon, "Taiwan, Technology Transfer, and Transnationals: The Political Management of Dependency," Ph.D. dissertation, University of California,

Berkeley, 1980, p. 327.

19. Alice Amsden, "Taiwan's Economic History," *Modern China* 5, no. 3 (July 1979), p. 362.

20. Huang Chi, pp. 140, 161; see also Su Bing, *Taiwan's 400 Year History: The Origins and Continuing Development of the Taiwanese Society and People* (Washington D.C.: Taiwan Cultural Grassroots Association, 1986), pp. 74–75.

21. Huang Chi, p. 158.

22. *Ibid.*

23. Walter Arnold, "Bureaucratic Politics, State Capacity, and Taiwan's Automobile Industrial Policy," *Modern China* 15, no. 2 (April 1989), p. 184; Huang Chi, p. 160.

24. Huang Chi p. 149.

25. Simon, p. 309.

26. Su Bing, p. 78.

27. *Ibid.*, p. 80.

28. Personal communication from Marc Cohen, March 20, 1990.

29. Thomas Gold, *State and Society in the Taiwan Miracle* (Armonk, New York: M. E. Sharpe, 1986), p. 71.

30. Huang Chi, p. 115; see also Neil Jaccoby, *U.S. Aid to Taiwan: A Study of Foreign Aid, Self Help, and Development* (New York: Praeger, 1966), p. 138.

31. Huang Chi, p. 153.

32. *Ibid.*, p. 157. In what some observers see as an effort to pressure the KMT for approval, Wang has threatened to set up his naphtha cracker in China.

33. Simon, p. 386.

34. Ichiro Namazaki, "Networks of Taiwanese Big Business: A Preliminary Analysis," *Modern China* 12, no. 4 (October 1986), pp. 516–517.

35. *Ibid.*, p. 515.

36. Personal communication from Linda Gail Arrigo, April 3, 1990. Such officials were derisively referred to as *tsui tai ching* or "handsome, Taiwanese, and young."

37. Namazaki, p. 525.

38. Simon, p. 387.

39. Statistics from James McGregor, "Growing Clout of Taiwan's Work Force Is Giving New Shape to Labor Relations," *Asian Wall Street Journal Weekly*, April 10, 1989,p. 2; Joseph Lee, "Labor Relations and the Stages of Economic Development," *Industry of Free China*, April 1989, p. 26; Chin Pei-Hsiung, p. 61.

40. Chin Pei-Hsiung, p. 61.

41. Lin Chung-Chen, "The Relations of Structure and Government Role to Income Distribution."

42. Chin Pei-Hsiung, p. 100; also John Ni, "Foreign Investment Policy and Export Orientation: A Case Study of the Republic of China," in Seiji Naya *et al.*, eds., *Direct Foreign Investment and Export Promotion: Policies and Experience in Asia* (Resource Systems Institute, East-West Center, University of Hawaii, 1987), pp. 265–267.

43. Chin Pei-Hsiung, p. 100.

44. Pan Chih-Chia, cited in Huang Chi, p. 126.

45. Alexander Caldwell, cited in Huang Chi, p. 127.

46. John Ni, p. 267.

47. Chu Yun-Han, "Authoritarian Regimes under Stress: The Political Economy of Adjustment in the East Asian Newly Industrializing Countries," Ph.D. dissertation, University of Minnesota, 1985 (distributed by University Microfilms International Dissertation Information Service), p. 68.

48. Interview with Taiwanese entrepreneur who wishes to remain anonymous, conducted by Talleyrand Lin, Taipei, May 1988.

49. Simon, p. 352.

50. Douglas Sease, "U.S. Firms Fuel Taiwan's Trade Surplus," *Asian Wall Street Journal*, June 8, 1987, p. 1.

51. Huang Chi, p. 190.

52. Quoted in Sease, p. 1.

53. Lin Chung-Cheng.

54. Huang Chi, p. 189.

55. Simon, p. 350.

56. *Ibid.*

57. Personal communication from Linda Gail Arrigo, April 3, 1990.

58. Huang Chi, p. 190.

59. John Ni, p. 260. At the most general level, foreign investment is catergorized by source as "overseas Chinese" and "nonoverseas Chinese."

60. Simon, pp. 256–257.

61. John Ni, p. 260.

62. Joseph Grunwald amnd Kenneth Flamm, *The Global Factory* (Washington, D.C.: Brookings Institution, 1985), pp. 69–70.

63. *Ibid.*, p. 18.

64. Gold, p. 79.

65. Huang Chi, p. 179.

66. *Ibid.*, pp. 192–193.

67. *Ibid.*, p. 207.

68. *Ibid.*, pp. 208–209.

69. Simon Long, *Taiwan to 1993: Politics versus Prosperity*, Special Report 1159 (London: Economist Intelligence Unit, 1989), p. 68.

70. Huang Chi, pp. 224–225.

71. *Ibid.*, pp. 226–227.

72. Some analysts sense that aside from coopting labor, one of the reasons for the KMT's passing the Labor Standards Law has been to discipline Taiwanese small and medium capital and defuse potential opposition to KMT policies.

73. Personal interviews with Chiou I-Jen, deputy secretary general of Democratic Progressive Party (DPP), and Yao Chia-Wen, DPP chairman, by

Walden Bello, Taipei, May 10, 1988.

Chapter 15. The Structural Squeeze

1. Werner International, "Spinning and Weaving Labor Cost Comparisons," New York, Spring 1989.

2. Huang Chi, "The State and Foreign Capital: A Case Study of Taiwan," Ph.D. dissertation, Dept. of Political Science, Indiana University, 1986 (distributed by University Microfilms International Dissertation Information Service), p. 218.

3. Chu Yun-Han, "Authoritarian Regimes under Stress: The Political Economy of Adjustment in the East Asian Newly Industrializing Countries," Ph.D. dissertation, University of Minnesota, 1987 (distributed by University Micro-film International Dissertation Information Service), p. 115.

4. Simon Long, *Taiwan to 1993: Politics versus Prosperity*, Special Report no. 1159 (London: Economist Intelligence Unit, 1989), p. 68.

5. *Ibid.*, p. 34.

6. Wenlee Ting, *Business and Technological Dynamics in Newly Industrializing Asia* (Westport, Conn.: Greenwood Press, 1985), p. 85.

7. Kung Wang, "Development Strategies of the Automobile and Parts Industry of the Republic of China," Paper prepared for International Motor Vehicles Project Forum, Acapulco, Mexico, May 1989, p. 12.

8. Long, p. 64.

9. Huang Chi, p. 210.

10. Long, p. 68.

11. Huang Chi, pp. 166–167.

12. Denis Simon, "Taiwan, Technology Transfer, and Transnationalism: The Political Management of Dependency," Ph.D. dissertation, University of California, Berkeley, 1980, p. 378.

13. *Ibid.*, p. 499.

14. Huang Chi, p. 189.

15. Simon, p. 502.

16. *Ibid.*, pp. 496–497.

17. Long, p. 34.

18. Wenlee Ting, p. 84.

19. *Ibid.*, p. 87.

20. Long, p. 34.

21. Andrew Tanzer, "Dawn out of Sunset," *Far Eastern Economic Review*, September 4, 1981, p. 55.

22. Liang Kao-Shu and Liang Ching-Ing, "Trade Strategy and Industrial Policy in Taiwan," in Thornton Bradshaw, ed., *America's New Competitors* (Cambridge, Mass.: Ballinger Publishing, 1988), pp. 74–75.

23. "ROC Textile Industry Facing Hard Times Ahead," *Trade Opportunities in Taiwan*, February 1, 1988, p. 18.

24. Tanzer, p. 55.

25. "Textile Workers Demonstrate Near U.S. Institute," *Agence France Presse*,

November 8, 1988, reproduced in *FBIS: China*, November 8, 1988, p. 70.

26. James McGregor, "Taiwan Firms Head Overseas as Costs Increase at Home," *Asian Wall Street Journal Weekly*, August 14, 1989, p. 1.

27. Werner International, "Cost Comparisons."

28. Tanzer, p. 56.

29. Liang Kao-Shu and Liang Ching-Ing, p. 62.

30. "Shrinking Profits Hurt Taiwan Manufactures," *Far Eastern Economic Review*, February 25, 1988, p. 72.

31. Long, p. 79.

32. Chu Yun-Han, p. 191.

33. Konomi Tomisawa, "Development of and Future Outlook for an International Division of Labor in the Automobile Industries of Asian NICs," Briefing Paper for the First Policy Forum, International Motor Vehicle Program, May 5, 1987, pp. 25–26.

34. Simon, p. 503.

35. *Ibid.*, p. 446.

36. Kuo Wen-Jeng, "External Learning Effects and Export-Led Growth: An Investigation of the Taiwanese Experience," Ph.D. Dissertation, Cornell University, 1987 (distributed by University Microfilms Dissertation Information Service), p. 14.

37. Tomisawa, pp. 45–46.

38. *Ibid.*, p. 46.

39. Chu Yun-Han, p. 213.

40. Kung Wang, p. 7.

41. Chu Yun-Han, p. 215.

42. *Ibid.*, pp. 215–216.

43. Walter Arnold, "Bureaucratic Politics, State Capacity, and Taiwan's Automobile Industrial Policy," *Modern China* 15, no. 2 (April 1989), p. 204.

44. Kung Wang, p. 9.

45. Andrew Tank, *Automotive News*, September 29. 1988, p. 29; Maureen Chu, "Automobile Importers in Taiwan Expect Moderate Profits This Year," *Asian Wall Street Journal Weekly*, March 6, 1989, p. 24.

46. Tank, p. 30.

47. *Ibid.*, p. 29.

48. Tomisawa, p. 34.

49. Tomisawa, p. 68.

50. Alison Maitland, "Aided by a 'Reverse Brain Drain,'" *Financial Times*, Section 3, October 10, 1989, p. v.

51. Ashoka Mody, "Alternative Strategies for Developing Information Industries," Paper prepared for Industry Development Division, Industry and Energy Dept., World Bank, Washington, D.C., October 1988, p. 16.

52. Morris Crawford, *Programming the Invisible Hand: The Computerization of Korea and Taiwan* (Cambridge, Mass.: Center for Information Policy Research,

Harvard University, 1986), p. 63.

53. Mody, p. 16.

54. "Competition Worries Taiwanese Manufacturers," *Electronic Business*, December 10, 1986, p. 43. Liang Kuo-Shu and Liang Ching-Ing note that "the electronics industry is tightly ruled by technological change, and local producers are still very much in the business of assembling components and computer peripherals, with high technology inputs being imported." Liang and Liang, p. 63.

55. Crawford, p. 64.

56. Ashoka Mody, "Recent Evolution of Microelectronics in South Korea and Taiwan: An Institutional Approach to Comparative Advantage," Unpublished paper, Boston, 1985, p. 12.

57. *Ibid.*, p. 8.

58. Eduardo Lachica, "U.S. Firms Curb Pirating of Their Products in Asia," *Asian Wall Street Journal Weekly*, March 20, 1989, p. 1.

59. *Ibid.*

60. James McGregor, "IBM's Clout Overcomes Taiwan Cloners," *Asian Wall Street Journal Weekly*, September 2–3, 1988, pp. 1, 20.

61. *Ibid.*, p. 20.

62. George Gilder, *Microcosm: The Quantum Revolution in Econmics and Technology* (New York: Simon and Schuster, 1989), p. 225.

63. *Ibid.*, p. 224.

64. Dori Jones Yang, "Taiwan Isn't for Cloning Anymore," *Business Week*, September 25, 1989, p. 208.

65. *Ibid.*

66. *Ibid.*

67. Philip Liu, "Emperor of Taiwan's Computer Industry," *Electronics Business*, October 15, 1988, p. 96.

68. David Sanger, "PC Powerhouse (Made in Taiwan)," *New York Times*, Business Day section, September 28, 1988.

69. "In the U.S., the Chips Are Up," *Asiaweek*, March 10, 1989, p. 50.

70. Yang, p. 208.

71. Wenlee Ting, p. 84.

72. Sanger, "PC Powerhouse."

73. Don Clark, "Sun Gets Taiwan Clones, Intel Fights Back," *San Francisco Chronicle*, June 22, 1989.

74. *Ibid.*

75. Crawford, p. 79.

76. Sanger, "PC Powerhouse."

77. Yang, p. 212.

78. "Competition Worries Taiwanese Manufacturers," p. 32.

79. Maitland, "Reverse Brain Drain," p. v.

80. Mody, "Alternative Strategies" p. 16.

81. Mody, "Recent Evolution," p. 15.

82. Mody, "Alternative Strategies," pp. 20–21.

83. Sanger, "PC Powerhouse."

84. Mody, "Alternative Strategies," p. 28.

85. "Competition Worries Taiwanese Manufacturers," p. 28.

86. Personal interview with Tom Wang, Taiwan expert at Dataquest, by Walden Bello, San Jose, March 16, 1989.

87. "Competition Worries Taiwanese Manufacturers,"p. 28.

88. Long, p. 69.

89. "U.S. Computer Firms Go Shopping in Taiwan," *Electronic Business*, December 10, 1988, p. 156.

90. *Ibid*.

91. Shigezaburo Kabe, "Taiwan's Stock Market a National Pastime," *Japan Economic Journal*, February 24, 1990, p. 24.

92. Crawford, pp. 76–77.

93. Mody, "Alternative Strategies" p. 24.

94. Personal interview with Tom Wang, Dataquest, San Jose, March 16, 1989.

95. Bob Johnstone, "Diverting the Brain Drain," *Far Eastern Economic Review*, January 28, 1988, p. 70.

96. Personal interview with Tom Wang, Dataquest, by Walden Bello, San Jose, March 16, 1989.

97. Johnstone, p. 70.

98. Interview with Sun Microsystems engineer who wishes to remain anonymous, by Walden Bello and Stephanie Rosenfeld, Mountain View, CA, April 26, 1990.

Chapter 16. Taiwan's Dilemmas

1. Personal interview with Michael Hsiao, by Walden Bello, Taipei, May 12, 1988.

2. James McGregor, "Taiwan Firms Head Overseas as Costs Increase at Home," *Asian Wall Street Journal Weekly*, August 14, 1989, p. 18.

3. "Taiwan's Little Secret," *Economist*, February 17, 1990, p. 75.

4. McGregor, p. 20.

5. Paul Mooney, "Taiwanese Eager for New Policy Allowing Investment in China," *San Francisco Chronicle*, February 21, 1990, p. A15.

6. Hirotsugu Koike, "Uniden, Weston Pioneer Move to Philippines," *Japanese Economic Journal*, August 13, 1988, p. 6.

7. Simon Long, *Taiwan to 1993: Politics versus Prosperity*, Special Report no. 1159 (London: Economist Intelligence Unit, 1989), p. 55.

8. Personal interview with Lin Chung-Cheng, Taipei, May 12, 1988.

9. Julia Leung, "Taiwan's Army of Illegal Workers Grows," *Asian Wall Street Journal*, January 7, 1988, p. 7.

10. Long, p. 55.

11. "Small Enterprises Hire Mainland Workers," *China Post*, November 8, 1988, reproduced in *FBIS: China*, November 16, 1988, p. 73.

12. Clark Roberts, "Workers: Foreign and Cheap," *Bang* (Taipei), November 1988, p. 35.

13. "Plan to Deport Illegal Foreign Workers Prepared," *China Post*, December 6, 1988, reproduced in *FBIS: China*, December 13, 1988, p. 76.

14. Timothy Flanagan, "Amahs Underground," *Bang*, November 1988, p. 33.

15. Roberts, p. 35.

Singapore Adrift
Introduction to Part III

1. Ira Magaziner and Mark Patinkin, *The Silent War: Inside the Global Business Battles Shaping America's Future* (New York: Random House, 1989), p. 47.

2. *Ibid.*, p. 46.

3. Lim Chong Yah *et al.*, *Policy Options for the Singapore Economy* (Singapore: McGraw-Hill Book Co., 1989), p. 17.

4. "Singapore Revising Laws to Deal with 'Wealthy Beggars,'" *Sing Tao International*, March 21, 1988, p. 5.

5. Quoted in James Clad, *Behind the Myth: Business, Money, and Power in Southeast Asia* (London: Unwin Hyman, 1989), p. 144.

Chapter 17. The Making of a Transnation Haven

1. Survey cited in Chong Li-Choy, "Singapore's Development: Harnessing the Multinationals," *Contemporary Southeast Asia* 8, no. 1 (June 1986), p. 65.

2. Lim Chong-Yah *et al.*, *Policy Options for the Singapore Economy* (Singapore: McGraw-Hill Book Co., 1988), p. 255.

3. *Ibid.*, p. 261.

4. *Ibid.*, p. 262.

5. *Ibid.*, p. 248.

6. *Ibid.*, p. 250.

7. Lee (Tsao) Yuan, "Singapore: The Role of the Government in Export Success," Unpublished manuscript, Singapore, 1988, pp. 22–23.

8. Lim Chong-Yah *et al.*, p. 255.

9. Quoted in *ibid.*, p. 256.

10. Koh Ai-Tee and Lee (Tsao) Yuan, "Whither the Local Entrepreneurial Spirit," *Straits Times*, March 9, 1988.

11. Quoted in James Clad, *Behind the Myth: Business, Money, and Power in Southeast Asia* (London: Unwin Hyman, 1989), p. 129.

12. Interview with high Singaporean executive who wishes to remain anonymous, Singapore, April 7, 1988.

13. Lim Chong-Yah *et al.*, p. 265. Subcontracting might have increased in the late 1980s, with the migration of more Japanese companies to Southeast Asia as the yen appreciated in value. However, the big Japanese corporations also tended to bring their suppliers with them to Southeast Asia.

14. Interview with high Singaporean executive who wishes to remain anonymous, Singapore, April 9, 1988.

15. Lim Chong-Yah et al., p. 268.

16. Quoted in Clad, p. 129.

17. Lee (Tsao) Yuan, p. 24.

18. Koh Ai-Tee, "Saving, Investment, and Entrepreneurship," in Lawrence Krause, Koh Ai-Tee, and Lee (Tsao) Yuan, eds., *The Singapore Economy Reconsidered* (Singapore: Institute of Southeast Asian Studies, 1987), pp. 92–93.

19. Economic Committee, *The Singapore Economy: New Directions* (Singapore: Ministry of Trade and Industry, Republic of Singapore, February 1986), p. 129.

20. Interview with high Singaporean executive who wishes to remain anonymous, by Walden Bello, Singapore, April 7, 1988.

21. Koh Ai-Tee, "Saving, Investment, and Entrepreneurship," p. 94.

22. Lim Chong-Yah et al., p. 270.

23. Interview with high Singaporean executive who wishes to remain anonymous, by Walden Bello, April 11, 1988.

24. Gary Rodan, "The Rise and Fall of Singapore's 'Second Industrial Revolution,'" in Richard Robison et al., eds., *Southeast Asia in the 1980's* (Sydney: Allen and Unwin, 1987), p. 159.

25. Economic Committee, *The Singapore Economy*, p. 44.

26. Rodan, p. 166.

27. *Ibid.*, p. 167.

28. Lim Chong-Yah et al., p. 265.

29. Ira Magaziner and Mark Patinkin, *The Silent War: Inside the Global Business Battles Shaping America's Future* (New York: Random House, 1989), p. 63.

30. Gary Rodan, *The Political Economy of Singapore's Industrialization* (London: Macmillan Press, 1989), p. 176.

31. Magaziner and Patinkin, p. 51.

32. Interview with high Singapore executive who wishes to remain anonymous, by Walden Bello, April 7, 1988.

33. Economic Committee, *The Singapore Economy*, pp. 51–53.

34. Chong Li-Choy, p. 62.

35. Quoted in *ibid.*

36. See "Foreign Worker Levy Rise a S'pore Matter: B. G. Lee," *Straits Times*, November 9, 1988.

37. Abby Tan, "Japan Urged to Upgrade Quality of Its Investments in Singapore," *Straits Times*, December 3, 1988. A Singapore business leader, cited in the same report, said that unless Japan upgraded the quality of its investments, Singapore's increasing dependence on Japan for foreign investment "could have ominous consequences for Singapore's economic prospects, leading to substantially slower growth and even a drop in living standards."

38. Thomas Sim, "Singapore Disk Drive Makers Spin Export Profit," *Japan Economic Journal*, October 1, 1988.

39. "Electronics Industry May be Slowing Down," *Straits Times*, November 18, 1988.

40. Economic Committee, *The Singapore Economy*, p. 61.

41. Lawrence Krause, ""Industrialization of an Advanced Global City," in Lawrence Krause *et al.*, "The Singapore Economy Reconsidered," p. 74.

42. Interview with high Singaporean executive who wishes to remain anonymous, by Walden Bello, Singapore, April 7, 1988.

Chapter 18. Controlling the Labor Force

1. Research and Statistics Department, *1988 Singapore Yearbook of Labour Statistics* (Singapore: Ministry of Labour, 1988), p. 52.

2. Frederic Deyo, *Dependent Development and Industrial Order* (New York: Praeger, 1981), pp. 37–38.

3. M. R. Stenson, quoted in Basu Sharma, *Aspects of Industrial Relations in ASEAN* (Singapore: Institute of Southeast Asian Studies, 1985), p. 64.

4. Chan Heng Chee and Baid Ul Haq, eds., *S. Rajaretnam: The Prophetic and the Political; Selected Speeches and Writings* (New York: St. Martin's Press, 1987), pp. 272, 277.

5. Hans Luther, "The Repression of Labour Protest in Singapore: Unique Case or Future Model," *Development and Change* 10 (1979), p. 293; *1988 Yearbook of Labour Statistics*, p. 52.

6. *1988 Yearbook of Labour Statistics*, p. 51.

7. *Ibid.*, pp. 3, 51.

8. Sharma, p. 65.

9. *Ibid.*, p. 68.

10. Noeleen Heyzer, "International Production and Social Change: An Analysis of the State, Employment, and Trade Unions in Singapore," in P. S. J. Chen, ed., *Singapore: Development Policies and Trends* (Kuala Lumpur: Oxford University Press, 1983), pp. 124–125.

11. Quoted in *ibid.*, p. 125.

12. Quoted in Patrick Daniel, "PM Praises Singapore Trade Unions," *Straits Times*, November 18, 1988.

13. AWARE (Association of Women for Action and Research), "Women in Singapore," Manuscript for publication, Singapore, February 5, 1988, p. 2.

14. *Ibid.*

15. Lai Ah-Heng, "Economic Restructuring in Singapore and the Impact of New Technology on Women Workers," in Cecilia Ng, ed., *Technology and Gender: Women's Work in Asia* (Kuala Lumpur: Women's Studies Unit, Universiti Pertaniab Malaysia and Malaysian Social Science Association, 1987), p. 114.

16. *Ibid.*, p. 118.

17. *Ibid.*, p. 114.

18. Aline K. Wong, "Planned Development, Social Stratification, and the Sexual Division of Labor," p. 213.

19. Statement in Seah Chee-Meow, ed., *Trends in Singapore* (Singapore: Institute of Southeast Asian Studies, 1975), p. 135.

20. Wong, p. 213.

21. "The Price of Foreign Labour," *Straits Times*, November 19, 1988.

22. Lai Ah-Heng, p. 126.

23. *Ibid.*, p. 112.

24. *Ibid.*, p. 128.

25. Noeleen Heyzer, *Working Women in Southeast Asia: Development, Subordination, and Emancipation* (Philadelphia: Open University Press, 1986), p. 108.

26. Lai Ah-Heng, pp. 126–127.

27. Quoted in James Clad, *Behind the Myth: Business, Money, and Power in Southeast Asia* (London: Unwin Hyman, 1989), p. 140.

28. Leong Chan-Teik, "Somkid Back in S'pore with a Job and a Smile," *Straits Times*, November 3, 1989, p. 25.

29. Lim Chong-Yah *et al.*, *Policy Options for the Singapore Economy* (Singapore: McGraw-Hill Book Co., 1988), pp. 405, 438.

30. "The Price of Foreign Labor," *Straits Times*, November 19, 1988. It is likely that the actual number is much higher. As Gary Rodan points out, in 1978 the government's claim that work permit holders numbered 40,000 was contradicted by the Selangor Graduates Society, which estimated that there were as many as 120,000 Malaysians alone in Singapore. Gary Rodan, *The Political Economy of Singapore's Industrialization* (London: Macmillan, 1989), p. 138.

31. *Straits Times*, November 17 and December 6, 1988.

32. See Lee (Tsao) Yuan, "The Government in the Labour Market," in Lawrence Krause *et al.*, eds., *The Singapore Economy Reconsidered* (Singapore: Institute of Southeast Asian Studies, 1987), p. 211.

33. Statement of Lee Hsien-Loong, paraphrased in "Government Cannot Have Total Hands-off Policy on Wages," *Straits Times*, November 25, 1988.

34. Chong Li-Choy, "Singapore's Development: Harnessing the Multinationals," *Contemporary Southeast Asia* 8, no. 1 (June 1986), p. 62.

35. Steven Erlanger, "What's Killing Thais? Nations Bicker," *New York Times*, May 8, 1990.

36. *Ibid.*

37. *Ibid.*

38. Pang Eng Fong and Linda Lim, "Foreign Labor and Economic Development in Singapore," *International Migration Review* 16, no. 3, 1982, p. 561.

39. Lee (Tsao) Yuan, p. 188.

40. Economic Committee, *The Singapore Economy: New Directions* (Singapore: Ministry of Trade and Industry, February 1986), p. 109.

41. *Straits Times*, January 14, 1989.

42. Francis Seow, "The Role of the Bar Associations in the Protection of Human Rights in the LAWASIA Region," Unpublished paper, undated, p. 10.

43. *Ibid.*

44. Philip Jeyaretnam, *First Loves* (Singapore: Times Books International, 1987), p. 149.

45. Francis Seow, "Human Rights and the Constitution of Singapore," Unpublished paper, undated, p. 12.

46. Chew Soong-Beng, cited in "Maids' Ban Set to Disrupt S'pore Lifestyle," *Sing Tao International*, February 29, 1988, p. 6.

47. *Ibid.*

48. Interviews with Filipino domestics in Singapore, by Walden Bello, April 8–10, 1988.

49. Gerry de Silva, "Sri Lanka Guarantees Quality of Maids," *Straits Times*, January 12, 1989.

50. "It's Against the Law to 'Lend Out' Maids," *Straits Times*, November 25, 1988.

51. Interviews with Filipino domestics in Singapore, by Walden Bello, April 8–10, 1988.

52. Interview with Filipino seaman who wishes to remain anonymous, by Walden Bello, Singapore, April 10, 1988.

53. Luther, p. 297.

54. Leong Chan-Teik, p. 25.

Chapter 19. Brave New Isle

1. Manuel Castells, "The Developmental City-State in an Open World Economy: The Singapore Experience," BRIE Working Paper no. 31, Berkeley Roundtable on the International Economy, University of California, Berkeley, February 1988, p. 47. Castells bases his description on the insightful work of John Clammer, especially *Singapore: Ideology, Society, and Culture* (Singapore: Chopmen Publishers, 1985), pp. 159–169.

2. Chua Beng-Huat, "Re-opening Ideological Discussion in Singapore: A New Theoretical Direction," *Southeast Asian Journal of Social Science* 11, no. 2 (1983), p. 38.

3. Quoted in Ian Buruma, "Fear Haunts Successful Singapore," *San Francisco Chronicle*, Briefing section, June 15, 1988, p. 1.

4. Quoted in Chua Beng-Huat, p. 38.

5. Clammer, p. 161.

6. Chua Beng-Huat, "Pragmatism of the People's Action Party Government in Singapore: A Critical Assessment," *Southeast Asian Journal of Social Science* 13, no. 2 (1985), p. 41.

7. Quoted in Francis Seow, "The Role of the Bar Associations in the Protection of Human Rights in the LAWASIA Region," Unpublished paper, Manila, undated, pp. 11–12. As his source, Seow cites the *Straits Times*, April 20, 1987.

8. Goh Chok-Tong, "Singapore into the 1990's: Changes But Constancy," in Fletcher School of Law and Diplomacy, *A Conference on Singapore and the U.S. into the 1990's* (Medford, Mass.: Fletcher School of Law and Diplomacy, Tufts University, November 6–8, 1985), p. 53.

9. *Ibid.*, p. 54.

10. Lee Hsien-Loong, "Westernisation—The Problem Singapore Is Trying to Solve," *Straits Times*, January 12, 1989.

11. This idea of cultural ballast was expressed by Lee Kwan-Yew in his National Day Rally Speech in 1978: "A person who gets deculturalized—and I nearly was, so I know this danger—loses his self-confidence. He suffers from a sense of deprivation. For optimum performance a man must know himself and the world. He must know where he stands. I may speak the English language better than the Chinese language because I learned English early in life. But I will never be an Englishman in a thousand generations and I have not got the Western value system inside; mine is an Eastern value system. Nevertheless I use Western concepts, Western words because I understand them. But I also have a different system in my mind." Quoted in Clammer, p. 22.

12. Lee Siew-Choh, quoted in N. Balakrishnan, "Pledge of Allegiance," *Far Eastern Economic Review*, February 9, 1989, p. 37.

13. Philip Jeyaretnam, *First Loves* (Singapore: Times Books International, 1987), p. 121–122.

14. Abdullah Tarmugi, quoted in N. Balakrishnan, "Pledge of Allegiance," *Far Eastern Economic Review*, February 9, 1989, p. 37.

15. Clammer, p. 166.

16. Francis Seow, p. 9.

17. Quoted in *ibid.*, p. 8.

18. Chua Beng-Huat, p. 39.

19. Seow, p. 11.

20. *Ibid.*, p. 10.

21. James Minchin, *No Man Is an Island: A Study of Singapore's Lee Kuan-Yew* (Sydney: Allen and Unwin, 1986), p. 255.

22. *Ibid.*

23. Lim Chong-Yah *et al.*, *Policy Options for the Singapore Economy* (Singapore: McGraw-Hill Book Co., 1988), p. 113.

24. Seow, p. 11.

25. Lim Chong-Yah *et al.*, p. 115.

26. James Clad, *Behind the Myth: Business, Money, and Power in Southeast Asia* (London: Unwin Hyman, 1989), p. 134.

27. "Birth of Another Nation," *Economist*, March 10, 1990, p. 37.

28. *Ibid.*

29. Lim Chong-Yah *et al.*, p. 113.

30. Clad, p. 134.

31. "Birth of Another Nation," p. 37.

32. *Ibid.*; also Minchin, p. 248.

33. Minchin, p. 248.

34. Manuel Castells, Lee Goh, and Reginald Kwok, "Economic Development and Housing Policy in the Asian Pacific Rim: A Comparative Study of Hong Kong, Singapore, and Shenzen Special Economic Zone," Monograph 37, Institute of Urban and Regional Development, University of California, Berkeley,

June 1988, p. 288.

35. Lim Ching-Yah *et al.*, p. 17.

36. Minchin, pp. 249–250.

37. Stanley Bedlington, *Malaysia and Singapore: The Building of New States* (Ithaca, New York: Cornell University Press, 1978), p. 221.

38. *Ibid.*, pp. 221–222.

39. *Ibid.*, p. 222.

40. Chua Beng-Huat, "Public Housing Policies Compared: U.S., Socialist Countries, and Singapore," Working Paper no. 94, Dept. of Sociology, National University of Singapore, 1988, p. 21.

41. John Clammer, "Peripheral Capitalism and Urban Order: 'Informal Sector' Theories in the Light of Singapore's Experience," in John Clammer, ed., *Beyond the New Economic Anthropology* (New York: St. Martin's Press, 1987), pp. 192–193.

42. Quoted in Castells, Lee, and Kwok, p. 361.

43. *Far Eastern Economic Review*, March 24, 1988, p. 26.

44. "Dhana: Clear, Open Policies Needed to Prevent Enclaves," *Straits Times*, January 7, 1989, p. 16.

45. *Ibid.*

46. Castells, Lee, and Kwok, p. 310.

47. Bedlington, p. 223.

48. Castells, Lee, and Kwok, p. 359.

49. *Ibid.*

50. Amnesty International, quoted in *Report of the International Mission of Jurists to Singapore, July 1987* (Geneva: International Commission of Jurists, October 1987), p. 10.

51. Francis Seow, "Human Rights and the Constitution of Singapore," Unpublished paper, Singapore, undated, p. 3

52. *Far Eastern Economic Review*, January 22, 1987.

53. Interview with Singaporean businessman who wishes to remain anonymous, by Walden Bello, April 11, 1988.

54. Milton Friedman, "A Welfare State Syllogism," Speech at the Commonwealth Club, San Francisco, June 1, 1990.

55. *Ibid.*

56. Mary Lee, " The Primed Minister," *Far Eastern Economic Review*, September 15, 1988, p. 15.

57. *Ibid.*, p. 16.

58. Go Chok-Tong, p. 54.

59. Interview with Singaporean businessman who wishes to remain anonymous, by Walden Bello, April 11, 1988.

Chapter 20. Uncertain Future

1. Andrew Baxter, "Singapore: Priorities for Expansion," *Financial Times*, Section 3, November 13, 1989, p. i.

2. John Clammer, "Peripheral Capitalism and Urban Order: 'Informal Sector' theories in the Light of Singapore's Experience," in John Clammer, ed., *Beyond the New Economic Anthropology* (New York: St. Martin's Press, 1987), pp. 192–193. See also Chua Beng-Huat, "Public Housing Policies Compared: U.S., Socialist Countries, and Singapore," Working Paper no. 94, Dept. of Sociology, National University of Singapore, Kent Ridge, 1988, p. 21.

3. Iyanatul Islam and Colin Kirkpatrick, "Export-Led Development, Labour Market Conditions, and the Distribution of Income: The Case of Singapore," *Cambridge Journal of Economics* 10 (1986), pp. 120–121.

4. David Sanger, "Singapore Aim: High Tech Future," *New York Times*, May 15, 1990.

5. See, among others, "Foreign Worker Levy Rise a S'pore Matter: B. G. Lee," *Straits Times*, November 19, 1988.

6. Gerry de Silva, "Levy on Foreign Maids to Go Up Next Month," *Straits Times*, December 4, 1988.

7. "Foreign Worker Levy Rise."

8. Andrew Baxter, "Maintaining the Balance," *Financial Times*, Survey, November 13, 1989, p. ii.

9. Abby Tan, "Japan Urged to Upgrade Quality of Its Investments in Singapore," *Straits Times*, December 3, 1988.

10. Simon Elegant, "Singaporeans Say the Government Exaggerates Brain-Drain Problem," *Asian Wall Street Journal Weekly*, October 16, 1989, p. 18.

11. *Ibid.*; see also "Birth of Another Nation," *Economist*, March 10, 1990, p. 37.

12. "Birth of Another Nation," p. 37.

13. Sanger, "Singapore Aim."

14. Elegant, p. 18.

15. *Ibid.*

16. "The Phantom of the Opera," *Economist*, November 11, 1989, p. 41.

17. Elegant, p. 18.

18. Interview with Singaporean lawyer who wants to remain anonoymous, by Walden Bello, Singapore, April 6, 1988.

19. Linda Lim, comments at Singapore's Second Industrial Revolution panel discussion, Conference on Singapore and the U.S. into the 1990's, Fletcher School of Law and Diplomacy, pp. 33–34.

Conclusion: The NICs, the Future, and the Third World

1. As Mark Clifford writes, Korean farmers "may also be able to take advantage of a new health awareness in the country, with people increasingly willing to pay more for organic produce. A popular television program lat year [1989]...which advocated and organic vegetarian diet, spurred a boom in chemical-free vegetables and fruits. While the craze has cooled down more farmers are returning to traditional methods. "It's Tough Going on the Land," *Far Eastern Economic Review*, June 28, 1990, p. 48.

2. Interview with Ju Gau-Jeng, member of Legislative Yuan, by Walden Bello, Taipei, May 9, 1988.

3. On this point, we found illuminating the comments of a *Japan Times* editorial on Eastern Europe's economies: "Command economies have the power to jumpstart large-scale industrialization, but they are unable to maximize efficiency. Such countries expand economically by making huge investments in productive capacity, but they cannot produce efficiently enough to compete with those of the Western industrialized world. This explains why the Eastern nations were relatively successful at an early stage of development but have somewhat stagnated since." "Capitalism's Coming Crisis," *Japan Times*, December 29, 1989, reproduced in *FBIS Daily Report: East Asia Supplement*, January 8, 1990, p. 58. We would add that stagnation was caused not only by the absence of markets but also the lack of democratic consultation on the direction of the economy.

Glossary

ASEAN (Association of Southeast Asian Nations). A political and trading bloc composed of Singapore, Malaysia, Thailand, Indonesia, the Philippines, and Brunei.

ASICs (application specific integrated circuits). Sophisticated integrated circuits or logic chips that are especially designed for semicustom uses. Unlike mass-produced DRAM (dynamic random access memory) chips, which are usually designed and fabricated by the same firm, ASICs are increasingly designed by specialized design houses, then sent to foundries for fabrication into chips.

bit. Binary digit or the basic unit of information in a binary numbering system. A bit is usually denoted one or zero. Eight contiguous bits make up a *byte*, the fundamental data word of digital computer systems. A byte is the basic unit of measure for storing memory in computers. A *kilobyte* is a unit of memory measurement equal to 1,024 bytes and a *megabyte* is a unit of memory measurement equal to 1,048,576 bytes.

B.O.D. (biological oxygen demand). This refers to the amount of oxygen required by microorganisms (such as bacteria) to utilize organic matter (such as sewage) as food and convert it into $CO_2H_2ONO_3$. If the B.O.D. is higher than the oxygen available, radical changes occur in the chemistry and biology of the system, as microorganisms outcompete fish and other oxygen-dependent life. As fish die, they add to the quantity of organic matter, making the B.O.D. soar even higher.

chaebol. A Korean conglomerate whose component corporations are usually in diverse areas of production, many of them unrelated. Unlike publicly traded corporations in the West, ownership of the chaebol is held by families.

comparative advantage. A controversial concept in neoclassical economics that claims that the greatest economic gains accrue to a country when it specializes in those products that it can produce at least cost (compared with other products) because of natural endowments, like cheap labor. This concept has been attacked as a conservative idea justifying the maintenance of third world countries as producers of primary products or low-value-added labor-intensive manufactured goods while reserving for the developed countries the production of high-value-added manufactured goods.

disk drive. A central component in a computer, a disk drive consists of rotating platters on which information is magnetically stored and read by a mechanical head mechanism that moves across the platter to seek out the desired bit of information. Typically, the average time required to locate a bit of information is around 15 milliseconds.

DPP (Democratic Progressive Party). The main opposition party in Taiwan.

DRAM (dynamic random access memory). The most common type of semiconductor memory chip used in computers. Unlike *SRAM* (static random access memory) chips, DRAMs require a refresh circuit every two milliseconds (thousandths of a second) during which all the capacitors are recharged in order to store input data. Data stored in a SRAM, on the other hand, remains there until changed or until power is terminated. The most advanced chip that now exists is the working prototype of the 64-megabit chip produced by Hitachi, which can store up to 64 million bits of information. In George Gilder's words, DRAMs "are the [microelectronics] industry's supreme example of the dominance of capital and manufacturing. The densest of microchips, capable of reading or writing between 1 and 16 million memory bits, DRAMs are by far the most difficult of chips to fabricate."

EPB (Economic Planning Board). The "superagency" staffed by technocrats that has had a strong directive role in economic development in Korea owing to its power to engage in long-term macroeconomic planning as well as to its control over government spending for private and public projects.

EPROM (erasable programmable read-only memory). A type of memory chip on which a program can be written electronically that does not lose its contents even if power is removed. Stored information can be erased by exposure to ultraviolet rays and the chip can be reused by "burning" new information into it.

Excel. The best-selling subcompact car produced by Hyundai Motors.

export-oriented industrialization. The strategy of industrialization followed by the newly industrializing countries (NICs), which takes advantage of low-wage labor and undervalued currencies to secure markets for a country's labor-intensive exports in advanced industrial countries.

GATT (General Agreement on Tariffs and Trade). A multilateral body that provides the framework for negotiations on international trade in commodities, agriculture, manufactures, and services. GATT negotiations have generally aimed at liberalizing international trade in goods and services through tariff cuts and the dismantling or lowering of nontariff barriers. The current round of talks, which began in 1986 and is scheduled to be completed in 1990, is known as the Uruguay Round.

HCI (heavy and chemical industries) drive. The economic strategy to develop heavy and chemical industries launched by the Park Chung-Hee government in Korea in the early 1970s. The drive's objective was industrial deepening, or providing more depth to the economy and promoting more integration among the industrial sectors.

higher-value-added industries. Industries characterized by capital-intensive or skill-intensive production processes. These processes are said to add more value to a product per unit of labor compared to unskilled, labor-intensive production processes.

highly leveraged corporation. A corporation that has a high debt to equity ratio, meaning that its operations and expansion are heavily dependent on debt incurred from banks and other financial institutions.

integrated circuit. The basic building block of microelectronic systems, the integrated circuit consists of thousands of transistors or circuits and other components crammed onto a tiny silicon chip.

ISI (import substitution industrialization). A strategy of industrial development that promotes the replacement of imports with locally manufactured goods by erecting tariff or nontariff barriers against selected imports. Thus, if a locally manufactured car sells for $10,000 and an imported model's selling price before entering the country is $8000, a 100 percent tariff on the latter will raise its local price to $16,000, making the locally produced car substantially less expensive to the local consumer.

KMT (Kuomintang) party. The ruling political party in Taiwan. The KMT fled to Taiwan in 1948 after losing the civil war in China to the Communist party.

microchannel bus. Proprietary—that is not public or open—32-bit expansion bus architecture introduced by IBM for its high-end PS/2 computers. The microchannel is not compatible with existing peripherals and adapters designed for the AT expansion bus of the earlier IBM PC. With proprietary architecture and components, the PS/2 computer is very difficult to clone.

micron. One-thousandth of a millimeter or the width of the human hair, a micron is a measurement of the width of a circuit on a silicon chip. Circuit widths have now shrunk to less than a micron, allowing semiconductor manufacturers to cram more circuits into a tiny piece of silicon.

microprocessor. The so-called computer on a chip, the tiny microprocessor contains more than one million transistors and performs the same function as the central processing unit (CPU) in a regular computer. "By putting entire programmable systems on chips," notes George Gilder, "microprocessors have vastly reduced the cost and extended the reach of computing power."

MITI (Japan's Ministry of Trade and Industry). By targeting selected strategic industries for development and backing them with financial resources and protection from foreign competition, MITI is regarded as the force that led Japan's economic renaissance after World War II. The Economic Planning Board in South Korea is said to be patterned after MITI.

naphtha cracker. A facility that breaks down or "cracks" the petrochemical naphtha into, among other substances, ethylene, which is used to make many different kinds of plastic.

OECD (Organization for Economic Cooperation and Development). Formal international organization made up of the developed countries. Includes Japan, Western European and Scandinavian countries, Australia, New Zealand, the United States, and Canada.

OEM (original equipment manufacturing). Refers to a system in which a foreign buyer provides design and other specifications, as well as quality control, for a product to a third world or NIC manufacturer. The resulting product is then sold in developed country markets under the buyer's brand name, e.g. Schwinn bicycles made by the Taiwanese company Giant.

open architecture. A computer system in which system specifications are made public and components are nonproprietary and commercially available. This makes cloning relatively easy. Firms like IBM and Sun Microsystems have made some of their computer systems open to encourage the industry and the public to accept these systems as the industry standard.

PAP (People's Action Party). The ruling party in Singapore whose dominant figure is Lee Kwan-Yew.

reverse engineering. A laborious and time-consuming process of technology acquisition that proceeds by taking apart the components and processes that are embodied in the final product and tracing them to their simpler, earlier stages.

stepper (step-and-repeat-exposure system). A system of making DRAMs and other chips that uses a beam of light of very short waves with high precision to imprint patterns on an oxidized silicon wafer. The surface exposed to the light is then removed, leaving a clear channel for a circuit.

structural adjustment. A euphemism for a program of wrenching change in a third world economy in return for loans from commercial banks, the World Bank, and the International Monetary Fund. Among the elements of structural adjustment are privatization of government enterprises, drastic reduction of the government budget deficit, devaluation of the currency, elimination of subsidies, elimination of price controls, dismantling of trade and investment barriers, and cuts or restraints on wages. The objective of structural adjustment programs is to shift much of production away from serving the domestic market to satisyfing export markets. Thus, structural adjustment programs have been attacked as thinly veiled attempts to raise foreign exchange earnings in order to pay off a country's foreign debt.

structural unemployment. Unemployment created by elimination or marginalization of certain strata of the labor force, for instance, unemployment of significant numbers of unskilled workers as unskilled labor-intensive processes are phased out and production is automated. Structural unemployment also results when investment shifts from low-value-added labor intensive industries like textiles to higher-value-added but technology intensive industries like electronics.

work station. High performance personal computer optimized for professional applications in fields such as digital circuit design, architecture, and technical drawing. Typically contains ample memory, fast and powerful processing circuits, and sharply defined on-screen images.

zaibatzu. The name for conglomerates in pre-war Japan which consisted of a cluster of corporations around a holding company. The Korean chaebol are said to be patterned after the Japanese zaibatsu.

Selected Readings

Out of hundreds of primary and secondary sources consulted for this book, we have selected the books, articles, papers, and periodicals in English that were particularly useful for our purposes. While some of the following may not be easily accessible, we nonetheless list them because they represent some of the best work in the field. This listing is meant to be selective, not exhaustive.

NICs General

A useful introduction to the NICs is *The Political Economy of the New Asian Industrialism*, edited by Frederic Deyo (Ithaca: Cornell University Press, 1987). An excellent review of the regional conditions surrounding the emergence of the NICs is Bruce Cumings' "The Origin and Development of the Northeast Asian Political Economy: Industrial Sectors and Political Consequences," *International Organization* 38, no. 1 (Winter 1984), pp. 1-40. Robin Broad and John Cavanagh marshal evidence pointing to the demise of the NIC model in their convincing "No More NICs," *Foreign Policy*, no. 72 (Fall 1988), pp. 81-103. Kent Calder investigates the imbalances in the NICs-U.S.-Japan relationship in his "The North Pacific Triangle: Sources of Economic and Political Transformation," *Journal of Northeast Asian Studies* VII, no. 2 (Summer 1989), pp. 3-17. The *Bulletin of Concerned Asian Scholars*, published in Boulder, Colorado, occasionally carries good articles on the NICs. The *Far Eastern Economic Review*, which comes out of Hong Kong, is indispensable for information on the latest economic and political developments in the NICs. Also useful are the *Economist*, *Financial Times*, and *Asian Wall Street Journal*.

Korea

A suggestive comparison of political and economic evolution in South Korea and Latin America is Bruce Cumings' "The Abortive Abertura: South Korea in Light of Latin American Experience," *New Left Review*, no. 173 (January–February 1989), pp. 5–32. Two indispensable works on the history, structure, and dynamics of the Korean economy are Alice Amsden's *Asia's Next Giant: South Korea and Late Industrialization* (New York: Oxford University Press, 1989) and Tony Michell's "From LDC to NIC: The Republic of

Korea: Employment, Industrialization, and Trade, 1961-1982," an unpublished manuscript prepared for the International Labor Office. "The Korean Economy," an unpublished manuscript by Song Byung-Nak, a former technocrat under the Park Chung-Hee government, provides an interesting conservative interpretation of the development of the economy. A fascinating glimpse into the military defense dimension of Korea's heavy industrialization is provided by Moon Chung-In's "South Korea: Between Security and Vulnerability," in James Everett Katz, ed., *The Implications of Third World Military Industrialization* (Lexington, Mass.: Lexington Books, 1986), pp. 241-266. One of the most informative and realistic comparisons between Japanese and Korean patterns of industrialization is John Wilson and Sheridan Tatsuno's "South Korea: Following the Leader," published in *Strategic Issues* series in February 1989 by the San Jose, California-based research firm Dataquest, Inc.

Two very useful works on Korea's labor movements are *South Korea's New Trade Unions* (Hong Kong: Asia Monitor Resource Center, 1987); and Jang Jip Choi's "Interest Conflict and Political Control in South Korea: A Study of the Labor Unions in Manufacturing Industries, 1961–1980," Ph.D. dissertation University of Chicago, 1983.

"Saemaul Agriculture: South Korean Farmers Prop Up Export-Oriented Economy," by Phyllis Kim, is a solid, two-part critique of Korean rural development policies which appeared in 1980 in Vol. 12, no. 1, pp. 2-11 and Vol. 12, no. 3, pp. 56-65, of *AMPO: Japan-Asia Quarterly Review*. Also indispensable for understanding developments in rural Korea is Mick Moore, "Mobilization and Disillusion in Rural Korea: The Saemaul Movement in Retrospect," *Pacific Affairs* 57 (Winter 1984-85), pp. 577-598. Peter Hayes and Lyuba Zarsky's unpublished paper on "Nuclear Electric Futures in Developing Countries of the Asia Pacific," written in 1984, provides a thorough critique of the Korean nuclear energy program. *Business Korea* and *Korea Business World*, both published in Seoul, are trade journals which periodically carry good articles on the structural crisis of the Korean economy.

Korea Report and *Korea Update*, both of which are published in Washington, D.C., carry informative pieces on political and economic developments.

Taiwan

Two excellent, critical overviews of Taiwan are Marc Cohen, *Taiwan at the Crossroads: Human Rights, Political Development, and Social Change on the Beautiful Island* (Washington, D.C.: Asian Resource Center, 1989) and Thomas Gold, *State and Society in the Taiwan Miracle* (Armonk, New York: M.E. Sharpe, Inc., 1986). Simon Long's *Taiwan to 1993: Politics Versus Prosperity*, Special Report 1159, published in London by the Economist Intelligence Unit in 1989 describes the latest trends in Taiwan's economy. Two Ph.D. dissertations which are probably the best in their respective topics are Huang Chi, "The State and Foreign Capital: A Case Study of Taiwan," Indiana University, 1986; and Denis Simon, "Taiwan, Technology Transfer, and Transnationalism: The Political Management of Dependency," University of California, Berkeley, 1980. Also very useful for information and analysis of various aspects of Taiwanese society is an unpublished manuscript by Richard Kagan entitled "The Taiwanese Miracle," Institute for Food and Development Policy, San Francisco, 1982.

On class formation, class conflict, and class domination in Taiwan, the following are enormously useful: Michael Hsiao, "Development Strategies and Class Transformation in Taiwan and South Korea: Origins and Consequences," *Bulletin of the Institute of Ethnology*, no. 61 (Spring 1986), pp. 183-216, published by the Academia Sinica in Taipei; Ichiro Namazaki, "Networks of Taiwanese Big Business: A Preliminary Analysis," *Modern China* 12, no. 4 (October 1986), pp. 487-534; Chin Pei-Hsiung, *Housing and Economic Development in Taiwan*, Working Paper no. 438 (Berkeley: Institute of Urban and Regional Development, University of California at Berkeley, 1988); Hsu Cheng-Kuang, "Political Change and the Labor Movement in Taiwan," a paper presented at the 84th Annual Meeting of the American Sociological Association in San Francisco, August 9-13, 1989; and two articles by Linda Gail Arrigo: "The Industrial Work Force of Young Women in Taiwan," *Bulletin of Concerned Asian Scholars* 12, no. 2 (April-June 1980), pp. 25-38; and "Economic and Political Control of Women Workers in Multinational Electronics Factories in Taiwan: Martial Law Coercion and World Market Uncertainty," *Contemporary Marxism*, no. 11 (Fall 1988), pp. 77-95. An informative handbook on the recent history of the labor movement in Taiwan is Ho Shuet-Ying's *Taiwan—After a Long Silence* (Hong Kong: Asia Monitor Resource Center, 1990).

On the environment in Taiwan, probably the most comprehensive survey of the wasteland that the island has become is *Taiwan 2000: Balancing Economic Growth and Environmental Protection* (Taipei: Academia Sinica, 1989). Also useful are Michael Hsiao and Lester Milbrath, "The Environmental Movement in Taiwan," a paper prepared for the Sino-U.S. Binational Conference on Environmental Protection and Social Development, Taipei, August 20-25, 1989; and Sheldon Severinghaus, "The Emergence of an Environmental Consciousness in Taiwan," a paper read at the 1989 Annual Meeting of the Association for Asian Studies, Washington, D.C., March 17-19, 1989. The vicissitudes of Taiwanese agriculture are discussed by George Kuo in his "Not by Rice Alone: Hunger for Justice in Taiwan," *Food Symposium 88 Newsletter,* which came out in Tokyo in 1988. Also valuable for understanding contemporary agararian society is Michael Hsiao, "State and Farmers in East Asia with Special Reference to Taiwan," a paper prepared for the Conference on "Directions and Stratregies of Agriculture Development in the Asia-Pacific Region," which took place at the Academia Sinica in Taipei on January 5-7, 1988. Wang Sung-Hsing and Raymond Apthorpe's *Rice Farming in Taiwan: Three Village Studies* (Taipei: Academia Sinica, 1974) is an enlightening study of the interaction of the state, small peasants, and production technology at the village level.

Bang, an English-language monthly that catered primarily to Taipei's expatriate community occasionally carried well-written stories on the environment, labor, the economy, and politics until it discontinued publication early in 1990. The *Occasional Bulletin: Taiwan Church News* put out by the Presbyterian Church of Taiwan is an excellent source for grass roots environmental, human rights, and aboriginal news. Also useful for news on current political and economic affairs are *Taiwan Communique,* which comes out of Washington, D.C., and the *NATPA Bulletin* published in Chicago by the North American Taiwanese Professors' Association.

Singapore

Perhaps the outstanding critical work on Singapore's economy is Gary Rodan's *The Political Economy of Singapore's Industrialization* (London: Macmillan Press, 1989). Also useful is Manuel Castells, *The Developmental City-State in an Open World Economy: The Singapore Experience,* BRIE Working Paper, no. 31, published in 1988 by the University of California's Berkeley Roundtable on the International Economy. Koh Ai-Tee and Lee (Tsao) Yuan's short piece "Whither the Local Entrepreneurial Spirit?" *Straits Times* (Singapore), March 9, 1988, serves as a good counterpoint to official explanations of the decline of local entrepreneurship. *Policy Options for the Singapore Economy* by Lim Chong-Yah and associates, published by McGraw Hill Book Company in Singapore in 1988, is a good compendium of economic statistics, though the analysis is highly orthodox.

Two insightul works on different aspects of Singaporean society by John Clammer are his *Singapore: Ideology, Society, and Culture* (Singapore: Chopmen Publishers, 1985) and "Peripheral Capitalism and Urban Order: "Informal Sector' Theories in the Light of Singapore's Experience," in John Clammer, editor, *Beyond the New Economic Anthropology* (New York: St. Martin's Press, 1987), pp. 188-201. A good treatment of the place of women workers in Singapore is Lai Ah-Eng's "Economic Restructuring in Singapore and the Impact of New Technology on Women Workers," in Cecilia Ng, ed., *Women's Work in Asia* (Kuala Lumpur: Women's Studies Unit, Universiti Pertanian Malaysia and Malaysian Social Science Association, 1987), pp. 107-135. Philip Jeyaretnam's *First Loves* (Singapore: Times Books International, 1987) is a well-written short novel that subtly surfaces the social contradictions of everyday life under the Lee Kwan-Yew regime. James Minchin's *No Man Is An Island: A Study of Singapore's Lee Kuan-Yew* (Sydney: Allen and Unwin, 1986) is probably the definitive biography of Singapore's strongman. Oppositionist Francis Seow's "Human Rights and the Constitution of Singapore," an unpublished paper, is one of the most insightful treatments of the state of human rights in that country. *Southeast Asia Business*, which comes out of the University of Michigan in Ann Arbor, carries useful periodic assessments of economic trends in Singapore, many of them written by Linda Lim.

Industrial Sectors

An excellent analysis of the difficulties facing the textile and garments industry in the NICs is Ashoka Mody and David Wheeler, "Towards a Vanishing Middle: Competition in the World Garment Industry," *World Development* 15, no. 10-11 (1987). On the autmobile industry, the following are indispensable references: Kim Byung-Kook, "Export-Promotion Strategy Reevaluated: A Case Study of the Korean Automobile Industry," Ph.D. dissertation, Harvard University, Cambridge, Mass., 1982; Konomi Tomisawa, "Development and Future Outlook for an International Division of Labor in the Automobile Industries of the Asian NICs," Briefing paper for First Policy Forum of the International Motor Vehicle Development Program, Cambridge, Mass., May 5, 1987; and Walter Arnold, "Bureaucratic Politics, State Capacity, and Taiwan's Automobile Industrial Policy," *Modern China* 15, no. 2 (April 1989), pp. 179-214.

A very useful comparative analysis of the development of the automobile and information industries in Taiwan and South Korea is Chu Yun-Han's "Authoritarian Regimes under Stress: The Political Economy of Adjustment in the East Asian Newly Industrializing Countries," Ph.D. dissertation, University of Minnesota, Minneapolis, 1987.

On the electronics, microelectronics, and computer industries in the NICs, we found the following works by Ashoka Mody very helpful: "Alternative Strategies for Developing Information Industries," Paper prepared for Industry Development Division, Industry and Energy Department, World Bank, Washington, D.C., October 1988; "Recent Evolution of Microelectronics in South Korea and Taiwan: An Institutional Approach to Comparative Advantage," unpublished paper, Boston, 1985; and *Korea's Computer Strategy*, Case 0-686-070 (Cambridge, Mass.: Harvard Business School, 1985). Another invaluable resource is Morris Crawford, *Programming the Invisible Hand: The Computerization of Korea and Taiwan* (Cambridge, Mass.: Program on Information Resources Policy, Harvard University, 1986).

A good source of information on trends in electronics in Korea is *Electronics Korea*, which comes out of Seoul. Lenny Siegel's *Global Electronics*, published in Mountain View, Calif., occasionally carries articles on developments in semiconductors and computers in the NICs.

Index

Resource Guide

The following organizations provide excellent information on and analysis of political, social, and economic trends in Korea:

The North American Coalition for Human Rights in Korea
Suite 302, 110 Maryland Avenue NE
Washington, D.C. 20002
(202) 546-4304
The coalition assiduously monitors the human rights situation in South Korea and produces the monthly publication *Korea Update*, (subscription $18/year).

The Korean Information and Resource Center.
Suite 5, 1314 14th Street NW
Washington, D.C. 20005
(202) 387-2551
The Center provides timely analyses of U.S-Korea relations and political and economic trends in the Korean peninsula. It publishes the bimonthly *Korea Report* (subscription $12/year).

The Committee for a New Korea Policy
33 Central Avenue
Albany, New York 12210
(518) 434- 4037.
The committee's *Korea Pamphlet* series provide concise analyses of political developments, trends in U.S.-Korea relations, and human rights issues (subscriptions $18/year first class, $12/year fourth class).

Trends in the human rights situation in Singapore can be obtained from:

Asia Watch
1522 K Street NW
Washington, D.C. 20005
(202) 371-0124

The following organizations provide excellent information on developments in Taiwan:

Formosan Association for Human Rights
17 Arthur Place
Montville, New Jersey 07045
(201) 227-8579

Formosan Association for Public Affairs
538 7th Street SE
Washington, D.C. 20003
(202) 547-3686

Asia Resource Center
P.O. Box 15275
Washington, D.C. 20003
(202) 547-1114
The Center publishes the bi-monthly *Taiwan Communique* (subscription $12 fourth class; $18 first class).

About the Authors

Walden Bello is the author of, among other books, *Brave New Third World? Strategies for Survival in the Global Economy (1989), American Lake (1987),* and *Development Debacle: The World Bank in the Philippines (1982).* Currently executive director of the San Francisco-based Institute for Food and Development Policy (Food First), he has taught at the University of California at Berkeley and, as a political exile during the Marcos dictatorship, worked in Washington, D.C., as a lobbyist and advocate for democratic rights in the Philippines. Currently also a research fellow at the University of California's Center for Southeast Asian Studies, Bello obtained his Ph.D. in sociology from Princeton University in 1975.

Stephanie Rosenfeld is a research associate in the Newly Industrializing Countries (NICs) Project of the Institute for Food and Development Policy. Her articles with Walden Bello have appeared in a number of publications, including the *Ecologist, World Policy Journal,* and *Multinational Monitor.*

About Food First

The Institute for Food and Development Policy, better known as Food First, is a non-profit research and educational center focussing on issues of food and democracy around the world. Founded in 1975 by Frances Moore Lappé, author of *Diet for a Small Planet*, and Joseph Collins,the Institute has worked to change accepted views on the causes of and solutions to world hunger. More recently the Institute has been actively promoting the vision of participatory, equitable and ecologically sustainable development in the Third World.

Becoming a member

Nearly all of our income comes from our members and from sales of our books. We accept no contributions from government sources. Our research is independent, free from ideological formulas and prevailing government policies. Would you support our efforts by joining Food First? For more information, and a free catalog of our publications, write or call:
The Institute for Food and Development Policy
145 Ninth Street,
San Francisco,
California 94103, USA
(415) 864-8555
Fax (415) 864 3909